Few occupations make as significant moral demands on their practitioners as policing. Yet no occupation has been as poorly prepared for the moral demands laid on it. But now, in response to mounting public concern and an increasing interest in police ethics, there are signs of change. John Kleinig's book has been written to address that new concern and interest.

This book is the most systematic, comprehensive, and philosophically sophisticated discussion of police ethics yet published. It offers an in-depth analysis of the ethical values that police, as servants of the community, should uphold as they go about their task. The book considers the foundations and purpose of police authority in broad terms but also tackles specific problems such as: accountability, the use of force, stratagems used to gain information or trap the criminally intentioned, corruption, and the tension between personal values and communal concerns.

Offering the fullest, most rigorous and up-to-date treatment of police ethics currently available, this book will make an ideal textbook for courses on applied ethics in philosophy departments or police and criminal justice ethics in departments of criminology and law schools.

The ethics of policing

Cambridge Studies in Philosophy and Public Policy

GENERAL EDITOR: Douglas MacLean

The purpose of this series is to publish the most innovative and up-to-date research into the values and concepts that underlie major aspects of public policy. Hitherto most research in this field has been empirical. This series is primarily conceptual and normative; that is, it investigates the structure of arguments and the nature of values relevant to the formation, justification, and criticism of public policy. At the same time it is informed by empirical considerations, addressing specific issues, general policy concerns, and the methods of policy analysis and their applications.

The books in the series are inherently interdisciplinary and include anthologies as well as monographs. They are of particular interest to philosophers, political and social scientists, economists, policy analysts, and those involved in public administration and environmental policy.

Mark Sagoff: *The Economy of the Earth*
Henry Shue (ed.): *Nuclear Deterrence and Moral Restraint*
Judith Lichtenberg (ed.): *Democracy and the Mass Media*
William Galston: *Liberal Purposes*
Elaine Draper: *Risky Business*
R. G. Frey and Christopher W. Morris: *Violence, Terrorism, and Justice*
Douglas Husak: *Drugs and Rights*
Ferdinand Schoeman: *Privacy and Social Freedom*
Dan Brock: *Life and Death*
Paul B. Thompson: *The Ethics of Trade Aid*
Jeremy Waldron: *Liberal Rights*
Steven Lee: *Morality, Prudence, and Nuclear Weapons*
Robert E. Goodin: *Utilitarianism as Public Policy*
Robert K. Fullinwider (ed.): *Public Education in a Multicultural Society*

The ethics of policing

JOHN KLEINIG

John Jay College of Criminal Justice
City University of New York

PUBLISHED BY THE PRESS SYNDICATE OF THE UNIVERSITY OF CAMBRIDGE
The Pitt Building, Trumpington Street, Cambridge, United Kingdom

CAMBRIDGE UNIVERSITY PRESS
The Edinburgh Building, Cambridge CB2 2RU, UK   www.cup.cam.ac.uk
40 West 20th Street, New York, NY 10011-4211, USA   www.cup.org
10 Stamford Road, Oakleigh, Melbourne 3166, Australia
Ruiz de Alarcón 13, 28014 Madrid, Spain

First published 1996
Reprinted 1997, 1999

Printed in the United States of America

Typeset in Palatino

A catalog record for this book is available from the British Library

Library of Congress Cataloging in Publication Data is available

ISBN 0 521 48206 2 hardback
ISBN 0 521 48433 2 paperback

Contents

Preface

For the most part, the ethical concerns of police have been ignored by academic writers. Not entirely; though when you compare the scholarly attention given to legal ethics, medical ethics, business ethics, ethics in government, and so on, police ethics comes off very poorly. Police novels, films, documentaries, and journalistic essays often do much better (and, alas, worse) in representing and exploring the ethical dimensions of police work.

My own interest in police ethics was first stimulated in 1984, when the then Commissioner of the New South Wales Police Service, John Avery, invited me to conduct a session on police ethics for an Officer Training Conference at the Australian Police College, Manly. His invitation came at almost the same time I was unexpectedly awarded a Fulbright grant to spend a year as Scholar-in-Residence at John Jay College of Criminal Justice at the City University of New York (CUNY). Though I did not then translate my nascent interest into any extended reflection and teaching, the College nevertheless welcomed me into an environment that had close links with police work, and by the end of my time there, when I returned to Macquarie University in Australia, I was sufficiently intrigued and emboldened to offer a course in police ethics.

I was subsequently to return permanently to John Jay College in September 1986, and found myself with the now-fascinating yet daunting responsibility of preparing courses in police ethics for undergraduate, graduate, and doctoral students. Accompanying the challenge, however, was the encouragement of my students, many of whom were actively involved in police work.

Breaking into a new field is an awesome experience, especially if one wants to have not only the narrow view but also the broader one. And the latter would not have been possible had I not been provided with the almost ideal conditions of a 1990–91 Fellowship in Professional Ethics in the Harvard University Program in Ethics and the Professions. My debts to that Program, and to the City University of New York's Scholar and Creative Incentive Award schemes, are enormous. Several people in the Harvard Program were particularly supportive: Arthur Applbaum, Allan Brett, Dennis Thompson, and Kenneth Winston were willing to put up with half-baked drafts and ideas, and I was also given the opportunity to present drafts or related materials to the Austinian Society, the Seminar in Ethics and the Professions, and Society for Social Theory. Other Harvard colleagues, Mark Moore and the late Judith Shklar, were sources of inspiration during that year.

Subsequently, I was able to present two drafts of the material to students in the CUNY criminal justice and philosophy doctoral programs. They elicited lively and penetrating discussion, and if it can be said that the numerous active and ex-police officers in the classes kept my feet on the ground, it can no less be said that some of the philosophy students kept me on my toes. A sabbatical leave gave me the opportunity to make final revisions of the manuscript. My efforts were facilitated by the hospitable environments of Ben Gurion University, the Australian National University, and the University of Western Australia.

Various parts of the material in this book have been tried out at conferences and colloquia, and several patient friends and colleagues have read and commented on them. Although I mention Howard Cohen, Michael Davis, the late Dan Guido, Tziporah Kasachkoff, Haim Marantz, T. Kenneth Moran, and Robert Young, I am sure there were others who in reaction or in conversation substantially contributed to my thinking. Long-suffering readers have Douglas MacLean and Cambridge University Press to thank for the fact that the script has been substantially shortened.

This is, perhaps, the point to acknowledge the permanent debt I owe to two of my earliest mentors – now, alas, deceased – Julius Kovesi and Stanley Benn. I can only hope that they would have approved of the work that I present here. I count myself fortunate to have been able to learn from two philosophers who so combined intellectual acuity with caring humanity that I have always felt comfortable in the scholarly discipline to which I have devoted myself.

Chapter 1

Introduction: ethics and police ethics

1.1 READERS' GUIDE

In preparing this volume, it has been my intention to address the interests of several kinds of readers. The lack of a reasonably comprehensive and scholarly discussion of police ethics is responsible for the formal structure that I have adopted – one that begins with wider and more abstract questions of moral theory and political philosophy before engaging with the more explicit concerns of operational police officers – and it is probably only those with a theoretical interest in police ethics who will feel tempted to read the book straight through. Most others, I suspect, will have a more limited interest in some of the specific challenges that confront operational officers and detectives in their day-to-day activities. Nevertheless, because some of the theoretical background bears importantly on the subsequent argument, it should not be ignored altogether.

For the reader who is interested only or primarily in the "hard moral questions" that confront police officers, I suggest that a beginning be made with Chapter 2, Section 2.4, in which I argue that the police role is most satisfactorily construed as a form of social peacekeeping. In fulfilling that role, police will often find themselves caught between the real and ideal, between competing factions and groups, between the public they serve and the culture of their own organization. Does this role, with its peculiar challenges, give police certain moral prerogatives that "common morality" would eschew? This general question is taken up in Chapter 3, Section 2 and should probably be read as a background to the topics taken up in Part II. Chapters 6 and 7 will be clearly of central importance to topically motivated readers, and the section headings should be sufficiently self-explanatory to enable such readers to select the issues they find of most interest. I would, however, also recommend that Chapter 4 not be skipped, because it raises significant questions about the environment within which police decision making takes place. It might then be followed by Chapter 9, which canvasses additional problems generated by that environment.

Readers whose interest lies with the "hard cases" of street policing may not want to work through Part III. Yet it offers the beginnings of what I see as

a crucial area of police ethics, problems that are largely managerial or organizational in character. Police ethics is often conceived of and taught as
though its problems occur exclusively at the police–community interface.
Yet many of the problems at that location have their genesis or are at least
exacerbated by issues that arise within the organization, and are handled by
police managers. Ideally, an encounter with police ethics, particularly for
those who are pursuing a career in policing, will move progressively from
street problems to managerial problems. And it is to be hoped that the topics
of Part III will be seen as a natural extension of street issues, well suited to an
advanced course in police ethics.[1]

I am very conscious that every issue canvassed in this long book cries out
for further elaboration both philosophically and practically. The problems of
authority, role morality, affirmative action, loyalty, privacy, coercion, and
deception, to mention some of them, have generated large and sophisticated
literatures whose complexities have been barely touched upon. But by the
same token, the concrete decisions that first line police officers and police
managers must make on a day-to-day basis are more diverse and finely
nuanced than the various situational circumstances to which I have alluded
in the text. Nevertheless, it is my hope that in bringing into some sort of
engagement these disparate yet connected enterprises, I will have eased the
transition from one set of concerns to the other, and that there will be
increased traffic between the two, to the mutual benefit of both police and
the communities they serve and to which they belong.

1.2 ETHICS

In projects of the present kind, in which philosophical argument is brought
to bear on matters of practice, it is commonly complained either that their
roots in more general ethical theory have been ignored or obscured or, by
contrast, that some general ethical theory is treated like a mantra or formula
from which practical conclusions can be unproblematically derived. Sometimes, unfortunately, especially in regard to textbooks in applied or practical
ethics, the latter complaint is well founded. For my part, I should make it
clear that I believe the relationship between general ethical theory and practical decision making to be very complex, certainly not linear, and that a
critical process in such decision making is *judgment*, not simply deductive
inference.[2]

The first complaint is more difficult to deal with. Such is the complexity of
the issues dealt with in practical ethics that any detailed concern with more
general theoretical concerns in ethics (or politics or religion or . . .) is likely
to be squeezed out by space or other more focused considerations. And such
is the complexity of ethical theory itself that any attempt to encompass it
within a work devoted to practical concerns is likely to appear superficial.
To satisfy one's critics one should follow Sidgwick by writing *The Methods of
Ethics* before turning to *Practical Ethics*.[3]

Given these constraints, I cannot hope to accommodate the otherwise reasonable demand for a more general framework. However, it may assist if I set out in a brief space some of the larger parameters within which this volume has been written. This at least will help to locate my approach to police ethics within the broader framework of intellectual and philosophical inquiry.

I begin with the general assertion that as part of the increasing differentiation of human cultural and social life, and the human desire to understand and control that life and its environs, we have developed a network of complex and increasingly specialized deliberative enterprises. Some of those enterprises, such as philosophy, mathematics, theology, and physics, have fairly abstract or theoretical cores. Their scope tends toward the universal and cosmic. They have, however, applied counterparts in undertakings like practical ethics, arithmetic, religion, and engineering. Other inquiries, such as history, sociology, and psychology, also have significant theoretical underpinnings, but tend to be oriented more specifically to understanding various aspects of the human condition. Their focus is not so much the cosmos or natural world as a specific presence within it. And associated with these inquiries, though not as specific derivations from them, are various more practically oriented concerns such as morality, law, politics, and etiquette.

This very sketchy representation is not meant to be more than suggestive. It is not intended to indicate much more than that these and other human deliberative enterprises are to be viewed as the constructs of a collective – albeit not always shared – human inquiry into the rich world that confronts us and into which we have been initiated in our human communities. These deliberative enterprises and activities represent a progressive or at least a competitive but cumulative articulation of our experience of, and coming to terms with, that world.

In saying that these various human inquiries are "constructs," I do not want to suggest that they are merely spinning in a vacuum, unrelated to some "reality" out there. Rather, they arise out of our engagement with that "reality" and are attempts to accommodate it in ways that enable us to understand and deal with it. Nevertheless, in speaking of these human activities as constructs, I also intend to suggest that what we conceptualize scientifically, historically, ethically, and so on, does not so much "mirror" that outer world as "embody" it through our *interests*. We structure the world of our inquiry by means of certain standpoints and orientations that belong distinctively to us as the kinds of beings we are. It is because we have the brains we have, the senses we have, the physical and social needs we have, and so on, that we structure the world in the ways we do.

Now, there is a problem about this to which I want later to return – an assumption that we can specify the kinds of beings we are, and the standpoints that we have, and that there is some kind of identifiable unity to the subjects of these deliberative enterprises. But for the moment I want to leave this assumption aside.

Focusing more specifically on morality or ethics and ethical concerns, how do they fit within the larger schema that I have sketched?[4] My initial suggestion here is that as far as the interests that inform our deliberative engagement with the world are concerned, a very broad distinction can be drawn between those that are theoretical and those that are practical. On the one hand, we have an interest in *understanding* ourselves and our world; on the other hand, we are actors in that world and have a *practical* interest in determining what we are to do. These are not, of course, unconnected interests. What we are to do will obviously depend on what options are there for us, and what options we perceive there to be for us will obviously connect with how we understand ourselves and the world to be. The connection may even be closer than that. Our very interest in understanding how things are may itself reflect a concern to act on the world in which we are enmeshed. Likewise, some of our practical concerns are designed to enhance our ability to understand ourselves and our world.

The distinction between theoretical and practical interests can be somewhat crudely used to distinguish between the so-called sciences – physical and social – and more practical enterprises such as law, morality, economics, and politics. Or, maybe more accurately at this point, the distinction not only helps us to differentiate between the theoretical sciences and practical enterprises such as morality, law, and politics, but also between the theoretical and the applied sciences, such as engineering, mechanics, architecture, and accounting.

There is, then, a further question about the ways in which we might want to differentiate practical activities such as law, morality, politics, and religion. In approaching this, it is helpful to recognize that one feature of human deliberative activity is its concern with choice. Humans are not merely the observers of – or elements within – an intersection of forces over which they have no control, but are positioned as actors who, by their choices, can make a difference to outcomes. And in the service of that practical choice-bearing activity, we have developed a very complex structure of evaluative concepts: some, like good and bad, right and wrong, virtue and vice, are general; others, such as murder, stealing, hypocrisy, democracy, and constitutionality, are more specific. Some characterize specific acts or choices; others deal more with ways of being or traits of character that lead to choices of certain kinds: courage, patience, honesty, conscientiousness, for example.

These evaluative concepts are of many kinds, and all of our practical activities are informed by some range of them. It is by means of them that we make or assess the various choices or options that confront us.[5] Perhaps our richest stock is to be found in connection with those deliberative activities that are concerned primarily with the question: How are we to live? They are concerned, that is, with the enterprises of religion, politics, law, and morality.

The religious quest is probably the most encompassing, but also the most problematic of these practical inquiries. Its basic concern is even more synoptic than: How am I to live? For it asks: What is the meaning of life? Why am I here? These are ultimate, synoptic questions with strong practical overtones. Whether they are answerable or even intelligible is fairly hotly debated, and even if they are intelligible and answerable, it is sometimes claimed that they are religious only in the broadest of senses – in which, say, humanism or Sisyphian nihilism can be understood as forms of religious outlook. Thus, whether a god or gods need figure in religious inquiry is not something to be taken for granted.

But, leaving aside the potentially ultimate and synoptic dimensions of the fundamental religious interest, each of politics, law, and morality is concerned with the way in which we conduct our lives. They are not, of course, the only practices concerned with that (consider, for example, economics, etiquette, and protocol), but they are arguably the major ones. Only *arguably*. For someone of a Marxist persuasion might plausibly claim that the bodily needs of humans are of such fundamental significance that the interests involved in meeting them ought to be included in, if not given priority over, other human practices. On such an understanding, certain "economic" realities will form the base on which the superstructures of morality, law, politics, and religion are to be erected. Although I shall leave these and similar debates aside, I do not wish to minimize their importance.

In claiming that politics, morality, law, and the like, are concerned with the way in which we conduct our lives, I have particularly in mind our *social* lives – our interpersonal interactions, either direct or as mediated via communal or institutional structures. It is the social character of these activities that I think helps us to understand why they are also the major ones in our lives. For, whatever else we may want to say about humans – as reasoners, toolmakers, political animals, or whatever – we are social beings. Not only are we products of a social existence, but it is generally through, though not as mere epiphenomena of, social life that we realize our distinctive characters. The importance of this should become clearer after I make one further suggestion.

This suggestion is that a certain precedence can be observed with regard to normative social practices such as politics, law, and morality.[6] In contemporary philosophical inquiry and also I think in everyday life, it is common for moral interests to be accorded some sort of practical priority. In the philosophical literature, this is usually expressed in the thesis that moral considerations are overriding. In practical life, it is displayed in the fact that we tend to bring both legal and political determinations before the bar of morality rather than subject moral determinations to the judgments of law and politics. Morality gets the final say.

Of course not everyone takes that view. Some would divorce morality from law and/or politics altogether, and see them as belonging to completely separate domains. Others might give legal and/or political considerations some priority over those deriving from morality. Even in the philosophical literature, there are those who question the overridingness of moral considerations.[7] And of course in real life situations moral concerns might lose out to legal or political pressures, or, perhaps more often, to considerations of expediency. The issue is one of status rather than of influence. As

Bishop Butler wryly observed of conscience: had it power, as it has authority, it would rule the world.[8]

The foregoing caveats aside, the generally held view, and one to which I am sympathetic, is that moral or ethical considerations have a normative priority in practical decision making, particularly where one's actions will impinge on the lives of others. Even this, however, requires some clarification. For overridingness is understood in different ways. R. M. Hare, for example, considers overridingness to be a conceptual feature of moral considerations, a formal characteristic that defines a consideration as a moral one. And he sees moral beliefs and utterances as being constituted by considerations that combine overridingness with prescriptivity and "universalizability."[9] I, on the other hand, tend to understand the relation of overridingness to morality rather differently, and would suggest instead that the reason why moral considerations are overriding is not because, by definition, any overriding consideration functions as a moral consideration, but because the substantive interests to which morality is directed have a theoretical priority in our decision making. Overridingness, in other words, is a substantive rather than a merely formal feature of morality.

Why is this so? To answer this, it is helpful to return to a consideration of what it is to be a human being, or, if you like, a person. Again, what I say will raise as many questions as it answers. But I think it has at least the appearance of plausibility.

We do not come to be the kinds of beings we now are and perhaps aspire to be as the result of a simple process of maturation. It is not enough that, once delivered from our mother's womb, we are left to be. Unlike trees, which, springing naturally from the soil, are fortuitously nourished by the rain and sun until they achieve their full maturity – an unfolding of "pre-ordained" inner structures – humans come to be what they are only through their communal engagement with others, through a process of interaction and learning.

For this to come about, for humans to aspire to be and to be what they aspire to be, they must interact and be disposed to interact in certain kinds of ways. Their experience of the world must be of a relatively firmly established kind. Not any form of interaction is conducive to human flourishing: that we know from child and social psychology, from oppressive and destructive legal and political regimes, and so on. At least in the early stages of their development, humans need social stability, predictability, and affection, if they are to flourish. If the bonds are too tight or too loose, some form of crippling, breakdown or *anomie* is very likely to result.[10]

It is, I believe, our interest in these primary forms of human interaction that constitutes the core of morality. As I see it, morality is human life viewed *sub specie humanitatis*. It is *human* life and flourishing at its most general and basic level that is of central concern to morality. Without that, everything else is in jeopardy. The doctrine of universalizability, then, is not to be seen as a formal feature of morality, but rather as a consequence of our concern with human life at its most general level. Morality is centrally (albeit not exclusively[11]) constituted by those attitudes and standards of conduct that hold between human beings wherever they are.[12] In essence, or at least in aspiration, morality – the moral sphere – is concerned with what we are in our relationships with each other, individually, collectively, and institutionally. I phrase it in this way, because morality is concerned with *being* and not just *doing*, or at least not in doing divorced from being. Thus morality is concerned not just with rules and principles, but with virtues and character, with reasons and attitudes as well as conduct. And it is concerned with these *sub specie humanitatis*, and not *primarily* from the standpoint of, say, an American or Caucasian or male or police officer perspective (though these tend to get in our way, and in certain contexts may even be relevant).

How does morality thus construed link up with, say, law and politics? The classic answer to this has been that, on its own, morality does not provide a sufficient guide for life. Our practical commitment to moral authority is fragile at best, and in the increasingly complex interactions of ever-expanding communities, there is a need for institutions to establish social ground rules, to coordinate human interactions, to execute justice, and to provide incentives for compliance. Governmental authority, with its legislative powers, is one of the institutions that makes up for the practical failure of morality (and more generally of unplanned human coordination) in an imperfect world.

I think the foregoing helps us to see how morality, law, politics, and religion might intersect and complement each other in human experience. If you start with the view that *we* – being how we understand ourselves to be – have an interest in conducting our lives in a manner that will enable us to flourish in the ways in which we seem capable, it becomes easier to see why moral judgments are often – as they are by Hare – defined as prescriptive, universalizable, and overriding. And it also becomes easier to see why others (such as G. J. Warnock[13]), who prefer to define morality in terms of a certain content – say, that which contributes to the good or harm, well being or otherwise, of human beings – take the position they do.

Moral *theory* not only abstracts from but also helps to shape this lived experience. It attempts to offer a systematic understanding of the considerations that inform our moral sensibilities and judgments, considerations that will both explain, justify, and appraise our attitudes and choices. In the present work I shall not be concerned in any detailed and general way with moral *theories* – with, for example, the advocacy of deontological as against consequentialist, or intuitionist as against natural law, theories. Suffice it to say that I believe it essential to any adequate moral theory that it accommodate both deontological and consequentialist considerations.[14] Only so can the full richness of our moral experience be encompassed. If that accommodation can be achieved without loss within a single coherent framework, then that is all to the good. But if not, and moral theory becomes a Procrustean bed to which our moral life must be conformed, then moral theory will have lost its claim to our serious attention.

I conclude with a few additional comments about the differences between law and morality. I do so partly because legal and moral requirements often parallel each other, but more importantly because they are often confused (at least in the context of criminal law), and in the realm of police ethics what is legally allowed is often taken to articulate the bounds of the morally permissible.

Despite certain congruities and convergences, there are some very important differences in the character and content of moral and legal requirements. These differences help us to understand why morality is accorded a normative primacy in practical affairs; that is, law is to be judged by reference to morality, and not vice versa. One major difference is that law, unlike morality, is concerned primarily with conduct, and not with character. So long as a person physically conforms to some legal requirement, he or she has generally done all that can be legally demanded. The reasons and motives for that conformity are not normally relevant. Moral requirements, however, are centrally concerned with reasons, motives, and intentions, and more generally with the character that expresses itself in conduct. Morality, as I noted earlier, is concerned with what we *are* in our relationships, and not just with what we *do*. True, what we do to some extent shows what we are; but it does not unambiguously do so. This is one reason why it is only when a person breaks the law that we ask questions about motives, intentions, and so on. For although the law is not terribly interested in why we conform to it when we conform to it, it is a different matter when we do not conform. For then some penalty may be exacted, and, in line with the normative priority I have already noted, there is a moral demand that the legal process take into account intentions, motives, attitudes, and so on, so that any penalties are *justly* imposed.

Central though the foregoing difference between law and morality is, it is not the only important difference. Law, unlike morality, is jurisdictionally limited. What the law legitimately requires may differ from one state to another, and from one country to another. Moral values, however, we are inclined to apply more universally. Just because morality is concerned with the basics of human interaction we do not expect it to be geographically or historically or culturally determined. In fact, of course, it is considerably influenced by such factors. Yet these culturally and historically idiosyncratic overlays we generally aspire to remove or at least to universalize. Laws, on the other hand, we much more readily accept as jurisdictionally limited. And along with that, we accept that laws, but not moral requirements, can be created and changed by authoritative fiat.

One implication of this – to be taken up again in later chapters – is that we should not expect "police ethics" to characterize a distinctive type of ethic, but rather to be the expression of a more general ethic within a police context. The ethical demands on police are the ethical demands under which we are all placed, by virtue of our common humanity; they are, however, demands colored by the specific roles that police have and shaped by the circumstances under which they must decide.

PART I

Professional ethics

Chapter 2

Moral foundations of policing

Police are occupied with peacekeeping – but preoccupied with crime fighting.

Jesse Rubin[1]

As long as human societies have existed, the police function has been needed. Social coordination and harmony have never flourished without some form of executive authority. Sometimes the executive task has been shared among many; at other times, and increasingly with the division of social labor, it has devolved upon selected individuals, organized and coordinated to provide that service effectively and efficiently. What we now most generally refer to as policing usually dates itself from the formation, in 1829, of the London Metropolitan Police, a legislatively mandated organization designed to provide round-the-clock service to a community confronted by diverse needs and fears. The "principal object" of the Metropolitan Police was "the Prevention of Crime,"[2] and although, along with the detection and conviction of offenders, this has ever since been the central and distinctive concern of police organizations, it is clear even from the first instruction manual that police were expected to have a much wider social role as "problem busters" or "crisis managers."

On what *moral* basis can we justify the existence of an organization with the powers customarily vested in police? By what morally preferable alternative means might we contemplate the provision of police services? How widely should police authority and responsibility be permitted to extend? It is to these general questions of political morality that the present chapter is directed.

Like many others who have considered these questions, I begin with social contract theory, because some version of that theory permeates most liberal democratic thinking, and appears to offer good prospects for a theory of accountable policing. Yet, as will become clear, I am not altogether comfortable with naked contractualism, because it belies much of our communal and historical experience as inheritors and perpetuators of cultural traditions, albeit traditions that can and indeed ought to be open to the scrutiny of those who are their bearers. And so I offer an account of the police role as "social peacekeeping," understood not so much as a function of social homogeneity as of social cooperation in the pursuit of the varied ends to which, as individuals and groups, we may choose to devote ourselves. To understand those ends, however, we need an appreciation of cultural histories and traditions, and must focus not only on the present and future, but also on the past that has yielded, and gives much significance to, the present.

2.1   CONSENT AND TRADITION

The justificatory framework for what we now understand by policing antedates its organizational manifestations by well over a century. In his *Second Treatise Of Civil Government*,[3] John Locke maintained that life outside of civil government – life in what he calls "a state of nature" – would be beset by certain "inconveniencies," deficiencies that would prompt rational individuals, desirous of preserving their fundamental rights, to forsake this natural state for a civil one. Although, according to Locke, humans are endowed by their Creator and by virtue of their rational nature with certain basic rights – to life, liberty, and property – their ability to exercise and secure those rights is severely hampered by several features of the human condition. These deficits of the human condition include ignorance, carelessness, partiality, and lack of power, almost surely guaranteeing that life in a state of nature will be characterized by fear, insecurity, and arbitrary interferences. In such circumstances, Locke believes that it would make sense to exchange certain of one's freedoms for the greater security of rights promised by some form of civil government.

Locke is not content to present only a general argument for government, one designed to do no more than reconcile a theory of fundamental rights with the exercise of governmental power. He is quite specific about the particular deficiencies attending a state of nature and about the kinds of governmental institutions that would rectify them. In Chapter 9 of the *Second Treatise*, he identifies three kinds of deficiencies, and nominates their institutional remedies. First of all, the Law of Nature, that fundamental standard of right and wrong, is inadequate to the task of guiding and coordinating the everyday affairs of humankind. Although this moral law is discernible to the eye of reason, our partiality, ignorance and negligence distort or obscure its dictates, and it needs to be supplemented by "an *establish'd*, settled, known *Law*, received and allowed by common consent to be the Standard of Right and Wrong, and the common measure to decide all Controversies between [people]." A legislature is called for.

But a shared law, whether natural or positive, is not sufficient to rectify the defects of a state of nature. Laws need to be applied to particular cases, and in a state of nature this will be done idiosyncratically and arbitrarily. It is, Locke believes, a manifest fact of human experience that those who need recourse to law are likely to be biassed in their interpretation of its provisions; and where their own interests are not immediately involved, their commitment to its application is likely to be half-hearted. So, Locke writes, there needs to be instituted "*a known and indifferent Judge*, with Authority to determine all differences according to the established Law." A judiciary is called for.

Without power, however, the authority to make and apply law will come to nothing. In a state of nature, Locke observes, offenders are unlikely to offer themselves for punishment or penalization, and those who have been wronged or who stand to gain from the law may not have the power to make good their claims or position. Civil government will provide "*Power* to back and support the Sentence when right, and to *give* it due *Execution*." Institutions for law enforcement are called for.

Locke thus provides a neat and persuasive justification for the emergence of those various agencies of law enforcement – police, corrections, probation, and parole – that represent for many citizens the most immediate and visible expression of governmental authority and power. And, not surprisingly, it is social contractarianism that figures most prominently in contemporary justifications of the institution of policing.[4]

The contractarian strategy for governmental and police authority can be seen as *moral*, and not merely pragmatic if viewed in the light of the moral problem that generates it. Put in Lockean terms, it is the problem that government, any form of government, just because it places constraints and limits on beings who have certain inherent moral rights, is morally suspect. The core of that tradition, and indeed of most liberal thinking, is that mature individuals have a status that casts a moral shadow over any constraint that is placed on them. There is a moral onus on those who limit the freedom of others to provide a justification for that limitation.

Yet the social contract theory, though deeply entrenched in our cultural rhetoric of individual rights and government by consent, cannot be simply presumed to provide the whole, or even an unambiguous, justificatory story. There are hard questions that need to be faced, both generally and specifically. At the most general level there are problems concerning the existence, interpretation, range and basis of the rights that government is supposedly instituted to guarantee; the underlying conception of the bearers of those rights; and the quality and validity of the consent that liberal democracies are able to secure. More specifically, there are problems concerning the particular forms to be taken by the various institutions of government, and the most appropriate way of separating and delegating social responsibility. The role of police cannot be presumed to be timelessly settled by, say, Locke's simple tripartite division.

We cannot expect to address all these issues here; yet neither ought we to ignore them, if we wish to provide an account of policing that is attuned to both the realities of everyday life and the demands of moral theory. And so I shall indicate only briefly why an account such as Locke's needs to be amplified, amended, and supplemented if it is to retain its place within an account of police authority.

2.1.1   *The purposes of government*

According to Locke, the chief end of government is the protection of individual life, liberty, and property. No longer is that simple statement sufficient. At the time it was enunciated, it represented an assertion of individual moral claims against the oppressiveness of feudal, monarchical, and other authoritarian regimes. Since then, particularly with the formation of more democratic political structures and the rise of potentially oppressive forces outside of government (industrial and corporate powers), there has been a general shift toward the positive contribution that government may be able to make to human welfare. The right to government protection against invasions of life, liberty, and property has been reinterpreted to include the government securement or provision of what will enable those rights to be enjoyed, supplemented by other social, political, and welfare rights.

There has been, of course, no unanimity about the wisdom or justifiability of the foregoing shift, and in our current social environment the political divisions that exist between "left" and "right" manifest the tension that exists between those with more and less expansive views of the role that government should take in providing for human well-being. This tension can create confusion and difficulty for police officers, who, as agents of government, may at some times be unclear about what is expected of them and at other times be expected to offer services that they may not think it their business to provide.

2.1.2   *The bearers of rights*

The picture of human nature and human social life presented by early social contract theorists carries with it the strong suggestion that our capacities for speech, imagination and reflection preexist their civil (and social[5]) embodiment, and that civil society is simply a mechanism for preserving what is already in – albeit precarious – existence. But human life is much more deeply embedded in relatively complex social structures than this account suggests. Humans as we conceive of them do not emerge from the womb fully formed, nor do their distinctive capacities develop, like pubic hair, out of a genetic blueprint, as the (mostly) natural outcome of physiological maturation. What is most characteristically and distinctively human is the result of a long process of learning. And this process of learning is essentially social. It requires the ongoing engagement of human beings, and if it is to be at all successful, this social environment must be characterizable in certain relatively determinate ways. Determining the exact nature of these social conditions must be a matter for empirical research as well as normative reflection. But it will almost certainly include an environment characterized by care, stability, moral sensitivity, diversity of experience, interaction with others, attention to individuality, and so on.

What this means is that human social life cannot be completely resolved into relations governed by consent. Our social existence is governed as much by inherited traditions[6] – linguistic, cultural, moral, and political – as it is by structures and institutions for which our consent may and should be sought. In an important sense, we become the bearers of traditions before we become consenting agents, and the consenting agents we become will be determined in part by the traditions within which we have been nurtured. Of course, traditions are neither fixed nor inaccessible to critical scrutiny, and they may, over time, be abandoned or transformed. Indeed they *ought* to be responsive to changing situations and the progress of thought. But there is a dynamic tension here, a dialectic, that excludes a simple either/or attitude to consent and tradition.

Police work itself, and the authority vested in it, is not (and has not historically been) simply the outcome of some social contract, but it is also the expression and to some extent the perpetuator of an ongoing form of social life. What was "initiated" in 1829 was as much the outcome of a long tradition as it was a deliberate choice to create something "new."

To some extent police are expected to act as conservators of a tradition. What is more, for police themselves the work is not simply an acceptance of contractual responsibilities, but also a participation in ongoing traditions. The loyalty that police have for each other, like the loyalty of citizens to their country, is no mere fidelity to the terms of a contract, but the outcome of commitment to a way of life that has become partially constitutive of their identity. The education of police is not just the impartation of skills, but induction into a form of life. It is characterized as much by ritual and tradition as by expertise. Consent is not excluded, but it is conditioned.

Our participation in a variety of communities – families, ethnic and religious communities, political associations, and professions – informed by their distinctive traditions, brings with it the possibility of conflict, and draws attention to the importance of a personal formation that fosters individuality, and of structures that will provide opportunities for consent (and dissent). A personality constructed out of traditions that offer minimal freedom of choice risks fragmentation when those traditions come into conflict. And though refuge from such conflict can possibly be found within the walls of some single, all-encompassing tradition, such as a religious tradition, this option, though available to individuals, cannot easily be generalized. Social life of any diversity will carry within itself the seeds of struggle and accommodation.

2.1.3 *The manipulation of consent*

Were atomistic or individualistic social contractarianism considered the sole justification for our acceptance of governmental authority, our existing institutions and structures would be in dire moral straits. For the opportunities for consent and the quality of consent generally available to us would cast serious doubt on the validity of those institutions and structures.

Within most liberal democratic communities, consent is thought to be executed by means of the franchise. At periodic elections, and in the processes leading up to them, citizens have the opportunity to register their will, and to have their individual preferences count equally with those of others in determining representation, and, less directly, social policy. The franchise is not, perhaps, the only vehicle through which the popular will may be expressed. Referenda, petitions, demonstrations, and media publicity all provide channels through which advocacy, consent and dissent may be expressed. Yet they are generally considered secondary to that provided by the franchise.

All, however, are limited as vehicles of consent. Voters are not given much choice about the particular form of government they will have, the limits of its mandate, or the institutions through which it will exercise its authority. They are, rather, socialized into an existing range of structures, expectations and institutions, and their choices are to a significant extent limited by these. And when we come to actual practices of government – the influence of party machines, the prepackaging of policies, the gerrymandering of electorates, and manipulation by the media – we see much that compromises the integrity of the freedom that is supposedly honored by atomistic contractarian consent. In other words, government by consent operates within a framework provided by already existing ways of social being and doing. Although these traditions are in some measure responsive to change, and, in fact, do change over time, they are not as open to criticism and revision as simple atomistic contract theory would lead us to expect.

Locke himself was aware of the awkward fit between his notion of an original contract and its application to an ongoing civil society. He knew there was a problem "how far any one shall be looked on to have consented, and thereby submitted to any government where he has made no expressions of it at all." He found refuge in a notion of "tacit consent," supposedly given when a person has benefitted from the provisions of an existing governmental authority.[7] But though consent may sometimes be tacitly given, what Locke extends it to accommodate, and what full-fledged contractarian justifications of the existing order must also require, almost certainly stretches the concept beyond the bounds of its legitimate use.[8] Perhaps the idea of tacit consent has some residual point in hypothetical contractarian theories, which focus on some account of what (suitably defined) rational beings *would* consent to. Here, though, it has to be recognized that one vital connection with classical contract theory – *actual* consent – is missing.

We may, however, give a more generous (albeit problematic) interpretation to the Lockean notion of "tacit consent." If we see such tacit consent not as a substitute for the "original consent" that brings people into civil society, but as a "sign" that an ongoing civil order is fulfilling the contractarian mandate (what rational beings would consent to) and therefore may lay claim to our obedience, we give some weight to the ongoing customs, traditions, values, and expectations of a community over and above what has been explicitly agreed to by its members. True, there will be an ongoing dialectical interplay between the expectations of tradition and the moral requirement of consent, but it will generally have the form of a fraternal debate rather than of negotiations between rival powers.

Even though traditional and contractual expectations may well achieve some sort of mutual accommodation, it is important to recognize their theoretically different character. Traditional expectations are more immediately rooted in affective bonds and communal ties than they are in voluntaristic, deliberative accords. Contractual expectations, on the other hand, are explicitly deliberative and calculative. In practice the distinctions begin to blur. Like love and marriage, loyalty and fidelity, friendship and partnership – indeed, like morality and law – traditional and contractual relations, and the rights and obligations that go with them, exist in something of a dynamic tension, each having its place in human social life, and neither easily sustainable without the other.

Police work must take account of this fuller background to governmental authority. Were policing to involve no more than a mechanical enforcement of laws defined by a legislature, as Locke sometimes seems to envisage, there would be some reason to ground it in an explicit contract. But police work has evolved into far more than this. Strict law enforcement comprises only a part of that work, and perhaps only a small part, and even in that part the need to exercise discretion in how law is enforced requires that police appeal to something beyond the explicit terms of any contract. If police are not to lapse into private decisions about how they are to act, they must be attuned to the cultural traditions and *mores* that inform the world they serve.

2.2 POLICE AUTHORITY

The "inconveniencies" of the state of nature are generally said to provide a sufficient reason for rational individuals to cede some part of their freedom to governmental control. But if what I have thus far argued is on the right track, this justification is too simple. We are initiated into a world of social rights and obligations before we acquire the capacity to appreciate the nature and accept the responsibilities of contract, and to a large extent these traditional rights and obligations provide a framework within which our contractual rights and obligations are voluntarily acquired. True, the traditions themselves may be revised, but, like Theseus's ship, they are reconstructed gradually, while we are still aboard, and using materials that have been fashioned en route. Some contemporary contract theories of government, by focusing on hypothetical rational consent rather than actual consent, have tended to marry these dual sources of social rights and responsibilities, for in such theories the canons of rationality have become the bearers of tradition.[9]

But whether we focus on traditional rights and obligations or on those rights and obligations for which some more contractualized justification can be sought, governmental action is to be understood, in the first instance, as an exercise of *authority* rather than of naked *coercive power*.[10] I say, "in the first instance," because the ability to enforce its will is of course integral to the idea of government. Social contract theory was developed in response to that recognition as a way of reconciling the coercive power of government with a particular conception of the rights of human personality. But governmental coercion, to the extent that it has not degenerated into dictatorial coercion, is a normatively constrained form of coercion. Although authoritatively sanctioned, the coercive dimension of government obtrudes itself only when the normative force of its requirements fails, when the "majesty" of law is denied or not heeded. Government does not merely command us, it obligates us, albeit with the threat of sanctions should we transgress its requirements.

These are, of course, normative rather than merely descriptive observations. Although, for reasons to be indicated below, the persistence of governmental *authority* will almost surely depend on the government's conformity to this understanding, unless it is perceived to have right as well as might it will lose its character as the source of law and social order, and it will become indistinguishable from the gunman, bully or tyrant for whom threat is the modus operandi. What is more, even when the might of governmental authority is exercised, it is not simply might per se, but a normatively constrained force, deemed appropriate to the normative requirement that has been disobeyed.[11] Individual actions of government or its agents may be more readily characterizable as those of the authoritarian or "tough," but so long as these do not become too pervasive, the institution will retain its authoritative character.[12]

The notion of authority has a certain complex unity, though many writers have been more inclined to focus on the complexity than on the unity. It is quite common, for example, to differentiate three kinds or forms of authority: (1) positional, or de jure, authority (someone's being *in* authority); (2) actual, or de facto, authority (someone's *having* authority); and (3) expert authority (someone's being *an* authority).[13] And, by those who have made such a differentiation, it is usually claimed that these different kinds of authority are conceptually independent. Someone who is *in* authority may not *have* authority or be *an* authority. Someone who *has* authority may not be *in* authority or be *an* authority. Someone who is *an* authority may not *have* authority or be *in* authority. And it is indeed sometimes useful to make these distinctions. But they should not be allowed, as they frequently are, to obscure the centripetal forces that make them all instances of *authority*.

Authority is not a property that people possess, like body weight or skin color or recessive genes, though it is just possible that these could, rightly or wrongly, enter into attributions of authority.[14] Authority is centrally and essentially a *normative social relation*, an accorded status. Someone who is in authority or is an authority or who has authority is someone who is acknowledged by others as being in a position to do or require or know whatever happens to be the object of that authority. Someone with authority possesses a normative resource such as a right, entitlement or power. There is a consensual but not exclusively contractual element to the possession of this resource. Tradition no less than contractual agreement may sustain authority. In liberal societies, individual political authority, both de jure and de facto, may depend to a significant degree on something approaching contractual consent. But parental authority may be acknowledged for moral or customary reasons that cannot easily be construed contractually. Of course, like all traditional roles and statuses, that of parental authority may be reviewed and be reconceptualized. But the authoritative standing of parents does not initially depend on a negotiated understanding.

What links positional, actual and expert authority is not simply their being socially sustained; there is a certain content to that social support. Underlying every recognition of authority is the presumption that the person (or officeholder or group member) is "in the know." The bearer of authority is presumed to be informationally equipped to engage in or require certain conduct or to pronounce on particular matters. It is not usually necessary that authorities be "experts" in the usual sense; experts, to be sure, are "in the know," but to be "in the know" you do not have to be an expert. It is often argued that the most important quality a police officer can possess is a reasonably informed "common sense," and a recognition that officers manifest this in their work may be sufficient to sustain the presumption that a police officer is relevantly "in the know."

What we are talking about here is a *presumption* of knowledge that sustains authority, not the *possession* of knowledge that would justify it. One of the arts (or wiles) of politicians – and probably of many others in or with authority – is to maintain the appearance of being "in the know" even if there is no substance to back it up. Or, no less problematic, it is to seek to discredit those who *are* "in the know," so that they will lose or fail to achieve the authority warranted by the knowledge they in fact possess.

Police authority, as a form of governmental authority, will to some extent depend on the recognition accorded to "the powers that be." If the government of the day loses credibility, this may well be reflected in the authority the police are seen to possess.[15] But the authority of police officers will also depend on the way in which they conduct themselves, on whether *they* are perceived to be "in the know" with respect to the matters over which they have jurisdiction.[16]

Several factors make the public recognition of police authority highly volatile. As enforcers of law and maintainers of public order, they may be the executors of unpopular policies, and their activities may be perceived as being more oppressive than authoritative. And because there may be uncertainty or conflicting views about their social role, and hence about the matters on which they are expected to be "in the know," there may be a hiatus between police service and public expectations. Further, because a good deal of police work involves discretionary judgment, there is considerable room for judgments that are, or may appear to be, arbitrary, inconsistent, or unfair.

This volatility is exacerbated by two additional factors: the fact that police are given primary responsibility for the social use of coercive power, and the unifying significance of the police uniform.[17] Along with the coercive power that is given to police there also goes a heavy responsibility. We do not lightly waive our right to self-defense. And in cases in which a police officer abuses his or her authority, the uniform makes for a ripple effect. Because a police officer loses or at least obscures his or her particular identity under the uniform, what that officer does is frequently taken to characterize the police as a whole. And so, when police administrators attempt to take refuge in the idea that police corruption is to be construed on the model of "a few bad apples in the barrel," their failure to convince can sometimes be attributed not merely to the fact that the corruption is more systemic than officially acknowledged, but also to the unifying symbol of the uniform.

2.3 PRIVATE VERSUS PUBLIC POLICING

To this point I have assumed that policing is appropriately regarded as a governmental activity – whether national, state, or municipal. Even if it is insisted that the allegiance of police is to law rather than to the partisan concerns of an incumbent power, nevertheless law, whether federal, state, or local, is an expression of ongoing governmental authority, and police services are generally paid for from public revenues.

It is one thing to argue that a viable social community needs police services, but it is quite another to assume that these should be publicly provided. If, as it appears, it is not self-evident that the provision of educational and medical services is a governmental responsibility, why should we assume that police services ought to be provided from the public purse? The question is not posed *in vacuo*. There has been a growing demand for private policing, a demand that has already been realized in a variety of private investigational and security services.[18] And volunteer groups of various kinds have assumed or supplemented various police functions.

Policing may be "private" in more than one way.[19] It may be privately organized and privately paid for, privately organized and publicly paid for, publicly organized and privately paid for, and privately organized as a nonpaid or not-for-profit service. Some of the discussion to follow is more appropriately associated with one rather than another form of "private policing."

The argument for privately organized and paid-for police services can be mounted in several ways. Most radically, it can take the form of an anarchist eschewal of governmental power, a considered belief that any concentration of power will ultimately jeopardize the rights that it is intended to secure. A detailed exploration of this position belongs elsewhere.[20] Less radically, it can be argued that the policing function can be most efficiently handled by private contractors. This practical argument may have its source in two different considerations. The more general one is that government bureaucracies tend to be less efficient than private service providers, since competition ensures an optimal use of available resources. The more specific reason is that the existing publicly provided resources are inadequate and need to be supplemented from private sources. This, presumably, is the view of businesses that make use of private security services: they judge that their needs are in excess of what is publicly available. Communities, too, might supplement their existing personnel resources by employing private contractors. More significantly, it may be the view of certain groups in the community, in places in which it is considered that "the social contract" leaves them with less than they might have expected, that "private" or "community-owned" police services should replace those that have been publicly provided.[21]

The more general claim, that the private provision of police (and other) services is likely to be more efficient, and therefore better, looks more plausible in theory than in practice. If it is seen as an argument for the exclusively private provision of police services, serious questions of justice will have to be confronted. Those who cannot afford police services, and who may well be most in need of them, will be left unprovided for.[22] Historically, we have seen no reason to believe that such people will be adequately shielded by the "Invisible Hand."[23] As a community we have not been able to tolerate the provision of educational and medical services on this basis. The trickle-down theory is just what it says, and those who do not have their own access to resources suffer significantly in comparison with those who do. Even less, I believe, could we tolerate what would become the maldistributive outcome of private police services.

What may seem to be more plausible is the public funding of private police services, the contracting out of police work to private agencies that must tender for their services.[24] But recurrent scandals surrounding governmental recourse to private defense and building contractors suggests that this, too, may not be anything more than a theoretically attractive solution: The real marketplace is no paragon of efficiency or justice. The problems may not be insuperable, for the government holds the purse strings and it may also set standards and determine levels of accountability. In the correctional area, at least, there is some evidence to suggest that private agencies may do *no worse* than those over which the government has direct control. For the internal politics that so often characterizes governmental activity may be just as, if not more, destructive of the delivery of just and efficient services as the bridled workings of the profit motive. Still, this is hardly an encouraging prospect.

An intermediate position, according to which private policing is taken as the norm, and is supplemented by the public coverage of those unable to afford it, might also be contemplated, though it, too, may leave much to be desired. As public medical patients have often observed, the quality of treatment they receive, whether from public practitioners or from medical personnel who also care for private patients, is often markedly lower. We have no reason to believe that it would be otherwise in respect of the publicly covered clients of private police service providers.

In considering the demerits of private policing, we should not pass over or ignore the serious deficiencies of public policing. Were that not the case, the arguments for the private provision of police services would hardly be worth mounting. And it may well be the case that the argument for one rather than another of the foregoing alternatives will look stronger or weaker depending on the prevailing social environment. Just as our beliefs concerning the appropriate form and role of government have undergone change as social circumstances have changed, so too may our beliefs about the best way of satisfying our police needs.

A more attractive option may be to view private police services as supplementary to those that have been publicly provided. It can be argued that some social activities make greater demands on police services than the public purse is able to finance, and that these might reasonably be provided on a private basis. This is what in effect happens when individuals and companies hire or employ security personnel or private detectives, and it is in some ways analogous to private payment for educational and medical services over and above those that can be secured through other means. Although this practice may sometimes lead to jurisdictional conflicts or even to conflicts of interest, some version of it may represent a judicious response to the scarcity of social resources. Of course, there is a serious problem for the community whose *basic* police needs cannot be fully met from the public purse.

Even if it is possible to develop an argument for the provision of some private police services, important problems will have to be confronted. But they may have their source in jurisdictional and industrial factors as much as any private/public distinction. We already find such problems in the relations between firefighters, ambulance personnel, and police officers, and between local, state, and federal police officers. Their activities converge in various situations, and some determination of authority and responsibility must be made. That determination is probably made more easily in the case of private and public agencies, because it is generally accepted that the institutions of government take precedence. But in any case it will be necessary to develop structures of accountability that will minimize the "inconveniencies" that generally make the state of nature such an unattractive alternative to civil society.

2.4   THE POLICE ROLE

To this point I have assumed that Locke's executors of the legislative will are police officers as we generally understand them to be. But in a complex society this executive function is in fact much more dispersed. Internal Revenue agents, housing and FDA inspectors, "meter maids," court officers, public safety officers and bailiffs, among many others, have executive functions in the Lockean sense. Their roles are often more circumscribed and clearly defined than those of police officers, and for the most part they do not have the same individual resources of coercive force as police officers.

So what, then, is the *police* role? It should first be noted that in speaking of a "role" we are referring to more or less determinate social relations that are governed by certain norms. Roles are not constituted simply by habits or patterns of conduct. They are structured by obligations and responsibilities, rights and privileges. We may occupy various roles – familial, occupational, and associational – and our roles may change over time. To be the occupant of a role we must be aware of the relations associated with it and the norms governing it. We do not play roles blindly. In the case of many roles, we expect, partly because of the norms involved, and partly because of the importance accorded to those roles, that those who occupy them will not only be aware of, but also be committed to what the roles demand of them.[25]

Can we provide any general account of the "police" role that will give coherence to our understanding of policing and an indication of its appropriate scope and limits? On one reading of Locke, the role of police is centrally concerned with effecting the rule of law. From this executive goal there flow the various duties and privileges of police officers. But although there is significant support for this understanding within the police community and in popular police mythology, the reality of police work suggests otherwise. Studies have revealed that only a small proportion of police work is devoted to crimefighting.[26] Most police time is spent in various social service activities – intervention in family crises, searching for lost children, rescuing animals, directing traffic, supervising crowds, visiting schools, assisting the elderly, and so on – or in various administrative tasks. No doubt some police specialist groups spend much more of their time in strict law enforcement activities; but for the majority of police officers that is not so.

It does not of course follow from this that the police function ought not to be conceived of as crimefighting. It is at least arguable – and many police officers do argue – that policing has been deflected from its raison d'être, and needs to be reorganized round what they see as its central functions: the prevention of crime and the prosecution of criminals. Yet there is nothing sacrosanct about the crimefighting model, or the Lockean tradition. In the same way as we now have an expanded conception of the role that government may legitimately play in our lives, we may also have an expanded conception of the role that police should have in our communities. Just as government is seen as having a welfare as well as a protective function, so we may see police as having a social service as well as a law enforcement purpose.

The issues here are as much empirical as ideological. For they concern not only the appropriate bounds of governmental authority but also the optimal way in which that authority may be expressed. Some might want to argue that the optimal use of those with police powers is to be found in their exclusive attention to law enforcement, other social services being provided by specialists with different training and skills. But this division of labor is almost certainly at odds with the structure and demands of social life. There is much to be said for a strict division of labor in a factory setting, where the processes are limited and controlled, but in the complex environment of urban and suburban society a firm division of this kind is unrealistic. So-called domestic disputes, for example, are not either exclusively law enforcement or exclusively social work matters. They may be both (and other things), and it may be difficult to tell in advance which need is most pressing, or how it is best addressed.[27] Crowd and traffic control, too, may involve a convergence of functions. So too may the search for a missing person. There is something to be said for a response that is able to accommodate a variety of social needs.[28]

In order to deal with this complexity, but also to provide some sort of normative shape for the police function, writers on police matters have developed a variety of models of police work.[29] These models are designed to provide ways of structuring our understanding of the police role so that its legitimate limits can be determined. The strengths and weaknesses of these models highlight some of the major issues in contemporary police work.[30]

2.4.1 *The crimefighter*[31]

The major attractions of this self-explanatory model are its pedigree and simplicity. Classical social contract theory perceives such a role for police. Just as an army is needed to protect us from the barbarian without, a police force is required to protect us from the barbarian within. Thus the role has a clear rationale and a simple definition.

But there are serious practical and moral problems with the model. Violations of law vary in their seriousness, and violators differ in their depravity. Even if all violators of criminal law act in a manner that is properly considered antisocial, they do so in different ways. There is a morally relevant distinction to be drawn between the person who cheats on his taxes and the mugger, between the shoplifter and the rapist, between the person who parks illegally and the carjacker. The crimefighter model tends to obscure this. Criminals are "the enemy," "the bad guys," and police and the law-abiding community are "the good guys." This strong dichotomy between "them" and "us," normal in wartime and so easily cultivated in police circles, frequently fosters a form of police conduct that is inimical even to the purposes of crimefighting. For police come to see their role punitively, and not simply custodially; they are inclined to treat suspects as though they are guilty criminals; and, not surprisingly, skepticism and cynicism often characterize police attitudes toward the public at large.

As in military engagements, police work runs a risk of excess. Indeed, the problem may be exacerbated in police work because, unlike defending armies, which often (and no doubt prefer to) operate on or beyond territorial borders, police conduct their crimefighting activity in the midst of our ongoing social life. The dangers of innocents being caught in the "crossfire" are considerable. Privacy may be invaded, entrapment may be induced, life and limb may be jeopardized.

One way of ameliorating this problem is to set crimefighting activity into a wider framework of social service so that police will be less inclined to dichotomize their social world and so to jeopardize some of the values, such as liberty and justice, that they are employed and empowered to preserve. One of the difficulties here is that many police *like* to see themselves as crimefighters, and even though their actual work is much more diversified, the attitudes associated with the crimefighting model frequently pervade these other activities.

Even if crimefighting ought not to be seen as the raison d'être of police work, we need to remember that, aside from the armed forces, the police constitute our major social repository of coercive power. And for this reason any model of policing that fails to take into account their authority to employ force will be inadequate. This is so even with regard to those police who, in some societies, are generally unarmed.

However, as the following models indicate, the coercive possibilities of the police role can be accommodated within a wider understanding than that provided by the crimefighter.

2.4.2 *The emergency operator*[32]

Howard Cohen states that, besides law enforcement, peacekeeping and the provision of social services constitute "the authoritative social interventions characteristic of police work."[33] He notes, however, that since there are other social agents, public and private, who provide these latter services as professionals (social workers, psychologists, clergy, and so on), it is not clear what appropriate place remains for police involvement in their provision. It is Cohen's contention that as long as police are limited to offering emergency assistance of these kinds, they may be accorded authority to do so. They have what he calls a "stand-in authority": "they make decisions and take action where designated authorities cannot or will not."[34]

I do not believe that Cohen wishes to limit this sort of authority to police[35] or to suggest that this is the only authority they have. Rather, stand-in authority places an appropriate limit on police involvement in the provision of social services. Whereas others may also act as emergency stand-ins, the ubiquity and experience of the police in dealing with people will make them the most appropriate stand-ins where professionals are not available.

Once we accept that only a small proportion of police work is involved with crimefighting, Cohen's position might be taken to imply a serious downgrading of much police activity. Police social service authority will be seen as temporary and provisional, the product of an untimely conjunction of events rather than of any particular social skills or expertise that police possess. Perhaps this is as it should be. Nevertheless, as Joseph Betz points out, there is a dimension to the provision of these services that Cohen's account overlooks. The fact that police will often be succeeded by professionals (doctors, social workers, marriage counselors, and so on)

> does not mean that the police had no role in the situation if the doctor or marriage counselor got there first. The police do not stand in for them; the police handle the situation when it is not yet a problem which the doctor or marriage counselor can handle. . . . They have their own full authority for their own kind of situation, not half of somebody else's authority for someone else's problem.[36]

Cohen's apparent downgrading of police peacekeeping and social service authority may well serve only to reinforce the view that real police work and police authority is constituted by crimefighting, for only in that role will police be perceived as having more than stand-in authority. And that would go contrary to Cohen's intentions. As Betz puts it: "Police are not crimefighters out of their element doing social work; they are emergency resource personnel who usually do social work but are competent in crime control as well because of their monopoly on coercive force."[37]

But even with this emended understanding of police authority, the characterization of police as emergency operators seems both too broad and too narrow. It is too broad because many other emergency resource personnel can be so designated – ambulance operators, firefighters, and so on. It is too narrow, because much police work does not seem to be easily characterizable as a response to some social emergency – community-oriented policing, for example, in which the avoidance of emergency situations might seem to be more to the point.[38] The second element in Betz's account might therefore seem to provide the appropriate distinguishing feature, their monopoly on coercive force. So argues Egon Bittner.

2.4.3 *The social enforcer*

Bittner believes that the unifying feature of police work, and the source of police authority, can be found in the likely need for coercive intervention: "The role of police is to address all sorts of human problems when and insofar as the problems' solutions may require the use of force at the point of their occurrence."[39]

Bittner's model has several attractions. It seems to do justice to many of the situations in which police are involved. Not only in their crimefighting role, but also in many emergency situations, police are appropriately involved in part because they are repositories of coercive power. Domestic and other confrontations may require forcible intervention, and access to coercive force may be needed at demonstrations and accidents to ensure crowd and traffic control. The model preserves the strong identification that police feel with their possession of coercive power while at the same time extending their role beyond that of crimefighting. And at a theoretical level, the model coheres well with the traditional liberal understanding of police agencies as communal reservoirs of coercive power.

But there are also serious drawbacks to the model. As it stands, Bittner's account is too broad. Police are not the only members of society whose authority to use coercion is recognized. Parents are usually accorded the authority to use some coercion in relation to their children; school teachers, too, may be granted limited coercive authority. "Bouncers" in nightclubs may use force to remove the unruly; and in similar vein there are various private security agencies with recognized coercive powers. Even citizens are granted powers of arrest and detention in certain circumstances. But Bittner's account is also too narrow. Many police activities – for example, informing a woman of her spouse's death in an accident, giving safety lectures to school groups, searching for missing amnesiacs, opening locked car doors, and running youth programs – do not call attention to their access to coercive force.

An even greater problem for Bittner's model is that it focuses too directly on the coercive dimension of police authority. Although it is true that police are authorized to use force where necessary to carry out their responsibilities, we should not confuse their role with means that are available to them in their performance of that role. That confusion perpetuates one of the features of police work that many people find most problematic, the tendency of police to resolve issues by means of force and threat. Citizens frequently complain that their encounters with police are intimidating, that threat is used when negotiation would have been more appropriate, and that force is resorted to when mediation was called for. Certain features of police culture have reinforced this: the emphasis on physique and "street smarts" and a disdain for formal education, the macho values that are fostered and savored, the encouragement often given to "come on strong,"[40] and the resistance to and masculinizing of female officers. We need a model of police work that acknowledges the nonnegotiable force at police disposal without transforming it into the police raison d'être.

2.4.4 *The social peacekeeper*

It is this characterization that seems to me to offer the best potential for accommodating in a practical and normatively satisfactory way the varied tasks that police are called upon to perform.[41] One of its virtues lies in its deep historical roots, allowing us to see its contemporary manifestations in evolutionary rather than revolutionary terms, as the historical bearer of a tradition rather than as some johnny-come-lately bandaid for our social problems. Continuity blends with change, history with contemporary need.

The origins of the model can be found in the Anglo-Saxon notion of the king's peace, a zone of tranquillity that was originally local, personal, and seasonal, but which was gradually extended to encompass the whole realm, not merely during the life of the king, but in perpetuity.[42] Breaches of the king's peace were crimes, subject to fines. In republican society, the king's peace became the public peace, a social environment characterized by ordered liberty. Modern-day police have become its guardians.

On this understanding, the peacekeeper model does not stand over against the crimefighter model or social service model (as is the case in many discussions[43]), but it embraces them. It is grounded in the recognition that there are many things that may and do disturb the peace or tranquillity of a community, not just crime, but disaster, noncriminal social conflict, the movement of people, and even large gatherings. The role of the police is to ensure or restore peaceful order.

Communal peace as I understand it here is not simply a matter of some externally imposed structure (law enforcement), but of a perceived security, of ordered liberty. It has a significant psychological as well as a behavioral dimension. Police, to use Wayne Hanewicz's terminology, are there to distribute psychologically satisfying closure on social conflict.[44] Perhaps that puts it too reactively: the role of police is not simply to resolve social conflict, but, so far as possible, within a reflective and ongoing framework of values and traditions, to minimize its likelihood. Police have preventive, deterrent, and crowd / traffic control functions as well as mediatorial and law enforcement ones.[45]

Perhaps the foregoing is still expressed too negatively. The functions of police are not limited to keeping a lid on the sources of social disorder. Within the bounds of the resources that are available to them, they may engage in forms of social assistance that actually enhance the quality of social life, not only deterring crime and disorder and dissipating fear, but actually fostering social trust and cooperation. That, indeed, is often seen as a key element in community policing.

Such peacekeeping is not to be confused with pacification. Although police generally function as agents of government, it is to democratic governmental authority that the peacekeeper model is intended to apply. In so-called police states, in which police function to impose the will of government against the people, their function is one of pacification rather than of social peacekeeping.

Hanewicz suggestively links the peacekeeping function of police with a deeper human need for ordered experience. Ordered experience, he claims, is not simply a desirable end, but essential to human life as we wish it to be. At the most fundamental level, it is provided by conceptualization – that by which we render the perceptual field intelligible; at the social level, the "need is met in its most elementary form by predictability in behavior, by commitments, roles, social institutions."[46] But these commitments, roles, and social institutions are not fully self-sustaining for the same reason that Locke considered the state of nature to be deficient. There is need for an independent "other" to ensure or restore the order that we need, to help maintain and create conditions under which trust can grow. Police constitute part of that "other," and, given adequate training in discretionary responsiveness as it relates to public law and policy, they are able to contribute to the need we have for a peaceably ordered social environment.

So understood, the peacekeeper model is broad enough to encompass most of the work that police do, whether it is crimefighting, traffic control, or intervention in crisis situations. But what is more important is the irenic cast that it gives to police work. Although the model has room for the use of nonnegotiable force, its instrumental or subservient character is emphasized. The use of coercion to enforce the law or settle disputes is not appropriate just because police are socially recognized repositories of coercive power or because they have coercive power at their disposal, but because in their peacekeeping role such means have become necessary. If police are seen as possessors of authority and not simply as wielders of coercive power, and if that authority is vested in their perceived ability to preserve and restore a peaceable social order, then their use of coercion becomes a last (albeit sometimes necessary) resort rather than their dominant modus operandi.

Again, my purpose in emphasizing "peacekeeping" is not to downplay the importance of "crimefighting." Law enforcement is indeed the "hard edge" of police work. Crime can generally be considered to constitute the most serious and worrisome disturbance to a peaceable social environment. But just as the peacekeeping perspective refocuses our attention from coercive force to authority, it does the same for law enforcement, when that is viewed as an element of peacekeeping.

There is one final reason not to downplay the importance of crimefighting, a reason rooted in the historical origins of the peacekeeper model in the notion of the king's peace. The king, as protector of the realm, was concerned primarily with a public rather than a private order and peace. What we speak of as "civil" or "private" disputes are not generally the concern of police. Their commitment is to a broader peaceableness, to fostering and maintaining an order that is not exclusive to the concerns of particular individuals, but focuses on concerns that have wider social ramifications. Crimes, though often committed against individuals, are seen as violative of that wider social order. "The People" take action. Civil claims or breaches focus on action in its private aspect, and police involvement will normally be limited to what might be called the public ramifications of such actions.

The problem, of course, is that the private–public distinction, problematic enough in theory, is sometimes even more difficult to make in practice. Domestic disputes are now seen as falling within the domain of police concern, but school demonstrations generally do not. What happens in such cases is that police must judge whether a particular form of disorder has reached a point at which wider social order is implicated. In many cases, unfortunately, police–community relations have been strained by poor or controversial judgments in this area.

It is primarily in terms of social peacekeeping that I shall understand the police role in this book. Having regard to the values we associate with peace, a climate of trust in which our human selves may flourish in community with others, I suggest that, if taken seriously, this conception could provide the basis for a profoundly renovating and conciliatory style of policing through which both police and community might be brought together in a joint and mutually supportive enterprise.

Chapter 3

Professionalism, the police role, and occupational ethics

I never did or countenanced, in public life, a single act inconsistent with the strictest good faith; having never believed there was one code of morality for a public and another for a private man.

Thomas Jefferson[1]

How you cling to your purity young man! How afraid you are to soil your hands! All right, stay pure! What good will it do? Why did you join us? Purity is an ideal for a yogi or a monk.

Jean-Paul Sartre[2]

There is, admittedly, a certain vagueness to the idea that police are social peacekeepers. Yet, as I have indicated, this characterization is not without content or even normative significance. In the present chapter, I want to focus on another way in which this conception of the police role may be given clearer definition: the claim so integral to much contemporary police rhetoric, namely, that policing is a *profession*, and that police are professional peacekeepers.

Viewed historically, policing has not had the high status associated with the traditional professions. Police have usually come from groups with low or only modest social, economic, and educational status, and entry qualifications have focused as much on physical characteristics and technical proficiency as on intellectual aptitude. Given the nature of much actual police work, and the way in which it is often conceived (police as enforcers), this emphasis is probably not surprising. This is not to imply that policing has been a low-status occupation, along with unskilled labor or janitorial work. The "commanding" uniform, the power and social responsibility associated with the police role, and the opportunities policing has provided for job security and career advancement, have made police work attractive to many, and among some groups (for example, the Irish in New York, Boston, and Los Angeles) a favored career choice. Colored minorities (and women) have not been welcomed into the police "fraternity," and for some this exclusiveness has constituted a positive element in policing's status.

But what has been historically true is no longer as obviously so. There have been significant social changes with respect to the place of minorities and women in the work force. As well, from August Vollmer's 1936 treatise, *The Police in Modern Society*,[3] to the present, there has been a loud though not uninterrupted call for increased professionalism on the part of police, and for the recognition of policing's essentially professional status. Although some practitioners have resented what they see as the downgrading of the old "beat cop," and many commentators have bemoaned the gap between rhetoric and reality, the shortcomings have often been construed as contingent and remediable.

The call for professionalization has to be understood against a background of historical reasons why police work has not been accorded a high social status. Low entry requirements have no doubt been one factor, and the emphasis on mere "order maintenance" another. But more important has been the lack of social independence of police – their historical links with the political machine and organized crime, and their susceptibility to corruption. Such links may have been stronger in the United States than in Great Britain, and the corruption more systemic. But probably for that reason policing in Great Britain is generally accorded higher status than it is in the United States.

Advocates of police professionalization have argued that, by raising the status of police work through professionalization, job morale will be boosted and pride engendered, greater public respect fostered, a better quality of intake attracted, services improved, efficiency increased, and corruption curbed. Not only the police themselves, but also many academic commentators on police work have argued that professionalization would function as a partial panacea for policing's ills.

These expectations, however, have depended on certain questionable assumptions about both the nature of the professions and the police role. In this chapter I will consider some of the problems that confront policing's search for professional status (3.1.1). In addition, I shall point out several moral dangers in professionalization (3.1.2), and the preferability of professionalism as a personal and organizational goal (3.1.3). I shall also consider the extent to which professional status can be thought to confer special moral privileges on its bearers (3.2).

3.1   THE PROFESSIONS, PROFESSIONALIZATION AND PROFESSIONALISM

3.1.1   *What is a profession?*[4]

It is not easy to give an uncontroversial account of what constitutes a profession. The social status generally attaching to professions (as distinct from mere occupations), has conduced to something of a stampede for the kudos attached to professional status, and the notion has become distended and imprecise. It is no accident that Harold Wilensky skeptically asked: "The Professionalization of Everyone?"[5]

If, however, we take the so-called "classical" or "learned" professions as paradigmatic, some reasonably well-defined contours can be discerned. I shall use these as a basis for considering the professional status or aspirations of police work. I shall contrast this account of a profession with one proposed by Michael Davis. Although I take issue with Davis I believe that his approach reveals a very important dimension of *professional conduct* that I will later distinguish from the social status of *professionalization*.

3.1.1.1 Provision of a public service.

It has been important to the character and status of the traditional professions of law, medicine, architecture, education, and theology that they have been thought to offer a valuable public service. Their practitioners have provided highly skilled and knowledgeable assistance in respect of some of our most important interests – our negotiations with others, our bodily integrity, our need for shelter, our intellectual development, and spiritual destiny. Members of the professions have been bearers of considerable public trust, and in the conduct of their activities are often privy to the most private details of people's lives. For this reason, there has usually gone with professional status a strong tradition of provider-client confidentiality. Although this individual provider-client confidentiality has sometimes expressed itself in ways that are inimical to the wider public, it has been generally believed that the overall public interest is best served by maintaining a firm practice of privacy in provider-client relationships. *a groups commitment for some benefit*

Michael Davis believes the provision of a public service to be a relatively contingent feature of professional status. He contends that what essentially defines a profession is the mutual commitment of a group of persons to some moral ideal, persons whose work for that ideal benefits from their group membership.[6] Though this ideal is commonly constituted by the benefit that it offers a wider public, that it does so is largely accidental.[7] I believe that rendering this connection merely contingent underplays the social significance of the professions. It is *just because* members of the professions provide a highly valued public service that we become so exercised by the ideals to which they are devoted, and the ways in which those ideals are expressed.

When looked at from the perspective of public service, policing poses no special difficulties. There is little doubt that police provide, or are expected to provide, an important public service. Our interest in a peaceable social order is of highest importance, and through their activities police are capable of making a significant contribution to an order of secure tranquillity. Their doing so, moreover, may require a level of trust between provider and client for which confidentiality would be appropriate. Police officers are often cognizant of, and need access to, details of people's lives that would normally be regarded as private.

But professional status is not constituted simply by the fact that a public service is provided. Bank managers and loans officers also perform an important public service, and at the same time have or require access to details of a person's life (for example, financial status) that should be kept confidential, because private. Yet we do not normally regard what they do as a profession.[8]

3.1.1.2 Code of ethics. Because the services provided by the professions touch on people's most important and/or private interests, professionals are generally governed by a "code of ethics." The collective adoption of such a code is often taken as a sign of a vocation's or occupation's true professionalization. The professional code comprises a public set of constraints under which members are pledged to operate, and is intended to provide a tangible basis for public trust (see Chapter 12, Section 12.4).

In regard to this last comment, Davis would demur. On his view, the purpose of a code of ethics is not primarily to mediate between the providers and users of services, but between the providers themselves. As he understands it, "a code of ethics is primarily a *convention between professionals*" that is intended to optimize the coordination of their professional activities.[9] The code prescribes how, if they are to pursue the *telos*, or ideal, that is implicit in their activity (whether it is health, justice, or peacekeeping), professionals can do so with the best results, and with the least cost to themselves and those they care about. What is at stake in the code is the integrity of their activity, and not the maintenance of some public trust.

Although, as I shall later suggest, there is an important truth in what Davis says, I believe that it is just as, if not more, important to see professional codes as public assurances as it is to see them as integrity-enhancing conventions between professionals. Not that there need be any inherent conflict or tension between these two ends, for maintaining the integrity of the professional activity will generally contribute to the public good and thus sustain the public trust.[10] But the possession of professional status is a form of public recognition, and unless the standards that enhance the integrity of professionals are publicly available there will be some reason to doubt the commitment to excellence in service.

Codes of ethics are as much for the benefit of the public served as they are for the professional. They offer a guarantee to those who use professional services that certain standards will be observed in their delivery. But since there is also an internal dimension to that recognition, those who violate the code of ethics may jeopardize their standing as recognized members of a particular profession. For the code helps to unify otherwise separated practitioners into a professional community. [undergone public review]

Police organizations have often promulgated codes of ethics, and this has been largely coincident with endeavors to professionalize policing.[11] In the United States, Vollmer's protegé O. W. Wilson's Wichita "Square Deal" Code (1928) became the precursor of the International Association of Chiefs of Police Law Enforcement Code of Ethics (1957; 1991), still the most widely used of all law enforcement codes. Already in the 1938–39 Report of its Committee on the Professions, the IACP had stated that an essential element of professionalization consisted in the promulgation of a code of ethics that would prescribe standards of conduct for relations of members of the professions with the public and each other, and would provide a grounding for public service that would transcend exclusively economic considerations.

But the possession of a code of ethics is not of itself or even in association with the provision of a public service sufficient to constitute an occupation a profession. Many commercial enterprises (for example, store chains, manufacturers, publishers, appliance repair companies) and fraternal service organizations (for example, Rotary, Lions) have codes of conduct which not only link those who are covered by them, but also seek to assure their publics of the high standards that they observe. However, the members of such bodies may not be regarded as professionals, despite the importance of the public services they provide.

3.1.1.3 Special knowledge and expertise. More than anything else, the services provided by the professions are not "ordinarily" available with anything like the degree of sophistication or expertise that the professional is able to provide. The ordinary socialization of human beings does not give them the competence that professional service offers. As the etymology hints, professionals are special by virtue of what they profess. They possess a scarce social resource, "higher" learning: knowledge and skill that is generally available only to those who have undertaken a long and arduous program of study. What is more, the practical services provided by the professional tend to demand sophisticated knowledge and expertise that only the professional can provide at an acceptable level. Once an occupation has achieved professional status, the level of knowledge and expertise provided by its practitioners tends to become the social standard. Less, except in an emergency, will not normally do.

Davis would probably not dispute part of this account. For, to the extent that a profession is constituted by a group of persons who are dedicated to some practical ideal, it is to be expected that its members will devote more than ordinary attention to the outworking of that ideal. And that will bespeak a proficiency and knowledge concerning the ways of realizing it. But because, for him, the (contingently social) ideal to which the members of the professional group mutually devote themselves need not be served by the members of the profession in the way in which the profession has in fact chosen to serve it, "an occupation does not need society's recognition in order to be a profession."[12] I would suggest, on the contrary, that granting an occupation the status of a profession is to give it a form of social recognition, and that this recognition is granted only if the occupation's implicit ideal is pursued in a manner that is believed to serve an important social interest in a unique or at least superior way.

It is at this point that the case for considering policing a profession begins to look problematic. Many would argue that police work requires "common sense" more than anything else, and that beyond that police officers need to be "jacks of all trades" rather than masters of some one. They are not even like general medical practitioners, for the knowledge they are required to have for most of the tasks they perform is generally available, albeit not always to the particular persons they are assisting.[13] Hence Howard Cohen's attribution to police of a stand-in authority with respect to their social service role.[14]

More, however, may be said on behalf of police expertise, especially in its modern urban manifestations. In its law enforcement aspect, for example, police must now have a fairly detailed understanding of the law, lest people be wrongfully arrested. Hostage negotiators, bomb squads and emergency teams are often carefully selected and highly trained. In their investigative role, police must master increasingly complex technology and have expertise in scientific methods of detection. And in their general social service function, they have to be rapidly responsive and highly sensitive to the complexities and changing character of social life. If, indeed, police are to be considered social "problem solvers," then they will require a much more extensive knowledge than is conveyed by the idea of "common sense." Arguably, in-service programs and additional training requirements have transformed modern urban police from critical stand-ins to innovative and highly skilled service providers.[15]

But there is a tension here that is not easy to resolve. The requirements of highly specialized knowledge, on the one hand, and broadly-based competence, on the other, tend to pull in opposite directions. To some extent it is overcome by a division of labor within policing. At the patrol level, the emphasis will be more heavily on broadly-based competence than on highly specialized knowledge and expertise. But in various specialist units the knowledge and expertise required may be much more like that characteristic of the traditional professional. Even so, there is still a significant gap between the specialized knowledge and expertise required of most police officers and that traditionally associated with the professions. In-service training programs are not really comparable to the course requirements for admission to medical or legal practice. The skilled detective is more like a skilled mechanic than an engineer. *patrolmen are not professionals while detectives, bomb squads, SWAT etc are professionals*

3.1.1.4 Higher education. The issue may be brought into sharper relief by the frequent assertion that professional status requires the successful completion of a college or university degree.[16] A craftsman may need to undertake a long and arduous study or apprenticeship before mastering his craft. And when he does he will possess a knowledge and expertise not evident in others. But this does not make the craftsman a professional in the requisite sense. Perhaps this can be explained in part by the more marginal service that the skilled craftsman provides. But it is also thought to relate in part to the kind of knowledge supposedly possessed by the professional. The practical expertise of the professional is often said to be embedded in theory, in a grasp of the general principles governing the service, and not simply in the practical knowledge and skill of the craftsman or copyist. This is what distinguishes the architect from the draftsman, the engineer from the mechanic, the educated from the merely trained. The professional is not simply a technician; he or she is believed to possess an insight into and understanding of his or her work that the technician neither has nor requires.

In this respect, certainly, police have traditionally differed from members of other professional groups. The academic requirement for entry into police work has generally been no more than a high school diploma and six months of academy training. And even less is sometimes considered sufficient. This, however, is not to deny the strong pressures sometimes exerted to demand more of police: Some larger departments have begun to require some college education, if not as a prerequisite for entry then at least for promotion. Informing these pressures has been the rhetoric of professionalization.

At a departmental level, the upgrading of police work and police preparedness has expressed itself in the movement for professional accreditation. In the United States, where policing is organized on the basis of geographical and political divisions, the call for professionalization initially foundered on the lack of national cohesion. In the 1960s and 1970s, three major efforts to develop programs for upgrading the quality of law enforcement were instituted – the President's Commission on Law Enforcement and the Administration of Justice (1967), the National Advisory Commission on Criminal Justice Standards and Goals (1973), and the American Bar Association/IACP Standards for the Urban Police Function (1973; 1979). But it was not until 1979 that a serious effort was made to give effect to these attempts at police professionalization. At that point, four major law enforcement organizations – the International Association of Chiefs of Police (IACP), the National Organization of Black Law Enforcement Executives (NOBLE), the National Sheriffs' Association (NSA), and the Police Executive Research Forum (PERF) – sponsored a Commission on Accreditation for Law Enforcement Agencies (CALEA) to develop and administer a set of national law enforcement standards. In 1980 CALEA was incorporated as a private, nonprofit corporation; applications for accreditation were accepted in 1983; and the first police department was accredited in 1984. Five-yearly accreditation now functions as an "independent" statement that the quality of service offered by a particular law enforcement agency is what one might expect from professionals.

To be accredited, law enforcement organizations must not only meet several hundred individual standards of competence, but, as an expression of their commitment to public service, they must also adopt a statement of mission or purpose and values. By 1994, well over two hundred departments (including one in Canada) had been accredited, with almost one thousand others progressing toward accreditation.[17]

Yet, despite this press for individual and departmental upgrading, there remains a strong resistance to the conception of professionalization that is being fostered among police. Only a small fraction of departments is involved in seeking accreditation, and there are clearly different schools of thought on the wisdom and appropriateness of individual "educational upgrading." In 1967 Arthur Niederhoffer referred to a "simmering internecine conflict" in the police establishment between defenders of an "old" school who felt that what police needed for success was common sense and street experience, and many newer recruits who felt that modern-day policing required a college-type education.[18] To some extent that tension still exists, because it is reflective of a clash between proponents of two conceptions of the police role – between those who believe that police work is about maintaining law and order, and those who see it in broader and more creative social service terms, as reflected in the social peacekeeper model.[19]

The macho law-and-order approach is often strongly represented in police unions, and this has sometimes constituted an additional barrier to professionalization in its traditional sense. Although unions often use the rhetoric of professionalization, and for economic and status reasons may strongly support it, their actual demands often serve to impede moves toward professionalization as I have so far outlined it. Where there is insistence on seniority as a condition for promotion, resistance to increased educational demands that would prejudice "old hands," reluctance to allow that abuses may have occurred, a militant interest in and focus on "fighting power," a contempt for social service and "community policing," and so on, the professionalization that is advocated with gusto is likely to be compromised.

These impediments aside, we may still doubt whether the upgrading of police education and the accreditation of law enforcement agencies bring policing to the point of professional eligibility. For one thing, we may want to distinguish between what it is desirable for police to have and what it is essential for them to have. It may be very desirable for police to have a college education without it being essential to the acceptable performance of the services they are called on to provide. But mere desirability is probably not enough for the purposes of professionalization. A higher education would probably benefit people in many occupations – secretarial, clerical, administrative – without there being any broad agreement that they could or should constitute professions. Even though a college education probably broadens the mind, sharpens one's reasoning processes, and makes possible a tolerance for ambiguity – all valuable attributes in a police officer[20] – they do not establish police work as a profession in the strong sense. For the higher education that is recommended for police officers, unlike that associated with, say, law, medicine, and architecture, need not have any very direct relation to the way in which they will conceive and perform their duties.

3.1.1.5 Autonomy and discretionary authority. Because of their grasp of the general theoretical principles informing the service they provide, professionals are usually accorded a great deal of autonomy in the way in which they render their service. The service they provide is not dictated by a rigid and closely defined set of rules but by judgment and skill anchored in a thorough grasp of the principles governing the service. This is not to deny that there will be rules to which professionals will be expected to conform; however, such rules will not generally prescribe a narrow course of behavior but will leave professionals with considerable scope for creative counsel and conduct. Their discretion is likely to be quite considerable.

Broad discretionary authority might also be thought a characteristic of policing. But the de facto discretionary power available to police cannot be assumed to be identical with that possessed by professionals (see further, Chapter 5, Section 5.1). For one thing, though police discretion might be necessitated in part by variety in the circumstances that require police intervention – so that no set of rules could fully encompass them – the principles that inform police decisions would probably be those of common sense rather than those operative in the application of specialized knowledge. Such discretion, although extensive, is also severely constrained by the hierarchical character of the police organization. The fact that superiors are likely to be held jointly responsible for the conduct of subordinates militates against the possession of a large amount of de jure discretion. Much of the so-called discretionary behavior of police officers is really just unsupervised conduct. *professionals are not governed by a central authority*

Unlike most traditional professionals, public police officers are, and must remain, employees. They are not independent suppliers of the services they provide. Doctors in hospitals frequently act in a consultant capacity or have the option of going into private practice. Employed lawyers and architects may aspire to partnership or at least to a large degree of institutional autonomy. Academics have the freedoms and protection of tenure. Even members of the clergy tend to be relatively free from centralized control, provided they work within their "code of office." Unlike professional employees, police find that not only are their hours, salary, and general working conditions centrally controlled, but even many of the decisions they are called on to make.

In recent years, however, a number of police administrators who have recognized the inherent tension between professional discretion and the paramilitary organization of their departments have sought to replace what is called "rule-driven" policing with policing that is said to be "value-driven." Acknowledging that the increasingly bulky Patrol Guides have become impossibly detailed, that even so they frequently fail to address the subtle operational needs of officers, and that following their endless directives is most often a function of supervision, they have made some effort to encourage approaches to decision making that look not merely to behavioral guidelines but to the values implicit in the confronting situation and the values to be realized by the decisions to be undertaken.

A department that is value driven will not do away with all rules and/or guidelines. The issue is one of perspective and emphasis – what you start from, and how you move from there, not necessarily what you finish up with in practice. Take high-speed pursuit policy, for example. A department may promulgate guidelines for high-speed pursuits that tell Radio Motor Patrol officers when they may and may not engage in high-speed pursuits, what procedures they should follow with respect to the use of sirens, barlights, radio contact with base, accidents, handling of the suspect after a pursuit, and so on. Or it may, as has occurred in some cases, remind police of their role as social peacekeepers, set out the public and personal safety priorities to be observed, and then seek to show how, in enunciating various practical guidelines regarding occasions for such pursuits and procedures that should be followed, these are practically expressive of those fundamental goals and values.[21] *Don't understand the importance of*

Ideally, such values ought not to be simply institutional or "departmental" values, but also values of the officers who are expected to act on them. Although it is possible that in a rule-driven department these values are implicit or were at least operative in the minds of those who developed the rules and guidelines, if they are not made explicit, and then linked in a substantive way to the rules and guidelines that they inform, it is hardly surprising that officers will view them opportunistically and legalistically, effectively cut off from their motivational ties in values.

But admirable though the sentiments informing value-driven policing are, and supportive as they are of guided professional discretion, we are probably still a long way from realizing this form of policing in most police departments. Even within professedly value-driven departments, the existing hierarchical structure and political accountability of management make it unlikely that, even if they should be granted it, line officers will be permitted to exercise significant professional discretion within ethical guidelines. The value-driven guidelines are still top-down deliverances, and are sometimes conjoined with concrete guidelines in what seems to be an almost fortuitous manner.[22]

3.1.1.6 Self-regulation. Although the professions focus on individual autonomy, their practitioners have, over time, tended to institutionalize themselves into professional certifying (and decertifying) associations. It is argued that this ensures "quality control" of the services they provide. And for the most part it does. But institutionalization has also been used to protect the economic and other interests of members, and the rhetoric of quality control is sometimes a rationalization for self-serving interests.[23]

Hand in hand with institutionalization has gone a demand for self-regulation. It is asserted that professionals themselves should be the ones to pass judgment on the quality of their services, for, as possessors and dispensers of scarce knowledge and expertise, they are in the best position to determine whether a service is being properly provided.

Police have fairly consistently claimed the same privilege. In their use of coercive and deadly force they have often acted in ways that others have felt to be improper. But they have responded by arguing that, as the socially approved executors of coercive and deadly force, knowledgeable and trained in its utilization, it is for them to determine whether it has been appropriately – that is, "professionally" – employed. Unless some gross violation such as a violation of the criminal law is involved, they have claimed that it is for them alone to determine whether one of their number has acted unprofessionally.

There is something to be said for the police position. Because of the nature of their work, police may be expected to have acquired a body of experience and knowledge of situations superior to that of the individuals who seek their assistance. Moreover, it is often difficult for outsiders to appreciate the constraints and pressures under which police must work. Because police must frequently intervene in situations that threaten the peaceable order we ordinarily enjoy, the vantage point of an outsider may give a distorted picture of the officer's situation. "Monday-morning quarterbacking," with "the 20/20 vision of hindsight," is not always reasonable.

But we should not take such demands at face value. It is well known that the traditional professions have frequently taken refuge behind the screen of valid and limited self-regulation as a means of circumventing public accountability. This has happened sufficiently often to mute claims for self-regulation. Such claims as can be made for self-regulation depend on the very specialized character of professional knowledge and expertise, and hence on the difficulty of regulating them from the outside. It is doubtful whether police can lay claim to such specialized knowledge. Even if it is difficult for individual outsiders to have the range of experience available to police and an empathetic appreciation of the constraints and pressures under which police have to work, the difficulty is as much affective as epistemic. It is not really beyond the ability of an outside collective with active moral sensitivities to appreciate the exigencies under which police work and the merits of the choices they must make. Underscoring this is the fact that what has often been at stake when the police use of coercive and deadly force has been questioned is the general moral issue of the appropriate occasions for using such force, and not simply the individual circumstances surrounding some particular use of it.

On the basis of the foregoing six factors – the provision of a public service, the promulgation of a code of ethics, the possession of special knowledge and expertise, the requirement of higher education, the according of autonomy and discretionary authority, and the grant of a privilege of self-regulation – it is difficult to see police work in general as qualifying for professional status. No doubt, with an increasing division of police labor, and increasingly sophisticated knowledge and expertise being demanded in some areas of policing, the argument for ascribing to some police some form of professional status will appear stronger. But it is also clear that a great deal of the work that police do, and that they will probably continue to do as part of their social peacekeeping role, does not require anything like the specialized knowledge and expertise normally presupposed by professional status.

For writers like Michael Davis, I suspect, this conclusion will almost surely appear too strong. Davis believes that all that is essential is the commitment to a certain *telos* or ideal, best served through association with others of like mind.[24] But this fails to do justice to the self-understanding of the phenomenon of professionalization. Nevertheless, as I indicated at the beginning of this section, I believe that Davis's conception points to something important about professional activity – about *professionalism* rather than about the *professions*.

But before we attend more closely to that distinction (3.1.3), let us consider whether there is anything to be lost in denying that policing warrants professional status.

3.1.2 *The moral problems of professionalization*

To this point I have not questioned the assumption that professional status is a good thing, or that it is worthwhile for police officers to strive for increased professionalization. If we start, however, not from what might be called the conceptual expectations of professional status – which emphasize expertise, ethical conduct, learning and individual responsibility, features that might incline one to a positive view of professional status – but instead from the social manifestations of professionalism, there emerges a somewhat different picture: of élitism, paternalism, exploitation, alienation, and discrimination. As conceptualized, professionalization represents the *idealization* of a phenomenon whose actual social worth is considerably more problematic than suggested by the account I have provided. These problems, furthermore, are not easily remediable, being to some extent endemic to the social status sought by and accorded to professionals.

As possessors of somewhat arcane knowledge and refined skills – knowledge and skills that are believed to be of great practical importance – professionals possess considerable social power. That power is concentrated and protected, and to a large extent exploited, and access to the services associated with it are often limited by ability to pay. This does not reflect on professional conduct exclusively, but points more generally to problems that occur when humans have the opportunity to exercise power over each other. Power, as Shelley observed, "like a desolating pestilence, pollutes whate'er it touches."[25] Obviously, institutionalizing that power may not do much to alleviate the situation.

At one level, the power available to professionals has made them the envy of others. Their indispensability to the social services they provide, their control over how they provide them, and their relatively small numbers, have given them high social standing. It is this enviable social standing and its perquisites that have been significantly responsible for what has now become a stampede to professionalize other occupations. Engineers, psychotherapists, nurses, school teachers, accountants, and even secretaries, insurance agents, and real estate brokers have fought, along with police officers, to gain public recognition as professionals. The increasing division of labor and growing sophistication of the work involved in various occupational roles has given some assistance to such claims. And in some cases they have been successful: Engineers were already being given professional recognition in the late nineteenth century.

Still, professional status as a form of social recognition is hard to come by. Though people desire it for themselves, they are slow to recognize it on the part of others, as this accords to others an autonomy that diminishes their own control over the services that those others provide. In relinquishing, or even in sharing, control, especially when they are vulnerable, people need to have confidence in those to whom they entrust some of their most important affairs. Less admirably, precisely because professional status is taken to involve membership in an élite group, then, if that status is accorded too easily its currency will be downgraded. In the words of the pithy, if snooty, aphorism: If everybody's somebody then nobody's anybody.

But the fact that professionals constitute a social élite with considerable power over people's lives, taken together with the fact that that power has often been abused, has given rise to a backlash against professionals and professionalization. In some cases this backlash has had its origins in a form of social egalitarianism, a reaction against the social class differentiation that tends to go with membership of a profession. But sometimes the response has been less sweeping and has taken the form of calling attention to some permanent dangers that confront the drive for professionalization. I mention three in particular.

3.1.2.1 Professional paternalism. "Professions," George Bernard Shaw remarked, "are conspiracies against the laity."[26] Shaw's cynicism aside, it has, nevertheless, been common for professionals to believe that the special knowledge and expertise they possess entitles them to decide what will be best for those whom they serve. Although we are most familiar with this paternalism in the fields of medicine and law, examples abound in the other professions. And to the extent that police see themselves as professionals, the same temptation will be, if it is not already, present.

I do not want to take the position that professional paternalism is always unjustified. But I think it is usually unjustified. And it is unjustified because of the presumption that it embodies, that the professional's judgment should take precedence over the choices of clients. The professional paternalist figures not only that he or she knows better than others what will be in their best interests, but that he or she is entitled to make those choices for them. This is deeply problematic. For individuals, as choosers, have a certain claim on the way in which they live out their lives. Though others may advise, the responsibility and privilege of determining their path is theirs. On its face, paternalism is not merely intrusive but insulting.

But apart from the arrogation to oneself of the prerogatives of others that professional paternalism involves, it is frequently misguided. In medicine this is particularly clear. A doctor may be well placed to determine what would be most appropriate medically for a patient. But the decision to submit to a particular treatment regimen cannot be presumed to be a simple medical decision, that is, a decision about bodily or physiological well being.[27] Rather, because it is a decision that may involve the whole of a person's life, it must take into account not only the person's medical needs, but also involve his or her quality of life, psychological well being, religious beliefs, economic and family situation, hopes and expectations, factors that are not usually as well known to the doctor as they are to the patient. And even if they are, the weight that is given to each of them is for the patient to determine, not the doctor.

As police begin to see themselves as professionals they too will be tempted to use such knowledge and expertise as they have as a justification for determining how best they may render service to others. It is easy to see how, in situations involving domestic violence, disturbed persons, and crowd control, police, either individually or collectively, might make decisions that will not have an adequate regard for the objects of their attention. In their hands this may be a particularly dangerous power, for police are often taught to assert their authority by "coming on strong." The assertion of "superior" knowledge is coupled with coercive power.

3.1.2.2 Alienation. Although professionals become privy to serviceable knowledge and expertise that others lack, they are not by that fact better able to judge what will best serve those others. The knowledge, indeed, may alienate them from others. This is because professionals tend toward specialism rather than generalism, toward the minutiae rather than the whole.[28] The complaint that someone is unable to see the wood for the trees can frequently be made of professionals who have abstracted the focus of their concern from the rich context in which it is located, and have concentrated instead on the intricacies and details of one part or system. Theory as well as practice becomes fragmented. The more specialized the professional becomes, the smaller the portion of human life that falls within the ambit of his or her attention. The holistic *human* dimensions of service are often lost.

Police officers, like physicians, often meet people at critical points in their lives, and their attention is directed to some particular aspect of those lives. That is the aspect that primarily engages their attention and expertise. Yet its full appreciation may require contextual supplementation that they are not in a position to provide. To the extent that police officers begin to see themselves as professionals, they will be tempted to lose touch with the more informal contextual features of people's needs, and will focus more narrowly on "scientific" solutions to critical situations.

A slightly different form of alienation is brought about and reinforced through the esoteric words and ways that are engendered by professionalization. Here it is not a distancing from client needs so much as a denial of client access that is at issue. Professionals withdraw, or are initiated into, a world of their own jargon and of arcane rituals and practices that limit the availability of their knowledge and expertise to nonprofessionals and which thus create and sustain the mystique of what they do. Although some of these things may be important to the aura that often surrounds their activity, they may – as we are learning in the case of many legal forms and rituals –

contribute little to the advancement of the human interests to which they are ultimately directed. Part of their function is to sustain solidarity and control.[29]

3.1.2.3 Discrimination. The "learned" professions demand highly specialized knowledge and expertise that is normally attainable only after a lengthy period of training. This restricts access to the professions, and where societies have a history of discrimination members of groups that have been discriminated against are likely to be underrepresented. Poorer socioeconomic backgrounds compounded by inappropriate or inadequate educational opportunities conspire to underprepare such people for places in professional schools.

As police press for increasing professional status and its accoutrements, it will be found that economically and educationally disadvantaged groups will find access progressively harder. This may not always occur at entry level, but only later when promotion is in question. In itself, differential access might be seen as tragic rather than discriminatory, should it be established that adequate provision of the services in question requires long and arduous training. But if the pressure for higher entry standards serves only or mainly to increase the status of police work, without demonstrated need and some corresponding improvement in police service, then the differential access will not merely perpetuate existing social discrimination in some passive way, but in addition will exacerbate it. It will constitute a further and unnecessary barrier to members of those groups who already labor under the effects of social discrimination.

3.1.3 *Professionalism vs. professionalization*

The traditional professions have a noble rhetoric, but a less noble history. Their institutional form and power have enabled and even encouraged them to operate in a self-interested and discriminatory manner, and in some respects may have even detracted from their ability to achieve their public goals.[30] Energies that should have been directed to public good have instead been devoted to the self-serving concerns of the profession. Autonomy has become a shield against accountability. Although professionals possess an enviable expertise, the institutionalization of that knowledge/expertise has encouraged a form of tunnel vision or collective hubris resistant to correction and scornful of alternative and sometimes better ways of doing things.

But the failure of the professions to live up to their ideal of disinterestedly providing the best possible service should not be allowed to obscure the significance of that ideal. What we need is "professionalism sans professions," as John Kultgen felicitously puts it.[31] Professionalization is a social process in which some purveyors of a service organize themselves to be the primary or recognized providers of that service, establishing that title through such means as certification, continuing education, and the promulgation of a code of ethics. To the extent that service providers are successful in gaining recognition for these efforts, in law and in society at large, they will acquire the status of a profession. But the ideal is apt to get lost in its trappings, and may inevitably get lost, so long as professionalism – a dedication to doing what one does out of a commitment to it, with a determination to do it to the best of one's ability – is believed to belong exclusively to the professions.

For the proponent of professionalism, self-regulation is a matter of disposition rather than of institutional self-monitoring, ethical conduct is not constituted by conformity to a code, but by a commitment to providing service that is respectful of those who are affected by it, and recognition is predicated on the quality of service that is provided rather than on the institutional qualifications of the providers. To the extent that institutional self-regulation, codes of ethics, and certification have a place, it is because they manifest the internal self-regulation, respect, and competence of service providers. In no way should they constitute a substitute for them. Professionalism thus understood is a reasonable goal for police and for those myriad others who currently aspire to a professional upgrade. The spinoff of course *will* be an improvement in social status, not measured, however, by income or power but by the appreciation of a client public that is capable of recognizing work well done.

It is this ideal of professionalism that informs – though overextends – Michael Davis's account of a profession. There is commitment to an ideal in the service one is providing or activity in which one is engaging. But, whereas for the professions some form of collective engagement or commitment is necessary to the furtherance and realization of that ideal, in the case of professional conduct no such membership or even a sense of collective self-identity seems to be necessary. A janitor or cleaning lady, without associational affiliations, may view and accomplish his or her work with the same professionalism as a skilled surgeon.

What I am proposing is not intended as an argument for deinstitutionalizing the professions. To argue for that would be almost as unrealistic as arguing for a society without law. For though we can expect professionalism from professionals to the extent that we can expect people in general to have regard for each others' interests, that is a fragile expectation, and professional ideals, like social ideals, will need to be monitored, safeguarded and fostered by formal means. There is more to it than institutional rules and disciplinary mechanisms, however. Even professionalism is not constituted solely by individual good will in the provision of a service. Unless there is some community of those who see it as their joint task to improve the quality of a particular service, it is unlikely that individual service providers will be able to achieve very much. Inter alia, a professional is someone whose work reflects the best that can be achieved in the area.

A professional attitude and professional conduct can reasonably be fostered in and expected of police officers. For what this requires is not, or at least not first and foremost, higher education or a formal code of conduct or institutional self-regulation, but a dedication to service, and to providing it as competently as possible. The institutional structures of professional status are, or at least should be, subservient to that service.

However, the dominant structure of police organizations creates a daunting problem for the implementation of professionalism. Their hierarchical character, marked by a tightly stretched chain of formal accountability, fosters a mentality of rule-following instead of wise judgment, a concern with the internal repercussions of decisions more than with their appropriateness. It is well known that first line officers are as much guided by maxims such as "cover your ass," "don't make waves," and "never trust a boss," as they are by judgments of the appropriateness of their response to the circumstances confronting them.[32] And to the extent that this is so, professionalism in policing will be difficult to attain and maintain.

As noted earlier (3.1.1.5), in police departments that have sought to replace rule-driven with value-driven decision making, there has been some recognition of the structural impediments to professionalism. Yet the hierarchical traditions of policing die hard, and management's desire for a trouble-free image tends to undermine the emancipation of police officers from quasi-military supervision and regulation. Perhaps this is inevitable, given the nature of the work that police are called to do. Because their work is frequently inconvenient to or even invasive of individual members of the public they are pledged to serve, they are subject to many pressures and temptations to compromise the trust that is placed in them. And just as ordinary social life must be monitored by law, so too must police work be subject to regulation and supervision.

3.2 ROLE MORALITY

Whether or not we view police as professionals, their occupation of a social role carries with it certain privileges and duties. I have defined their role as one of social peacekeeping, and hinted at the duties that may follow from it, given the need for a social order suited to the flourishing of human beings like ourselves. There will of course be problems of intersection, as police activities connect up with those of public mediators, social workers, ombudsmen, security personnel, and so on. And there may be no firm way of separating them. It may be necessary to give procedural no less than substantive norms a significant place in the definition of their duties.

But leaving aside these problems of intersection, we need to confront a critical ethical question that attaches to their occupancy of a social role. The question is of ancient pedigree, and is generated by the tension or conflict that may (and sometimes does) arise between the requirements of a social role and what are seen to be the requirements of a more universal and mundane morality. Is there a special morality that attaches to social roles that differs from and that may sometimes take some kind of precedence over the requirements of ordinary morality? May police, by virtue of their role, use means to achieve their ends that transgress the bounds of what is ordinarily morally permissible?

The questions themselves stand in need of some clarification, for it is not obvious what is meant by "role morality" and "ordinary morality."[33] Is role morality to be identified with the codified standards that are set by professional organizations, and here contrasted with the ordinary standards of human intercourse that operate between us outside our professional or occupational roles? Is role morality to be identified with certain normative resources (such as authority to command) and responsibilities (for example, the obligation to render aid) that "go with" being the occupant of a particular social role, the presumption being that occupants of that role have knowledge, skills, capacities, and so on, that are not possessed by nonoccupants who are thereby ineligible or unfitted for those normative resources and responsibilities? Is role morality to be thought of as a special derivation of practical principles and standards from the specific features of a professional role, and thus to be distinguished from a more universal morality that attaches to humans by virtue of their humanness? These are some of the many possibilities.

It is also unclear how these two moralities, though different, may be related. Those who insist on the distinction usually do so because of a certain precedence that they sometimes wish to give to role morality. But it is not always clear what kind of precedence they have in mind. Do they mean that because of the relations they have with those they serve, the occupants of professional roles may possess rights and responsibilities that supersede those they would possess in the absence of those relations? For example, may a defense lawyer's commitment to his client justify the cruel, unfair and demeaning cross-examination of a sincere but vulnerable prosecution witness? Will it justify the maintenance of client confidentiality even when doing so will lead to a gross perversion of justice? Or does the assertion of precedence imply instead that the occupants of professions or occupations have knowledge, skills, and so on, that justify or require their doing things that others would not be justified in doing or be required to do? Thus, for example, may a physician employ an experimental therapy without first obtaining the patient's informed consent? Or yet again, does the assertion of precedence simply amount to the view that the occupants of particular social roles are morally enabled or required to act in ways that, from the point of view of our "ordinary moral consciousness" would be immoral? Do the needs of criminal investigation permit police officers to engage in whatever deception is likely to advance the process of discovery? Do police officers owe each other loyalty that would be excessive were it to be manifested in and by others?

This is a mixed bag of questions and cases, and a variety of responses is probably called for. In some cases we may want to question the so-called entitlement, or burden, that is attributed to the role occupant. In other cases we might want to explain and justify the difference by reference to the specific circumstances of the role occupant (say, the possession of a particular skill) that is morally relevant to the act for which some entitlement is claimed. Or, more generally, we may want to explain and justify the difference by reference to the social benefits of having a practice in which occupants of a particular social role are accorded certain entitlements, or burdens, even though the morally relevant particulars of a specific situation would seem to demand a different course of action. But do we also, perhaps, sometimes want to say that there *just is* a different morality applicable to the occupants of certain social roles, and that though what they do in that role is contrary to standards of some universal morality, we must (in some sense of that word) somehow swallow that? And if we must "swallow" it, does this mean that their occupational morality overrides (or may override) the demands of universal morality, or that although they may or must do what they do, they are left stained by it?

The last of these questions we shall tackle in a later section (3.2.2). Here I want to focus more specifically on the one that precedes it: whether the occupants of roles have entitlements and obligations that sometimes require them to act in ways that, from the point of view of "ordinary" or "universal" morality, would be wrong. In *The Moral Foundations of Professional Ethics*, one of the seminal contemporary discussions of this topic, Alan Goldman has argued that no general answer to this question is possible. Some role relations are subject to norms and principles at variance with "ordinary moral demands," whereas others are not.[34] Parents and children have obligations to each other that they do not have to others. Judges have obligations that may require them to make determinations at variance with what would ordinarily be considered morally best. But he does not extend this to lawyers, doctors, business people (and, we may presume, police), groups that are sometimes inclined to claim moral obligations and privileges not countenanced by "ordinary morality."

Unfortunately, Goldman's thesis is not stated with the kind of clarity that enables a direct response. For what he does is to provide a justification – based on what he refers to as "ordinary morality" – for the special obligations and privileges of members of families and judges, and to the extent that he provides this, he seems to undercut the special status that is claimed for members of those groups. Or at least, what is undercut is not their status, but the apparent contrast between "ordinary morality" and "role morality." And so his thesis loses what intuitive clarity it may have had. Parents bring their children into being, and thus bear a special relation to their well being; judges are called and trained to provide a form of adjudication that is intended to complement a social order in which individualized moral decision making fails to provide closure. What seems to be special is not their status, but circumstances created by or implicit in their status, or the knowledge and skills that go with their status. And this seems to echo a commonplace of moral reflection, namely, that situational factors count.

The more radical possibility is explicitly endorsed by Benjamin Freedman.[35] Starting from a distinction between what he calls "nonacquired" and "acquired" morality, Freedman suggests that nonacquired – "ordinary," or "natural," morality – may sometimes conflict with acquired morality – those obligations that I acquire through some act of mine, such as promising. And it may be the case that what I have promised to do – depending on the case – will conflict with and take precedence over some other moral requirement (whether, say, a nonacquired obligation to offer assistance, or even another acquired obligation arising, say, out of another promise). Role, or professional, morality he sees as a form of acquired morality, because the professional binds himself/herself to an ordering of values that will sometimes conflict with those reflected in "ordinary" morality.[36] Freedman makes it clear that the conflict that may result from this professional role is not removable by reference to the additional obligation acquired by the adoption of a particular role or by reference to the professional's skills or to some authorization that the professional is granted. It is, he believes, an acquired obligation to do what may be actually immoral (from the standpoint of ordinary morality). That there is an *actual* conflict here can be seen by taking the perspective of someone who is not yet the occupant of a particular professional role, but who, as an ordinary moralist, is about to commit himself to a role known to warrant him to act in ways he currently considers to be immoral: "This warrant is not available from the [person's] current moral world but, rather, either by reference to a future moral world or perhaps by reference to some compendious moral world (which includes allowable transitions between worlds which are warranted)."[37] In other words, it is only by reference to the perspective of a professional world not yet entered, or some – as yet unarticulated – overarching moral perspective, that certain acts, currently perceived as immoral, will be able to be justified.

Unless some form of Freedman's "compendious" alternative can be developed, it is not easy to comprehend how what is warranted by the professional's role can be incorporated into a justificatory story that can retain some grip on the assent of those who must subject themselves to the professional's ministrations. No doubt professionals perform important social functions, and these provide some basis for granting them certain privileges (and no doubt for imposing on them certain special obligations). But it is very difficult to see how the social importance of the roles played by professionals might warrant their acting in what, from the perspective of an ordinary person, is an immoral manner. It is not simply that the ordinary person *qua* ordinary person would not be justified in acting in that manner; it is that from the moral point of view of the ordinary person the role occupant is acting immorally. Freedman's position leaves us in a moral limbo.

To escape from this limbo, while yet recognizing that professionals may be subject to standards that others are not, one must, I believe, appeal to some unitary, albeit complex, "ordinary morality." A possible structure for such an appeal has been outlined at length and with great clarity by David Luban.[38] Referring to this structure as "the fourfold root of sufficient reasoning,"[39] Luban suggests that where *apparently* immoral conduct is justified by reference to a role, the justification will go through only if:

1. The conduct is essential to the fulfillment of the role obligation.
2. The role obligation is essential to the role.

3. The role is essential to the institution.
4. The institution is justified.

In other words, the norms that govern the role must ultimately be rooted in a set of justificatory reasons that sustains the institution within which the particular role is embedded. Those justificatory reasons belong to what is called "ordinary morality."[40]

Thus, a lawyer's aggressive questioning of a nervous witness can be justified only if it can be shown to be essential to fulfilling the lawyer's role obligation to provide zealous advocacy; zealous advocacy in turn must be shown to be essential to the role of a defense lawyer; the presence of a lawyer must be shown to be essential to the adversary system, and the adversary system in turn needs to be justified as a social institution. Each link in this chain is important, and weaknesses are cumulative. In some cases it may be very difficult to justify the institution in question; in other cases we may want to call into question the essentiality of some feature of the system as it currently exists.

Items of problematic police conduct that are sustained by reference to police role obligations will need to pass through a similar process of reasoning. Individual acts of coercion or deception by police need to be shown to be essential to, say, their obligation to enforce the law; they in turn need to be established as an essential part of their peacekeeping role as police officers; police work itself needs to be shown to be an essential and thus legitimate concern of government; and government itself needs to be justified.

Lethal force → detain criminal → necessary for peace → measure institution of police is justified

3.2.1 Selves and roles

I believe, then, that the issue is miscast if it is construed as a conflict or competition between "role morality" and "ordinary or common morality." This is made even clearer by the fact that there is no ordinary or common morality that is not, at least in part, role-oriented. We can appreciate this if, as Luban himself suggests, we undertake a metaphysical inquiry into the self. Moral agents are neither, at one extreme, "bare selves" nor, at the other, mere "clusters of roles." They are, rather, structured to be both deliberative individuals and the occupants of a variety of social roles, some of which may be professional roles.

The reasons for this are to be found in the empirical conditions of our world, conditions about which I have already had something to say (see Chapter 1, Section 1.2). We do not emerge into the world pre-programmed, needing only the wherewithal for survival to take our place in society. Our emergence as moral agents is crucially dependent on forms of social interaction (broadly, nurture and education) that constitute us as distinctive individuals (usually with a particular name, a particular language, a particular family, a particular social structure, a particular polity). Furthermore, although, as individuals, we can reflect upon the forms of interaction into which we have been initiated, and may seek to alter (criticize, remodel)

Can it be on a smaller scale?

them, we do so, not from some Olympian standpoint, but while sailing on Theseus's ship. The repairs we make have to take account of the fact that we are passengers. We view the conditions of our existence not *sub specie æternitatis* but, at best, *sub specie humanitatis*. I say "at *best*." In fact, the so-called "common morality" on the basis of which we may choose to criticize "role morality" is already the morality of a person who is, for example, a parent, and/or Protestant, and/or twentieth-century American, and/or police officer, and so on, and whose moral perceptions and deliberations are colored by these facts. Some of these acculturations are properly incorporated into our moral positioning; others corrupt our reflection. Unfortunately, the imagination and abstraction of which we are capable will enable us to see only some of the contours of the ship on which we travel: we never see all at once or enough to settle permanently the issues that present themselves to us.

Nevertheless, there is, as I have noted (see Chapter 1, Section 1.2), an aspirational dimension to our moral reflection. If we think of morality primarily as something governing the interaction of complex "selves" or "humans" (ignoring, for present purposes, the otherwise challenging claims of Zen Buddhists, animal liberationists and deep ecologists), then we will want to do some cultural discounting, or at least "contextualization," so that we become aware and take account of the influence of personal and cultural idiosyncrasies. We will want to look beyond, albeit through, our own cultural acquisitions to the *fellow humans* with whom our interactions occur. But this will not evacuate our morality of all reference to roles – particularly our familial, social, tribal, and perhaps national ones; it will simply call into question certain idiosyncratic features of those roles that serve to denigrate or otherwise undermine the essential and rich humanity of others.

The standpoint of "eternal reason" and "ideal roles" is not one which the occupants of time and history can hope or should even try to achieve. "The view from nowhere"[41] is always the view from somewhere, albeit an expanded somewhere (which is not to say that each vantage point is as good as any other). One of the things that helps to give the social and political tradition of liberalism its contingent strength is the place that it accords to the values of tolerance and open mindedness, values that enable us to expand our horizons, to overcome some of the limitations of our subjectivity. This is not to espouse an easy relativism, but to recognize our finitude and partiality, our embeddedness in history, and to demand that our dealings be accessible to public scrutiny.

Thus, to return to the issues of roles, I suggest that a strict separation of professional and ordinary morality will deny to ordinary moral selves access to an important form of practical reasoning. It will imply that the compartments that make up our lives do not have adjoining doors, but open out onto the world in their own ways. It is of course just possible that our human experience is fundamentally incoherent, that we are saddled, as part of our human condition, not merely with mystery but with fundamental contradiction (since in taking upon a particular role professionals do not cease from

2nd phenomenon happening alongside the primary, a useless accompaniment

being ordinary humans). But we need rather more than some assertion that such is so if we are to go down this path. The arrogation of moral prerogatives by professionals is not enough.

I would suggest instead that our metaphysics of the moral self – the ordinary moral self – must contain both impersonal or universal and particularist elements. The moral life must accommodate our being both human and particular humans, ordinary people and role occupants. Both cohere for both are required if our status as moral agents is to be secured. True, they stand in some sort of dialectical tension not unlike – it is, indeed, part of – that between individual and community. Our human individuality is created through and expressed in community, though not as its epiphenomenon, and under certain conditions it may be stifled by community's bonds. Pursuing and maintaining some sort of dialectical balance is integral to our ongoing life as moral agents.

Issue of obligations not morality

If this is so, then I do not believe there is a distinctive problem about professional roles: they are just more formalized expressions of a tension that we all have to deal with in our everyday lives: our responsibilities to our family, friends, country, and so on versus our more general responsibilities to others. If there is a tension, it is between universal and particular obligations, not between common or ordinary morality, on the one hand, and professional role morality, on the other. There are some obligations that we have by virtue of our common humanity, by virtue of the fact that we are sensitive and reflective choosers in a world of sensitive and reflective choosers. We have obligations of respect; we may not injure or exploit. But there are also obligations that we have by virtue of our standing in more particular relations to others. Some of those will be almost universal – filial and familial obligations, for example. Others, however, will attach to us only as the articulation of our selves initiates us into various social roles, be they professional or public – as doctor, police officer or politician.

3.2.2 *Dirty hands*

relating to a offspring

I have suggested that what appear to be tensions between so-called ordinary morality and role morality are tensions common to us all, since we are all confronted by universal and particular demands. Morality, so-called ordinary morality, is itself a complex phenomenon, and our assumption of particular professional roles is a manifestation of that complexity rather than a further addition to it. Along with my rejection of a simple contrast between ordinary and role morality, I have also rejected the view that the demands of one should necessarily or always take precedence over the demands of the other. What, by virtue of being a police officer, a person ought to do, does not override what some "ordinary morality" might allow; nor, for that matter, does what some alien "ordinary morality" prescribes take precedence over what a person ought to do as a police officer. There is a univocal albeit complex moral universe, and it will depend very much on the particular situation whether the fact that a person is a police officer makes some normative difference with respect to what is morally acceptable.

But just because morality is not bifurcated into a dualism of self-contained "ordinary" and "role" requirements, we may be confronted by demands that appear to be both incompatible and unresolvable. I do not have in mind here the dilemma that results when the considerations supporting competing demands are so equally "weighted" that there is no reason to submit to one rather than to the other. This sort of case might just as well be settled by the flip of a coin or the drawing of lots. Nor do I have in mind the situation in which we are regrettably faced with a choice between two evils, and where it is at least possible to argue for the propriety of choosing the lesser of those evils. Rather, I have in mind conflicting demands that are seen as being in some sense incommensurable, and where the idea of some bottom-line moral comparability and resolution seems out of place. It is often argued that those who occupy professional or public roles are particularly vulnerable to such "impossible choices" – in which, no matter what they do, some egregious wrong will be done. In particular, it is argued that by virtue of their role responsibilities they sometimes "must" violate the canons of ordinary moral decency. They must, as Sartre put it, "dirty their hands."[42]

In policing contexts, the case of Inspector "Dirty Harry" Callahan is frequently taken to illustrate the phenomenon.[43] Callahan, we learn, is given the "dirty" jobs, and he does them in the way that seems appropriate to the kind of jobs they are – "dirtily." He it is to whom the San Francisco mayor and police commissioner turn when the city is held to ransom by a sociopathic killer, Scorpio. When "standard" methods fail to stop him, and the triumphant but vengeful Scorpio places a ransom and time limit on the life of his hapless fourteen-year-old hostage, Ann Mary Deacon, it is Callahan who delivers the ransom. But Scorpio reneges on his promise to release the girl, he brutalizes and taunts Callahan, and then wounds his partner. In trouble over the partner's presence at the scene (in violation of an agreement between the City and Scorpio), and incensed at what he sees as the cowardice of a city and police administration, "Dirty Harry" determines to pursue justice and Scorpio in his own way. The discovery that Scorpio is the groundkeeper at Kezar Stadium prompts Harry, against the advice of another partner, to break into Scorpio's quarters, and pursue him onto the playing field, where Harry first shoots Scorpio in the leg, and then grinds his foot into the wound to extract the information he needs concerning the girl's whereabouts, though it is now highly probable, and in fact the case, that she is dead. At least it will yield a body as evidence. Scorpio is taken into custody, but must then be released, because, although the girl's body is recovered, and a murder weapon is found in Scorpio's quarters, Harry, as an agent of the state, has violated Scorpio's constitutional rights by virtue of his illegal entry, torture, and the denial of medical attention and legal counsel. Harry is ordered to remove himself from the case, but he has already determined on a campaign of personal harassment that he hopes will bring Scor-

pio down. Scorpio, however, neatly turns the tables on Callahan and trans-
forms the harassment into a serious complaint against Callahan and the
police department. In a final confrontation, Scorpio commandeers a bus load
of school children, and demands money and a plane out of the country. The
city acquiesces, but on the drive to the airport Callahan engages Scorpio in a
terrifying (to the children) shootout that ends in the grounds of a quarry
with Callahan and Scorpio alone and face to face at last. Callahan taunts
Scorpio, and the latter is "suckered into" the move that "enables" Callahan
to put him beyond the reach of an uncertain law. Callahan's final act is to
hurl his badge into the quarry waters.

The movie encourages us to think that had Harry not done what he did,
he would have fallen short of the *telos* underwriting his role and the moral
obligation to do what he could to ensure a just and beneficial outcome. He
did what had to be done, but in doing it he dirtied his hands. But though his
hands are dirty, we are encouraged to think that they are not filthy. The ends
he has pursued, the motives with which he has pursued them, and the
necessity of the tactics that he has used, "justify" what he has done, and
distinguish his case from one where, say, an officer, out of self-interested
motives, or in the exercise of authority, unnecessarily violates the standards
he or she is sworn to uphold. So it is argued.

The case of "Dirty Harry" is just one of a great number of cases in which it
is said that one must "dirty one's hands." The phenomenon is of ancient
vintage, and forms the core of some of the great Greek tragedies – of Orestes
and Agamemnon, for example. But the modern-day characterization is different. The writers of the Greek tragedies often appear to suspend final
judgment, seeing in the "tragic" decision that "must" be made a moral
perplexity if not indeterminacy, evidence, perhaps, of life's lack of moral
coherence. Its latter-day exponents, however, follow Machiavelli's *Prince* by
not only accepting the need to dirty one's hands, but also seeing it as being
in some fairly strong sense morally "appropriate" or "necessary":

> A man who wishes to make a profession of goodness in everything must
> necessarily come to grief among so many who are not good. Therefore it is
> necessary for a prince, who wishes to maintain himself, to learn how not to be
> good, and to use this knowledge and not use it, according to the necessity of
> the case.[44]

A prince who hopes to survive *and to serve*, cannot afford to be wise as a
serpent and harmless as a dove; he must also be a hawk. And so the verdict
has usually been in contemporary discussions. Certain acts are characterized
as being "justified yet wrong." And attention has shifted from the issue of
the correctness or appropriateness or justifiability of the decision to the
character of the person who has had to make it, and the response that we
should make to those who act in this way.

Michael Walzer, the most influential contributor to recent discussions of
the issue, takes it as "given" that public life requires dirtying one's hands:
sometimes, in the fulfillment of one's public commitment, one must choose

to do what it is wrong to do.[45] Walzer speaks of the decision alternately as "right," "the right thing to do in utilitarian terms," "justified," and "what we ought to do." The problem for him is how we should then proceed: whether to regard the person as a hero, should he or she "pull it off;" as a tragic figure who has sacrificed his or her soul in doing what had to be done; or as having discharged a responsibility for which expiatory punishment would nevertheless be appropriate. Walzer himself favors the last option, though he is troubled by the absence of social mechanisms for administering such redemptive suffering.

Two distinct issues will confront us here: First, to reconsider whether we are in fact sometimes faced with situations in which all the options are "wrong" or "evil," but in which one course of action would be "justified" as "necessary." And, second, if that is so, to ask what we are to say of the person who has had to make such a choice.

Walzer himself has no doubt about the genuineness of the moral dilemmas that give rise to "dirty hands" situations. He does not think dirty decisions always avoidable; nor does he think the options can be redescribed so that the decision may lose its immoral taint. He instances a reform-oriented political candidate who must make a deal with a dishonest ward boss to win an election. Or, more dramatically, he envisages a situation in which one must torture terrorists to save a community from destruction by bombing. The examples may be multiplied.[46] In policing contexts, it is sometimes suggested that sting operations of the kind involved in the ABSCAM investigations,[47] or the giving of false testimony to ensure that a public menace is "put away," or the illegal wiretapping of a sophisticated organized crime figure, might, along with the kind of action taken by Dirty Harry, sometimes be "necessary" and "justified" though "wrong."

There is, of course, some question as to whether all of these are characterizable as "dirty hands" situations in the full sense intended by Walzer (wrong acts justifiably chosen). And behind that there is the more important question whether *any* of the decisions in question should have been as it was: we are being asked to accept the view that occasions arise in which a person "must" dirty his or her hands. In any case the situations are of many different kinds. Sometimes they appear to be of a kind in which, if the agent does not violate a moral requirement, someone else will do worse.[48] In other cases the choice between the terrible alternatives is not thrust upon the person as a result of some other agent's machinations, but is presented to the agent as a way of dealing with an ongoing situation.[49] There are further differences. In some cases, the agent is faced with the choice of "doing" x lest y happen; in others the choice is to "allow" x lest y be done: the distinction between doing and allowing is often said to possess intrinsic moral significance.[50] Consideration also needs to be taken of the fact that in some cases the agent's choice situation may have come about as the result of some prior culpable choice of the agent; in other cases it may have arisen "innocently" – where the agent has not painted him/herself into a dirty corner. We are not dealing with a simple[51] or isolated[52] phenomenon.

Consider the larger question: whether we should accept the view that it is
sometimes "morally necessary" to dirty one's hands. Here I remain uncon-
vinced that the situations usually put forward to illustrate the phenomenon
show that we are "justified" in dirtying our hands: at least, we need to know
more about the situations that are said to require it than we are generally
given. Take Walzer's example: a reform-minded political candidate who
may not be able to succeed without making a sweetheart deal with a corrupt
ward boss. So perhaps he should not. Maybe he should take his chances
(without support) or seek to serve the public in other ways. The example as
it is presented does not give us enough information for a clear decision. And,
to take Walzer's second example, maybe it is not wrong to torture terrorists
who are threatening to kill, say, thousands of innocent people. Is the moral
constraint against torture so strong/absolute? We can grant that the classic
defense of torture (truth *über alles*) is inadequate. But is it not possible to act
so evilly that the right not to be tortured may be overridden or forfeited?
Must torture dirty one's hands, as Walzer assumes?

The usual response here is to claim that even if these particular examples
are not sufficiently developed to establish what they are intended to establish, they could nevertheless be elaborated or amended to make the requisite
point. Or at least other examples could be given. Politics, in particular, and
other forms of public office, must sometimes be engaged in in that way if
good is to have any chance to triumph. It is "glib moralism" to think otherwise, Bernard Williams suggests.[53] Unless the good are sometimes willing to
dirty their hands, evil people will find it within their means to cause untold
havoc. *This is just the way things are.* As Michael Stocker puts it: "Dirty hands
reminds us of the perhaps archaic view that the immorality of the world can
irredeemably stain our acts and lives. They show that not only our own
immoralities, but also another's immoralities, can make it impossible to
avoid doing what is evil."[54] The doctrine of dirty hands is thus like a secular
version of a certain interpretation of the doctrine of original sin – we are
located in a world of wrongdoing in which guilt is properly even if un-
willingly our lot.

This may be so, at least I have no knockdown argument against it. It may
be that we have no choice in the end but to be occasional "foxes and lions." It
may be that there is no place, except accidentally, for people who are "wise
as serpents and harmless as doves."[55] It may be that the call to be the latter is
simply a counsel of perfection, a representation of what we might aspire to
be, rather than a prescription we can ensure we can carry out. It may be that
the only morality we can actually live with is a "morality of the second best."

But I also think that the concession to dirty hands may register no more
than acquiescence in a pragmatism that poses as realism. It may be, as
Kenneth Howard suggests, that "politics is not how you find it but what you
make it. Walzer, it seems, gives up."[56] The point here is not to deny that we
may sometimes be confronted with terrible choices, situations in which our
only choice is between x and y, and in which, whatever choice we make, we

will have done something terrible and for which guilt may be an appropriate response. The world of our moral reflection just may sometimes present us with impossible choices. Nor do I want to deny that the choice between x and y may sometimes be such that even if our choice of x is justified, we will experience moral qualms. That a choice is justified does not show it to have been an easy one to make or stomach. But neither do the feelings that may accompany a hard choice show it to have involved wrongdoing, even if those feelings are appropriate. What I am somewhat skeptical of is whether we can sometimes be said to be "justified" in making a choice that nevertheless involves us in wrongdoing. It is the willingness to accommodate a certain form of incoherence in moral theory that I find troubling. My own reading of many of the actual cases that are put forward to show that some people sometimes must dirty their hands suggests that when we fill out the details a little more, and look at the options more carefully, the hands look more sweaty than dirty, or more filthy than dirty. And further, that some of the hypothetical examples that are put forward suffer from the lack of detail that we would expect to have in an actual situation, and so we are forcing our moral intuitions in circumstances for which they have not been properly prepared.

As I indicated, I have no way of showing that we could never be placed in a position where we would have to dirty our hands. And I am prepared to allow that in rare cases we may be faced with choices that are so terrible that no particular choice will be "justified" or "appropriate" and that it will be our lot to be the agents of wrongdoing. We may have to make genuinely tragic choices. But I am not convinced that the kinds of examples normally adduced to illustrate such situations establish anything that we can speak of as "the justifiability of doing wrong." Although Walzer's own concern to confront the guilt of those who dirty their hands is an advance on Machiavelli, philosophers have often been too willing to accommodate and ameliorate the claims and analyses of those for whom some acceptable dirtying of the hands has seemed to be an inevitable feature of the human condition. In the context of police ethics, this seems to me to be a particularly dangerous failing, for police, like politicians, seem to be peculiarly drawn to self-justification.

In contrast to Walzer and others, I want to suggest that the emotive concomitants of the hard decisions that are sometimes said to involve the dirtying of hands may often be characterized and explained in ways that do not involve the appropriate guilt of real wrongdoing. And rather than suggesting that, at bottom, our moral life lacks coherence, I would suggest that even though coherence is sometimes difficult to perceive, it is better to work on the assumption that it exists than to accept that one must sometimes dirty one's hands.[57]

Take first the moral qualms that hard decisions sometimes involve. *If* our choice is as it should be in such a case, then we need not characterize our residual feelings as those of "guilt," "remorse" or even "compunction," though "regret" and "anguish" may be more acceptable. Unfortunately, writers on the topic tend to move alternately or indiscriminately between these feelings, as though they are somehow of a moral piece. But there are important distinctions to be made here. There are distinctions between being, being found / held, and feeling guilty. And feelings of guilt and remorse are to be distinguished (for we may feel guilt concerning our wishes and desires, whereas remorse is focused on our actions; feelings of guilt, though not of remorse, may be objectless; remorse involves repudiation, a sense of guilt need not). Compunction (a pricking of the conscience) conveys a nice sense of moral unease; it tends not to be as strong as a sense of guilt, and, unlike remorse, which succeeds the act, accompanies the decision to act. Regret and anguish may be felt in the absence of any sense that one has done wrong (and no repudiation need be involved): Wishing that it had been otherwise or that one did not have to do as one did does not imply wishing that one had done otherwise, or the belief that what one did was wrong. Shame need not be connected with anything of moral significance or over which we have control; it is associated with self-exposure (of ourselves as we find ourselves to be, and not as we like to think of ourselves or like others to think of us). Maybe the casual running together of these emotions gives phenomenological support to the idea that one is sometimes right to do what is also wrong. For it is surely true that some things that it is right to do are regrettable, and sources of great anguish. But it does not follow from an understandable anguish or from justifiable feelings of regret at what we have had to do that we have acted wrongly and are therefore right to feel guilt or remorse or even compunction.

Other feelings and emotions too may be involved in so-called dirty hands situations. Anger and resentment may be felt at having been placed in a situation in which important values, principles and commitments have had to be sacrificed. Frustration and discombobulation may be felt at the inability to keep one's most important values and projects together in a coherent life-plan. Sadness, despair, heaviness of heart and grief may accompany the recognition that we cannot relate to others as we would wish.[58] These reactions may feed our anguish and regret, but they need not imply guilt.[59]

We can, in fact, suggest several alternative accounts for the squeamishness that is felt when hard choices have to be made. Different accounts may be appropriate to different cases:

1. Most straightforwardly, the strong emotions felt may be those of anguish, regret, agony, or grief, without there being any implication that one did wrong for which it is appropriate to feel guilt. Feeling bad about a decision one has had to make is not the same as feeling that one has acted badly. If a police officer finds he has to arrest a friend, particularly one who is a police colleague, he may feel bad about it – even that it contravenes the prevailing expectations of friendship and loyalty – but this need imply no staining betrayal, only an agonizing regret that this should have come in the way of

their friendship and brotherhood. It is not an "impossible choice," but it may well be experienced as acutely.

2. More subtly, the feelings may take the form of an unease grounded in the substantial moral risk involved – where, for example, for the sake of an overwhelming but uncertain *future* benefit, a *present* sacrifice is made that, in the absence of that benefit, would not be justified.[60] A decision of that kind is not something a person can be casual or blasé about: the rightness of the decision is to some extent determinable only by reference to future outcomes, and *in the meantime* a strong moral expectation has been contravened. The chooser takes the same moral risk that anyone does when, knowing his finitude and what at one level this requires of him, he chooses the part of God. But hand wringing is not the same as hand dirtying. Hands that have been wrung may need drying rather than washing.

Although the film suggests otherwise, suppose that Dirty Harry had reason to think that Ann Mary Deacon was still alive. Given that time was running out, that *might* have justified – morally, at least – use of the third degree on Scorpio. This, of course, is not to suggest that what Harry did could have been condoned: there is good reason to think that he might have been able to get the information he needed with considerably less force than he actually used. Nevertheless, there are situations in which, for some sufficiently good end, a moral risk can be taken that will – and perhaps ought to – leave one morally nervous should what one risks not come off.[61]

3. A different kind of unease may be grounded in judgmental uncertainty, in which complex tradeoffs of important values are involved, and it is not easy to be sure that the sacrifices were really justified. As is clear from debates in moral theory, it is not easy to develop a single currency in terms of which moral problems can be discussed and resolved. Sometimes we speak of balancing or weighing values; yet the values and/or norms to be balanced or weighed are not sufficiently commensurable for such a simple comparison. We must exercise a form of judgment that does not have certainty attached to it, and attached to that uncertainty may be the anxiety and heaviness of heart that go with a decision having serious moral consequences.

The issue of judgmental uncertainty often arises where "values" and "principles" come into conflict. Paternalism may involve this sort of uncertainty. Police officers are obligated to pursue the welfare of those they encounter, yet not everyone in need seems willing to accept assistance. Benevolence is pitted against liberty. Does a great good "outweigh" a relatively small invasion of liberty? Or does liberty act as a principled side-constraint on the doing of good? Police may be greatly exercised over such issues, especially when dealing with street people, domestic abuse, and harassment situations. Their intervention may be rebuffed by those at risk, further complicated by their uncertainty whether the refusal of assistance is truly or sufficiently voluntary.

benevolence is pitted against liberty

4. A different kind of unease may arise from our recognition that stand-points, and not simply values, can have a certain incommensurability at-tached to them. Consider the case of the aspiring politician who enters into the sweetheart deal with the corrupt ward boss. Assume that he is able, subsequently, to introduce the reforms he has pledged. Assume, too, that he has had to fulfill the agreement he made with the ward boss, say, to award certain contracts to a company with which the boss is associated. Maybe, from the point of view of most of his constituents, he has been a good representative. But, were they to learn of the circumstances, what about from the point of view of the contractors who lost out as a result? From whose point of view are we to assess the politician's conduct? Our actual points of view, no matter what we may aspire to, are neither *sub specie æternitatis* nor even *sub specie humanitatis*, but something more time- and culture- and condition-bound.

In a liberal and urban society, particularly one marked by strong racial, ethnic, and/or class contrasts, police will find themselves having to adjudi-cate in situations where fundamental standpoints are diametrically opposed. If the law is clear on the issue, they may not find it hard to know how to handle the situation; but if it is a dispute that has its origins in cultural, religious and familial traditions that are alien to the officers involved, it may be difficult to negotiate a satisfactory resolution that will not offend against a sincerely held standpoint. They may feel very uneasy.

5. A further possibility is that unease arises because the moral prohibition is so strong and the circumstances for overriding it are so rare that we will almost inevitably feel bad about having to do so, even though we may be and may even consider ourselves to be justified. Where what has had to be brought about involves the sacrifice of innocents, in which no appeal to desert can be mounted, we may experience moral turmoil, regret, and even guilt. For most of us, such situations are not likely to be sufficiently common as to enable us to adjust our emotions to what, intellectually, we may believe to be the case.

In a hostage situation, where an innocent hostage has already been killed, police may face a serious dilemma about whether to storm a stronghold, and seriously risk further innocent deaths (either from their own weapons or those of the hostage taker), or to continue attempts at negotiation even though the prospects of a satisfactory outcome have already been substan-tially diminished by the death of one hostage. The same kind of situation seems to be an almost inevitable part of war, where, even if it is in some sense "just," innocents will get caught up in the crossfire.

6. Finally, we may need to accommodate those cases in which the guilt is real enough, and appropriate, but has its origins in some prior wrong deci-sion that we have made and that has created a "dirty hands" decision. Here we might be reluctant to say that our choice of *x* was justified; perhaps the best we can say is that it minimized the costs of a previous bad decision.

Suppose a police officer intervenes in a dispute, but does so clumsily and insensitively, worsening rather than ameliorating it. Should the officer then find that he must use deadly force on one of the participants in order to defend himself or another, he might put forward a defense-of-life justification, but also appropriately feel guilty at the ineptness and thoughtlessness that aggravated the situation.

The foregoing alternatives may not account for all those cases in which there appears to be some kind of moral remainder even though one has done what, in the circumstances, was the best that one could do. They are, however, meant to force a reappraisal of the view that public officials, in particular, will have to dirty their hands. The danger of the dirty hands doctrine lies not so much in the incoherence it suggests in our moral landscape or even in the emotional toll that it may exact, but in the "benign accommodation" that it may provide for "violations of the moral order."[62] For public officials have an unfortunate history of either denying their involvement in untoward conduct or, if found out, of seeking to justify it as necessary – of taking refuge in the Casa Machiavelli.

As I have already noted, it is not my intention to deny that we may sometimes be presented with choices in which the alternatives leave us without any "right answer," in which, no matter which way we go, we will do badly and will experience not mere regret but actual guilt, for we have been the agent of great wrongdoing. But I think it important that we not dress up such decisions as being in some sense morally "justified" or "right" or "what ought to have been done," even if they are politically or professionally advantageous.

The real significance of dirty hands cases, I would suggest, is not that they demonstrate incoherence or that, "in a world governed by demons" we are justified in making use of "diabolical powers."[63] They show us instead the complexity of moral life and warn us against the simplistic moralism so often associated with moral decision making and moral theorizing. The normative resources of moral life are rich and varied, and accommodating them all cannot be achieved by an easy recourse to the simple metaphors that we often employ: balancing in the scales, making tradeoffs, filtering, weaving webs, and so on. Even if, ultimately, the process is one that requires we find some sort of judgmental "reflective equilibrium," how we achieve that is ultimately *an exercise of judgment* rather than recourse to some formulaic device or strategy. This, however, is far from conceding some deep incoherence in our moral world.

What, then, do we need to look at when confronted by situations that threaten to dirty our hands? Obviously we need to see what issues are at stake – what principles may be infringed, what benefits are to be gained, what values realized. Are there other options that do not generate the same perplexity? We need to have some sense of the importance of those principles, benefits, and values. We need to have some idea how likely it is that the benefits or values in question will be attained; and whether, as a consequence of attaining them, other values may be jeopardized. We may need to know something about how the hard decision arose, whether as a matter of happenstance, someone else's immoral behavior, or perhaps through culpable conduct of our own. What, exactly are we being asked to do – to initiate something, to refrain from interfering with a course of events, or to omit something that we might otherwise be expected to do? If important principles or values are to be sacrificed, who will be the losers? Will they be innocents, or (like Scorpio) people whose guilt might render them liable to evil consequences in any case? In deciding the issue one way or the other, what will our motives be? Will our concern be for the good of others, for some abstract value or principle, or for our own purity or gain? Are we willing to be held to account for what we do?

All of these, and perhaps other, questions may be brought into play by the so-called dirty hands phenomenon. And we must somehow exercise our judgment with respect to the interplay of those that do in the case at hand. So far as the story of Dirty Harry Callahan is concerned, we have to take into account the havoc that Scorpio has caused, is causing and, if not stopped, will almost certainly continue to cause. There is the fourteen-year-old girl who has been "buried," the school bus of children that he has commandeered, the holding of a city hostage, the fear that has been created. But we also need to remember that Dirty Harry has himself "contributed to" some of these circumstances through his earlier violations of Scorpio's rights, enabling Scorpio to continue on his sociopathic way. In addition, Dirty Harry has good reason to believe that he is too late to save the fourteen-year-old girl's life, and we need to remember that his passion to bring Scorpio to "justice" has left him with a wounded partner. No doubt the fact that it is Scorpio who is tortured (and not, hypothetically, an innocent close relative of Scorpio), and that it is Scorpio who is shot in the end, weigh somewhat in Harry's favor, though the final killing seems not only gratuitous, but also shortcircuits the admittedly imperfect processes of justice that are generally important to the orderly progress of social and civil life.

In Carl Klockars's discussion of Dirty Harry, there is one other factor that bears comment and development. Klockars believes that dirty hands situations occur and, indeed, that they regularly impinge on the police role. He also thinks, however, that the temptations for police to get their hands filthy are sufficiently strong to hold those police who dirty their hands responsible for what they do, to the point of punishing them. But in doing this, he notes, we should "recognize that we create a Dirty Harry problem for ourselves and for those we urge to effect such punishments," since the dirty means have been employed to achieve "some unquestionably good and morally compelling end."[64]

The issue of accountability in so-called dirty hands cases is a tricky one. It was Walzer's view that the "Catholic" tradition that he favors, in which the dirty hero is tainted but may "redeem" himself through expiatory punishment, nevertheless lacks a social mechanism for ensuring that redemptive punishment.[65] But the problem goes deeper than that, because those who accept the phenomenon of dirty hands usually think it integral to the achievement of the consequences that make dirty conduct justifiable that as far as possible its agents (at least if they are public officials) conceal the dirt from those to whom they are accountable. As Machiavelli put it, if great things are to be done a wise lord not only cannot and ought not to keep faith, but there will never "be wanting to a Prince legitimate reasons to excuse this nonobservance."[66] Because even the Prince speaks as vox populi, so that what *he* does for us *we* do, lest he be seen to deny the virtues of citizenship on which the state depends, he must cover his dirty hands with white gloves. *That*, for Machiavelli, is why the official who is inescapably "found out" must resign or be punished.

Machiavelli's "political realism" here determines not only the need for dirty hands, but also encompasses the issue of accountability. Although Walzer professes to be a realist, he collapses into romanticism by advocating expiatory punishment in situations for which accountability generally needs to be avoided. His claim that if the "moral politician . . . were a moral man and nothing else, his hands would not be dirty; if he were a politician and nothing else, he would pretend that they were clean,"[67] underestimates the need for secrecy. The realistic politician may have to pretend that his hands are clean, at least until he gets decisively found out, and his pretense can be seen for what it is.[68]

In contrast to Walzer, Klockars democratizes dirty hands by seeing in the demands and burdens that we place on police an unreasonableness that should disturb our sense of peace. Dennis Thompson likewise claims that, because elected public officials are our agents, what they do also implicates us.[69] Does this then suggest that there is something hypocritical about punishing dirty-handed officials should they be found out, even if we have mechanisms of punishment available to us? Who are *we* to cast stones? Or, as Alan Donagan puts it: "If citizens are unwilling to forgo what can only be obtained by actions they are unwilling to do themselves, they are not entitled to exact penance from anybody they appoint to do them on their behalf."[70] And might not a similar question be asked in relation to the police, who find themselves between a rock and a hard place, on the one hand constrained by various constitutional and moral requirements, and on the other expected to achieve certain results, despite the "inefficiencies" created by those constraints?

Perhaps it is the feeling of hypocrisy that makes our responses to discovered and merely dirty (rather than filthy) hands so awkward and unpredictable. But a feeling of hypocrisy may not be necessary, even were we to accept – as I have sought not to – that some dirtying of the hands may be inevitable. We could still expect from the exposed official some form of self-inflicted punishment (say, resignation). That might acknowledge not only the appropriateness of punishment, but also the inappropriateness of *our* inflicting it. Of course, it still leaves unsettled what should be done in the case of an official who refuses to resign.

Nevertheless, *if* we want to take the democratic thesis seriously, I think that even this should be the occasion for some form of embarrassed awkwardness. For although the particular dirty decision is made by the politician or police officer without our explicit agreement, the fact that we expect or even demand of our officials that they be prepared to make decisions of this general kind – allowing, of course, that we agree with Machiavelli, Weber and Walzer – should leave *us* compromised as well. Thompson, interestingly, thinks that the secrecy that surrounds dirty hands is not something we can be said to have consented to, and that a framework for dirtying hands can be articulated in the public arena, making anything beyond an initial secrecy unnecessary.[71] He may be right. Certainly we would do better to make the outer boundaries of political and police decision making matters of public discussion than to leave it to police and politicians to decide on their own the appropriate parameters for their decision making. Nevertheless, if some of those dirty decisions, to be "justifiable," will need to be kept secret ("damage control"), there is likely to be a significant penumbra of uncertainty about those limits.

One of the reasons why Thompson seeks to democratize dirty hands is to allow for a partial refocusing of our response from punishment to the compensation of its victims, from retribution to reparation.[72] This may be a helpful refocusing. We should note, however, that the question of a "duty of reparation" may arise even if hard decisions do not result in the dirtying of hands. Police officers and politicians, even if justified in doing things that leave innocents or others as "victims," may nevertheless have a duty to ensure that some form of compensation is given. Guilt is not needed for that.[73]

area of partial illumination surrounding the darkest part of a shadow

PART II
Personal ethics

Chapter 4

Institutional culture and individual character

When an organization wants you to do right, it asks for your integrity; when it wants you to do wrong, it demands your loyalty.

Author unknown[1]

Loyalty in the police department means you're willing to lie for someone else.

Bill McCarthy[2]

Our cultural ideology places much store on the individual and on the values of individuality and autonomy. And at some level that is probably as it should be. Yet individuals do not generally exist and act in isolation but as integral parts of various evolving cultural and institutional structures and groupings. Our identity as individuals is constituted in part by our roles and communal memberships. So it is with police. When a recruit enters the police academy, it "does more than give him a job; it defines who he is."[3]

The interplay of, and tension between, individual and social identity generates some of the central and most difficult questions of moral, social, and political philosophy and practice. The very relations that are essential to our formation and that constitute the matrix for our ongoing activity may also overwhelm us. That is no less true of police character and culture than it is of our common experience. Individual integrity and group loyalty are simultaneously expected of police officers, and some of the most difficult problems, both moral and psychological, that officers face concern the ordering of these two demands.

This situation is psychologically ameliorated but morally exacerbated by another tension that police confront. They are held to high personal standards by a community that they often come to perceive as hypocritical. They are expected to be moral exemplars in a social environment that breeds moral cynicism. This tends to reinforce the values of peer group membership and to erode the demands of individual morality. Or, to put it another way, group culture tends to reconfigure individual moral demands so that they sit more easily with the demands of group membership. We do not have to be skeptical of the sincerity of Sergeant Stacey Koon when he argued that what was done to Rodney King was completely within the bounds of proper police procedure.

In this Chapter I propose to look at some of the ethical issues raised by the tension between the individual and the group, between police and the wider community. I focus particularly on two issues, those of loyalty and of cynicism.

4.1 POLICE CULTURE

Talk of "police culture," as of any other culture, makes it appear much more monolithic than it really is. There are significant differences between "management culture" and "street cop culture,"[4] differences between different groupings within ranks – between uniformed and nonuniformed officers, and between those and detectives – between one department and another, and between police in one country and those in another. At the same time, however, were we to deny that there is anything distinctive about police culture we would fail to recognize important contours of the environment within which police have to exercise their moral judgment. Police officers who travel beyond the boundaries of their own jurisdiction or overseas know that they are part of a large "brotherhood," and that when they encounter police in other places certain features of their experience are likely to be shared.

Although police officers in democracies are expected to be public servants par excellence, they are, at least in larger urban settings, remarkably distanced from the public they serve. To a significant extent, this is a product of their law enforcement and order maintenance roles. As frequent bearers of "bad news," they have, as it has been put, "a built-in public relations problem."[5] Even though law enforcement and order maintenance may not comprise the larger part of their regular activity, police tend to be perceived, and indeed tend to perceive themselves, as law enforcers first and foremost, and in the United States, at least, their visibly armed presence appears to confirm this. As law enforcers they are seen as monitors of human conduct, standing *over against* rather than *with* their client public, and police soon find that this perception interferes with their ability to maintain normal social relations.

Because it is part of the task of police to be impartial enforcers of the law, and because they have this responsibility (to some extent) even when "off-duty," they can easily find themselves socially uncomfortable. There is frequently an expectation that friendship will have to be sacrificed to the demands of law enforcement. A good deal of social life and intercourse may concern itself with or involve infringements of legal requirements, and the presence of a police officer in a social setting can therefore be problematic for both the officer and others. In addition, open socializing sometimes provides the occasion for complaint and recrimination. Police officers, like doctors and lawyers, often find that knowledge of their occupation turns a social occasion into an opportunity for consultation or complaint. Sometimes the complaints concern the police themselves. Because their work includes law enforcement and order maintenance, and brings them into contact with the fringes of society, police develop ways of dealing with situations that do not always sit easily with liberal culture. And so stories of police misconduct and brutality may well surface in social situations; police can find themselves the target of animosity for acts for which they had no responsibility and which may not have even been adequately represented in the media. Therefore it has not been uncommon for police to avoid regular social contacts, finding the company of their own less awkward, less threatening, less demanding, and more relaxing. No doubt shift work and irregular days off exacerbate this situation, but they are hardly responsible for it.[6]

Police, then, tend to have diminished social contacts with the community they serve. They become alienated from it, and an "us–them" mentality develops. Frequently they gain little support from other members of the public. Police often complain that if *they* find themselves in trouble no one comes to their assistance. Other police alone can be relied upon for assistance. That sense of the reliability of other police is affirmed and confirmed by the 10–13 (officer needs assistance) call. Indeed, the spectacle of exaggerated police response to a 10–13 call graphically manifests their sense of isolation and bonding. What ordinary citizen could expect a similar concentration of assistance or such a short "estimated time of arrival"?

As if to compensate for their alienation from ordinary society, there are features of police culture that reinforce their identification with each other. Whether or not police actually spend a great deal of time in high-risk situations, much in police socialization emphasizes the dangers of police work, and of the need for mutual dependence. Police soon learn that there's no better friend than another cop, especially a partner, and that there is virtually nothing a cop will not do for a partner. An intense loyalty develops, which finds expression not only in acts of great heroism, even recklessness, on behalf of another cop, but also in the notorious "blue wall of silence" that shields miscreant cops behind the "ignorance" or, as McCarthy observes, the lies of their fellows.

It is sometimes argued that this picture has changed, or at least "softened." Following some of the corruption scandals of the 1970s, and with increased accountability and a growing recruitment of minorities and women, police departments have become more open to outside scrutiny and less defensive. The "blue wall of silence" has, it has been suggested, gone the way of the Berlin Wall, and, particularly in an era of community policing, police officers have become partners with the communities they serve rather than a somewhat feared presence patrolling its boundaries.

But although I believe that there is some truth in these claims, it is at best a fragile and contingent truth, and most of the changes have been changes of degree rather than in the deeper culture of policing. The success of accountability mechanisms depends significantly on the existence of a culture of dispositional accountability; police still put "blue" before "black;" and the media is still treated with deserved suspicion. More importantly, just because police have the powers and responsibilities that they have, and their internal organization remains hierarchical, they remain persistently subject to pressures that tend to alienate them from the wider communities they serve and bind them to their own lateral groupings.

4.2   POLICE LOYALTIES

There is a certain complexity to the loyalties police have for each other, a complexity born out of the competing demands that are made of them. Carsten Stroud has spoken of a horizontal and vertical loyalty felt by police officers, a divided loyalty reflective of the different relations that police have to each other and to their work.[7] The primary loyalty of police often seems to be the horizontal loyalty of peers – partners most intensely, but also other first line or street officers. It is the loyalty that closes ranks after a police riot;[8] it is the loyalty that rushes to the scene of a 10–13 call; it may well divide line officers from management; and it is revealed in maxims to "cover one's ass," not to trust "bosses," and not to "make waves." This peer loyalty is to be distinguished from the loyalty that one feels toward the hierarchy, the vertical loyalty to the police administration and/or organization. The latter is likely to be felt/expressed most keenly in situations in which the police department itself is under attack. Then, line officers and management are expected to stick together against a critical, ignorant and unsympathetic media or public.

Donald Schultz, however, in dedicating his book on problems in criminal justice "to those Police Officers Whose first Loyalties are to Principles, not Men,"[9] clearly has a different contrast in mind. There it is not the administration or organization that is counterposed to peers, but certain ideals of policing, a particular conception of police work. Probably much the same conception lies behind Bill McCarthy's contrast between the loyalty he found manifest in the police department (as a willingness to lie for a fellow officer) and his own conception of loyalty: "Loyalty to me meant that I would always be the way I promised to be for another person."[10] Although this speaks explicitly only of a certain kind of personal integrity, of being true to oneself and one's commitments, without particular reference to any principles of policing, such as one might find in a code of ethics, it is most probable that the "promise" was intended to reflect a particular conception of what police work ought to be, rather than anything more private and idiosyncratic.

How are police to resolve the tensions created by these competing loyalties? What loyalties should they be encouraged to develop? How should these loyalties be weighted in relation to their other obligations? More generally, is it desirable to cultivate loyalties, or do they, as David Hume suggested, hold "less of reason, than of bigotry and superstition."[11] In what follows I shall argue that although loyalties are important, they are easily corrupted, and, particularly in police work, need to be reconceptualized if they are not to contribute to the disrepute into which police departments have often fallen.

4.2.1 *The uneasy virtue of loyalty*

Loyalty has had a very mixed press. On the one hand, Philip Pettit has remarked that "the ideal of loyalty is at the heart of commonsense morality."[12] And not only commonsense morality. If Frank Macchiarola is to be believed, it is also at the heart of organizational morality. Speaking after his appointment in 1976 as Chancellor of the New York City public school system, he stated, "I look for two things in my people: loyalty and competence, and in that order."[13] On the other hand, as the quote from Hume and the epigraphical maxims at the beginning of this chapter indicate, loyalty also has its detractors. Like patriotism, even loyalty in general is seen as "the last refuge of scoundrels."[14] The point has been forcefully expressed by Harry Blamires:

> Loyalty is in itself not a moral basis for action. Loyalty to a good man, a good government, a good cause, is of course a different matter. But in these cases, where one stands by a man, or a government, or a cause, because it is good, one is standing by the good. The basis of action in these cases is moral in that one is serving the good; and thus the concept of loyalty is redundant. One can therefore say fairly that whenever the virtue of loyalty is quoted as a prime motive or basis for action, one has the strongest reasons for suspecting that support is being sought for a bad cause. There is no need to drag in the pseudo-virtue of loyalty if genuine values are being served in the course that is recommended. In this sense it may be said that loyalty is a sham virtue exploited to give a bogus moral flavour to amoral or immoral actions. We breathe the word "loyalty" and immediately a sentimental warmth floods our minds. We get the emotional kick which properly accompanies decisions made in the interest of noble causes. Our complacency is cheaply earned. We have evaded the necessity to scrutinize policies with our best Christian judgement; we have acted in the way calculated to keep us in with the powers-that-be; we have followed the herd. We have done all this and at the same time acquired a cosy feeling in the stomach of virtuous achievement. Loyalty is a key concept in modern life; and it does enormous damage to our moral fibre.[15]

What accounts for these contrasting assessments? Is the value of loyalty purely a function of the value of its object? Is it a blind – or even worse, a blinding – attachment to some object? In what follows I wish to defend the value of loyalty, but also to suggest that it has features that make it vulnerable to exaggeration and distortion, and that these have corrupted its understanding in police work.

Loyalty is not a fairweather commitment. It has a self-sacrificial dimension. For the loyal person will, for the sake of the object of loyalty, set aside significant personal interests. A loyal friend is one who sticks by in bad times as well as good ones, someone who is willing to put him/herself out for the good of the other. A loyal police officer will be willing to jeopardize his safety and maybe even his life, for a partner.

Sometimes this commitment is viewed simply as an emotional bond – a sentimental tie, devotion to or affection for the object of loyalty that issues in unwavering support for it. So understood, loyalty does not need to recognize any moral constraints. It finds its expression in Stephen Decatur's (in)famous toast: "my country, right or wrong."[16] The police officer who would *never* give up a partner, no matter what the partner had done, is heir to such sentiments.

Yet although loyalty is often associated with strong bonds of affection, such feelings are not central or even essential to it. Although feelings are often involved, our loyalty manifests itself centrally through conduct – perseverance in our commitment to the object of our loyalty or in the fulfillment of our responsibilities to that object even though such perseverance will be costly. That is the specific virtue of loyalty.

The virtues are character traits and dispositions that we develop to govern our personal and social lives, to the end that they may be fulfilling and worthwhile. In the case of many virtues, their specific function is, as Philippa Foot puts it, to stand "at a point where there is some temptation to be resisted or deficiency of motivation to be made good."[17] Loyalty preserves us from self-diminishing and socially destructive self-interest and self-assertion.

There are, as Albert Hirschman has argued, important social benefits to loyalty that may easily be overlooked. Our valued human institutions[18] are usually far from perfect, and even if currently healthy they are always susceptible to deterioration. When decline occurs, there will be a tendency for those who rely on the institution to seek alternative means for realizing the ends for which they looked to them. Yet it is often better all round that such institutions undergo renovation than that they collapse from corruption or defection. It is Hirschman's view that where people have loyalty to institutions, they will be more willing to react to declines by exercising "voice" than by "exiting." Loyalty commits people to the regeneration of declining social institutions, even though this may involve some sacrifice on their part.

But although loyalty is an important social virtue, it may also go badly wrong. For not only may people acquire loyalties to evil institutions, but their loyalty to worthwhile institutions may sometimes blind them to other – and sometimes overriding – obligations and responsibilities that they have. In this respect loyalty is like sincerity and conscientiousness – virtues that it is important to have, but not sufficient to constitute one's conduct morally acceptable.

4.2.2 *The limits of loyalty*

If loyalty is to be rescued from the misuses and abuses to which it is prone, it is important that we gain a clear idea of the limits to which it ought to be subject.

As a general disposition, loyalty tends to be learned very young, and many of our most significant loyalties are acquired almost unconsciously as a part of our socialization. As noted earlier (Chapter 1, Section 1.2), we do not emerge from the womb fully endowed. Nor do we become endowed with our distinctively human qualities merely by surviving long enough, like seedlings that eventually grow to maturity. Mill's romantic metaphor of human nature as a tree, needing only room in which to grow,[19] is profoundly misleading in at least this respect. Almost uniquely, in order to develop and use and maintain our distinctive powers, we must pass through a long, and to some extent deliberately structured, process of learning. Only so will we come to display the characteristic marks of personality: speech, rationality, moral sensitivity, and so on. Our early learning necessarily takes place in a social environment. Language is acquired, emotions are shaped, will is focused and strengthened, and reason is developed, only through the complex social interactions of childhood and adolescence. And even in adulthood this does not generally change. Our human lives tend to be articulated and to thrive in joint or communal projects and activities. In a very important sense, our *human* identity has to be construed in social terms.

Our *individual* identities tend to be even more narrowly structured than this. Individually, we do not grow up to be generic persons, but members of particular families, speakers of particular languages, citizens of particular states, inheritors of a particular culture and traditions, friends with particular people, and so on. All these particular relations, traditions, and ambitions may and generally do become "ours," not only in the sense that we have them, but in the more deep-seated and constitutive sense that we conceive of ourselves in terms of them. They are not simply general facts about us, as is the fact of our being members of the species homo sapiens, or even specific facts about us, as our having large feet or hairy chests may be, but they are things that can be represented as partially constitutive of our particular individuality – as features of our being with which we identify ourselves.

It is in the realm of these constitutive relations, commitments, environments, traditions, and values that our most central loyalties tend to be located. Loyalty to the bearers, representatives or members of these traditions, commitments, structures, and groupings – as components of our particular identities – is often seen as our due. They are things to which we are often said to owe our allegiance independently of our prior consent and agreement. Most of our earliest and most abiding loyalties predate our capacity to consent to their objects. And it is partly for this reason that loyalty is often construed as a natural, nonrational or even irrational attachment.

Yet there are usually values associated with such loyalties, for the social institutions to which we become constitutively attached are bearers of significant values for us. Later we will voluntarily enter into other relationships that will become significant for us, and acquire other values against which our initially acquired loyalties will to some extent be measured. The process is generally one of gradual evolution, of growth and reassessment, in which continuities and discontinuities intermingle, and the individual seeks to retain a coherent sense of self in the midst of change.

A consequence of the way in which we are socialized and develop is that we generally come to acquire many loyalties. Some of them, and generally they will be our most deeply-rooted ones, will be personal; others will be abstract. We acquire loyalties to our families, our friends, our colleagues, to our God, our organization, to members of our ethnic group and our country-men. But we will also acquire loyalties to standards – to values and princi-ples and ideals – to a culture, and to a conception of what we are engaged in (as police officers, and so on).[20] For the most part these varied loyalties will cohere. Loyalty to one will not conflict or not conflict seriously with loyalty to another. Some loyalties will clearly take precedence over others. But occa-sionally we will experience serious and radical conflicts of loyalty, and we will be faced with an either/or decision. Does our chief loyalty lie to our partner, our department, the Commissioner, our family, or to the profession-al standards that are implicit in the kind of work that we do? These are not easy questions. They may be painful. And sometimes they will involve "defining decisions," in which we decide what sort of a person we will be. Because of the nature of their work, police officers may be faced with such decisions on a number of occasions during their careers.

In this connection, it is very important to recognize that when one loyalty is sacrificed to another it will not necessarily constitute *dis*loyalty to the other object of loyalty. Whether disloyalty is involved will depend on the reason why one object of loyalty rather than the other was chosen.

Real disloyalty is almost always constituted by the forsaking of an object of loyalty for self-serving and individualistic or self-assertive reasons. Where our own comfort, convenience, advantage, advancement or private vision is the reason for abandoning an object of loyalty, then and only then will our abandonment of that loyalty constitute disloyalty, a betrayal. But where our reason for forsaking an object of loyalty is some higher loyalty, say, to moral principle or professional standards, then, although we will not have been loyal to the forsaken object, neither will we have been disloyal.

This is an important point, especially in the context of policing, where loyalty to partner very often tends to be viewed absolutely. It is usually in the interests of those who take an absolute approach to their own particular loyalty, or who have something to hide, to characterize *every* forsaking of loyalty as disloyalty, every abandonment as a betrayal. This partially ex-plains the contempt characteristically shown for the whistleblower. He or she is characterized as disloyal, as though anyone who is not loyal must therefore be disloyal. And, as disloyal, is to be condemned.

Even though loyalties, especially personal loyalties, are often deeply felt, this does not put them beyond the bounds of moral and professional ap-praisal. We should not simply assume that what, as a matter of our natural development, acquires and perhaps demands our loyalty thereby deserves it, or that those to whom we owe our loyalty may demand what they like.

And the personal and institutional loyalties that may be expected of us as adults need to be *earned*. Or, if that is too strong an expectation, we should at least recognize that any such loyalty may be *forfeited*. Loyalty is not a morally insensitive commitment, but one that ought to be subject to the same scrutiny as any other value. Just as we may draw back from absolute truthfulness ("come what may") and strict justice ("though the heavens fall") in the name of compassion or benevolence, so too we may draw back from absolute loyalty in the name of justice or professional integrity. The self-sacrifice that we owe in loyalty is not the sacrifice of our integrity, but of our comfort and convenience, sometimes of our safety and private ambitions. We do not *owe* loyalty to those whose conduct has transgressed and undermined publicly acknowledged or professional standards any more than the sexually abused child, physically abused wife or oppressed minority group owe loyalty to their abusers. The loyalty that might normally be expected has been forfeited by the abuser. Of course, loyalty *may* continue to be given, but this loyalty will have cut itself off from the roots that make loyalty the valuable thing it is. The abuser, like the corrupt police officer, has betrayed what the particular group stands for, and has subverted the values that help make loyalty to it the worthy thing it is.

There is also a certain proportionality about what is properly owed as loyalty to another. Loyalty to one's organization does not require that one die for it, though it may require that one not leave it as soon as a better offer comes along, and it almost certainly requires that one not sell its secrets to another organization. Even loyalty to one's country or friends may not require a willingness to die for them. What loyalty demands will depend not only on the object of loyalty, but also on the particular interests that are at stake. If a friend is being falsely maligned, it might require only that one sticks up for the friend. Only if the friend is in immediate and grave physical danger may putting one's own life on the line be seen as an appropriate (though even here, perhaps, supererogatory) loyalty.

What counts as disloyalty will also vary according to the object. Public criticism of one's spouse may manifest disloyalty, but not criticisms of one's government's policies. What will be critical in such cases is the effect of one's conduct on the interests of the object of one's supposed loyalty. If those interests are unjustifiably undermined, and the object is injured in some way, then one's conduct might reasonably be seen as disloyal. But, as we saw earlier in the discussion of Hirschman, a critical opposition may actually manifest loyalty if it is directed (and likely to contribute) to the good of its object. In theory, one of the factors that enables a democracy to thrive is the presence of a "loyal opposition," ensuring that whatever policies are promulgated will be maximally beneficial.

Where does the foregoing leave police? First of all, they will most likely – and perhaps it is appropriate that they should – develop multiple loyalties, some related specifically to their work, some to objects outside it. It will be important that they have some rough ranking of those loyalties, so that when tensions or conflicts arise they will have an idea of where their priorities should lie. The critical situations will often be where the loyalty claimed or expected by a fellow officer conflicts with organizational or professional ideals.

Sometimes these conflicts may be agonizing. Consider the case of an officer who has been taunted by a particularly unpleasant suspect and who reacts by giving the suspect a sharp but not seriously damaging slap. The suspect lays a complaint. Suppose too that the department has become particularly sensitive to charges of excessive force, and is likely to dismiss the officer (with consequent pension loss) if the substance of the complaint is established. The officer's partner is asked what happened. Where do the partner's loyalties lie in such a situation? Even though it may reasonably be argued that the officer should not have allowed himself to be provoked into striking out, the partner may consider that the consequences for the officer, if the complaint is upheld, will be draconian. Does loyalty reasonably demand that he profess not to have seen what happened? In such a case we might be tempted to excuse the partner if he professes ignorance of what transpired. Yet, as we know, a case such as this is simply the gray edge of the code of (loyal) silence that has been so subversive of good order in police work.

The partner's dilemma may be increased by his knowledge that a good deal of police work takes place in what is seen as a morally gray area where values compete and "the moral way to proceed" is not always obvious, where force and deception are often integral to the achievement of worthwhile ends. A fellow officer who acts as though the world is morally black and white might be seen as a threat to fellow officers and to the success of the unpleasant and morally hazardous work they are often called to do. How many officers can claim never to have held someone too long or hit someone too hard or deceived someone unnecessarily or . . . ? Of course, we might want to claim that the dilemma has been created by a department with draconian rules, and that if a more reasonable response were taken to the assault then there is no doubt what the partner should do. But police work does not take place in a world where everything else is "fair" or "reasonable," and that is also the world in which the partner has to decide what to do.

However, it is one thing to claim, as I suggest here, that there is a gray area in which difficult decisions must be made about where one's loyalties should lie. It is quite another to think that such cases could be used to sustain anything as strong as the blue wall of silence found so often in police organizations. The police who refused to testify against their fellows in the Tompkins Square Park riot on Manhattan's Lower East Side, the police who turn a blind eye to and profess ignorance of serious corruption and misconduct on the part of their fellows, cannot justify their silence by claiming that they morally *owe* loyalty to their fellows. That they might sometimes do so shows the corrosive effect of a cynicism that reduces loyalty to a tribal value that insulates oneself and one's group against a hostile world.

Dilemmas of the kind that I have outlined are not susceptible of any formulaic resolution. Cases, with their particular nuances, have to be considered on an individual basis, and tradeoffs have to be made between considerations that are to a large extent incommensurable. The simplest solution that I can suggest is a purely procedural one: whether an officer would be prepared to defend his decision in a public forum. This is no test of moral correctness. It might function as a test of moral sincerity. But in this area, securing moral sincerity might itself be a very significant achievement (see further, Chapter 7, Section 7.1.2).

4.3 POLICE CYNICISM

The problems associated with police loyalty are closely tied in with the problem of police cynicism. In large measure, it is because police become cynical about morality and about the moral seriousness of those they serve that their loyalties become detached from the moral constraints that would moderate them.

The police experience of social and organizational morality is conducive to the development of moral cynicism. Where hypocrisy pervades public life, and the police organization itself displays a Catch–22 attitude toward its lower-ranked employees, cynicism is easily spawned. This cynicism allows their loyalties to become morally unfettered. Why should police officers qualify their loyalty to partners when all they see around them is evil, deceit and hypocrisy? Why testify against a fellow officer, someone who would be prepared to risk his life for you, just because he beat up some "lowlife" who was giving him a hard time? Why cooperate with brass who are more interested in their advancement and with media opinion than with truth and justice?

The issue of police cynicism was first discussed and researched at length by Arthur Niederhoffer, in *Behind the Shield: The Police in Urban Society*.[21] According to Niederhoffer, cynicism is an outcome of anomie, the alienation that one experiences when the belief structures of one's existing social world have been eroded, but have not yet been replaced.[22] The anomic person becomes cynical, that is, distrusting of the motives and rectitude of others, and generally skeptical of the moral order. According to Niederhoffer, police officers he interviewed within the New York City Police Department had become cynical, and had become so for two main reasons. One reason related to an internal struggle between two forms of policing: a middle-class based professional model versus an older traditional lower middle- and upper lower-class model. Officers found themselves caught between these two approaches, and became confused about their goals and values. The other reason was a disenchantment with the wider social world that police served, an unaccepting world marked by hypocrisy. Accordingly, their cynicism was directed toward both the police system and the wider society.

Cynicism is a matter of ethical importance for a number of reasons. Obviously, police officers who develop a cynical attitude will find it difficult to give a serious as against a merely pragmatic place to ethical considerations in their work. And this will have important implications for police professionalism. Insofar as professionalism involves a commitment to service and to providing the best service one can, then cynicism is erosive of the professional aspirations that police are encouraged to have. Any code of ethics that might be promulgated becomes simply a bit of window dressing, a public relations strategy. Niederhoffer goes further by suggesting that the press for professionalism is itself a source of cynicism for those officers who are unable to join the new professional élite. To the extent that the press for professionalism is construed or perceived as a press for professionalization, this might well turn out to be the case, since it will often carry with it the corrosive tendencies that we noted in an earlier chapter (3.1.2). But a genuine concern for professionalism is unlikely to contribute to cynicism. Only the already cynical will view it cynically.

It was Niederhoffer's contention that cynicism among police officers increased slowly but significantly in their first eight years of employment, and then gradually declined until retirement. Subsequent researchers have not always agreed with his findings. Some have argued that what Niederhoffer found was in some ways peculiar to the New York City Police Department, or at least to large urban departments, and was not as likely in smaller departments.[23] Others have questioned Niederhoffer's nexus between professionalism and middle-class values and its contrast with "traditional" lower class values.[24] And they have located anomie and cynicism in other factors, such as job-related stress (danger stress, and administratively produced stress), exacerbated by professional values that undermine protective group cohesiveness.[25]

However widespread police cynicism is, and whatever its causes, the moral implications are nevertheless profound. Central to cynicism is the lack of trust that is shown towards the objects of cynicism. And where that distrust is directed to both the police organization and the wider society, there is a corruption of the very conditions of a form of policing that takes seriously the idea of service to, and partnership with, the community. Indeed, the very idea of community policing, intended as a corrective to some of the cynicism that police feel toward the community, is itself viewed with cynicism by officers who see it as the latest fad or buzzword of police administrators seeking to improve their public and political image.

There is a deep and dangerous irony implicit in police cynicism, for one of the major functions of police as social peacekeepers is to safeguard and foster social conditions that will be sustained and characterized by trust. True, police are needed in part because that trust is fragile and has been compromised. Nevertheless, theirs is the task of preventing its further erosion, and even of helping to restore it. Should they become cynical toward what they do and those whom they serve, the growth of a culture of trust is less likely to be assisted. And we are all losers thereby, for it is only through the establishment of communities of trust that we are able to flourish as individuals.

It is, moreover, through such communities of trust that healthy loyalties will be developed. For loyalties shaped by communities of trust will be morally bounded loyalties. Loyalty will not be demanded, as the chapter's epigraph suggests, only when it is desired that one compromise oneself. Loyalty and integrity will be internally connected and mutually supportive. Maintaining one's loyalties should be an element in the maintenance of one's integrity.

Is it ever right to be cynical, or is cynicism a form of moral pathology? Perhaps we need to distinguish between a healthy skepticism and cynicism. Skepticism, like cynicism, involves disbelief. But skepticism is usually particularized. We may be skeptical about this or that particular proposition or explanation. We are not cynical towards them. Skepticism is usually based on rational doubt. Cynicism tends to be a generalized attitude – it may be toward politics in general or toward the police system, or more generally toward the public or humankind. The cynic has given up on the object of cynicism, a judgment that is not implicit in skepticism. Skepticism is usually based on rational doubt. Cynicism, however, usually reflects distrust, based on moral doubt. The cynic doubts motives, not reasons. Cynicism need not be nihilistic. Unlike skepticism, it is directed toward people and human institutions; skepticism, unlike cynicism, is shown toward beliefs or propositions. Whereas skepticism may be healthy, cynicism is unlikely to be so.

Police engage with a world that easily encourages cynicism. The kind of work that they do is likely to expose them to efforts to deflect them from the frequently unpleasant duties that they must fulfill. Frequently their work makes them privy to information about people that reveals the substantial hypocrisy of much public moralizing. Moreover, from the somewhat prurient media interest in police corruption and misconduct, they know that they are being held to standards that others do not themselves observe, often the very people who demand high standards of them.

Even within their own organization they see the evidences of manipulative bad faith. They see superior officers allowing themselves liberties that they would condemn on the part of those under them. They see departmental intrigues and politicking. They will see their own being made scapegoats for the failures of those above them. Where officers do stand up for what is right, they are not given the managerial support that might be expected.

In an environment of social and organizational hypocrisy, cynicism is an ongoing temptation. Cynics think that the air one breathes when walking the high moral ground is too rarified for survival. What really counts, what really keeps the wheels of institutional reality turning, are politics and organizational custom (proper channels, standard operating procedures, and networks – "hooks" and "rabbis").

But like many -isms, cynicism involves an excess, a loss of objectivity, a capitulation to "ideology." Although cynicism is often adopted as a survival mechanism, a means whereby officers may distance themselves from the moral, psychological, and emotional stresses that accompany their work, it is, ultimately, self-destructive. For it casts a pall on relationships that have the potential to be personally and socially fulfilling. And even if those relationships have become less than ideal, it does nothing to mend or restore them. Indeed, one of the most seriously destructive effects of cynicism is the fact that it infects the very means whereby we might seek to counteract it. That cynicism fails to reap its full self-destructive harvest is due only to the fact that there remain enough people who refuse to be overtaken by it, and who seek, in small or larger ways, to continue the search for a fulfilling social peace.

Chapter 5

Police discretion

The following General Instructions for the different ranks of the Police Force are not to be understood as containing rules of conduct applicable to every variety of circumstances that may occur in the performance of their duty; something must necessarily be left to the intelligence and discretion of individuals; and according to the degree in which they show themselves possessed to these qualities and to their zeal, activity, and judgement, on all occasions, will be their claims to future promotion and reward.

Colonel Charles Rowan and Sir Richard Mayne[1]

In a recent survey of discretionary decision making in the criminal justice system, Samuel Walker argued that discretion was "discovered" only in 1956, and that once discovered there were cries for its abolition.[2] Walker's point, as the quotation from Rowan and Mayne makes clear, was not that discretion did not previously exist, but that researchers into the criminal justice system had not taken account of its impact on decisions made within that sphere. Once it was seen how great was the impact of discretionary decision making on outcomes, there were calls for its abolition. The calls, it turned out, could not be heeded, and in any case were hardly justified. But significant steps were taken to control the way in which it was used.

The exercise of discretion is often said to be central to professional decision making. In providing their services, professionals are not slavish followers of rules and procedures, but are expected to make their own judgments about how their services might best be rendered. This expectation is grounded in the belief that they possess special knowledge and expertise relevant to the provision of those services, and that in making their decisions they will be drawing on that special knowledge and expertise.

The need for discretion in police work has often been taken as evidence that police are, or at least ought to be, professionals. However, as I have already briefly indicated (Chapter 3, Section 3.1.1.5), not only is policing a problematic candidate for professional status, but the discretion that police are called upon to exercise may not be altogether the same as that for which professionals are distinguished.

There is, in fact, a great deal of confusion about the idea of discretion, and, therefore, in discussions about the need for it and limits to it. So I want to begin with a consideration of different ideas of discretion before returning more explicitly to its meaning for policing and the professions. Once we have clarified that, we will be in a position to consider whether, what kind, and to what extent discretion is acceptable and/or to be fostered in police work.

5.1   IDEAS OF DISCRETION

We should not assume that the idea of discretion is univocal, even if there is a common root notion. Our English word "discretion" has its philological roots in the Latin *discretio*, which originally meant "separation" or "distinction," but in later Latin took on the related though distinct meaning of "discernment." We preserve this forking in the two English adjectives "discrete" and "discreet." Both have relevance to the present context.

In the latter sense, the person who shows discretion is one who manifests good, sound, careful or wise judgment in practical, and particularly interpersonal, affairs. In this sense, a police officer who handles a difficult case with discernment can be said to have acted with discretion.

Clearly, however, this wholly "commendatory" sense is not what is usually intended when people say that police officers have too much or too little discretion. What they are referring to is not an unqualifiedly commendable way of handling situations, but a *power* that police have to exercise their own judgment with regard to situations in which action is called for. That they exercise it well is not implied, except insofar as they are said to have too little! Indeed, the extent of their discretionary power is often a matter of considerable public concern, and there is frequently believed to be a tension between their authority under law and the exercise of such discretion. We hope that police will exercise their discretion with discretion, but we have no guarantee that they will do so.

The second sense of "discretion," in which it is seen as a power, links up with the earlier sense of "separation," for it refers to a power that police have to act as independent agents. In this regard, George Fletcher notes that German sociologists, when referring to police discretion, speak not of their *Ermessen* (discernment) but of their *Definitionsmacht* (power of definition), a power to determine how a situation will be dealt with.[3]

We are, however, not yet out of the woods. An ambiguity still remains. For "power" can refer either to an ability or capacity, or to a prerogative or authority. Both understandings can be found in discussions of police discretion. Kenneth Culp Davis, one of the most influential contemporary writers on discretion in law enforcement, has written that "a public officer has discretion whenever the effective limits on his power leave him free to make a choice among possible courses of action or inaction."[4] Here the emphasis is more on a capacity that police have than a prerogative that is theirs. By emphasizing the "effective" rather than, say, "legal" (or other normative) limits to their power, Davis recognizes that much police work is effectively unsupervised, and that *how* police handle a situation will de facto depend on the decision or choice of the officers concerned. Some writers have extended this understanding of "discretion" to encompass *any* voluntary decision by an officer. Clearly this latter extension evacuates the idea of discretion of much of its usefulness, and is certainly broader than Davis intends.

Yet though he intends less, Davis encourages such uncontrolled extension of the term. What he intends is a police decision-making power that is not completely covered by rules – where what police ought to do is not completely "spoken for" by laws, rules, regulations or other authoritative pronouncements. And his concern is with the appropriate limits to that power and the relative merits of legislative fiat, judicial review, and administrative rule-making as mechanisms for circumscribing it. But what he does by grafting on the idea of "effective" limits is to shift the emphasis from normative to executive mechanisms of control over police decision making. And from there it does not take much to see as discretionary any situation in which a police officer has the ability or capacity to decide how to proceed.

To speak of any situation in which police voluntarily decide what they shall do as one in which they exercise discretion trivializes the idea of discretion. So too, however, does the use of "discretion" to refer to any situation in which police are free from "effective limits on their power" to act. *Pace* Davis, if a police officer beats a vagrant in a back alley, he is not exercising his discretion either well or badly.[5] Even though the *effective* limits on his power leave the officer free to make this choice, this is not a situation in which it is appropriate to speak of the officer having or exercising discretion. It is a mistake to think that because something is effectively a matter of decision, it is therefore a matter of discretion.

The idea of discretion is best understood as a normative condition – as a permission, privilege or prerogative to use one's own judgment about how to make a practical determination. It is in this context that we can understand the recognition of professional discretion. Precisely because professionals are seen as possessing special knowledge and expertise in relation to their sphere of service, we accept their discretionary judgment. This of course is not the same as accepting that their discretion is used *with* discretion (discernment). But the link with a normative condition helps us to see how the two uses of "discretion" may be connected. We might speak of a rebuttable presumption that those to whom discretionary power is given will exercise it with discretion.

Discretionary authority may be recognized informally, or, more commonly, it will be acknowledged and perhaps even circumscribed in administrative or other documents. In acknowledging the need for officers to exercise discretion, it will *ipso facto* be presumed that those who exercise it are competent to exercise it.

5.1.1 *Broad and narrow discretion*

Even if it is not the case that every situation in which a decision has to be made is for that reason a situation in which discretion is authorized, we still need to make a further distinction between broad and narrow discretion, and to clarify the relation between them and the making of a voluntary decision or choice.

Consider a situation in which a police officer notices that someone is exceeding the speed limit by eight miles per hour. Unless we take the view that police are strictly required to enforce all the laws – a view with which I shall soon take issue – the officer may exercise his or her discretion as to an appropriate response. Should the officer ignore the breach, take the vehicle's number, or commence a pursuit? If the last, what level of pursuit should the officer be prepared to initiate? Following apprehension of the driver, presuming that it takes place, should the driver be reprimanded, ticketed, or even arrested (supposing the driver recklessly sought to avoid apprehension)? These are all likely to be discretionary matters because they lie within the officer's designated authority. It is not simply that the officer is capable of pursuing each of these options; *they are permitted to the officer*. Which of them will be the correct or best will depend on other factors in the situation. The officer will almost certainly have no discretion to ram the vehicle, fire shots, or beat up the driver after apprehension, even though the officer may voluntarily choose to do any of these things, and even though the officer may be able to get away with them.

In some cases, such as the one just considered, the officer's discretion may be quite broad: A large range of permissible options is available to the officer. In other cases, some aspects of the officer's discretion may be considerably limited: in the foregoing situation, if the officer proposes to initiate a pursuit, the officer may be required to radio that fact to a dispatcher/ supervisor. That will not be a matter about which the officer has any discretion. And if the supervisor tells the officer not to proceed with the pursuit, the officer will not have the discretion to continue with it, even if he could get away with doing so.

Generally speaking, the more serious the offense (in the case of a breach of law) the narrower we might expect the officer's discretion to be with regard to non-enforcement. At the same time, there may be increased discretion with regard to the measures that the officer may legitimately employ to apprehend the alleged offender. How expansive that discretion is will to some extent depend on situational factors. If an officer sees a man shoot a woman and then run off with her purse, the officer does not have the discretion to ignore the situation, even though he or she may have some discretion with regard to the employment of deadly force against the perpetrator. But if the brutal mugging takes place in a crowded shopping area, the officer may not have any discretion with regard to the use of a firearm.

Consider, however, a situation in which the offense takes place in a street where some though not many other people are present. Although the officer may have no discretion to use a firearm in a crowded area, he or she must make a judgment as to whether this constitutes a crowded area. Is this a discretionary judgment? We can call it discretionary if we like, but it is discretionary only in a narrower sense. It is discretionary in the sense in which every act of authority requires the exercise of judgment, because it must be determined what the situation is, what, if any, rules are relevant to it, and whether they are determinative. However, it is generally the further practical judgments, concerning the weight that relevant rules should have, and how they ought to be followed or applied, that we think of as involving discretionary authority.

To characterize judgments of this narrower kind as discretionary tends to invite confusion. For these interpretative judgments are better seen as necessitated by the exigencies of situations than as authorized prerogatives. There may of course be such a prerogative: It may be *for the officer* to determine what is and what is not a crowded area. And where there is such discretionary authority, how broad it will be might depend on the definiteness or vagueness of concepts: A rule forbidding the use of a firearm in a "crowded area" might allow for greater latitude of interpretation (greater interpretative discretion) than one forbidding the use of a firearm where it would "endanger bystanders," though "dangerousness" may itself be open to some variation in interpretation. But even if the concepts or rules to be applied are fairly clear, the situation may not be, and it will require some exercise of judgment (whether or not also of discretionary authority) to determine how it should be characterized. Generally, however, it is a broader practical discretion that characterizes professional authority rather than the judgment that is required whenever someone with authority is confronted by a situation that appears to impinge upon it.

5.1.2 *Forms of police discretion*

Let us now look more closely at the discretion allowed to police. In an earlier chapter I argued that the police role might be most usefully characterized by the idea of social peacekeeping (Chapter 2, Section 2.4.4). Although the idea of a social peacekeeper is not tightly constrained, it locates police work within a rich and useful conceptual and social context. For we recognize that one of the things giving human life its special character is a kind of order, a rational order and a social order. That order is fostered and maintained through a variety of social institutions, and police have a special, albeit not exclusive role in helping to ensure that an ordered peace remains achievable.

To this end police perform a great variety of social peacekeeping functions, from crowd and traffic control, through emergency assistance and dispute settlement to law enforcement. To provide the full range of these services they have powers of access and resources of coercive force that are not as unambiguously available to the rest of us. How they are to carry out their various responsibilities is a difficult, if not impossible, task to specify in advance, so varied and complex are the situations to which they are called to respond. And so we grant them some discretion in such matters. It may not be very considerable, and in some cases we may allow them none at all. On-duty police officers, unlike other citizens, are not generally given the option of standing to one side in an emergency situation.[6] In *Discretionary Justice,* Davis took the view that police had no legitimate discretion with regard to the enforcement of criminal law, though considerable discretion in respect of their social service functions. In his later *Police Discretion,* however, he revises that opinion, at least with respect to some criminal law.

Police discretion is a normative resource that police possess, one that authorizes them to use their considered judgment in certain ways in certain situations. It may be that they are authorized to determine *whether* a situation should have their intervention or whether to respond to some demand that is made. In other words, whether or not a particular situation falls within the ambit of their social peacekeeping powers may be a matter of discretion. Civil disputes generally do not have a claim on their involvement; where criminal conduct is involved, it almost certainly will. But often situations do not fall very obviously into one or the other, and the officer will have some discretion about the extent to which he or she should intervene.

Decisions of the foregoing kind encompass questions of scope, interpretation and priority. That is, police may exercise discretion about whether the issue in question is a police issue, about how to characterize it once it is acknowledged to be a police issue, and about whether, given competing demands on police resources, their resources should be expended on this issue rather than on some other.

Alternatively, when officers do intervene, they may be authorized to determine *how* they will intervene. Frequently their discretion in these matters is considerably less than is accorded those generally considered to be professionals, and this is because although it is *for them* to act, their knowledge and expertise is limited and only questionably superior to that of others. Their task in many of these situations will not be to act on the basis of individual professional judgment, but to give effect to a more general departmental or societal will. Although they will need common sense, individual officers are not deemed to possess superior professional knowledge.

5.2 · FOUNDATIONS OF POLICE DISCRETION

As I have argued, police discretion is not simply a decision-making power that police possess in virtue of the relatively unsupervised nature of their work. It is a normative resource that we grant them or recognize that they have. As such we should expect this authority or prerogative to be grounded in certain justifying considerations. In the case of the traditional professions, we recognize the public service to which they are directed and the superior knowledge and expertise of their practitioners as the basis for their (only partially constrained) authority to make their own (discretionary) decisions about whether and how their services are called for. Or, perhaps better, we are prepared to grant them discretionary authority only to the extent that we recognize them as having superior competence and skill in the provision of their public service. This authority, first recognized as a social phenomenon, may subsequently be given formal or legal recognition.

What can be said on behalf of police discretionary authority? Here we are not dealing with a unified situation. As we have noted (Chapter 2, Section 2.4), police work is very diverse, and can encompass many kinds of emergency assistance, crowd and traffic control activities, as well as law enforcement. We need not assume that police discretion is grounded in the same considerations in each of these cases.

An argument for granting discretionary authority would seem to be most easily mounted in regard to the social service and order maintenance activities that police perform, since such activities will almost always call for individualized responses. The relevant features of such situations are likely to be so variable that any discretion-limiting rules covering them are likely to leave a significant degree of latitude regarding the way they are to be handled. And so, given that there is a need for intervention of some sort, and for that intervention to be of an orderly kind, where order may not be easy to achieve, police, who have been granted the social authority to command "at street level," and who have usually been trained in some of the basics needed for handling such situations, are likely to be appropriate executors of needed discretion. It will, of course, be a limited discretion, since there are other specialists who may come to be involved, and whose discretionary authority may subsequently take some sort of precedence, at least with respect to some aspects of the situation. If firefighters or ambulance personnel or social workers also respond to a situation, there may be aspects of it that should be yielded to their judgment. But, as was earlier argued (see Chapter 2, Section 2.4.2), peacekeeping needs may extend beyond those dealt with by the professional, and so the presence of a professional may not dispense with the need for a police presence.

One of the most problematic forms of police discretion is that involved in selective law enforcement. It is especially problematic since a particular response sometimes appears to be prescribed by the rules under which officers work. Police are generally pledged to enforce all the laws, and to do so without partiality. It is largely on this basis that William Heffernan has questioned the appropriateness of most selective enforcement. Taking the New York City Police Department oath as his starting point, Heffernan claims that the officers' pledge to "enforce and prevent the violation of all laws and ordinances in force in the city, and for these purposes . . . arrest all persons guilty of violating any law or ordinance,"[7] requires full enforcement, within procedural limits set by the U.S Constitution. Leaving aside self-interested reasons for selective enforcement (favoritism, discrimination, and so on), Heffernan then considers four different types of "disinterested rule violations":[8] (1) meting out justice via violations of the Constitution; (2) meting out justice via selective enforcement of the law; (3) promotion of social order via violations of the Constitution; and (4) promotion of social order via selective enforcement of the law.

Heffernan believes that a police officer's oath has the force of a promise, a promise of full, Constitutionally-bound enforcement in return for employment. This obligation cannot be easily set aside – and certainly not for violations (1)–(3). In cases of type (4), Heffernan believes that provided certain institutional guidelines are met – review, publicity, *onus probandi*, and so on – selective enforcement can sometimes, though only with difficulty, be justified.

I think these constraints are too severe. For one thing, too much attention is paid to the enforcement clause of the police officers' oath, to the neglect or at least the underplaying of its other dimensions. At least in the case of New York City police officers, the commitment is to "preserve the public peace" and "protect the rights of persons" before there is any pledge to enforce and arrest. So, although a commitment to full enforcement is exacted, so also is a commitment to preserve the public peace and protect rights. This gives the oath an inherently problematic character. For what contributes best to the preservation of public peace may not always be compatible with enforcement and prevention of violations of laws and ordinances. In itself, a "disinterested violation" may stand in no more (or less) need of special justification than the refusal to engage in an unconstitutional preventive frisk.[9] May not the latter sometimes be as important to the protection of (others') rights as the arrest of lawbreakers is to law enforcement?

There is a further point that requires more attention than Heffernan provides. His analysis of promising, and of the obligations of promising, is abstracted from the varied contexts in which promises are made – for example, interpersonal situations, in which the promisor formulates the terms of the promise; institutional situations, in which the terms of a promise formulated by others are repeated and consented to; contractual promises; formal, ritualized occasions, in which an oath is solemnly made; and so on. Promising is never a light matter, but there are different social understandings permeating the varied contexts in which promises are made, and which may sometimes yield a less "legalistic" understanding than Heffernan's. All promises are intended to create reliance; but the kind of reliance intended and created, and the character of the obligation involved, might well differ with the kind of promise and the context in which it is given. It is true, as Heffernan observes, that "any prospective officer who declined to take [the oath] or who made public in advance his intention to adhere to it selectively would surely be denied the position he seeks."[10] But it does not follow from that that an officer who takes the oath is assumed to be committed to arresting the orderly participants in a family picnic who are drinking beer in a public park.

There are, nevertheless, two problems with the police exercise of discretion that do not have a clear parallel in standard cases of professional discretion. As agents of government, and particularly as the enforcers of its legal will, police are bound by principles of legality. Like the law that they are expected to administer and under whose rule they act, their decisions too should be clear, consistent, publicly accessible, and predictable. Allowing them discretionary authority might well appear to subvert these expectations. What is more, their exercises of discretionary judgment might appear to be incompatible with democratic principles. Unlike legislators, who govern by consent, police officers are appointees whose authority is executive rather than legislative. Discretionary decision making by police might be interpreted as a form of legislative activity.

These problems for police discretion are at best contingent. For one thing, discretionary judgment may be explicitly acknowledged and even expected. Such has been the case from modern policing's earliest days. As it was observed (with parliamentary approval) in Rowan and Mayne's *General Instructions* to the Metropolitan Police, the *Instructions* were not to "be understood as containing rules of conduct applicable to every variety of circumstances that may occur in the performance of their duty; something must necessarily be left to the intelligence and discretion of individuals."[11] Although the language of subsequent pronouncements by police officials, and of codes and oaths of office, has sometimes suggested something more restrictive – though generally as regards law enforcement – few have argued that police are completely lacking in discretionary authority. The contention has focused on the *extent* of that authority. The law does not cover every eventuality with which police must deal, and sometimes it may conflict with other purposes that police are pledged to fulfill. Some discretionary decision making can therefore be expected of police.

A similar response can be made to the claim that discretionary authority is undemocratic. There is nothing about discretionary authority as such that puts it beyond public scrutiny and consent. Discretionary authority may be granted in advance, within the limitations mandated by laws, regulations, and supervisory determinations. And particular exercises of that discretion, like exercises of judicial discretion, may be open to public review and discussion. As long as this is so, such discretion has every claim to be part of a democratic order. The "rule of law, not of men" is directed against arbitrary exertions of power, not against discretion. Discretion, as a normative resource, is a form of decision making power that is embedded in a rationale, and although that may not be sufficient to justify its every exercise, it is to be firmly distinguished from action based on personal preference. That authority may, as a result of public scrutiny, be broadened or narrowed via legislation, judicial review, or administrative rule making. As with the previous objection, the crucial issue regarding the democratic conformity of police discretionary authority will concern its limits rather than its general legitimacy.

The foregoing discussion has suggested several possible bases for police discretionary authority – its sheer necessity, some form of official sanction, and communal consent. Taken together they provide a fairly plausible case for recognizing a constrained police discretionary authority. Yet taken singly, each has its weaknesses as a full account.

5.2.1 *Necessity*

On the face of it, the fact that it is impossible for police to enforce all the laws all the time provides a strong argument for the exercise of discretion – at least with respect to selective enforcement.[12] Formal breaches of law occur constantly, and most of us are guilty of them many times over. Jaywalking, not fully stopping at stop signs or stopping too far forward at corners, exceeding the speed limit, removing property (pencils, stationery, paper clips, and so on) from our workplaces without permission, violating noise or pollution regulations, and so on, may all, strictly speaking, be prohibited. But we do not have the resources to enforce all these rules strictly; and even if we did have them it would be socially disruptive were strict enforcement to be instituted. So police *must* exercise discretion.

But a bare argument from necessity will not take us far enough. It builds on certain assumptions about the relative importance of enforcement, and of full enforcement, and these assumptions may need to be made good. Otherwise, all it may show is our need for more law enforcement, the need to invest greater resources in policing. It may show that while we presently need to *excuse* police for not enforcing all the laws, selective nonenforcement is nevertheless not *justified*.

We need an argument to show that even if the resources were available, police should selectively enforce the law. That there is some such argument is suggested by the penultimate sentence of the previous paragraph, which hints at the disruptive effect of full enforcement: pursuing one end of policing may subvert another. If, as I have suggested, we see policing primarily as social peacekeeping, and law enforcement as an element within that, then selective enforcement becomes a much more reasonable option, without the need to invoke a two-edged argument from necessity.

5.2.2 *Official authorization*

The various laws, rules, regulations and authoritative pronouncements governing police practice also provide a possible source for police discretionary authority. Although laws are themselves expressed in an exceptionless form, and police pledge themselves to enforce them all (what else might one expect them to pledge?), other equally authoritative directives appear to "soften" that generality, and encourage judicious and selective enforcement.

At first blush, the appeal to some form of official authorization for discretion may not seem particularly promising. For there is relatively little explicit encouragement, recognition, or requirement of discretion in regard to selective enforcement. Indeed, when Kenneth Culp Davis undertook his investigation of police discretion, he suggested that the opposite position tended to find a more prominent public representation, lest it were complained that police were failing to perform their duty or that they were performing it in a discriminatory manner.[13] However, there is some reason to think that Davis's evidence was somewhat incomplete, and that as the Metropolitan Police's *General Instructions* show there has always been an explicit as well as implicit recognition of the need for police discretion.[14] One does not need to "read between the lines" to see it. Where appearances suggest otherwise, it is usually because something has gone badly wrong, and police officials have wished to distance the untoward events from any outworking of departmental policies.[15]

However, although there is some official authorization for police discretion, it is sometimes half-hearted in practice. When something goes wrong, individual discretionary authority is likely to be denied. It does not, moreover, have the breadth and robustness of the discretion that characterizes the classical professions. Indeed, even the skepticism we show towards professional discretion when we get a "second opinion" presupposes a certain kind of commitment to the discretionary authority of professionals. It may not empower them to act without the consent of those they serve, but it certainly recognizes the importance of individual judgment in such matters. Were physicians expected to be mere spokespersons of a higher authority, seeking a second opinion would be more like "double checking." But in the case of police organizations, their hierarchical character and the vertical chain of responsibility that operates within them makes the discretionary authority of line officers inherently problematic.

Of course, even were there to be some reasonably clearly articulated authorization for police discretion, we would still need to inquire into its justifying grounds. Mere authorization is at best an intermediate justification. That authority is granted and/or recognized does not show it to be justified. Do police officers have some particular competence to decide in these matters? Is it given them simply as a convenient structuring of their social organization and decision making?

Once again, we are forced back to the fundamental grounds for police authority, and in particular to the normative considerations that delimit their social role. That they are expected to be and to function competently as social peacekeepers provides the key that we need to understand how they might be seen as authorized to exercise discretion. Like umpires in games, who are there to enforce the rules and penalize breaches, but are expected to do so with an eye to the wider purposes of the game, and its need to "flow," police officers, too, will know that an over-attention to law enforcement may undermine the needs of an ordered and peaceable social life and their role in conserving and promoting it. And so, although official authorizations may offer some form of confirmation, it is probably better to see such formal acknowledgements of police discretionary authority as a recognition and formalization of something that has its foundations elsewhere.

5.2.3 *Community expectation*

I have already traced the source of police authority to communal expectations and traditions. And so we should not be surprised to find that such discretionary authority as police have is also sustained by similar expectations, in particular by the belief that police are competent to exercise discretion wisely. The argument goes roughly as follows: Police authority is grounded in communal recognition; the understanding that those who are to be designated as police officers are competent to carry out various peacekeeping responsibilities. Along with that responsibility, the community also devotes a portion of its resources, and it is to be expected that, in a situation of relative scarcity, in which social peacekeeping figures as their general justifying aim, police will exercise discretion as to how those resources should be allocated and deployed. This authorization of discretion need not be formalized, but is implicit in the ongoing interaction between police and the community they serve.

The discretion of police is more constrained than that of other professionals. Since police authority, unlike that of other professionals, is not as directly linked to their possession of some complex and theoretical knowledge or expertise, it is more appropriately understood as a delegated power. Their discretion is correspondingly more open to public scrutiny and reconfiguration. The extent of police discretion, like the extent of police authority, is ultimately a matter of public determination.

Howard Cohen has argued that community expectations provide too narrow a base for the range of discretionary decisions that appropriately fall to police.[16] For one thing, he claims, it is not always clear what the community expects, and to speak, therefore, of community recognition is hyperbolic. In some matters, "the community" is not sufficiently au fait with the police activity in question (say, undercover work) to have a "voice." More often, perhaps, there will be no single communal "voice." The "community" itself is something of a construct, and its "speaking" is at best a fiction. It is not Cohen's view that we can conclude from this that police lack discretionary authority; he concludes, rather, that because they clearly have discretionary authority it must be based on something other than community expectation.

There is something to Cohen's argument. If police discretionary authority is made to rest exclusively on some kind of communal consensus, then it will remain very shaky. But communal consensus, though important, is not the only factor that contributes to the authority that police have. There are also communal values and traditions, those deposits of cultural history that give a community its character and distinctiveness. Although these too may reflect change and ambiguity, they may, taken together with whatever appears to represent an existing ethos and consensus, provide a social milieu that will sustain not only the general authority of police officers, but also their limited discretionary authority. The fact that this is a shifting authority ought by itself to present no problem. The idea of some fixed social authority is as anachronistic as that of the divine right of kings. Stability and order may coexist with change, so long as that change is not precipitate.

However, the communal and traditional support for police authority will serve only to explain it, rather than to justify it, unless there is also a presumption that those to whom it is given are also competent to exercise it. The "authority" relation will not exist without communal support, but its justifiability must rest on the general accuracy of the belief that police are "in the know" with respect to the matters on which they are acknowledged to have authority. Because police "expertise" is to a significant degree the expertise of common sense, their discretionary authority is much more easily determinable by public scrutiny than is the case with professional discretionary authority. And where such individualization of judgment is seen to manifest itself in unwise decisions, police will run the risk of having their discretionary authority challenged, restricted, and even removed.

Cohen's complaint, that the "community" is not sufficiently au fait with certain aspects of police work to constitute an appropriate source for police authority, shows, rather, that police authority is sometimes tenuously sustained. Although undercover investigations, which Cohen instances, could not be effectively undertaken if individual cases in which they were contemplated had first to be publicly scrutinized, nevertheless, various forms of undercover activity could be the appropriate object of public discussion without their use in particular cases being compromised. Thus, for example, Gary Marx's study of police undercover activity might provide the basis of a more general appraisal of police methods, and particular forms of that activity might gain more or less public support as a result.[17]

5.3 LIMITING DISCRETION

As I have tried to emphasize, leaving matters to police discretion is not the same as leaving those matters to their arbitrary judgment. Discretion is a normative resource, not a mere power or capacity, and it can be exercised well or badly. Police need to know something about how their discretion is to be exercised – something about the considerations that should come into play in making discretionary judgments, and how to balance them or trade them off.

The term "police" in the last paragraph can be understood collectively or individually. It is one thing to say that certain matters ought to be left to police discretion; it is another to say that they ought to be left to individual police discretion. As far as discretion is concerned, there are some things that police (collectively) are probably in the best position to decide. There are other things that ought to be left to the judgment of individual police officers. Striking some sort of balance between these two is one of the most problematic tasks for police policy makers. It is problematic, not only because of its difficulty, given the complexity of human situations, but also because it is so sensitive to political pressures.

The general problem of police discretion is that it may (and sometimes does) work itself out in a discriminatory manner. Left to their individual judgment, police officers may (and sometimes do) express the prejudices of their class, race, gender and cultural background. What is needed, it is generally considered, is some form of administrative rule making that will guide the exercise of police discretion without removing it. Discretionary options may be shaped by wider communal values and traditions, as well as practicalities, without being removed.

No administrative rule is likely to be sufficiently fine-grained to cater adequately for every contingency. But if it provides a context of reasons, of values and circumstances, it may set a tone and provide a framework for the exercise of discretion that will enable police officers to make wise judgments in the complex circumstances in which they are likely to find themselves.

Administrative rule making, as a way of mediating between the problems of partial discretion, on the one hand, and situational needs, on the other, has been strongly advocated by Davis. Yet, as he realizes, this devolution of responsibility has the potential to appear antidemocratic, for it takes "legislation" out of the hands of democratically elected law makers, and puts it in the hands of an authority that has not been elected or appointed for that purpose, and that may not be responsive to "the people."

Davis is sensitive to that concern, and suggests that police administrative rules should be promulgated only after opportunity has been given for "citizen participation and judicial review." This will allow for the formulation of a "police perspective" on matters calling for discretionary judgments to be made, yet one that will be sensitive to and moderated by other accountability mechanisms. This need not require publicization of the discretionary rules, because they might then be exploited. For example, should it be decided that the handcuffing of arrestees be made discretionary for offenses where no violence has been involved, wide public knowledge that that is so might be used to improper advantage by an arrestee. Nevertheless, the issue of handcuffing arrestees might properly be the subject of wide public debate.

This still leaves a need for criteria that will enable us to determine (1) where individual police discretion should end and administrative rule making should begin, and (2) what individual officers should take into account when making their discretionary judgments. More broadly it leaves us with a need for some way of determining (3) what discretionary rules should be left for the police to determine, and what ought to be set at a wider community level (through legislation, judicial review, and so on).

With regard to the first two of these issues Davis has relatively little to say. He notes, somewhat unhelpfully, that administratively promulgated rules are intended to "reduce unnecessary discretion without cutting into needed discretion," and that "the more general the question of policy the greater the rule content of the mix; the more the need for individualizing the greater the discretion content of the mix."[18] But these remarks leave untouched the issue of determining the *need* for individualization, that is, for discretionary judgment. How can we tell when a situation calls for individual judgment, and when it should be dealt with by means of an administrative rule?

We can get some sense of the need for and limits to police administrative rule making from the following example that Davis uses. Consider a state antigambling statute. It might be quite general. Its intention is to outlaw casinos, betting parlors, lotteries, and so on. But by implication it also outlaws certain kinds of social gambling, say, the convivial poker game between friends. Such activities, it might be argued, though strictly outlawed, are hardly those that were in the minds of the legislators, and, to the extent that they were, constitute marginal cases as far as the deployment of police resources are concerned. A police department, faced with the responsibility of enforcing such a general law, may therefore choose to limit its enforcement in something like the following terms:[19]

> In the absence of special circumstances, we do not ordinarily arrest for social gambling in the absence of (a) a complaint, (b) a profit from the gambling other than gambling winnings, or (c) extraordinarily high stakes. When we receive a complaint, we ordinarily investigate, but for first offenders we may break up social gambling without making arrests.

A rule of this kind acknowledges the appropriateness of some discretion regarding the basic rule outlawing gambling. The department itself exercises its discretion in deciding that it will not generally prosecute social gambling. It also acknowledges that if individual police officers are left to make their own discretionary judgments about the way in which the rule is to be enforced, inequity is very likely to be involved. So discretion is limited or channeled via the administrative rule. But this institutional discretionary limiting of individual discretion does not eliminate all individual discretion, as the rule itself makes clear by allowing that "special circumstances" may obtain and by indicating what is "ordinarily" done. It is recognized that "complaints" may be of different kinds, and leaves unstated what "extraordinarily high stakes" might be.

What is probably implicit in divisions of discretionary labor such as we have here is an "ear" to the kinds of distorting temptations to which the various parties might be prone. Individual officers will ordinarily be able to make fair discretionary judgments within the framework provided by the administrative rule. A police department might ordinarily be left to decide what kind of discretion it should exercise with regard to the antigambling statute. In some cases, it might be felt that neither individual officers nor departments can be trusted to exercise certain sorts of discretion, and that limits have to be imposed from without. That, presumably, is what lies behind the exclusionary rule. The temptation for police in general to trade off individual rights for evidentiary gains is so great that any control over such decisions cannot reasonably be left in the hands of administrative rulemakers.

Chapter 6

The use of force

I'd rather be judged by twelve than carried out by six.

Conventional police wisdom

Who overcomes
By force hath overcome but half his foe.

John Milton[1]

Most people are familiar with the police beating of Rodney King. Yet what was exceptional about the case was not the beating, but the fact that it was captured on videotape. Nor was the initial acquittal of the officers exceptional; what was exceptional was the fact that *despite* the videotape the officers were acquitted. Reports of police beatings, especially in circumstances such as Rodney King's, after a car chase, are not uncommon. But it is only rarely that police are held to have acted improperly. When Egon Bittner writes that "the role of police is to address all sorts of human problems when and insofar as the problems' solutions may require the use of force at the point of their occurrence,"[2] he feeds the image that police have of themselves as crimefighters, working in a human jungle whose law is force. That image licences most police force as necessary force. The onus is placed on others to show that it was excessive. Had the Los Angeles police considered themselves primarily as social peacekeepers, for whom recourse to force constituted a last and regrettable option, events would almost certainly have turned out very differently.

Nevertheless, I do not want to underplay the importance of force to the police role. To keep the social peace it is sometimes necessary to deal with people who are recalcitrant and/or dangerous. And if this is to be done effectively, coercive force will sometimes have to be used or at least threatened. Within the social life of liberal democratic régimes, police are acknowledged to be the primary repositories of that force – force that enables them not only to deter, apprehend, and restrain, but also to take life. Even if it is argued, as it is by many in the United States, that every citizen has a right to bear arms, the use of those arms against other human beings is considered appropriate only in situations in which a prepared police presence is lacking.

Police are the primary resources of social force not only in the sense that they are (usually) armed,[3] but also in the more important sense that they are authorized to bear arms, and to use them, along with other coercive and forcible measures.

6.1 MORAL DOUBTS ABOUT THE USE OF FORCE

That police are authorized to use force constitutes a problem, not especially or only because *they* are able to use it, but because the use of force by any human being against others constitutes a problem. The use of force needs justification, not just the police use of force, and it needs justification in general as well as in particular cases.

The general source of concern is simple enough. It is a certain view of human beings and of the life that is appropriate to them. Mature human beings are centers of action and reasons for action, agents capable of determining how they will make their way in the world, given their capacities and abilities, and the resources and opportunities available to them. As such centers of action, a certain respect is due to them. They have a basic (albeit not absolute) claim to be free from constraint and interference by others; that is, they have a claim to be permitted to live out their lives according to their own lights. The use of force against others constitutes a prima facie violation of the respect that is their due.

In the case of deadly force, the problem is aggravated, because the invasion is irrevocable. Not only does it (in most cases) impede or curtail one or other of a person's interests, but it effectively extinguishes the whole complex and pattern of interests that make up a life, including the interest in life itself. Without life, nothing remains to us.[4] In the case of deadly force, there is no room for mistake, for changes of mind, for remission or pardon, no room for compensating the person who is killed.

Although these represent the most powerful reasons for being concerned about the use of force, they are not the only ones, and they do not rule out the use of force to counter force. More radical positions may also need to be confronted, whether in specific cases or as frameworks for social policy.

One such view claims that the deliberate use of force, even if intended to counter force, is intrinsically and perhaps even absolutely wrong. On this view, the evil of using force is not neutralized by employing it to prevent or stop or even punish its use by others, but simply adds to the evil a further evil. Like the Amish depicted in the film *Witness*, whose sense of community, desire for reconciliation, and techniques of moral suasion are juxtaposed with "police methods" of dealing with the violence that has invaded their everyday life, it may be felt that violent resolutions of conflict, however called for they may appear to be, only debase the human, and alienate people further from what is appropriate to their high calling.[5]

The argument is often given a more consequentialist twist. The use of force is not only out of keeping with our nature but worsens our lot: violence breeds violence. Here the point is not that violence is "intrinsically and absolutely wrong," but that it offers no solution to, only an aggravation of, human conflict. It is argued that just because the use of force represents a nonrational and nonloving response to a situation involving conflict between rational beings, it does nothing to defuse, but serves only to perpetuate, and may even magnify the violence: "Those who live by the sword shall die by the sword."[6] The Oresteian cycle of violence cannot be halted by violence.

It is not really an adequate response to the radical pacifist argument that it is impracticable, for it may be replied, as it has been in other contexts, that it is not as though nonviolence has been tried and found wanting but that it has been found difficult and left untried.[7] Perhaps it *is* impracticable, the product of a view of human nature and of a human viewpoint that we have no strong reason to believe or to expect others to come to adopt. But this is not an arena in which decisive arguments come easily. We may also wonder whether force does constitute the unmitigated evil that the argument claims. Why may we not just as plausibly see it as a prima facie evil, sometimes justifiable as the "lesser of two evils," or as part of an "organic whole," acceptable when considered part of a totality (as in retributive punishment)? To pursue these questions at length would take us too far afield. For present purposes it is probably sufficient that the objections stand as notice of the seriousness of using force.

Nevertheless, we can see that authorizing the police use of force represents a very significant ceding of power, one that needs to be carefully regulated and monitored. Generally, some form of social contract argument has been advanced to limit that authority to police. For, once we recognize that humans do not always accord to each other the respect that is appropriately owed to them, that those whose rights are violated or threatened with violation are frequently not in a position to protect their rights or to ensure recompense for their violation, and that even if they are able to do so they would very likely overreact or otherwise show poor judgment, we can, it might be said, see the wisdom of placing the use of force in the hands of a chosen and trained few. We do better to vest such authority in police than in retaining it for ourselves to use as and when we see fit. It should, however, be clear that although our recognition of the police authority to use force can be construed as our consenting to it, the arguments for restricting the public use of force in this way do not require anything so formal as consent to be seen as a reasonable response to a social need. It is at least plausible that the argument for the police authority to use force be given a consequentialist form.

To grant that police should have the authority to use force is only the first step in any justification of their use of that force. Their authority is a constrained authority. We need also to consider when and how they should use it, and the kinds of coercive resources that should be made available to them. It is frequently complained, probably with justification, that police abuse or overstep their authority to use force. Such complaints can only jeopardize their authority, and, to the extent that the complaints are believed, police run the risk of transforming the perception of their actions from demonstrations of authority into exercises of despotic power.

6.2 INTERMEDIATE FORCE

The police use of force has come in many forms: nightsticks, clubs, saps and batons, handcuffs and velcro straps, hogtying, nets, armlocks, chokeholds, stun and Taser guns, tear gases and pepper spray, nutcrackers,[8] nunchakus,[9] water cannons, dogs, firearms, and high-speed pursuits.[10] They vary in their effectiveness and risks, some are obviously better suited to some situations than to others,[11] and some have been outlawed. What considerations should govern the use of such devices? I will begin with uses of force that are generally regarded as falling short of deadly force, so-called intermediate force.

The legal discussion provides a useful starting point, partly because of the considerations that it adverts to, partly because of the way in which the legal framework has changed. Until recently, two distinct tests were employed to judge whether the use of force was justified. One was – or, rather, incorporated – a subjective "good faith" test. It asked inter alia whether the officer applied force "in a good faith effort to maintain or restore discipline or maliciously and sadistically for the very purpose of causing harm."[12] The other was an objective "excessive force" test. It asked whether, given the "totality of the circumstances," the force used by the officer was excessive (or unreasonable).[13] Some uses of force that passed the first test would not pass the second. Occasionally, uses of force that would not pass the second test passed the first.

The "excessive force" test probably constitutes the better social policy, since it is more likely to be protective of the individual, and thus more in keeping with a cultural tradition that recognizes and seeks to curb public authority's tendency toward despotism. In a 1989 decision, the U.S. Supreme Court determined that it should constitute the sole test for police uses of force.[14] Nevertheless, a *moral* assessment of the police use of force cannot leave out of account the so-called "subjective" factors. An officer who applies force that might on "objective" grounds be considered "reasonable," but does so, not because that exercise of force happens to be reasonable in the circumstances, but *because* the subject is black, has acted badly, even if also prudently.

6.2.1 *Constraining factors*

The following five factors will be relevant to the ethical assessment of the use of force:

6.2.1.1 Intentions. It is not uncommon for police to use force as a means of punishment. An arrestee who gives trouble may be punished by means of a "tune up" or the tightening of his handcuffs. A ubiquitous troublemaker who has managed to avoid all or severe penalties may be "slowed down" or "deterred" by informal uses of force – an overnight stay in the lockup, a little rough handling – or be "taught" some other "lesson."[15]

But however deserved such measures may sometimes appear to be, they are improperly imposed and in that respect are unjustified. It is not for the police to inflict punishment. Their task in these contexts is to detain and restrain. It is for others to decide whether and what punishment is appropriate. There are good policy reasons for this, the kinds of reasons that lie behind the somewhat elaborate (albeit unwieldy) criminal justice system that we now have.[16] As Locke observed, our individual judgments concerning violations are easily clouded by ignorance, self-interest, and emotionality, and the division of labor represented in the criminal justice system is an attempt to overcome or at least to minimize those deficiencies. The system, of course, is an imperfect one, and for this reason police officers may consider that a little informally administered punishment will strike a blow for justice. But although their assessment of the system may be correct, it is unlikely that an arrangement whereby police were permitted to take it upon themselves to rectify its perceived deficiencies would work out any better. For by so doing they would turn us back toward the "state of nature" and the "inconveniencies" from which civil society was intended to deliver us. The point is not that in any particular case officers would act in a substantially unjust way, but that they would be acting on a maxim of action which, if universalized, would almost certainly result in significant injustice. The acts of police officers, no less than those of other members of society, must be open to public scrutiny.

6.2.1.2   Seemliness. Good faith on the part of officers is not sufficient to justify the use of force. It must also be seemly. The judgment in *Johnson*, which established the good faith test for reasonable force, appealed to the earlier decision of *Rochin v. California*,[17] in which a suspect's stomach was pumped to recover apparently swallowed evidence of drug possession. Here the court argued that the police methods "shocked the conscience," and were "bound to offend even hardened sensibilities." We need not suppose that the officers involved were acting maliciously or sadistically. They were, however, acting callously, with little thought or regard for what it was decent to do to a suspect. Not every means that is well intentioned and / or effective is *ipso facto* justified. Although, subsequent to the 1961 *Mapp* decision, in which the provisions of the Fourth Amendment were applied to the states, the Supreme Court has not used the 1952 *Rochin* decision to assess the use of force, the seemliness of a particular technique might still be considered relevant to our assessment of its moral appropriateness.[18]

One of the problems with torture or, more generally, use of the "third degree" to extract truth from a suspect is its almost unexceptionable unseemliness, its violation of human dignity. The intentions of the torturer may be high-minded – a desire to obtain truth, to see justice done – but treating someone in a way that undermines his capacity to make a rational response – literally, brutalizing him – is an unseemly affront.

6.2.1.3 Proportionality. The police conduct in *Rochin* was not simply unseemly but also disproportionate. Force used to achieve legitimate police ends ought not to be disproportionate to the seriousness of the offense that is alleged or threatened. Shooting someone who is suspected of committing only a minor offense violates the doctrine of proportionality.[19]

6.2.1.4 Minimization. Closely related to the doctrine of proportionality, though distinct from it, is what is sometimes known as the principle of "the least restrictive alternative."[20] The doctrine of proportionality is a deontological constraint; the doctrine of the least restrictive alternative is a consequentialist one. Police ought to use those means that are least intrusive, least constraining, and least harmful, compatible with the securing of their ends. If handcuffs will do, hogtying will not be justified. If police can take in a killer without using deadly force, then they should forgo the use of deadly force.

The principle of the least restrictive alternative needs to be moderated by the demands of policy. What, in a particular case, constitutes the least restrictive alternative, may not, if incorporated as a general practice, make good policy. If, for example, it is not necessary to handcuff a particular arrestee, since the latter poses no danger to himself or others, it could nevertheless be argued that the practice of giving officers discretion regarding the handcuffing of arrestees will produce costs (abuses, misjudgments) that outweigh the benefits of a more restrictive policy.

6.2.1.5 Practicability. Given that there is a presumption against the use of force, and also that certain police ends, such as the provision of public safety, apprehension of wrongdoers, and so on, may sometimes justify the use of force, we still need to have some assurance that its use will further the legitimate ends for which it is employed.

Generally, given the immediate goals of apprehension and restraint, police uses of force will contribute to their achievement. However, when more remote ends, such as the promotion of public peace, are taken into account, the issue may become less clear. In dealing with the public, police are often encouraged to come on strong, lest those inclined to resist cooperating are encouraged to resist. Coming on strong may sometimes be justifiable, but cannot be "standard operating procedure." Police need to be trained to discriminate between situations in which a "forceful" presence is necessary from those in which a less adversarial approach should be used. It is, of course, not good for police–community relations when police are felt to be overbearing. But more importantly, tactics that intimidate, and make some more compliant, may also motivate others to avoid police encounters, and to elude questioning. This may then aggravate the situation and lead to an escalation of force. Where exacerbation of the situation occurs, we can hardly say that the force was justified, even though it may have become necessary to achieve a particular end.[21] Were police to see themselves primarily as social peacekeepers, they would be less inclined to "overkill" in their dealings with both ordinary citizens and those whose disruptive activities properly require their intervention.

6.2.2   *A survey of techniques*

Because police must sometimes use force to achieve their ends, because the use of deadly force is only rarely appropriate, and because different exercises of force are appropriate to different situations, police have developed a range of coercive devices that generally fall short of being exercises of deadly force. Each of these devices has its particular advantages and drawbacks, and there is value to considering their specific features and problems, as a further articulation of the ethical reflection to which police are committed. Here I consider the advantages and problems associated with several such techniques, before drawing some general conclusions about intermediate uses of force.

6.2.2.1   Handcuffs. There are several problems associated with the use of handcuffs. One was brought into the public arena a few years ago, when a prominent politician was arrested for the alleged misuse of public funds. He was led out from his office in handcuffs in front of waiting TV cameras, a situation that a friend, the then Mayor of New York, considered demeaning and unnecessary.[22] The politician in question was not charged with an offense that involved physical violence; he gave no indication of being uncooperative; and he was made out to be a criminal even before conviction (the charges were, in fact, eventually dropped). Apart from the TV cameras, there was nothing very special about this incident (though some people saw the fact that he was cuffed in front rather than at back as an aggravation of its demeaningness). The New York City Police Department, along with many other police departments, had a policy of handcuffing every arrestee.[23] The incident did, however, raise questions about the need for rigid adherence to it, and whether there ought to be some room for officer discretion.

At first blush, a rigid policy does seem to violate the requirements of proportionality and least restrictiveness. At least it appears so when specific cases are examined. But policies take (or should take) their shape from practices and not from isolated cases, and those who defend the policy argue that the costs of allowing officer discretion here would outweigh its benefits. Basically, handcuffing on arrest is seen as an insurance measure. Being arrested is a significant event; and the more "respectable" a person is, the larger its impact is likely to be. It may not be easy to predict how a person will react to such a situation. Perhaps the arrestee will not try to run for it;

but might he be overwhelmed by an impulse to commit suicide? Is the person HIV positive, and may he therefore pose a special danger in the event of a scuffle? Handcuffing secures police officers against such unknowns. And, in the unlikely event of some particularly untoward outcome, it may also be thought to protect departments against liability.

There is a further consideration, at least in a community where class and race tend to converge. White-collar criminals, who will tend to be predominantly white, are likely to benefit from such discretion, whereas members of poorer minorities will not, and they will continue to experience the humiliation of handcuffing. This may be so, not just because the latter are more likely to be involved in crimes of violence or are more likely to "get ideas," but because they are *perceived* stereotypically, and their dangerousness is magnified. A policy of handcuffing all arrestees may therefore be seen to minimize the opportunities for racial discrimination.

Still, that does not resolve the issue completely. Ignorance is relative, and some offenses are sufficiently minor (for example, misdemeanors) to make it extremely unlikely that unwanted outcomes will occur. Where a person's place of residence is known, the offense is relatively minor, and there is no reason to believe that the arrestee will be uncooperative, there would seem to be good reason for not subjecting that person to the humiliation of handcuffing. The racial issue is more troubling, but need not be a complete barrier to some officer discretion. A department may well monitor handcuffing practices to see if discretion is being exercised in a discriminatory manner.

A second problem, one that may also bear on the former, concerns the abuses to which handcuffing may lend itself. I do not mean situations in which its use would not be justified at all, but cases where it is employed injuriously. Because of their design, handcuffs may be used not only to restrain, but also to punish, torture, or vent anger. Arresting officers may easily tighten handcuffs so that they cause excruciating pain or even nerve damage. Although officers are trained in their use, that is no guarantee that they will not be misused, and there is some evidence that the vengeful overtightening of handcuffs constitutes one of the most common forms of police brutality.[24] The injury may also be psychological. Handcuffing a person in front rather than behind, parading a handcuffed person in public, and the use of straps rather than a ring to which an arrested person is clipped when transported, may be thought to constitute unnecessary humiliations of a person who, it must be remembered, has not yet been convicted of the offense for which he or she is being arrested.

Given such possibilities for abuse, we might be more cautious about requiring all arrestees to be handcuffed. At least there should be some effective recourse for those who believe that handcuffs have been improperly used on them.[25] Alternatively, some thought could be given to redesigning handcuffs and developing use policies that would diminish the likelihood of excessive force, injury and indignity. In some situations, for example, velcro straps might be more appropriate and less open to misuse.

6.2.2.2 Batons and nightsticks. Most line officers in urban areas carry some form of baton. They are a staple of police equipment, along with a firearm, handcuffs and radio. They vary in design, though their smooth rounded contact surface is intended to minimize the likelihood of permanent injury.[26] They may be used defensively or to subdue, and if used judiciously can usually achieve their end without repeated applications.

Obviously the possibility of causing serious injury is one reason for the restrained use of batons. Officers need to be trained in their use, in how and when to use them. But an equally serious concern is their unnecessary use. Officers frequently use them to move the sleeping or slow homeless or other vagrants out of public areas. This may sometimes be reasonable, but often it becomes routinized, and an expression of the officer's impatience and contempt rather than a needed "come along." And when it is needed, it may be used more vigorously than necessary. A sleeping vagrant may usually be awakened as effectively by a sharp tap on the bottom of a shoe as by a jab to the ribs or stomach.

6.2.2.3 Stun and Taser/dart guns. These guns,[27] capable of delivering a low amperage 50,000 volt charge when triggered against another's body, are designed to subdue fractious citizens in a manner that is effective, nonlethal, nondamaging, and, for officers, likely to reduce their own risk of injury. According to one technical report, a charge that lasts less than a second will "startle and repel the subject," a charge between one and two seconds will cause a subject to lose balance, and a three to four second charge will "incapacitate a subject, causing disorientation and leaving him weak and dazed for five to fifteen minutes."[28]

The great virtue of stun and Taser guns appears to be that when used properly they are unlikely to have long-term effects. Unlike batons, which may cause skull fracture, or firearms, which may well cause death, stun and Taser guns appear to have few serious side effects. Sometimes there are what appear to be burn marks, though these are not permanent, and in the case of Tasers, the darts may occasionally need to be surgically removed. Although there is a possibility of the shock causing cardiac arrest, or other damage if applied to the head, thus necessitating caution in their use, the probability of such outcomes appears to be small.

There are two concerns associated with stun and Taser guns. One is voiced by the police who use them; the other is voiced by citizens who are anxious about abuse.

Police have expressed doubts about the effectiveness (85–90 percent) of stun and Taser guns. They have not always proved effective on the two classes of people against whom they would seem to be most appropriately used. Mental patients and large, aggressive subjects (particularly those under the influence of drugs such as PCP) are not always disabled by such devices, and a reliance on them, where they are used as alternatives to deadly force, could place officers in unanticipated danger. Some such claim was made by the officers responsible for Rodney King's beating. According to their account, the Taser used against Rodney King was ineffective, and they remained in danger of injury as he sought to regain his feet.

Ironically, the very fact that stun and Taser guns have few after effects contributes to their abuse, and this lies behind the concern of citizens. Like black jacks (saps) and rubber truncheons, which can be used to torture, punish or otherwise victimize those in police custody, without leaving clear evidence of the brutality involved, there have been well-publicized cases in New York and Los Angeles in which police have used stun and Taser guns against otherwise physically cooperative or restrained subjects.[29] These instances of abuse have led the NYPD to restrict their use to specialist groups or specially trained users.

Incident-driven policy making is, as I suggested earlier, fraught with dangers. Yet in this case we have some reason to believe that the incidents were not isolated, and that monitoring in any other way would be difficult. Achieving accountability, where it is not internally motivated, may sometimes require inconvenience and the development of policies that are less than optimal.

6.2.2.4 Chokeholds. Among the measures used by police to bring people under control are chokeholds. Several years ago they came into the public spotlight because of a number of deaths associated with their use, particularly in Los Angeles.[30]

Various forms of chokehold have been employed, but the two major types are generally referred to as the "bar arm" and "carotid" restraints/holds/controls. In both cases there is compression of the soft structures of the neck – the larynx is depressed, restricting the flow of oxygen to the lungs, and the carotid arteries are constricted, preventing blood from getting to the brain. Effectively applied, chokeholds can bring a person under control in a very short time.

But just because of the particular body structures involved, chokeholds can also be very dangerous, and, as the Los Angeles experience shows, quite a number of deaths and permanent injuries resulted.[31] Had it been plausibly argued that chokeholds were necessary, this might have been regarded simply as an unfortunate cost of carrying out police work. But the fact that many large urban jurisdictions did not include chokeholds in their array of defensive measures strongly suggested that other alternatives might well have been available.[32] And even if there had not been alternatives, there might still have been an argument for training officers to use the technique in a less dangerous way. Barry Creighton has argued that the carotid restraint, because pressure is applied to both front and back of the neck, is one of the most dangerous of some thirty-six martial arts choking techniques, and that only if it is used by someone experienced in martial arts can it be applied both effectively and nonlethally.[33] If Creighton is correct in this claim, then there may well be an argument for removing it permanently from the police arsenal.[34] Few police are likely to have the extensive training required to use it appropriately.

James Fyfe takes a slightly different tack, though one that may have a similar effect. He suggests, and the *Lyons* opinion supports this, that chokeholds should be classified as deadly force techniques, subject to the same constraints and monitoring as firearm use. He believes that this will lead to a much more circumspect and infrequent use of the technique, less likely to be a cause of death.[35] Indeed, its use in these circumstances will be permissible only because a police officer may use any means necessary to the defense of life.[36]

6.2.2.5 Tear gases and OC spray.[37] Like stun guns, tear gases (CN and CS) and OC spray have worked their way into the police arsenal as intermediate forcible techniques. They can be very effective in subduing unmanageable and aggressive individuals, and, on a larger scale, in quelling riots or dispersing crowds. Unlike firearms, batons and chokeholds, they are not as likely to cause significant and permanent damage. But though not as likely to cause persisting injury, tear gases at least are known to be capable of creating respiratory difficulties, of causing permanent eye damage, of triggering longlasting skin problems, and, in extreme cases, even of causing death. But more saliently, they are extremely painful to those on whom they are used, and thus offer an opportunity for officers to exploit them "maliciously, punitively, or unnecessarily."[38]

6.2.2.6 Dogs.[39] Dogs have been used in many facets of police work – for tracking down wanted persons, searching buildings, sniffing out drugs or explosives, preventive patrol, crowd control, subduing dangerous people, and so on. On preventive patrol they are able to cover an area that would normally require several officers. Generally, such dogs are highly trained, they diminish the risk to human investigators, and, when used to subdue dangerous people, they do not generally inflict serious injury. Sometimes, however, they do injure, and occasionally they kill, a factor that should restrict their use to situations in which they clearly constitute the least dangerous alternative.

What many have found more troubling about the use of dogs is the fear they evoke. Even if the dog causes no permanent physical injury, the psychological effect of a canine attack may be considerable and permanent, and this should be taken into account in considering the reasonableness of using them.

There is, however, a more subtle concern about the use of police dogs, a concern that may go back to days when dogs were sometimes used to hunt down slaves and other social outcasts as though they were animals. It is sometimes considered a demeaning practice to hunt and bring down a wanted person as though he were a hare or fox. Using a dog to protect oneself from assault is one thing, but, it might be argued, sending a dog out to track or bring someone down is another.

Although this constitutes only a limited objection to the use of dogs, it should not be disregarded or consigned to the category of "irrational prejudices." Even if its sources are historical and cultural, that is not a reason to ignore them. There is some analogy here with issues of privacy. We generally – at least within reasonable limits – respect a person's desire to keep certain matters private, even if other people, or those from other cultures, do not see those matters in that way. It does not take too much imagination to see how the use of dogs might have historical resonations with certain members of the community, and thus give us reason to be careful about their deployment.

In sum, then, given the overall peacekeeping mandate of police, the limited role that they have in law enforcement (protection and apprehension rather than punishment), and the variety of circumstances in which they find themselves, it is important that police develop a variety of low- and middle-range coercive techniques for achieving their ends when other alternatives are not available to them. There is still a great deal of room for improved methods and devices, and probably a great deal of room for alternatives that do not require the application of force.

It may not be easy to develop techniques or devices that will be free from risk or abuse. Indeed, there is an ironic sense in which the more risk free a device, the more easily it can be appropriated for abusive purposes. Great suffering may be caused by using techniques that leave few physical traces. Although the possibilities for abuse do not disqualify a device or technique from use, such possibilities indicate once again that the basic issue in police ethics is not regulation or supervision or structural arrangements but character. Regulation and supervision may diminish opportunities for abuse, but they need to be supported by the commitment of those whose conduct is at issue.

6.3 DEADLY FORCE

The police use of deadly force is generally restricted to firearms, though, as I have already suggested, in the case of chokeholds, it may also encompass other police techniques.[40] I shall later argue that it might reasonably be extended to cover high-speed pursuits.

I have already indicated the basic reason why deadly force is so problematic: its irrevocable and catastrophic invasion of an individual's most basic interests. But there are additional reasons why, in the case of police, the use of deadly force is particularly problematic. An obvious one is that as far as criminal suspects are concerned, it is the task of police to apprehend them and ensure that they are properly inducted into the criminal justice system. The use of deadly force appears to subvert that induction process. People are put to death without the benefit of representation or trial for an offense that is unlikely to carry a capital penalty.

In the case of criminal suspects, that may not seem so bad. At least that is how Justice Sandra Day O'Connor saw it in her dissenting judgment in *Tennessee v. Garner*. There she argued that the majority opinion's claim that "the suspect's interest in his own life need not be elaborated on," constituted a "blithe assertion [which] hardly provides an adequate substitute for the majority's failure to acknowledge the distinctive manner in which the suspect's interest in his life is even exposed to risk."[41] *Pace* O'Connor, it is not at all obvious that a suspect's interest in his life is so weak that it is forfeited or overridden or even weakened when he attempts to flee from a nonviolent burglary. Her claim that "a person's interest in his life" does not encompass "a right to flee unimpeded from the scene of a burglary" is surely correct. But it is a *non sequitur* to think that this in any way permits the use of deadly force against such a person. A person's claims to life are not diminished by such flight; whether the interest in preventing flight is so important that it overrides the claim to life will surely depend on other factors (whether the person is particularly dangerous, for example).

An additional complication is provided by the possibility that deadly force is used in a racially biased manner. Members of minority groups, blacks in particular, are shot or shot at disproportionately to their numbers in the population, and this may seem to provide clear evidence of racial discrimination.[42] Interpreting the figures is problematic, however, and several commentators have suggested that although blacks are more likely to be shot than whites, the proportions are not out of keeping with the relative numbers of blacks and whites involved in serious crime. But this may not be an altogether satisfying argument if the further argument, that the disproportionate involvement of blacks in violent crime is itself a consequence of societal and structural racism, can be sustained.

Another cost must be factored in – the cost to police officers themselves and other innocents. Because firearms are so lethal, and have to be handled with care, there will be accidental shootings and suicides that probably would not otherwise have occurred. To this must also be added the use of service weapons to settle marital and "bar room" disputes. In an attempt to minimize such shootings, some departments now discourage their officers from carrying weapons when they are off-duty.[43]

6.3.1 *The case for deadly force*

As I indicated earlier, the *police* use of force is most commonly justified by appeal to some form of social contract argument. This is thought to be most responsive to our conception of people as agents. The belief that police have been *authorized* to use force provides a means of reconciling their powers with the respect that we owe each other. But social contract arguments do not have the whole stage. After all, consent to some practice, though it may authorize it, need not justify it. And so various consequentialist and other arguments are also used to show why such consent – were it to occur and were it to be necessary – would be justifiable. Here I consider the two main arguments. Additional arguments will be canvassed when I discuss the development of deadly force policy.

Jeffrey Reiman has provided one of the more persuasive *social contract* arguments for vesting police officers with the authority to use deadly force.[44] As Reiman sees it, were individuals to live in a social environment lacking "shared rules and [a] public apparatus for administering and enforcing them" – what Locke called a "state of nature" – they would find its hazards and uncertainties so distracting that, as rational, freedom-loving beings, they would come to see the benefits of renouncing their freedom "to use force at their own discretion" for the sake of "secure freedom to live as [they want]," and of vesting their freedom to retaliate in a "public agency . . . that can use force in the name of the group."[45]

Where does this leave us with respect to the use of deadly force? According to Reiman, the contracting individuals (as potential victims) would not give up their (natural) retaliatory right entirely. In cases of *immediate* danger they would insist on retaining a right of self-defense. But there are circumstances in which they would not be in a position to exercise their right or in which they would not be aware of the danger to which someone was exposing them. And here they would agree to the use of deadly force on their behalf. However, the discretionary use of such force would need to be carefully controlled. Only where its use by public officials would have the effect of decreasing the likelihood of their being the victims of others' use of deadly force, would they, as rational, freedom-loving people, see any wisdom in permitting the official use of deadly force.

Capital punishment and the police use of deadly force would be official uses to which the contracting parties might contingently agree.[46] Of course, should such authorizations fail to lessen a community's exposure to deadly force, then the possibilities for caprice and mistake inherent in the practices thus authorized would undermine the basis for these authorizations, and the contracting parties would presumably withdraw their consent. That is often argued with respect to capital punishment: It is claimed that it does not deter, that there are no alternative social benefits of significance, and that mistakes occur sufficiently often to make it freedom-diminishing rather than freedom-enhancing.[47] The same might be argued with respect to the police use of deadly force – for it is only contingently the case that it is more beneficial than harmful.

On this view, as Reiman emphasizes, the power to use deadly force is to be thought of as "loaned" to police officers. The police are accountable for their use of it, not merely to their fellow officers, but also and especially to the public-at-large which has entrusted them with it.[48] Exercises by police of their authority to use deadly force must be open to public scrutiny and debate. And in the light of this, such authority might be withdrawn, or at least narrowed.

Of course, we might agree that the police authority to use deadly force be exercised on a purely discretionary basis. We might charge them with using it as they judge appropriate. But that has never been the case. The power is so considerable, and the consequences of mistake or abuse so serious, that any discretion the police are given should be quite limited. Reiman develops his own social contract argument to provide for some fairly specific limitations. (1) Police may use deadly force in their own self-defense, because every party to the contract would reserve his or her right to self-defense. And, he suggests, the same reasoning might provide that police officers be permitted to carry special weapons for their own defense, since their work exposes them to considerable risk. (2) They may use deadly force to protect the lives of private citizens, because the contract that establishes their authority is intended to provide citizens with protection. (3) With respect to fleeing felons or perpetrators of crimes in which no grave danger is present, the situation is less clear. Reiman suggests that it needs to be settled empirically: We need to determine whether a general policy in which police could use deadly force in these situations would contribute more to security than to insecurity. He suspects the latter:

> The questionability of the deterrence effect in general, the difficulties of making instant judgments on the scene, the level of police marksmanship, the similarity of crime rates in cities with very lenient gun-use policies as compared with cities with strict policies, and the terrible human and political costs of error, all support the conclusion that police ought not to use their weapons except where necessary to protect individuals against clear threats of grave danger to life and limb.[49]

As a possible objection to this "social contract" argument, Reiman considers Beccaria's opposition to the death penalty: Rational individuals would refuse to give anyone the right to take their lives, an argument that might be extended to the authorization of deadly force. But this argument, as he points out, is vulnerable to the reductio ad absurdum that it would be equally irrational for people to agree to being incarcerated or even punished, a conclusion that would undermine the criminal justice system which it was the point of the social contract to establish. Rather, it would be irrational for individuals to give others the right to take their lives *only* if giving them that right would place their lives in greater danger. No one has suggested that the contracted right would constitute a blank check for those authorized to take life.

An alternative approach to the police use of deadly force is more *consequentialist* in its focus. Here it is argued that, overall, society is better served if the major guardians of the social order – police – have the power to use deadly force. The police themselves sometimes propound this argument. They argue that, unless they have and are known to have the power to use deadly force, their authority will be ineffective. Here too, though, there appears to be an implicit, albeit contingent, limitation. The general welfare will not be promoted if the police use of deadly force is permitted in circumstances in which innocent parties are placed at greater risk than would be the case were their powers more circumscribed.

The difference between this approach and the social contract argument as Reiman develops it is minimal. This is because Reiman's focus is not on the *actual* consent of the "contracting parties" but on what rational individuals *would* consent to – and what they would consent to is what would maximize their welfare (here thought of primarily in terms of certain freedoms). The utilitarian justification focuses on the maximization of welfare as something that it would be rational to pursue. Other versions of the social contract argument, which emphasize actual rather than merely hypothetical consent, can be more easily distinguished from utilitarian arguments. But in their case, unless the consent is shown to be reasonable, it is difficult to see how it provides a *justification* as distinct from an *authorization*.

Reiman's argument, along with other arguments of its kind, is erected on the Lockean presumption that there exists some natural right of retaliation or self-defense that permits *killing* in self-defense (or in defense of the lives of others). This, of course, is not an uncommon presumption. And it is not usually questioned. Yet it is not at all obvious how it might be justified. One need not be an extreme pacifist to think that killing, as a particularly radical invasion of a person's interests, requires some special justification over and above that needed for other uses of force. How is it that the protection of one's own life or that of another takes precedence over the life of another? Is it that someone who *threatens* another's life loses claim to his own? Or that the claims of *innocent* life override those of "life-threatening" life? Or that so long as a person poses a threat to the lives of others, his right to life is *suspended*? These and other suggestions have been proposed, but all have difficulties that leave it unclear just what, if anything will sustain the base presumption.[50] Here, however, I take the opportunity only to note that it is a presumption, and that, like most presumptions, it may be challenged.

6.3.2 *The development of deadly force policy*

To get a better perspective on the appropriate limits for deadly force policy, it is useful to consider the course of its development through the common law tradition. It was this tradition, preexisting Independence, that was taken over or codified by the various States (occasionally with amendments). Judicial interpretation filled this out and sometimes qualified it.

The common law tradition dealing with the police use of deadly force is summed up by two privileges, one concerning "defense of life," the other concerning the "fleeing felon." In both cases, whether to defend life or to apprehend a fleeing felon, the use of deadly force by police officers has been sanctioned. In a particular case, both rules might be applicable: The fleeing felon might pose a grave danger to others. But the "fleeing felon" privilege is more encompassing, and has constituted the main focus of subsequent debate.

Both privileges have their main ideological underpinning in the moral doctrine of proportionality. According to this, police may be justified in using force to apprehend suspects, provided that the force is proportionate to the seriousness of the alleged offense or harm threatened. Translated into common law, this was thought to justify the use of deadly force not only to ward off deadly force, but also to apprehend a fleeing felon.

Obviously, the plausibility of this latter application of the doctrine of proportionality depended heavily on the way "felons" were to be identified. At the time the "fleeing felon" privilege took shape, felonies were relatively few in number, if not in incidence, and were meant to be distinguishable from misdemeanors by their perceived seriousness. They were for the most part punishable by death, and comprised homicide, rape, arson, mayhem, robbery, burglary, larceny, sodomy, prison breakout, and assisting a felon to escape. Because of their alleged seriousness, and the availability of a capital penalty, exercising the privilege was taken to be merely "the premature execution of the inevitable judgment."[51] Or, as the court expressed it in *Petrie v. Cartwright*, "it made little difference if the suspected felon was killed in the process of capture since, in the eyes of the law, he had already forfeited his life by committing the felony."[52]

Subsequently, several changes occurred to complicate this fairly neat picture. For one thing, the felony–misdemeanor distinction came to be drawn rather differently. In common law, the term "felony" was reserved for what were perceived as particularly grave offenses, offenses which, almost by definition, involved the forfeiture of a person's substantial rights. All other offenses were misdemeanors. That has changed. Currently, a felony is most commonly understood to be an offense for which a prison sentence of more than a year is imposed. A consequence of this has been a great increase in the number of felonious act-kinds. More importantly, in many cases in which the "fleeing felon" privilege was exercised, the use of deadly force no longer anticipated a subsequent death sentence. That was not only because of "due process" requirements, which loosened the connection between apprehension and conviction, but also because even serious felonies were no longer generally punishable by death. Indeed, given the gradual movement away from almost any use of capital punishment, the traditional rationale for the fleeing felon privilege came to look increasingly anomalous.

Other factors were also at work. Straightforwardly abusive exploitation of the fleeing felon privilege precipitated calls for greater restrictions on its use. Such "incidents," often highlighted by the media, prompted a tightening up of state legislative permissions or, in many cases, departmental policies and practices. This was so in New York, Kansas City and Atlanta – and, as I shall soon indicate, more dramatically and generally in Memphis (*Tennessee v. Garner*). No doubt the suspicion of racism in the use of deadly force – both in and independently of such incidents – also served to bring the privilege under scrutiny. For, as I noted earlier, in relation to the general population, blacks have been shot at disproportionately. Whatever that actually shows, it was a politically potent factor in forcing a reassessment of the fleeing felon privilege.

Two national projects also contributed to reassessment of the status quo. One was the American Law Institute's Model Penal Code, the final draft of which was completed in 1962. The Model Penal Code took a two-pronged approach to the police use of deadly force. It recommended that the use of deadly force be restricted to situations in which the apprehending officer believes that either:

1. The crime for which the arrest is made involved conduct including the use or threatened use of deadly force; or
2. There is a substantial risk that the person to be arrested will cause death or serious bodily harm if his apprehension is delayed.[53]

This recommendation both restricted and supplemented the fleeing felon privilege. It restricted it by confining the use of deadly force to certain forcible felonies – essentially felonies in which life is threatened. It supplemented the privilege by joining it with the "defense of life" privilege, which allows that an officer may employ deadly force when the person to be apprehended poses a serious immediate physical threat to the officer or others. Although several States subsequently adopted the Model Penal Code formula, some adopted it only to abandon or modify it later.

Some fifteen years after the Model Penal Code was finalized, the Police Foundation in Washington, D.C., with the strong support of its reformist President, Patrick V. Murphy, conducted a comparative national survey of provisions and practices in the police use of deadly force. The Report, published in 1977, noted the widely divergent policies and variable patterns in the use of deadly force round the country; it called for much closer monitoring of its use, and urged departments to develop more restrictive policies on its use. Its recommendations were in line with much that had been appearing in legal and criminological literature.

Nevertheless, the effects of these various pressures for change was modest. By the mid-1980s, when I think we could argue that these revisionary factors had been present for some time, four states still persisted with the common law privilege. Others – some nineteen – had codified that privilege, though in two cases the codified version carried some restrictions. Another two states had adopted verbatim the fairly restrictive provisions of the Model Penal Code. A further eighteen, though, had restricted the use of deadly force to situations in which the fleeing felon had committed a felony involving the use or threat of physical or deadly force, or was escaping with a deadly weapon, or was likely to endanger life or inflict serious physical injury if not arrested. The situation in the remaining states was unclear. Overall, it left almost half the states with something not very different from the old fleeing felon privilege.[54]

However, this picture is somewhat skewed by the fact that quite a number of police departments developed deadly force policies of their own that were considerably more restrictive than state law. An officer who acted within the bounds of the law in using deadly force might well violate departmental policy. Fear of civil liability was a factor in implementing these restrictive policies. Even so, many departments were content to follow existing state policies (or, as in the case of the Memphis Police Department, were willing to fall back on them when it suited).

Why was change so slow? Several considerations appear to have come into play:

1. The lack of political clout possessed by fleeing lawbreakers is surely relevant. A large portion of the populace is clearly unsympathetic to the rights of those who flee from the scene of a crime or attempt to escape custody. Although the situation was more volatile in the 1960s, a period that produced an unprecedented alienation between police and sections of the community, there was never a unified call for restraint. Along with the calls for greater restrictions on police power, there were also calls for increased or at least active expressions of police power.

2. Another important factor lay in the opposition of police, particularly police unions, to more restrictive rules. The growth of police unionism in the late 1960s and early 1970s found partial expression in a strong resistance to any policy changes that would diminish the options available to police officers or might appear to render them more vulnerable to danger.[55] Police administrators often concurred, though their concurrence was sometimes grounded more immediately in a fear of civil suits. They were led to believe that a tightening-up of rules relating to the use of deadly force would alter the relevant standard of care and thus make municipalities more vulnerable to civil actions. Occasionally it even appears to have been thought that if deadly force were not available up to its legal limit, police might be held liable for any harms subsequently caused by a felon who thus managed to escape.

The opposition of police unions to change is vividly illustrated by their reaction to the 1977 Police Foundation Report and Patrick Murphy's subsequent support for its findings.[56] In 1980, the International Union of Police Associations passed a resolution that sought to remove Murphy from his position "as President of a private corporation known as the Police Foundation and to boycott any organization or foundation that supports the Police Foundation." It sought to do this inter alia because Murphy had criticized "police officers' use of weapons," "notoriously accused our nation's police officers as the immediate cause of the riots that took place in the 60's," and had "further stated that a restrictive shooting policy not only reduces police shootings of civilians but does not result in any increased danger to police officers or a rise in crime." In the same year, members of the International Association of Chiefs of Police attending its annual meeting voted "by a 4-to-1 margin reaffirming [the Association's] support of laws and policies permitting police to shoot fleeing felony suspects."[57]

3. Finally, federalism and localism meant a fragmentation of knowledge, of political effort, and of reform. The 1977 Police Foundation Report went some way to overcoming that, at least in its call for record keeping and the sharing of experience.

The turning point – if we can speak of it as that – came in 1985, in probably the only way in which it could have come – a Supreme Court decision.[58] Errol Garner was a slightly built, fifteen-year-old black youth. He was shot while seeking to escape apprehension after he had apparently burglarized a vacant house ($10 was found in his possession). Although the pursuing officer did not believe that Garner was armed or even dangerous, the Memphis Police Department defended the officer's actions by appealing to the "fleeing felon" privilege. Had Garner not been shot, he would not have been apprehended.

In a 5–3 decision,[59] the Court extended a position it had taken earlier in *Terry v. Ohio*,[60] and argued that the police use of deadly force against Garner violated the Fourth Amendment guarantee against unreasonable seizure. There are several layers to the Court's *ratio decidendi*:

1. Extending *Terry*, the Court argued that the use of deadly force against a "fleeing felon" constituted a seizure under the Fourth Amendment, and therefore had to satisfy a reasonableness requirement. To this end it was necessary to "balance the nature and quality of the intrusion on the individual's Fourth Amendment interests against the importance of the governmental interests alleged to justify the intrusion."[61] The Court held that the use of deadly force against Garner was "unreasonable," when the diverse individual and governmental interests involved were taken into account. There was, on the one side, Garner's interest in life, and the societal interest in the judicial determination of guilt and punishment. On the other side there was the government's interest in Garner's apprehension, and generally in encouraging the peaceful submission of suspects, and there was also the property owner's interest in security. The Court argued that Garner's interest in life and the societal interest in due process overrode the other interests. It argued, moreover, that the interest in life would always prevail except where "it is necessary to prevent . . . escape and the officer has probable cause to believe that the suspect poses a significant threat of death or serious physical injury to the officer or others."[62] A significant threat, Justice White wrote, exists when a "suspect threatens the officer with a weapon or there is probable cause to believe that he has committed a crime involving the infliction or threatened infliction of serious physical harm."[63] This was not so in the case under consideration, which involved simple burglary.[64]

2. The Court further maintained that the reasonableness requirement was not satisfied by an appeal to the fleeing felon privilege – a provision that was enshrined in Tennessee state law and, more restrictively, in police department policy. Although of long standing, the privilege needed to be recast if it was to perform a task comparable to that which it performed when it originally evolved. Reference was made to the shift in the felony–misdemeanor distinction, to the fact that felonious conduct per se no longer attracted the death penalty, and to the original presumption that deadly force would most likely be used in hand-to-hand combat, when the apprehending officer himself would have been in physical danger.

3. Finally, the Court argued that there was no evidence that a more stringent policy, such as had been adopted in many police departments, would severely hamper law enforcement, or would be impossible to apply, or would

expose police to more danger or more litigation. The Memphis police had claimed that

> overall violence will be reduced by encouraging the peaceful submission of suspects who know that they may be shot if they flee. Effectiveness in making arrests requires the resort to deadly force, or at least the meaningful threat thereof. "Being able to arrest such individuals is a condition precedent to the state's entire system of law enforcement." Brief for Petitioners 14.[65]

But the Court was not convinced. It asserted that

> the use of deadly force is a self-defeating way of apprehending a suspect and so setting the criminal justice mechanism in motion. If successful, it guarantees that that mechanism will not be set in motion. And while the meaningful threat of deadly force might be thought to lead to the arrest of more live suspects by discouraging escape attempts, the presently available evidence does not support this thesis.[66]

And so we have arrived at a situation in which the police use of deadly force has been significantly limited – one in which the fleeing felon privilege has been all but subsumed under the defense-of-life privilege. Or at least that is how it looks at this stage.

In fact, the *Garner* ruling still leaves some issues unclear. For one thing, the Court's language seems to allow that deadly force may be used to apprehend a person who posed a threat while committing the offense, but no longer appears to do so. I guess the presumption is that a person who was prepared to use force on a particular occasion will be prepared to use it on some future occasion, and so must be apprehended immediately. It is not clear to me that this claim is empirically justified. Further, the Court does not really address the issue of its justifiability in situations where the need to use deadly force has been created by the police handling of a case. Nor did the Court address the question of racial bias in police shootings.[67]

The Supreme Court decision settled only the broad parameters of deadly force policy. Subsequent decisions could lead to refinements. But in the meantime the finer tuning of deadly force policy will continue to depend on state, local, and departmental regulations. Among the several issues that such policies need to address are:

1. The number and kinds of weapons and the ammunition that police should be permitted to carry
2. Whether off-duty police officers should be required, encouraged or even permitted to carry weapons
3. Whether warning shots or shots to summon assistance should be required, encouraged or even permitted
4. Training and recertification requirements for the use of weapons carried, incorporating both "shoot/don't shoot" and marksmanship training
5. Whether deadly force should ever be used against juveniles, or a more flexible standard of dangerousness should be employed

6. Risks to innocent bystanders (including the risks involved in shooting at and from a moving vehicle)
7. Circumstances for the display or drawing of firearms
8. Reporting policies relating to situations in which firearms are drawn, displayed or used
9. Procedures for reviewing firearm policy
10. Determining the degree of certainty required before using deadly force.

None of these issues is simple, and each needs to be sensitive to social and political factors as well as to the complex factual considerations that policies need to take into account.

Policy changes do not by themselves change practice, and one might reasonably ask whether the *Garner* decision can be expected to have an appreciable effect on police uses of deadly force. Unless and until police see themselves primarily as peacekeepers rather than as crimefighters, firearms will tend to be used unnecessarily. Nevertheless, it is Lawrence Sherman's opinion that this is one of relatively few areas in which policy change has already been associated with significant changes in practice. Police shootings have declined, and have done so at a time when violent crime has not. Sherman offers three reasons for the apparent success of such policy change:[68]

1. The difficulty of concealing the effects of the use of deadly force:[69] Police shootings tend to be publicly reported and publicly scrutinized.
2. The reluctance that many police have to using their weapons: Though there are exceptions, many police are deterred from using their firearms by the psychological costs,[70] and the anxiety caused by official and public inquiries into their use.
3. The changing understanding of the police role: From what may have been perceived primarily as a law enforcement role, policing has evolved into a more embracing social service or peacekeeping profession. Although the entitlement to use force has remained, it is not as the presenting factor but as a last resort. Negotiation rather than confrontation has been increasingly emphasized. And even where fleeing suspects are involved, the modern-day police force is better mobilized for orchestrated pursuit than it once was.

6.4 DEADLY FORCE AND HIGH-SPEED PURSUITS[71]

Although discussions of the police use of deadly force generally concern themselves with firearms, they might well be broadened to consider the "use of the deadliest weapon in their arsenal, the motor vehicle."[72] Pursuits involving police cars kill and maim more people each year than police firearms. Yet it is only since the late 1970s that discussions of police high-speed pursuits have taken seriously the idea that they should be covered by policy constraints similar to those of the more traditional forms of deadly force.[73] To some extent that is connected with the development of deadly force law itself. It took the

Supreme Court's *Garner* decision to constitute the use of deadly force a "seizure" under the Fourth Amendment, and this has paved the way for treating high-speed pursuits as exercises of deadly force. In a later Supreme Court decision, *Brower v. County of Inyo*,[74] it was held that setting up a roadblock and pursuing a fleeing driver into it constituted a "seizure" under the Fourth Amendment, and therefore had to pass the "reasonableness test." Thus it was not surprising when, in February 1991, the Texas Supreme Court explicitly stated that police policies governing high-speed pursuits should take their lead from those governing the use of deadly force.[75]

Although more deaths and injuries occur in the course of high speed pursuits than as the result of police firearm use, they are less dangerous. There is an obvious reason for this. Under current regulations, when police discharge their firearms, they *intend* to injure or kill. Police who engage in high-speed pursuits have more control over the situation and intend only to apprehend, preferably without injury. Nevertheless, there are inherent risks in high speed pursuits that make it appropriate that they be considered somewhat analogously to exercises of deadly force.

We can separate the moral questions posed by high-speed pursuits into those that bear on the issue of an *initial* pursuit, and those that relate to its becoming a high-speed or "hot" pursuit. In many cases the two questions will be addressed simultaneously.

6.4.1 *The decision to pursue*

It should hardly need to be said that the initial decision to pursue another vehicle – with a view to halting it – ought not to be made arbitrarily. In the absence of some public interest in their apprehension, travelers on public roads are privileged to have free passage. A "fishing expedition" will not suffice. The officers should have some reason to believe that the person stopped is violating or has violated some law, and that the violation is serious enough to warrant a stop.[76] Patrol officers, charged with enforcing the law and keeping the public peace, have a duty to ensure that public vehicular passageways remain free, safe and accessible. The decision to pursue, therefore, should normally be based on some reasonably grounded law enforcement, public safety or peacekeeping purpose.

Whereas the decision to pursue must override the privilege to free passage possessed by travelers on a public road, the decision to engage in a high-speed pursuit must confront several additional questions. This is because a high-speed or hot pursuit, unlike the initial decision to pursue and detain, poses a significant danger to life and limb. Here officers need to take into account: (1) the danger posed to the occupant(s) of the pursued vehicle; (2) the danger posed to innocent bystanders and other travelers; and (3) the danger posed to themselves.

1. If the decision to engage in a hot pursuit is made before the occupants of the pursued vehicle are aware that they are being pursued, the hot pursuit

may not place them in additional danger. On becoming aware that they are being pursued, they may halt. Sometimes, however, the awareness that they are being pursued will cause the occupants (or driver) of the pursued vehicle to seek to avoid apprehension, with a consequent increase in speed and in risk to life and limb. A speeding motor vehicle, or one that is being driven recklessly, imposes a significant risk of injury on its occupants.

Is the risk justifiable? At one level, we might say that the fleeing driver voluntarily assumes the risk. He chooses not to be apprehended, and the risks he takes are of his own making. And to a point that may be so. But talk of a voluntary assumption of risk is much too simple. Consider some of the possibilities:

(i) The driver of the pursued vehicle is an immigrant. He has broken no law, or is unaware that he has, but is fearful of police apprehension. For him, police pursuit means persecution. So he seeks to avoid apprehension.

(ii) The driver has had his automobile commandeered by a fleeing felon. He has a gun pointed at his head.

(iii) The driver has broken a law, and is aware of the fact, but panics when he hears the siren and realizes he is being pursued.

(iv) The driver has broken a law, and knows that is so. When he hears the siren he does not panic, but is determined to avoid apprehension. However, there are other passengers in the car who have not participated in either the lawbreaking or in the decision to flee.

(v) The driver has broken a law, and knows that is so. When he hears the siren he does not panic, but is determined to avoid apprehension.

Only in cases (iv) and (v) can we say with any sort of confidence that the danger is of the driver's own making. And only in case (v) can we say that of "all" the pursued parties. But even in that case we might ask the question: Was it reasonable of the pursuing officer to "structure" the driver's options in that way? Suppose the driver's only offense was to fail to stop at a *STOP* sign, even though this failure involved no immediate danger to other travelers. However, the driver does not want to be given a "ticket,"[77] and he seeks to escape apprehension (now, of course, violating other regulations, and posing a significant danger to himself, and maybe others as well). Continuing a pursuit in these circumstances may not be justified.

There is some reason, therefore, to engage in high-speed pursuits only where the alleged or suspected offense is serious enough to warrant the danger to which the fleeing driver is put.

This, however, might be thought to raise an interesting and difficult policy question. It could be argued that if it becomes known that patrol officers will not hotly pursue minor violators of the law, this will "encourage" minor violations or prompt minor violators to seek to escape apprehension, to the detriment of the public interest.[78] But although the general point is reasonable enough, and the immediate costs and benefits of a high-speed pursuit do need to be balanced against the longer-term costs and benefits of a policy embodying that decision, it is far from clear that this would justify a relatively unrestricted pursuit policy. Analogous to the Supreme Court's claim in *Garner*, the decision not to pursue minor violators hotly will probably have little effect on either the incidence of violations or the effectiveness of police.

The problem for police, however, is that the distinction between a "minor" and a "major" violator is "academic" at the point at which a pursuit becomes a high-speed pursuit. Even if what has initiated the pursuit has been a relatively minor infraction, police easily – probably too easily – assume that if a person refuses to stop for a minor infraction, there must be something much more serious that the person is hiding, something, moreover, that will be discovered if the pursuit is successful. It would be interesting to see some statistical data on this, to see how well such a presumption stands up. I suspect, though, that it would not hold up well. Of course, *even if* some "more serious" infraction is being concealed behind the attempt to flee, it would not follow that the risks generated by the high-speed pursuit would be justifiably taken.

2. Both the fleeing and pursuing vehicles pose a significant danger to other travelers on the road and any bystanders. There are numerous reports of death and injury caused to third parties as the result of high-speed chases. Obviously, the risk will vary from situation to situation: account will need to be taken of the amount of traffic on the road, the status and condition of the road, the speed and maneuverability of the vehicles, the skill and state of mind of the drivers.

The risk to bystanders and others provides a further reason for confining high-speed pursuits to situations where serious offenses are reasonably believed to be involved and there is good reason to believe that the occupants of the pursued car are strongly implicated. We are provided with a rather different application of Blackstone's dictum: "It is better that ten guilty people go free than that one innocent person be convicted."[79]

Where we are dealing with innocent third parties, such as bystanders, there is a particularly strong responsibility to avoid life-threatening risks. In the case of police officers and fleeing drivers, there is at least some basis for claiming that they have assumed some of the risks of their conduct. But innocent bystanders will have had the risk thrust upon them. The pursuer and pursued have initiated the risky behavior, and they have some control over its conclusion; the innocent third party has been caught unawares and has been offered no such choice.

Where an accident does occur, and an innocent bystander is harmed, complex questions of responsibility may arise. Suppose, in the course of the pursuit, the police vehicle goes through an intersection against the lights, colliding with a crossing car, and killing its occupant. Who is responsible? Should we hold the driver of the fleeing car responsible? After all, had he not sought to escape apprehension, the dangerous situation would not have occurred. Yet he was not directly responsible for the third party's death, and did not compel the patrol officer to drive the way he did or take the risks he did. Should we then hold the patrol officer responsible – since he was the immediate cause of the third party's death? But wasn't he doing his duty? If he had his siren and turret/bar lights on, and had slowed down at the intersection, had he not done everything that could be expected of him? Or was there more that could have been expected, had he been properly trained in pursuit driving? And if so, should the police department be held partially responsible for not providing better guidelines or training? Or might there be a wider responsibility, if advanced technology, enabling officers in pursuing vehicles to change traffic lights electronically, had not been fitted for budgetary reasons? Perhaps responsibility cannot be sheeted home to any one party, but must be shared, even by the bystander, the division varying, depending on the circumstances of the case.[80] I mention these possibilities, not to cloud the issue of responsibility, but simply to indicate that the tendency to search for a single person to "blame" when accidents occur, may blind us to a wider responsibility that should also be recognized.

3. Patrol officers engaged in high-speed pursuits also put themselves at risk. Although a person who chooses to become a police officer can be assumed ipso facto to have consented to a certain amount of risk, this does not constitute a carte blanche consent to risk. Or, even if it is *intended* as a carte blanche consent, it does not justify others in placing that person at excessive risk. There needs to be some balancing of risks and stakes. To expect police officers to place themselves at serious risk in order that minor violators will be apprehended is unreasonable and inappropriate.

It is therefore important that police departments develop policies to ensure that police officers not be required to place themselves (and others) at disproportionate risk. This could be assisted in a number of ways:

(i) by specifying who may engage in high-speed pursuits and in what vehicles such pursuits may be undertaken;

(ii) by detailing the kinds of circumstances under which a high-speed pursuit would normally be justified;

(iii) by providing appropriate training for patrol officers, so that they can handle high-speed chases;

(iv) by exploring alternatives to high-speed pursuit – radioing ahead to support vehicles, helicopter patrols, tracing violators through license plates, photographs, and so on;[81] and

(v) by requiring that all pursuits be monitored and subject to veto by the dispatcher or road supervisor.

6.4.2 *Departmental policies and driver discretion*

Decisions regarding high-speed pursuits may arise at several different points. In the midst of a pursuit, there may be occasion to decide whether or not to continue. Prior to a pursuit, it will be necessary to decide whether or not to initiate a pursuit. Before that, there will be decisions about what departmental policy ought to be. Departmental policies will focus on the appropriate occasions for pursuit, vehicles to be employed in pursuits, the training needed before it is permissible to engage in a pursuit, and the ways in which a pursuit must be conducted. Decisions will therefore need to be made about the extent of officer discretion in the matter of high-speed pursuits.

Many officers have argued that the variability of their circumstances makes it imperative that any policy be discretionary rather than restrictive. But the stakes involved, and the temptations to excess, make it more appropriate that discretion be restricted. Police officers can easily feel that the flight of someone they wish to stop constitutes both an insult and a challenge, and an officer who is experiencing the rush of adrenalin that is associated with a pursuit is not necessarily the best judge of what risks are and are not appropriate.[82]

Police pursuit training does not give adequate weight to the effects of an adrenalin rush. Not only does it affect an officer's judgment during a pursuit, but also afterward. One significant source of the injuries that occur pursuant to a pursuit was dramatically illustrated by the Los Angeles police beating of Rodney King.[83] Had the situation not been videotaped, his injuries would almost certainly have been incurred while "resisting arrest." It was not an isolated incident, and we should not, perhaps, have been surprised by it. Given the charge of emotion – of fear, anger, and frustration – felt by police who feel they have been held in contempt and placed at risk by the person they are now apprehending, it is not to be wondered that they let fly. Inexcusable as such conduct may be, it is likely to be protected by the code of silence, and thus not addressed by police management. Yet it *is* a management problem, to be dealt with, not simply by threatening first line officers, but by teaching officers how to release their emotions in less destructive ways.

Chapter 7

The use of deception

To tell the truth is a duty: but it is a duty only in respect to one who has a right to the truth.

Benjamin Constant[1]

Lying is the throwing away and, as it were, the obliteration of one's dignity as a human being.

Immanuel Kant[2]

Although the capacity to use force still remains central to police law enforcement activities, its importance has been increasingly rivaled by the use of deception. There have been several reasons for that. For one thing, it is no longer permissible to use third-degree tactics to elicit information and confessions from criminal suspects, and the measures adopted in many jurisdictions to ensure that coercion is not used have made it much harder to employ surreptitiously.[3] Although verbal statements and confessions are still, and will surely remain, admissible as evidence, there is little doubt that the courts have put increasing pressure on prosecutors to supplement their cases with "hard" material or physical evidence. In many cases that is not easy to do: The offenses do not involve "witnesses" (as is the case with much white-collar crime) or the witnesses are not complainants (as is the case with vice). So, over the past forty years police investigators have placed an ever greater reliance on deception as a means of accessing both material and verbal evidence.

At first the deployment of deceptive tactics occasioned some misgivings. Although civilian or criminal informants were unselfconsciously used, police who went under cover found that effective information gathering often forced them perilously close to the edge of illegality. The development of new technologies – wiretaps, bugging devices, and other forms of electronic surveillance – removed some of the risks of undercover work, but still had to take account of legitimate expectations of privacy. Even so, deception has

more and more become a mainstay of police investigation, and it is necessary to address the question: To what extent, if at all, may police rely on
deception in the furtherance of their law enforcement activities?

To answer that question, we need first to consider the more fundamental
problems of deception – what it is that makes it necessary to justify its use,
and what, if any, considerations will enable us to justify its use. For it is only
against that background that claims to its legitimate use can be established.
Then, using a helpful typology developed by Jerome Skolnick, we will consider the use of deception in three spheres of police work – investigation,
interrogation, and the giving of sworn testimony.[4] One form of investigative
deception, entrapment, will be considered in the next chapter.

7.1 THE MORAL PROBLEM WITH DECEPTION

Deception can be thought of as either "task" or "outcome."[5] As an outcome,
it refers to a condition in which a person has been misled with regard to the
truth. As an outcome, deception need not have come about intentionally.
Our senses, as Descartes memorably observed, may sometimes deceive us.[6]
Thought of as a task, however, deception does refer to an intentional activity,
to one of a range of communications intended to produce a false belief in
others. Conduct that is intended to deceive may not actually achieve its end.
But that does not make it less deceptive. One of the most controversial and
problematic forms of deception, lying, exploits language and consists in the
assertion of what is believed to be false with the intention that others should
take it as true.[7]

But there are myriad forms of deception, both verbal and nonverbal.
Deceptive practices can utilize gesture, expression, speech, silence, action,
inaction, or some device. Police deception itself takes many forms – the
withholding and distortion of information, lying, the employment of ruses,
the utilization of agents provocateurs, informants, decoys, sting operations,
wiretaps and bugging devices, the infiltration of suspect organizations, the
creation of "false friendships," manufacture of evidence, engagement in
"good cop/bad cop" routines, and so on.

It is as a task that deception possesses moral significance, though obviously were it never to achieve its intended outcome, it would be of little
interest. In the ethical literature, most attention is given to lying, and although that is partly because of features that attach particularly to lies, much
of what is said about lying is equally applicable to deception in general. Here
I will begin with a consideration of lying, and then turn to some arguments
that allegedly make a moral distinction between lying and other forms of
deception.

It is convenient, albeit slightly oversimplifying, to distinguish three kinds
of argument against lying. However, they need not be thought of as exclusive of others or of each other. Using familiar terminology, they can be
dubbed deontological, consequentialist, and contractarian.

Deontological critiques of lying concentrate on what are considered to be intrinsic features of lying. The following have gained wide currency.

1. Lying is said to violate a foundational "duty of veracity."[8] There is, it is said, a basic presumption in favor of truthfulness and against lying. For only if there is an expectation of veracity or truthfulness in human relations can such relations be created and subsequently survive. In some sense, truthfulness is constitutive of human relations. And only if human relations exist can there be human life in any morally significant sense. The liar acts in a way that is fundamentally inimical to the relation that is presumed by the untruthful communication.

2. Lying is sometimes said to subvert the natural purposiveness of language.[9] Language is a vehicle of communication, and a fundamental purpose of communication is the imparting of beliefs on which others may rely, or which they may at least take seriously. The liar exploits that purposiveness in a way that undermines its purposiveness and point.

This argument is closely linked with the previous one. The duty of veracity is a principle underlying communication, and language is integral to human communication and relationships.

3. Lying violates a principle of respect for persons. If we see human individuals as – to use Kant's phrase – ends-in-themselves, as developing centers of self-reflective and self-determining activity, sustained in that quest by a realistic hold on the world in which their reflection and activity takes place, they become objects of dignity to us, worthy of our respect. Lying negates that respect. The liar manipulates the world of others to ends of his or her own devising, in a manner that is subversive of the autonomy that is constitutive of others' dignity. The liar treats others as mere means – conduct that is made all the worse by the fact that he or she exploits the very processes that are integral to our status as ends.[10] Not only does the lie compromise our autonomy, but it is expressive of an essentially demeaning attitude on the part of another.

Another way of stating this argument is to say that the principle of respect for persons expresses the fundamental equality of rational beings: Their intercourse is to be mediated by reason and argument rather than by force or manipulation. Those who lie to others, and seek to manipulate them, impliedly place themselves "above" those whom they seek to deceive, as though they are entitled to structure the choices that are others' to make.

4. Lying fails to meet the formal ethical requirement of universalizability. Of all the deontological critiques of lying, Kant's is the most sustained.[11] It is also the most distinctive. According to Kant, it is a fundamental requirement of morality, as the activity of a rational being, that we act only on maxims that we could, without "contradiction," will to be universal laws. If universalizing the principle on which we act would undermine the possibility of our conduct achieving its purpose, it would be immoral to act on it. Were the

practice of lying universalized, it would no longer be efficacious, for it is a condition of the ability of lies to deceive that truthfulness be the norm.

Kant does not strongly separate the third and fourth arguments. At one point he cryptically writes that "lying is the throwing away and, as it were, the obliteration of one's dignity as a human being."[12] Not only does the liar violate another's being, but also his own. For he acts on a maxim under which others might, with as much reason, do the same to him. The liar acts on a maxim that would allow others to treat him as a mere means to their own ends. In lying, a person kicks out from under himself the very conditions for his own respectful treatment.

Consequentialist critiques of lying are oriented to the extrinsic effects of lying.[13] As in nearly all consequentialist arguments, these effects will tend to be contingent. We are talking about the likelihood or *probability* of consequences of a certain kind. Among the deleterious consequences said to be associated with lying, the following are often referred to:

1. Others are harmed. Insofar as people who are deceived are led to do what they would not otherwise have chosen, they are wronged, and therefore harmed in that sense. But they may be, and often are, harmed in more material ways. They may be defrauded of their possessions, placed at considerable physical risk, or caused great disappointment and unhappiness as a result of being lied to.

2. Social trust is destroyed. Someone who is lied to and discovers it is likely to be hardened as a result, thus diminishing the quality of interaction that he or she will subsequently have with others. Suspicion replaces trust as the environment in which interpersonal relations are conducted. With the undermining of social trust there comes an erosion of the human and social resources that enable human life to flourish.

3. The liar is himself harmed. One might distinguish a variety of possible harms that a liar may bring upon himself/herself. There may be a need for continuing and increasing evasiveness, lest one be found out; or a diminished credibility and the suspicion of others, should one be found out. Both of these are social impediments that could be considered harms. More controversially, one might posit some form of moral harm – a loss of integrity and a diminished ability to resist corruption in future.

It is a feature of exclusively consequentialist critiques of lying that they do not consider lying as such to be wrong. Any wrongness it has is contingent on its effects, effects that may or may not occur. As Bentham put it with characteristic directness: "Falsehood, take it by itself, consider it as not being accompanied by any other material circumstances, nor therefore productive of any material effects, can never, upon the principle of utility, constitute any offence at all."[14] In some sense, this constitutes a reductio ad absurdum of the consequentialist account. For there is implicit in the very characterization of an act as one of *lying* that it is morally suspect. Where a lie is considered to be morally acceptable, it must be characterized as "white" or "justifiable."

We do not have to call other lies "black" or "unjustifiable." That, barring some qualifier, goes without saying.[15] Of course, it is possible to claim that because certain kinds of acts produce bad consequences, we refer to them as lies, and that is why lying is wrong. But Bentham's point is rather different, since it presumes – correctly, I believe – that we can identify something as a lie or falsehood independent of any reference to its consequences.

Contractarian approaches to lying view language as a compact between people. It is a social device that we have developed and that we use to convey the truth as we see it. Any deviation from that constitutes a breach of an implied promise, unless there is an understanding that the context is one in which deception is permissible (say, a game of poker). Contractarian approaches are developed inter alia in the work of Grotius, W. D. Ross, and Charles Fried.

For Grotius, when humans "determined to make use of speech and similar signs," they agreed, at least tacitly, that what was "spoken, written or indicated by signs or gestures," would not be understood in a way that differed from "the thought of him who uses the means of expression." Otherwise, "the invention of speech would have been void of result." There would have been no point to the practice.[16] Ross subsumes the duty of truthfulness under that of fidelity, the latter being conditional on some prior commitment on our part. There is, Ross believes, an "implicit undertaking not to tell lies which seems to be implied in the act of entering into conversation (at any rate by civilized men), or writing books that purport to be history and not fiction."[17] "Every lie," Fried writes, "is a broken promise, and the only reason this seems strained is that in lying the promise is made and broken at the same moment. Every lie necessarily implies – as does every assertion – an assurance, a warranty of its truth."[18] The point is not that what is said *is* true, but that it is believed to be so.

The contractarian approach relies on our views about the keeping of contracts or promises, and to develop it fully we would need to consider why promises ought to be kept. Although there is not too much debate about the obligatoriness of promise keeping, there is little agreement about the grounds for it and the stringency of the obligation. For some there is an intuitive obviousness about the obligation; for others, the question is one of outcomes; for yet others it is the creation of reliance that grounds the obligation.[19]

As I indicated earlier, there is no need to see these different approaches to truth telling/lying as competing, exclusive, or exhaustive.[20] There is no compelling reason to reduce moral reflection to a common currency. The different approaches may, however, differ in the stringency of the obligations they generate. And this will have obvious relevance to the issue of police deception. The consequentialist and contractarian reasons appear to accommodate some lying more easily than some of the deontological reasons. If, as the consequentialist claims, lying is not intrinsically evil, but evil only because and insofar as it has deleterious consequences, then these may of course be counterbalanced by beneficial consequences. The social benefits of police deception, either in particular cases or in the use of particular strategies, may outweigh its detriments. And if lying is seen as a breach of promise or contract, we might see that promise or contract as contingent on a certain reciprocity or as overridable by other, more stringent obligations. Thus, it is commonly argued that the obligation to keep a promise exists or at least takes precedence only when the beneficiary has a right to what is promised. A promise to do evil need not be kept; nor need we speak truthfully to those who have no right to the information they are seeking. The intending murderer who wishes to know the whereabouts of his intended victim has no right to our knowledge of the same.[21]

7.1.1   *Deception and lying*

Lying, as I pointed out earlier, is a fairly specific form of deception, involving the use of language, and some of the objections to lying depend on the particular character and place that language has. Although there are other forms of deception that involve the use of language, yet do not constitute lying, there are many forms of deception that make no use of language, though of course they involve communication. Kant himself gives the example of a person who wishes to mislead others into thinking that he is going on a journey, and does so by packing his bags.[22]

   In view of the language-specific features of the critique of lying, we may wonder whether forms of deception that do not make use of language at all, or that do not use it in a manner that constitutes lying, are as open to moral question as lying. That they may not be has been suggested by Joseph Ellin.[23] Ellin, whose concern is with the use of deception in professional contexts, suggests that deception, though probably not lying, may sometimes be justified in the context of professional–client relationships. As intuitive evidence of the moral differentiation, he points to the way in which professionals who may be very reluctant to lie directly to their clients may have fewer qualms about deceiving them. He develops three arguments for considering such deception to be less problematic than lying.

1. Liars take greater advantage of our vulnerability than do mere deceivers. Crucial to Ellin's distinction between lying and other forms of deception is a distinction between that which is directly and immediately communicated and that which must be inferred. The liar who says "I am going away" directly and immediately provides a basis for our believing that he is going away. There is a presumption implicit in the mode of communication that what he asserts is what he intends us to believe. The person who packs his bags, however, conveys nothing so direct. We must *infer* from the fact of his packing his bags that he is going away.

   We can, Ellin suggests, more easily protect ourselves against mere deception than we can against lying. To avoid being deceived, we need adopt only a maxim of prudence: "Believe everything you are told, but draw no inferences unless supported by independent evidence." To guard against being deceived by lies, however, we will have to adopt the much more burdensome maxim: "Believe nothing you hear unless it is supported by independent evidence." That being so, we are more vulnerable to lies than we are to mere deception.

2. Liars are more responsible for the harms they cause than are mere deceivers. Just because a person who is (merely) deceived is deceived only because he inferred from what was done or said that something else was the case, he must take some responsibility for the false belief that he has acquired. The person who is merely deceived is an active participant in his own deception. The victim of the lie fails to verify a direct statement, but the victim of deception fails to verify a conclusion of his own *and* fails to seek confirmation of the speaker, and hence is more "responsible for" coming to hold his false belief.[24]

Ellin goes so far as to suggest that the deceived person is somehow "at fault" or "imprudent" in failing to verify the inference. This, I shall suggest, goes too far, and reveals a serious weakness in Ellin's account. For, insofar as the deceiver intends to divert the person from verifying an inference or tries to make the process of verification appear redundant, the attribution of fault or imprudence is surely excessive.

3. Lying, unlike mere deception, violates an implied contract that our assertions convey the opinions of those who make them. Following Ross, Ellin takes seriously the view that the duty of veracity is contractual – an implicit promise of straightforwardness, a commitment not to deceive. Lying, he suggests, represents a more serious breach of contract than mere deception. This may be in part because language, particularly when used assertorically, is essential to "*any* human society," whereas nondeception "is necessary only for a tolerable or decent society."[25] It may also reflect the explicitness of the "promise" that is involved when we make assertions, compared with the more implicit understanding that is involved in other forms of communication: "To speak at all is virtually to warrant that our words are true."[26]

Interesting as these arguments are, they are not, as I indicated, altogether convincing. The duty of veracity is concerned with straightforwardness in communication, and the person who deceives, *no less than* the person who lies, is not being straightforward. In both cases, our interest in having others deal with us openly is deliberately subverted. And the harms done by deception may be as serious as any brought about by means of lies.

It is true that we are often more willing to deceive than to lie directly. But this may not reflect a sense of the greater seriousness of lying, but only our deviousness. The fact that others had to make an inference from what we said provides us with an "out" should our deception be uncovered. We can more easily "relieve" ourselves of responsibility for what we did, by saying that the false inference was "theirs," although the fact that we *intended* that others believe what they wrongly did does not show that we are to be absolved or even that our responsibility is mitigated.

There is, in addition, something curious about the argument that liars take greater advantage of us than mere deceivers. If it is the case that the more trusting a person is, the more vulnerable that person will be to various forms of deception, then the most vulnerable people, in this view, will not be those who are vulnerable to lies but not to other forms of deceit, but those whose trust is such that they are likely to be deceived by nonlying deception no less than by lies. And therefore a grosser kind of exploitation will be involved in the case of those who are taken in not only by lies but also by other forms of deception.

Of course, some people are too easily taken in – they are gullible. That charge, to some extent, is implicit in Ellin's second argument, in which he attributes responsibility to the deceived for their deception. But is a person who fails to act on the maxim, "Believe everything you are told but draw no inferences unless supported by independent evidence," ipso facto gullible? As Ellin himself recognizes, the maxim is itself reasonably burdensome, and though there might be contexts in which it is wise to follow it (the limited caveat emptor of the marketplace), we ought to be able to presume that others will be sufficiently open and straightforward to ensure that the inferences we most naturally draw will be consistent with the beliefs of those to whose communications we are responding.

7.1.2 *Justifying deception*

Powerful as the arguments against deception are, they are, like arguments against the use of force, not obviously strong enough to rule it out in every circumstance. As long as there is only a strong presumption in favor of truth telling and openness, there may be circumstances in which some deception is permissible. Not everyone has a right to the truth from us, and withholding what others have no right to may sometimes require that we engage in some form of deception.

Where truthfulness will almost certainly result in great harm being caused, then its claims must be established in relation to another important precept, that we "do no harm."

There may, in addition, be contexts in which it is understood that some deception will occur. Certain social contexts, for example, where courtesies are to be observed, and where hyperbole or at least selective presentation is almost expected, will be amenable to some deception. These are contexts in which strict truthfulness does not really matter. Indeed, given our flawed natures, it would be a real problem were strict truthfulness insisted upon. Vanity may not be an admirable trait, but the cruelty of unadorned truthfulness is not thereby justified.

The deliberative process that pits truthfulness against harm is not of a simple utilitarian variety, in which what counts is only the bottom line. There is a moral risk, and often a moral cost, to deception that is not erased in those cases in which deception is, all things considered, justified (see Chapter 3, Section 3.2.2). In any case, harms, like truths, differ qualitatively.

In order to determine whether, all things considered, deception would be justified, Sissela Bok has suggested that deceivers should be prepared to submit their conduct to the public scrutiny of "reasonable" persons. This, in essence, is what happens when various forms of police deception come up for judicial review. Although the publicity requirement constitutes only a formal procedure for assessing the justifiability of deception, and will secure at best the endorsement of Public Reason, it may help to ensure that justification does not become hostage to Idiosyncratic Reason. In the case of deceptive practices, such as those used by the police, publicity is probably an important corrective to the partisan interests by which police might otherwise be tempted to justify it. The concern that police have for crime control may obscure the due process requirements that ought also to mediate that enterprise. The publicity requirement opens up for scrutiny practices that, by their very nature, are secretive and likely otherwise to remain so.

Publicity will not yield a timeless justification for this or that deceptive practice. That, however, is not because of the nature of deceptive practices, but because justification is inherently open-ended. Giving a justification of a practice is not like proving a theorem. Justifications are essentially responses to requests, requests grounded in what appear to be deficiencies in the practice. If a request is "met," the practice is said to be justified, at least with respect to that particular request. When all outstanding requests have been met, we are likely to speak of the practice as being justified *(simpliciter)*. But that is not to foreclose against some future request that may once again throw open the question of justification.

7.2 SPHERES OF POLICE WORK – SKOLNICK'S TYPOLOGY

In a perceptive discussion of deception in police work, Jerome Skolnick distinguishes three stages (or, as I would prefer to call them, spheres) of police work: the investigative, the interrogatory, and the testimonial.[27] They are generally concerned with the law enforcement aspect of policing, and mark out three distinct sets of conditions under which police and public confront each other. It is what broadly distinguishes these conditions that also distinguishes the three spheres, or stages, and gives them a normative role in the assessment of police deception.

In the investigative sphere, we are to assume that those whom police investigate are "at large." The police may not know precisely whom they are seeking, or, if they do, those whom they seek are at liberty (so far as the state is concerned) to do what they can to escape scrutiny and apprehension. True, they may not have the resources that will enable them to stay free for ever. At least we may hope not. Were police not to have a preponderance of power, the whole project of law enforcement would founder. Nevertheless, they are relatively free from authoritative government constraint, and apprehending them may present a considerable challenge to police ingenuity. The

cards are not inherently stacked in the favor of police. Skolnick sees circumstances such as these as allowing police the greatest latitude for employing
deceptive means.

The situation is somewhat different where the context is one of interrogation. For what is envisaged here is a custodial situation – generally, one in
which the party to be interrogated is under arrest. At least, it is a situation in
which the interrogated party is not free to come and go as he or she pleases,
and the police have control over the conditions under which the interrogation takes place. Where this is the case, significant constraints are placed on
the party who is interrogated, and this has some bearing on the permis-
sibility of deception, and on the kinds of deception that may be acceptable.

So far as deception is concerned, the testimonial sphere is the most problematic of all, because all the parties are under oath to "tell the truth, the
whole truth, and nothing but the truth." Here the constraints on deception
are usually thought to be absolute. For it is not the defendant who would be
deceived, but the court, and court proceedings constitute an arena in which
argument and reason are supposed to prevail. Yet because police testimonial
deception does occur, perhaps more frequently than we realize, and is sometimes considered justifiable by those who engage in it, we must consider
whether circumstances exist in which a moral niche can be carved out for it.

7.2.1 *Investigative deception*

Lawbreakers do not normally advertise their identity. The sanctions attaching to breaches of the law, particularly the criminal law, are intended not
only to punish but also to deter. No doubt their deterrent effect would be
greater were those who are tempted to break the law to know that they
would be punished. But, unfortunately with good reason, lawbreakers do
not usually count on being caught. Indeed, if they intentionally break the
law, they generally do what they can to avoid being caught. And the fact that
they are frequently successful in avoiding apprehension (and/or conviction)
is one of the reasons why the legal penalties fail to deter them.

People who are prepared to break the law are often prepared to be less
than straightforward in other ways. They are likely to engage in deception
and subterfuge designed to conceal their identity as offenders, subterfuge
that enables them to profit without penalty from the advantages given them
by their lawbreaking. The police who are charged with putting a stop to their
criminal activities or with apprehending them so that they may receive their
due punishment may find that unless they themselves engage in subterfuge
and deception, these lawbreakers will go free. Either the identity of the
lawbreaker remains a mystery to them, or they will fall short at an evidentiary level.

But should police engage in deception just because others do? And if they
may, to what extent may they employ it?

As I pointed out above, in what we have referred to as the investigative
sphere of police work the suspect is still "at large" and has a relatively

unrestricted opportunity to avoid detection and/or apprehension. It is very likely that the suspect will choose to avoid detection, and to do so may avail himself/herself of whatever means seem necessary. Those in pursuit will need some flexibility in regard to the strategies they use. They cannot presume that the lawbreaker will be discovered and apprehended as a result of straightforward inquiry. The use of deceptive tactics may be essential if the lawbreaker is to be reined in. We may have to "set a thief to catch a thief." Within the jungle, the law of the jungle must be heeded. Assuming, as we shall for present purposes, that the prevention and detection of "crime" are significant social goods, the availability and use of deceptive means will be (in broad terms at least) not only necessary but also justifiable.

A slightly different way of putting this, an adaptation of a point made earlier, is that inhabitants of the world of criminal activity, a world that by definition relies on force and deception, must expect that force and deception will be used to counter them. Criminals can hardly express surprise if they are investigated by deceptive means. They have every reason to expect that considerable ingenuity will be used in efforts to trap them.[28]

Nevertheless, there are problems confronting investigative deception. One significant problem is generated by the fact that there is no clear geographical or social division between the jungle and civilization, and unless there are some checks on police use of deception innocent citizens are going to get caught up in the cross fire – not only from the criminal, but also from the police side. Innocent bystanders, as well as innocent suspects, will be at risk. If police are to see themselves as peacekeepers (rather than as crimefighters), they must not lose sight of that fact. The key issue concerns the placement of appropriate checks on deception.

The major problem areas are: (1) targeting – the determination of those on whom deceptive techniques are going to be employed, and (2) the kinds of deceptive tactics that are permissible. But, in addition, account has to be taken of the costs to (3) police and their agents, as well as to (4) our social ethos and values.

7.2.1.1 Targeting. When it is argued that deception is a justifiable technique in the investigation of criminal activity, it is usually understood that the deception will be practiced against those who are reasonably suspected of having engaged in criminal activity, or at least against those who might have an interest in subverting the course of justice. But not all criminal investigation follows this pattern. Sometimes people are targeted without there being any reasonable suspicion that they have committed a crime or the crime under investigation. Sometimes personal, political, or other partisan factors may lead to a person's being targeted.[29] A particularly egregious example concerns Arthur Baldwin, the owner of a topless nightclub in Memphis, who was investigated following complaints from residents who were unhappy at having the nightclub in their neighborhood. The nightclub violated no zoning regulations, and so an undercover agent, Joseph Hoing, was detailed to go on a "fishing expedition," to see whether something could be laid on Baldwin that would serve to shut down the nightclub. After six months, during which time he befriended Baldwin, became his manager, chauffeur, gofer, and a resident in his house, Hoing managed to gain sufficient material evidence that Baldwin occasionally used cocaine. He was convicted, lost on appeal, and was denied certiorari when the case was submitted to the Supreme Court.[30] Not only was Baldwin targeted without there being any reasonable suspicion that *he* was engaged in any criminal activity, but he was targeted for an excessively long period, and in a way that invaded his most private domain. His case is an interesting one, for it indicates the way in which what turned out to be legally acceptable nevertheless transgressed the bounds of moral propriety.[31]

Sometimes it is not people who are targeted but activities. A spate of robberies, muggings, or a rash of corruption may lead investigators to use decoys, to set up sting operations, or otherwise to set traps for whoever may have been responsible. Obviously, operations such as these may run a significant risk of involving innocent or otherwise innocent people. And they may do so without constituting entrapment.

Innocent people may be victimized by such traps in more than one way. They may become unwittingly and innocently caught up in the elaborate deceptive net that police have set for criminals. Their phones are tapped, they become the victims of fraud, they unknowingly buy stolen goods, and so on.[32] Alternatively, they may be lured or otherwise influenced into criminal activities in which they might not otherwise have engaged. Most of us are in some measure vulnerable to criminal temptation, but are fortunate enough not to have our vulnerabilities tested. Government operations may provide the opportunity and inducement that we would otherwise have avoided.

Sometimes, in criminal investigation, the focus moves away from specific ongoing criminal activity, and undercover activity is used as a means of "testing" those entering into, or involved in, a particular kind of work. Such targeting is particularly problematic, since it is directed to future rather than to past or ongoing crime, and techniques may be used to induce those who would not otherwise have engaged in criminal activity to do so. Although such cases of inducement may not qualify for the legal defense of entrapment, they can involve the use of ethically suspect techniques. Under the heading of trickery, Gary Marx suggests that "(a) offering the illegal action as a minor part of a very attractive socially legitimate goal, (b) hiding or disguising the illegal nature of the action, and (c) weakening the capacity of the target rationally to distinguish right from wrong (or choosing a suspect who is already weakened),"[33] may be legally acceptable but ethically questionable. It was frequently charged that the techniques used to trap "corrupt" politicians in the ABSCAM case violated ethical, even if not legal, canons.[34] There is, moreover, a real question about whether and when integrity testing is an appropriate state task.

Marx suggests that the testing ought to be restricted to those situations in which (i) there is a well-documented pattern of prior infraction, and (ii) those tested are in positions of special trust or temptation. The issue in such cases, however, should always be: "Is he/she corrupt?" and not "Is he/she corruptible?"[35] The greater the emphasis on the latter, the closer the undercover activity gets to entrapment. But it may cross the line of moral impropriety well before it crosses that of legal impropriety.

7.2.1.2 Tactics. The courts, and our society generally, accept the limited use of several deceptive investigative techniques: informants, decoys, and agents provocateurs, wiretapping and bugging, fencing fronts (stings), the use of ruses to gain warrantless entry to premises, unmarked patrol cars, and concealed radar traps. Some are more controversial than others. What criteria should govern the determination of acceptable deceptive techniques, and with regard to those that are acceptable, how far may police go in using them?

In determining the acceptability of a technique, the discussion may focus on either the inherent features of the technique or the probable consequences of its use. With regard to the former, it is claimed that some deceptive techniques are so distasteful in themselves (for example, becoming intimately or romantically involved with the suspect) that they ought not to be permitted – either at all or unless the criminal activity in question is of a particularly heinous kind.[36] With regard to the latter, where a technique runs a high risk of (en)trapping an "unwary innocent" (for example, by offering an unrealistically attractive inducement), then there is a strong reason for prohibiting its use, at least in that context. However, as we have already noted, the moral limits of deception may be crossed before the legal limit (entrapment) is reached, and the evil of the technique may be disproportionate to the crime.

Skolnick talks briefly about the relative merits/demerits of depersonalized versus personalized deceptive techniques, for example, wiretapping versus the use of informants. Obviously, if a deceptive means is to be used to achieve a good end, we need inter alia to have some confidence that it will achieve that end, and that it will achieve it with fewer costs than the alternatives. It is arguable that the reliability of wiretaps will normally be greater than that of informants. A wiretap or bug "tells it like it is," whereas informants may mishear, misremember, misinterpret, misconstrue, or even fabricate what they are told. Although the active involvement of informants in information gathering may promise more information, their "interest" in what is being said or done can and sometimes does impair their capacity to be impartial gatherers. True, that will not always be so. And even wiretaps and bugs are subject to human error and interference. Tapes can be expertly "doctored," and there may be mistakes in transcription. Nevertheless, the use of electronic devices tends to have greater "neutrality" or "impartiality." An additional factor that might be offered in favor of wiretaps and bugs is that they lack the informant's exploitatively demeaning intrusiveness. It may be claimed that their impersonality keeps them from achieving the same access to the inner sanctum of the self as an informant, whose exploitation of trust (the "false friend") may enable him/her to gain entrée to a person's most private confidences in a manner that can be devastating to morale when that trust is betrayed.[37] However, just because bugs can be placed in private places or be used to tap private conversations, they too have a great potential for invading "inner" domains.

As we shall later see (Chapter 8, Section 8.1) there is a further, related problem with the use of informants: a greater possibility of entrapment. The dynamics of the suspect–informant relationship may influence the former to act in ways that, absent that relationship, would not otherwise have occurred. The suspect may be lured into previously uncontemplated, or at least unintended, criminal activity.[38] In some cases the defense of entrapment may be available; but in other cases the existing tests for entrapment may not be sufficient to exclude what is morally unacceptable deception.

The use of deceptive techniques in the case of so-called victimless crimes (vice) is a further problem area. Here, because of the nature of the offenses – the fact that there is no complainant – detection may not be possible without the use of deception. Yet it is at least arguable that in many such cases the costs of deception are not justified by the offense. Or at least, if they are, the case for prohibiting the activity in question needs to be made out more clearly.

7.2.1.3 Participant costs.

It is sometimes complained that the very nature of undercover work – its secrecy, deviousness, uncertainty, lack of close supervision, isolation, and the temptations it may involve – places special burdens on the police and others who assist them. Informants, of course, are often themselves criminals, but police may find that the work takes its toll on their own personalities and character. There are numerous anecdotal histories of undercover officers who have become complicit in the activities of those they were seeking to combat. Such problems are now generally recognized, and there is much greater supervision and support for those who go undercover. Nevertheless, the problem has not completely vanished.[39]

Informants, too, are unlikely to be edified by the work they do. Although many of them already live lives that leave much to be desired, their involvement in police work may give them little incentive or encouragement to make something better of themselves. They may be viewed in an excessively instrumental manner, their weaknesses exploited and their continuing illegal activities overlooked. The fact that they are sometimes victims of "institutionalized blackmail" can make it virtually impossible for an informant to leave his/her nether world.[40]

7.2.1.4 Social costs.

The proliferation of undercover operations, although intended to counter the increasing sophistication of criminal activity and to avoid the use of "strong arm" or unconstitutional tactics by police, may have unpleasant side-effects on our social ethos – how we view and what we expect of each other, of our leaders, and so on. Do we want to live in a society in which police engage in the kind of deceptive tactics that we sometimes read about? Maybe we think the cost is worth it: A bit of moral tattiness is not too heavy a price to pay for crime control, particularly if the deception in question is intended to control activities that cause injury, create fear, and erode social trust. But maybe we will find the moral shabbiness of some forms of police deception too threatening to a social self-image that we have, and we would be willing to put up with a higher level of the criminal activity in question, if that is what is at stake.[41] The ABSCAM investigations disgusted many Americans, not just because politicians proved so venal, but because government agents were permitted to use the undercover tactics they did. Maybe that disgust reflected something of a "class bias" (a revulsion that the middle class should be exposed to the same tactics as a social underclass), but at least the question has to be asked: What does it do for our sense of who we are and what our society represents that this or that kind of deception is sponsored by government officials?

More fundamentally, should we be tackling (at least some) criminal activity in another way – at its social roots rather than at its social flowering? There is something to be said for the complaint that our political structures are such as to encourage us to address social problems too late and too superficially. We focus on immediate, vote-getting responses at the expense of longer-term, less popular solutions. We (both citizens and politicians) are unwilling to engage in the fairly radical self-examination and restructuring that would, at some cost to immediate self-interest, help to eliminate some of the causes of the criminal activity that we now try to control by means of undercover work.[42]

There is the additional question of social trust. If the government itself sanctions or sponsors relatively unsupervised undercover operations, will we become increasingly suspicious in our everyday dealings with others, lest we find that our friends are "false"? To say that only those tempted to do wrong would have anything to fear underestimates the possibilities for, and evidence of, mistake and abuse in this area.[43] As Martin Luther King, Jr., learned, almost any person who seeks to improve society will create "enemies," and a process of discreditation may be initiated through the use of undercover means. Few of us are so upright that we would be able to withstand the close scrutiny of a dirt digger.

In all these problem areas, then, there will need to be a careful examination of both the conduct involved and its consequences. Deception is in itself problematic, and some forms of deception are more threatening to the values that straightforwardness expresses and secures. What is more, undercover work may do considerable damage, and be costly in social resources. Unfortunately, just because undercover work is under cover, it is often difficult to ascertain its effectiveness.[44] Some estimate of the costs and gains may become available where an undercover operation has been "successful" (itself a problematic label), but where it has not yielded positive results, it may go unreported, or be "snowed." Even at the investigative level, there needs to be some way to monitor and regulate the use of deception.

7.2.2 *Interrogatory deception*

Earlier I indicated a preference for talking of "phases" rather than "stages" of police work. This is because there is no simple transition or even progression from investigation through interrogation to sworn testimony. What I shall here call "interrogation" will be confined to custodial interrogation, though I suspect that the formal distinction between custodial and noncustodial interrogation is much too sharp to capture the variety of interrogatory environments that exists.[45] Even though a person who is in custody lacks control over the conditions of his interrogation (accepting, of course, that he may refuse to talk), those who are being noncustodially interrogated may also believe or feel that they are not completely free not to participate.

In some circles it has become popular to speak of an "interview" in preference to an "interrogation."[46] The intention is noble enough. The language of interview is "respectful," and the investigating officer is construed as a seeker of truth rather than as an accuser. But the characterization is too euphemistic. Although there may be some point to describing noncustodial interrogations as interviews, the use of "interview" to cover custodial interrogations mutes the essentially adversarial relationship that already operates in that situation. Once we recognize that a person is not to be taken into custody without "probable cause," the police will almost certainly interrogate with a view to confirming their suspicions rather than as part of some more neutral "search for truth." Indeed, the whole drift of the *Miranda* warning that "anything you say may be used in evidence against you" stresses that adversarial quality.

What distinguishes the investigative from the interrogatory phase, and what makes deception in the latter context problematic in a way that it is not in the former? Keeping in mind my earlier caveat about the gradual rather than sharp distinction between custodial and noncustodial interrogation, there would seem to be three linked differences that bear on the normative question.

1. The custodial situation is inherently coercive. The detained or arrested person is in custody, and may well feel threatened. He or she may be handcuffed, and the interrogating officer(s) may be armed. The manner of the interrogating officer(s) is likely to be unsettling. To exacerbate this advantage by means of deception may improperly favor the police. What is said to them may not be said *voluntarily.*

2. In custodial interrogation, the police have a decisive advantage over the arrested person. Within limits, they are able to control the terms under which the interrogation takes place: the physical conditions that operate, whom the person may consult, how long the interrogation will last, whether there will be opportunities for measured deliberation, and so on. Deception is a further weapon in their arsenal, and questions may be raised concerning the *fairness* of the interrogatory process.

3. The situation may undermine our confidence that we are discovering the *truth*. Because the interrogatory situation is inherently coercive, an innocent and timid person, unacquainted with or cowed by the interrogatory process, may react in ways that will be taken to imply guilt. Or a guilty person may be persuaded to confess to a more serious offense than the one he has actually committed. Deception may thus increase the likelihood of an innocent person being found guilty and the guilty being punished excessively.

Though linked, the three considerations are not identical. And the first and second are often regarded as being more fundamental in that they bear on the basic rights of suspects. Suspects do not lose their rights by virtue of their being suspects, and even if they are guilty they ought to be treated in ways that acknowledge their standing as moral agents. We need to ask: Would *this* person, whether innocent or guilty, with his/her specific psychological characteristics, and so on, and having no desire to confess, find the interrogation pressures overbearing?

However, those for whom crimefighting is what police work is about may choose to argue for the centrality of the third factor. Inbau and Reid, two "crime control" theorists and authors of a major textbook on police interrogation, have stated: "Although both 'fair' and 'unfair' interrogation practices are permissible, nothing shall be done or said to the subject that will be apt to make an innocent person confess."[47] Here the emphasis is on truth finding, and the need to reach the right conclusion. What constrains police interrogatory practices, for Inbau and Reid, is not their respect for the voluntariness of what is said in the interrogatory situation, but the need for reliability, the ability of interrogation to produce results that will not implicate the innocent. This "crime control" as against "due process" approach is both morally and legally problematic. For, as Welsh White puts it, the means of obtaining a confession should be "consistent with our accusatorial system of justice."[48] The onus is on the state to *demonstrate* guilt, as the outcome of a process of rational argument that establishes its conclusion beyond reasonable doubt. The state must therefore conduct itself in a manner that does not violate the defendant's right against self-incrimination, a right that is not waived if not voluntarily forgone.[49] It is true that one of the reasons for insisting upon voluntariness is the added assurance we have that any confession will reflect the actual guilt of the person who confesses. But that is not its sole or even primary raison d'être.

It was in line with the requirement of voluntariness and fairness that the so-called *Miranda* rules were established in 1966. These sought to ensure that confessions or other statements of an evidentiary nature were not obtained in violation of a suspect's right against self-incrimination and due process rights. They were to give the suspect a "continuous opportunity" to exercise that right.[50]

Several factors inform the *Miranda* decision: A person is innocent until proven guilty, it is for the state to establish guilt, and appropriate evidence is not provided by what has been coerced from the suspect or gained by fundamentally unfair means. And so the purpose of the *Miranda* rules is to create a bit of breathing space between the suspect and his / her accusers, to bring some equality into the relationship between the state and the arrested person.[51] Inbau and Reid, by their approval of "'unfair'" as well as "'fair'" interrogatory tactics, tend to subvert this basic requirement.

Legally, the *Miranda* protections rule out deception with respect to themselves; they represent a minimum for interrogatory contexts, exceptions to which would be legally unacceptable. This much is explicit in the *Miranda* decision itself: "[A]ny evidence that the accused was threatened, tricked or cajoled into a waiver will, of course, show that the defendant did not voluntarily waive his privilege."[52] But it does not automatically rule out all deception, and some interrogatory deception has been thought permissible. Those who have broken the law may be unwilling to confess to the fact even after they have been taken into custody. So long as they feel they have a chance of "getting away with it," they may continue to lie and dissemble, and there is an argument for trying to beat them at their own game.

So, the interrogating officers may engage in forms of deception that will fool the guilty into giving away more than they intended, or will convince them that they will not get away with what they have done. Various ploys are possible, some more acceptable than others. Most obviously, the arrested person can be lied to. The lies may concern the arrested person's rights, the quality of the evidence available to the police, the facts of the case, the real intentions of the investigator, and so on. But, in addition, information may be withheld from the suspect, half-truths may be told, the interrogatory situation may be structured so as to create a false sense of abandonment, or the manner of the investigators may display a false sense of "being in the know" (insinuation), or of power, or of friendship. No doubt there are other possibilities.

Obviously there are limits to the deception in which interrogating officers may engage. The deception must not be fundamentally unfair, or of a kind that will compromise the voluntariness of what is said or, secondarily, our reasons for being confident that what we believe was truthfully said was indeed truthfully said. That is why the *Miranda* privileges constitute a minimum, and why a person cannot be tricked into waiving his or her *Miranda* privileges. The latter, however, may not be all that uncommon. People in custody can be told that things will be easier if they waive their privileges; or the *Miranda* warnings can be read to them in a manner that interferes with their ability to appreciate what those rights amount to; or . . . [53] Law enforcement agents sometimes see *Miranda* as a hindrance to effective law enforcement.

But even if deception with respect to a person's *Miranda* privileges is legally outlawed, it would not automatically follow that such deception is also beyond the moral pale. It would be so only if we believed that there is an overriding moral obligation to do what is legally required. But that is likely to be too strong a claim. Not that laws ought to be broken with impunity or as a matter of convenience, for they are likely to embody more moral wisdom than we in our individual perceptions can boast, and there is always a further problem that arises when we turn what might sometimes be justified in an individual case into an institutionally recognized policy. As policy it may do more to endanger than to secure justice.

We need to ask about *Miranda*'s moral status, since it has not been without its critics.[54] We should not assume that because it represents the legal standard, it also embodies some unquestionable moral standard. Of course it may, up to a point. But it may also be too coarse. And subsequent case law has in fact sharpened its requirements in several ways.[55]

But leaving the problems with *Miranda* aside for the time being, what is allowable, once the *Miranda* rules have been observed? Is there any limit on the deceptive tactics that police may use? Suppose an arrested person waives his right to be silent and to have an attorney present. Can trickery be used to elicit a confession? The interrogation manuals respond with a clear "yes." In a post-*Miranda* edition of their book, Inbau and Reid state that "all but a very few of the interrogation tactics and techniques presented in our earlier publication are still valid if used after the recently prescribed warnings have been given to the suspect under interrogation, and after he has waived his self-incrimination privilege and his right to counsel."[56]

What controls should be placed on the use of deceptive tactics? The difficulties of spelling out general requirements might tempt us to operate on a case-by-case basis, to see whether, given the totality of circumstances, the arrested person was treated fairly and voluntarily yielded whatever information he/she gave. Welsh White, however, suggests that legal processes are not very well suited to establishing this. The fact-finding procedures are inadequate and the suspect will be placed at too much of a disadvantage. An alternative "objective" approach, which focused on particular tactics, and ruled some out as inadmissible, would circumvent this. However, White believes that this option might be too restrictive on police, since it would ignore the differing effect that different tactics have on different people. There are, moreover, variant uses of particular tactics, and what may be a problem with one use may not be a problem for another. So White suggests a via media, albeit one that is weighted in favor of due process expectations. He argues that certain techniques ought to be ruled out if their use on suspects would be such as to render it *likely* that any information elicited would have been extracted unfairly and involuntarily.[57] Among such problematic practices might be:

7.2.2.1 Deception about whether an interrogation is taking place.[58] In *Massiah*, the accused believed that the conversation he was having with his fellow accused was "private," and that the questions he was being asked to respond to were independent of the interrogatory situation. But unbeknown to him, his confederate had turned state's witness and was wired to record his responses. It was successfully claimed that this deception undermined

the accused's Sixth Amendment right to counsel. The police had taken unfair advantage of their position:

> Confinement of the suspect increases the power of the police in an important respect. Because the suspect's ability to select people with whom he can confide is completely within their control, the police have a unique opportunity to exploit the suspect's vulnerability. In short, the police can insure that if the pressures of confinement lead the suspect to confide in anyone, it will be a police agent. In view of the government's control over the suspect's channels of communication, it is blatantly unfair to allow the government to exploit the suspect's vulnerability by trickery of this type.[59]

Here it was the confinement that made all the difference. For in other cases where friends have "turned," the courts have been less sympathetic. In *Hoffa*, for example, Justice Stewart quoted approvingly from a dissenting opinion in *Lopez*: "The risk of being overheard by an eavesdropper or betrayed by an informer or deceived as to the identity of one with whom one deals is probably inherent in the conditions of human society. It is the kind of risk we necessarily assume whenever we speak."[60] But in *Massiah* the defendant's ability to confide in whom he would was severely circumscribed, and, so it was argued, he could not shoulder responsibility for the risk he took.[61]

7.2.2.2   Deception that distorts the meaning of the *Miranda* rules. Telling an accused person in the course of an interrogation that he no longer has a right to remain silent, or that his continued silence will be used as evidence against him, or by a new interrogator that his statements will not be used against him, and so on, will undercut the protection offered by the *Miranda* rules.[62] The rules are intended to ensure that certain minimum conditions are observed in the course of interrogation, and the foregoing ploys weaken those protections.

7.2.2.3   Deception that distorts the seriousness of the matter under investigation. A murder suspect may be informed that the victim is still alive, or that the offense with which he is being charged is not very serious, or that the victim was probably "asking for it." Alternatively, the seriousness of the offense may be magnified in the hope of prompting the suspect to confess to a lesser offense.[63] These ploys, designed to weaken the suspect's resistance to confessing, may also interfere with his ability to assess the desirability of continuing to assert his *Miranda* rights: "The effect of misrepresentation of the charge cannot be overestimated. If suspects ever engage in the type of rational deliberation implicit in a system that depends on warnings, it is a virtual certainty that their perception of the potential punishment will assume critical importance in deciding whether or not to confess."[64]

7.2.2.4   The assumption of nonadversarial roles by interrogating officers. In *Spano*, a police interrogator (Bruno), who was a childhood friend of the accused, falsely told the accused that unless he confessed he (the childhood friend) would lose his job and that this would be disastrous to his three children and pregnant wife.[65] In other cases, the interrogating officers have presented themselves as "father figures"[66] or religious counselors,[67] or have told the suspect that the murderer was not a criminal who deserved punishment but a person who needed medical care, and that he (the interrogator) would do all he could to help the suspect if he talked.[68]

The effect of taking a nonadversarial role, if manipulative enough, is to undermine the suspect's appreciation that what is said may be used in evidence *against* him or her. As the Court in *Miranda* put it, "[T]his warning may serve to make the individual more acutely aware that he is faced with a phase of the adversary system – that he is not in the presence of persons acting solely in his interest."[69]

7.2.2.5 **Tricks that take on the character of threats or promises.** Various deceptive possibilities are involved. The suspect may be placed in a lineup, and "identified" as the perpetrator of several more serious phony offenses. Or the suspect may be told that not confessing/confessing will have a bearing on the sentence.[70] A threat and promise may go together: It will be said that not confessing will lead to a heavier sentence, and confessing will lead to a lighter sentence.[71]

Included in such tricks is the "Mutt" and "Jeff" routine, in which one interrogator harangues and demeans the suspect, and the other offers sympathy; or in which one and the same officer moves between aggressive and fraternal roles. To what extent is the confession that may be elicited a function, not of Jeff's sympathetic treatment but of Mutt's threats and the desire to avoid them? Is it fair to accused persons that their honor and dignity as persons be called into question if they do not confess? Is this another version of the unacceptable practice of making suspects strip off their clothes? White believes so, though Abney argues that should the suspect feel too pressured by this form of interrogation, his *Miranda* right to silence may be asserted/reasserted.[72]

There may, of course, be some problem about characterizing a particular deceptive device as threatening or promissory, but the difficulties with deceptive practices that are threatening or promissory are clear enough. With false threats, the problem is that the voluntariness of the suspect's confession is called into question. With false promises, the suspect has been deprived of his ability to assess his situation and to determine whether or not it is worth his while to confess. In such circumstances, a fearful innocent may feel that there would be some value in "confessing." In each case it might be argued that "it is improper for the police to place a price tag on the right to remain silent in a context in which the bargain offered to the suspect is likely to prove illusory."[73]

7.2.2.6 **Repeated assurances that the suspect is known to be guilty.** This is much favored by Inbau and Reid: "Display an Air of Confidence in the

Subject's Guilt."[74] But although it is claimed that this technique will not induce an innocent suspect to confess guilt, this has sometimes been challenged: "When an individual finds himself disagreeing with the unanimous judgment of others regarding an unambiguous stimulus, he may yield to the majority even though this requires misreporting what he sees or believes."[75] Even though one would presume that the likely consequences of confession would have a strong countervailing effect on an innocent person, it is remarkable how manipulable people are, especially if they do not have their lives "together."[76] More often, a person might be persuaded into confessing to a more serious offense than to the one actually committed, say, second degree murder rather than manslaughter. Suspects do not necessarily have a fine sense of legal distinctions, and a suspect who actually feels guilty for what he has done may be susceptible to magnifying his offense.

7.2.2.7 The fabrication of evidence. A suspect may be confronted with manufactured "evidence" of his wrongdoing, thus misleading him with regard to the strength of the case against him. It might be asserted or implied that a partner has already confessed, even though that is not the case.[77] Or it might be claimed that he has been identified by an eyewitness, or that traces of his hair or blood, or his fingerprints, have been found at the crime scene. In *Cayward*, government investigators confronted a rape-murder suspect with fabricated investigative and laboratory reports, stating that his semen was found on the victim's underwear.[78] The court excluded the subsequent confession on the grounds of its unfairness to the suspect and the likelihood that "manufactured evidence," unlike mere "verbal assertions," was unduly coercive. The court also adverted to the possibility that a false *written* report might resurface at some later date, and for that reason its use should be discouraged.[79]

To this point, it has not been my purpose to question these suggestions for restrictions on interrogatory deception. They may be too severe. As White sees it, most of the foregoing illustrate the way in which *Miranda* might be applied even after waiver, and thus provide a way in which police uses of interrogatory deception may be limited. There are, however, very few bright lines here, and though some of the techniques sometimes subvert voluntariness, and some sometimes subvert the requirement of fairness, and some may sometimes subvert the cause of truth, there is no easy way of determining which techniques or which circumstances are likely to overstep the bounds of permissible deception. Perhaps the best we can do is to "flag" some techniques as problematic, leaving officers who use them vulnerable to challenge.

7.2.3 *Testimonial deception*[80]

Though there is reasonable latitude for police deception in the investigative sphere and some room for it during custodial interrogation, police deception in the giving of sworn testimony is seen as absolutely impermissible. In

Before Mapp. 67% found on person. In order to
adhere to ↑ only 16.5% were found on the
person where 83% was found dropped.

some forms, of course, it would constitute the crime of perjury; but even in
less explicit forms it seems to go contrary to the legal requirement that
witnesses tell "the truth, the whole truth, and nothing but the truth." Whatever the case in practice, there is little latitude here for any form of deception.

Yet it is well known that police have often engaged in testimonial deception. In one of the few empirical studies of police testimonial deception – a
series of comparisons of police reports before and after the Supreme Court's
1961 decision in *Mapp v. Ohio*,[81] – there was strong evidence that, in order to
comply with the constraints of *Mapp*, police regularly fabricated elements of
their testimony. The series focused on police reports of misdemeanor narcotics charges for the few months before and after the *Mapp* decision.[82] According to one replication, in 67 percent of 132 cases that came to court shortly
before *Mapp*, the narcotics were said to have been found hidden on the
defendant's person. In the remaining 33 percent of cases, the defendant was
said to have dropped the narcotics or thrown them to the ground. Of 97
cases prosecuted in a comparable period after *Mapp*, in only 16.5 percent of
cases was it claimed that narcotics had been found hidden on the person; in
the remaining 83.5 percent of cases it was asserted that the narcotics had
been dropped or thrown to the ground. Are we to explain this reversal by a
change in the practices of those in possession of narcotics, or is it more likely
that investigating officers, now aware of the constraints placed on them by
Mapp, tailored their testimony to conform to legal requirements?[83] "Dropsy"
testimony, as it came to be known, enabled law enforcement officers to
perpetuate some of the search and seizure practices that *Mapp* had outlawed.

Courtroom explanation for Mapp

Practices employed to search premises and seize incriminating items were
also affected by the *Mapp* decision. Entering closed and private premises
without permission or a warrant violates the Fourth Amendment protection
against unreasonable searches and also the right to privacy. Following *Mapp*,
investigating officers asserted with increasing frequency that they had simply happened by the premises in question, that the door was open or was
voluntarily opened to them, and that the incriminating evidence was in
"plain view." Though this was always possible, in many cases it was highly
unlikely. Evidence was being reconstructed to conform to legal requirements.[84]

Other forms for using deception

Other Supreme Court decisions made during the Warren years almost
certainly led to similar "accommodations." Subsequent to the *Miranda* decision, investigating officers would claim that confessing suspects had been
read their *Miranda* rights when in custody or that statements made without
the benefit of the *Miranda* warnings had been made noncustodially. Yet
those involved in the criminal justice process knew that on some occasions,
at least, such assertions were unlikely to be true or, if true, concealed deficiencies in implementation. However, establishing this without disadvantage to defendants was difficult, since suppression hearings would offer an
opportunity for damaging cross-examination, and so such breaches generally went unchallenged.[85]

Even though there is relatively little statistically structured empirical evidence that police engage in other forms of testimonial deception, there is a good deal of anecdotal evidence to suggest that police testimonial deception does not represent an occasional aberration. It would appear to occur quite commonly in sworn affidavits whereby police seek search warrants. In order to show probable cause, facts are created, reordered or inflated; sources are exaggerated; or nonexistent sources are cited.[86] In a recent, particularly tragic Boston case, after a police officer was killed during a drug raid, it turned out during preliminary hearings that a crucial informant mentioned in the search warrant did not exist. Murder charges against the alleged dealer had to be dropped, and two of the officers responsible for obtaining the warrant were convicted of perjury. During the trial, evidence was presented to the effect that "boilerplate" affidavits were common practice, since they provided a standardized formula for obtaining a search warrant with a minimum of judicial difficulty.

Other occasions for such deception occur when police plant evidence on a person whom they have other grounds for believing to be engaged in some form of criminal enterprise ("flaking"). Or they might increase the quantity of a drug found on a dealer ("padding"), to enable a felony charge to be laid rather than a simple misdemeanor, and so on.

Some of these deceptive practices are sufficiently well established for there to develop a specialized vocabulary round their use. That relating to testimonial deception in general is interesting, for it often draws on "cosmetic" analogies that indicate its deceptive character while downplaying its morally problematic status. Police who engage in testimonial deception are said to "fluff up,"[87] "firm up," "improve,"[88] "tidy up," or "shape"[89] the evidence, to "massage" their testimony, to "stretch" or "color" the truth or "shade" the facts. The Mollen Commission reported a new term of art: "testilying."[90]

Police officers who engage in testimonial deception may of course do so for a variety of reasons. Sometimes it may be to conceal criminal or negligent behavior, their own or that of other officers; or it may be to cover over their own or others' investigative incompetence. But it is not with these cases of testimonial deception that we are here concerned. A significant amount of police testimonial deception seems to be directed to the securing of serious and worthy ends – the control of crime, the conviction of those who are morally guilty, and social justice. It is not simply that the deception is directed to good ends, but police often take the view that what impedes their achievement of these ends and what necessitates their engagement in testimonial deception are deficiencies in the criminal justice system. They believe, therefore, that what they are doing is, in a broad sense, justifiable.

Consider a case in which police officers, investigating a drug-related murder, are led by slender threads of evidence to suspect the nightwatchman at a housing project. The project superintendent lets them into the watchman's "quarters," where, concealed behind a picture, they find a weapon that corresponds with the murder weapon. The suspect is arrested. As the case is being prepared, the prosecutor advises the police that their entry into the watchman's quarters *may* have been illegal, and, if so, the forensic evidence (their only strong evidence) will be inadmissible in court, resulting in the collapse of their case. The police decide to claim that through the window of the quarters they could see the butt of the weapon, and therefore had reasonable (and thus legal) grounds for entry. Justifiable testimonial deception?

The police who were involved in this case thought so. There are many similar cases, each of which rests on some of a variety of reasons that police use to justify what they do. Among those reasons are the following.

At the margins, though psychologically significant, there is an issue of morale. Police investigators are frequently expected to work long and hard under inhospitable conditions. The standards of proof required of the state, the procedural constraints under which police operate – particularly those relating to the Fourth and Fifth Amendment rights of suspects – and the hazards of "sharp" or "cunning" defense lawyers and unsympathetic judges mean that the odds are often felt to be stacked against them, threatening to bring a great deal of difficult work to nought. To have evidence excluded because of a "mere technicality" or a case lost because of "unreasonable" doubts sown in a jury's mind, can be very depressing for police. Job satisfaction, morale, and even the health of the law enforcement system may be felt to be at stake.

It is, of course, arguable that such demoralized reactions to failure in the courts are not justified. Their task has been to arrest, not to convict, and they can still take satisfaction in the fact that they have "done their part." Such a division, however, is in many ways a formal one, and police are bound to be affected if what they consider to be good work comes to nothing. The frustration may be intensified if the officer must later confront the person on the street. In some cases, particularly in detective divisions, promotion may be related to convictions obtained, and not simply to arrests. For convictions will be taken as an index of investigative skill. Losses in court, particularly if occasioned by factors beyond the officer's control, may therefore be particularly galling, and the temptation to inflate, reconstruct, or otherwise "improve" the evidence may be considerable.

Related to this frustration may be a more general frustration about the criminal justice system, particularly as it manifests itself in court proceedings. The Anglo-American judicial tradition is adversarial in nature. It is committed to the achievement of justice through the discovery of truth. To do this, it is structured so that the prosecution and defense may present before an impartial fact finder the strongest possible cases for their competing contentions, constrained by systemic rules that are designed to ensure equality of opportunity between the contenders and optimal conditions for fact finding. At least that is the theory. What police in fact encounter is rather different. For the major participants, justice seems at best a catch cry. Instead, winning is the name of the game. Contending lawyers are not interested in holding before the fact finder the most favorable construction of their client's case, so that the fact finder may be in a position to make an impartial assessment based on all the relevant data. Instead, they are verbal gladiators, determined to outflank and subdue their opposition, exploiting rather than abiding by the rules of combat. My impression in talking to police officers is that they have little respect for lawyers, and sometimes for judges, and that this assessment is often mutual. The police officer in court believes that he is in alien territory, where some are out to "get" him. The officer's obligations to the court are, therefore, qualified, and in the interests of a wider justice, to which the officer and victims are alone committed, testimonial deception is thought to be sometimes justified. It constitutes a strategic move in a game whose ends have become obscured.

Although the courtroom may be an alien environment for the police officer, it can be made easier by a friendly prosecutor. Police and prosecutors are often on the same side, and it can sometimes be as important to the prosecutor as it is to the police officer that a conviction is secured. If the case is at all important, an "aggressive" prosecutor may see it as a stepping stone to something else. For this reason, pressure or encouragement to engage in some form of testimonial deception may come from the prosecutor's office.[91]

The concern for justice may be formulated in a somewhat different way. As police easily see it, justice is not a processual abstraction, the outcome of set procedures, but the achievement of a just result in circumstances that police consider to be dispositive. Although procedural constraints have their place, they can also impede the achievement of a just result.[92] Many police officers, along with others who take a "crime control" approach to the criminal justice system, have felt that the exclusionary sanctions of *Mapp* and *Miranda* are too constraining on government agents, and that they impair the processes of justice (criminals being convicted). The exclusionary rules have been painted as criminally inspired and subversive of effective law enforcement.[93] In the light of opposition to the stringency of such rules, both their own and others', police may feel that the interests of justice will sometimes be served best by breach-and-concealment.

A further justificatory source for this willingness to engage in testimonial deception might be found in two general factors. First, the targets of their deception are often themselves deceivers and, it is felt, deserve no better from others. To use deception against them is only to play according to rules by which they themselves operate. In seeking to deceive the community, its officers, and the victims of their conduct, such people may be considered to have forfeited their right to truthfulness, and police may not feel too much compunction about "tidying up" or "tailoring" their testimony to meet constitutional requirements. They are, after all, not fabricating evidence against the innocent, but against those whom they have every reason to believe to be guilty – people who, generally, will have a history of lawbreaking.

Such an attitude fits comfortably into an environment where deception is otherwise available to police in the prosecution of their law enforcement activity. Jerome Skolnick notes how odd it appears that "the law permits the policeman to lie at the investigative stage, when he is not entirely convinced

that the suspect is a criminal, but forbids lying about *procedures* at the testimonial stage, when the policeman is certain of the accused's guilt."[94]

The idea that testimonial deception might be justified does not appear
that strange, given that deception can be justified in other circumstances.
Indeed, it would appear that the circumstances under which police are
generally willing to engage in testimonial deception are just those that
would normally justify the use of deception – the avoidance of evil and
production of social good. When police engage in testimonial deception, it
might be claimed, criminals get what they deserve, society is protected (for a
time, at least) from their predations, and an "ordered liberty" is secured.
Those who breach the community's rules with impunity are shown that they
may not benefit from it. We are reassured in the processes of an orderly
society.

Although these do not exhaust the arguments that might be advanced in
favor of limited testimonial deception, they constitute the major ones. Are
they strong enough to secure a niche for the practice?

It is doubtful whether they do. Although there may seem to be a simple
progression from investigative deception through interrogatory deception to
testimonial deception, there is, in fact, a radical shift. The police officer who
lies under oath is not deceiving the suspect but the court. And in deceiving
the court the officer is corrupting a system that respects persons by placing a
premium on rational processes of inquiry and judgment. The court represents our attempt to introduce equality and impartiality into the processes of
justice by making judgment depend on arguments presented to a fact finder
who must decide, in criminal cases, whether the truth has been established
beyond reasonable doubt. This latter requirement acknowledges the singular importance of the defendant's rights, lest state power be abused and
individuals be sacrificed to some larger good. The court and its procedures
are also an acknowledgement of the limitations attached to our individual
understanding and judgment and of the need for a multilayered structure of
investigation and inquiry, lest partisan concerns be reflected in determinations of guilt. The police officer who dissembles on the stand in the name of
social justice or even the victim's rights has failed to appreciate that what he
or she considers to be procedural impediments to successful conviction are
more appropriately seen as attempts to acknowledge the rights that should
be accorded every citizen within a free society.

Officers who, on the basis of their own certainty that a defendant is guilty,
seek to manipulate the court's consideration of the evidence, take it upon
themselves to deny what the whole criminal justice process is intended to
assert, namely, that as individuals we are not well positioned to pass judgment without a process of open public scrutiny. This is not to deny that an
officer will ever have a better fix on the facts than the court will be able to
achieve. The point is that, if testimonial deception is accepted as a practice in
cases where officers sincerely believe that the cause of justice will be better
served by testimonial deception, that very cause is likely to suffer. Further,
and of crucial importance in this case, if deception is permitted at this stage

of the proceedings, there will be very little control over its use. The very nature of the activity, its secrecy, puts it beyond easy surveillance. In contrast to deception at the investigative and interrogatory spheres, whose legitimacy may be tested in court, if, at the point of closure – the court – deception is permitted, it will not be open to scrutiny. In other words, permitting deception in the testimonial sphere would subvert the very institution by means of which we are able to monitor its use during the investigative and interrogatory phases of police work.

Of course, this still leaves us with the problem of police frustration, the aggravation of seeing undoubted offenders avoid the judgment of law. One response is simply to deny the relevance of police frustration – to say, if you like, that if police cannot do their job well enough to secure convictions, that is no reason to cook the books. But this does not take sufficient account of the inadequacies of the criminal justice system and, perhaps, of the constraints under which police have to work. Testimonial deception, however, does not constitute an adequate response to its deficiencies. Unlike civil disobedience, which constitutes a legitimate form of protest in a liberal society, testimonial deception represents at best a secret protest. Generally, police resolutely deny that they engage in it.

In suggesting that police do not have any adequate justification for testimonial deception, I do not want to be taken to be endorsing an absolute principle. It is, of course, possible that a system will become so corrupt that testimonial deception becomes a serious option. An officer whose testimony would consign a Jew to a death camp or return an escaped slave to servitude might reasonably reconsider his or her compliance with the requirements of truthful testimony. But such cases, at least in a society characterized by reasonable freedoms, are likely to be extremely rare.

It is the secrecy of testimonial deception that is at the heart of the problem. If it is the generally shared opinion of police officers that the adversarial system has become, if not a charade, then an unruly ball game, and that deception is the only way to play, this is something they need to bring to the attention of the public that expects them to "deliver." That they can hardly do if the pressures for and incidence of testimonial deception are underplayed or denied. And if the exclusionary rules make unrealistic demands of police officers, crippling their investigative work, then a public that has supported those rules needs to be made aware of the costs it must pay to keep them in place. It may be prepared to pay those costs. "Due process" theorists will probably be willing to accept them. But if it is not, as is the case with some "crime control" theorists, then it should enter into dialogue with the police about suitable modifications or alternatives. That discussion cannot take place as long as police continue to engage in testimonial deception, and then seek to deceive the public about its occurrence.

Chapter 8

Entrapment

And the woman said, "The serpent beguiled me and I did eat."

Genesis 3:13

Human nature is weak enough and sufficiently beset by temptations without government adding to them and generating crime.

Justice Felix Frankfurter[1]

Keith Jacobson, a middle-aged bachelor, lived with and looked after his parents in a small Midwestern rural town, where he drove a school bus. In February 1984 Jacobson made a mail-order purchase of two nudist magazines, *Bare Boys I & II* and an advertising brochure, from Electric Moon, a Californian distributor of pornographic materials. At the time he purchased these materials, it may have been legal for him to do so. Soon after, however, the laws relating to the distribution of child pornography through the mails were tightened up. Federal agents raided Electric Moon, and, using a mailing list they found, commenced a sting operation against people whom they suspected might be violating the laws relating to pedophilia and child pornography. In Keith Jacobson's case, the sting operation consisted of five separate ventures, engaged in over a period of almost two and a half years, and involving eleven "approaches." In the first of these ventures, a letter and invitation was sent from an organization calling itself the "American Hedonist Society." The AHS purported to be ideologically committed to pleasure and happiness as the sole goods in life. A survey and membership application were enclosed, along with advertisements. Jacobson filled out a membership, and indicated his interest in materials depicting preteen sex. But despite quarterly newsletters, he ordered nothing. This was followed by an approach from an organization calling itself "Midlands Data Research," canvassing attitudes on sexuality, particularly those relating to preteen sex. Jacobson again expressed interest in receiving information, but he did not answer the survey. A follow-up questionnaire and letter were sent. A third operation involved an approach from the "Heartland Institute for a New

151

Tomorrow," which claimed to be a lobbying organization founded to promote and protect sexual freedom of choice. It urged Jacobson to participate
in the MDR survey. He completed a HINT questionnaire, however, and later
received a letter and list from the HINT Director, encouraging him to write
to those with similar "backgrounds and interests." Although Jacobson failed
to respond, he received a pen-pal letter from an undercover postal inspector,
"Carl Long," in which Long indicated his own proclivities, and sought to
know Jacobson's. Although Jacobson indicated a sexual interest in adoles-
cent males, he did not seek to obtain materials through Long, and failed to
respond to Long's third letter. The final two operations involved the mailing
of catalogues to Jacobson, one from "Far Eastern Trading Co.," purportedly
based in Hong Kong, the other from "Produit Outaouais," supposedly based
in Quebec. Jacobson was assured that any materials that were sent would
not run foul of customs. Eventually Jacobson succumbed, and ordered one
magazine, *Boys Who Love Boys.*

After picking up the package from the post office, Jacobson was confronted by postal inspectors at his house. A subsequent search of the house
revealed no other pornographic materials. He was charged with receiving
prohibited materials through the mails, convicted, and sentenced to two
years' imprisonment. He appealed to the Eighth Circuit Appeals Court,
claiming entrapment, but the appeal was rejected.[2] The Supreme Court
granted certiorari, and in April 1992, in a 5–4 decision, upheld Jacobson's
claim and overturned his conviction.[3]

In the United States, entrapment constitutes a legal limit on the government's use of deception in investigation. It is a defense that, if established,
will result in the acquittal of a person charged with a criminal offense. But, as
the split decision in *Jacobson* shows, and the previous history of such decisions confirms, it has not always been clear what makes for entrapment or
why it ought to function as a defense.

Broadly speaking, entrapment occurs when an agent of government
(most usually, but not always, a police officer) initiates a course of action that
induces an otherwise innocent person to commit a crime in order that the
government may then prosecute. However, as will become clear, whereas
for some jurists the emphasis is to be placed on the "inducement" and its
subjective antecedents, for others the emphasis is to be placed on the "creative" conduct of the government agent.

With the revealing exception of *Jacobson*, most judicial discussions of entrapment, including those that have taken place in the U.S. Supreme Court,
have involved the clash of what are usually referred to as "subjective" and
"objective" approaches. The former has generally appealed to conservative
"crime control" members of the Court, the latter to its more liberal "due
process" members. The Court has consistently favored the subjective approach, a factor that was undoubtedly influential in shaping the somewhat
unexpected course of argument in the *Jacobson* case.[4] I shall look at each of
these approaches in turn – their strengths and weaknesses – before considering *Jacobson* and then offering an alternative of my own.

8.1 THE SUBJECTIVE APPROACH

In *United States v. Russell,* (then) Justice Rehnquist argued that the defense of entrapment can be made out "only when the Government's deception actually implants the criminal design in the mind of the defendant."[5] His words echoed those from an earlier Supreme Court decision in which Chief Justice Hughes had argued that the defense can be sustained "when the criminal design originates with the officials of the Government, and they implant in the mind of an innocent person the disposition to commit the alleged offense and induce its commission in order that they may prosecute."[6] In this approach, the primary emphasis is on the defendant's mental state, on whether or not, prior to the inducements offered by state officials, the defendant was *disposed* to commit a crime of the particular type with which he/she is now charged.

Informing the subjective approach is a desire to protect innocent defendants. The purpose of the defense, according to Chief Justice Warren, is to draw a line "between the trap for the unwary innocent and the trap for the unwary criminal."[7] Where the "disposition" to commit the alleged offense has been "implanted" in the mind of an "innocent" person, the line separating permissible deception and entrapment has been crossed. The defendant is no longer culpable.

But what is involved in "implanting," such that it should diminish culpability? Consider the following cases:

1. Abel would be averse to committing an *x*-type crime. However, Agent Baker plays on Abel's sympathies and persuades him to commit an *x*-type crime.
2. Abel has not considered the commission of an *x*-type crime, though would contemplate the possibility should the occasion arise. Agent Baker presents Abel with the opportunity to commit an *x*-type crime and persuades him to do so.
3. Abel has an inclination or disposition to commit an *x*-type crime, but has not formed any specific intention to commit one. Agent Baker gives Abel the opportunity and encouragement to commit an *x*-type crime. Abel responds affirmatively.
4. Abel intends to commit an *x*-type crime, and needs only the opportunity to do it. Agent Baker makes it possible for Abel to commit the crime in question.

According to the theory (though not always the practice) behind the subjective approach, the defense of entrapment can be made out in cases (1) and possibly in (2), but not in (3) or (4).[8] For in cases (1) and (2), but not in cases (3) and (4), the intention has been implanted in Abel's mind. Even though, in case (3), the intention is still general rather than specific, it is claimed that Baker does no more than provide the water that will determine whether or not the seeds of criminal conduct are already there.

However, if the issue is one of *culpability* for the *x*-type crime, isn't Abel just as culpable in cases (1) and (2) as in cases (3) and (4)? Suppose, in cases (1) and (2), that Baker had been a private citizen rather than a government agent. Then Abel could not claim in his defense that Baker had implanted the intention in his mind, rendering him nonculpable. At the very most what Baker had done would be a mitigating factor. This is why Eve's remark about the beguiling serpent carries no weight. The fact that her eating of the forbidden fruit was not previously contemplated and in fact was resisted is no excuse or defense. So the issue in entrapment does not seem to be a simple one of lack of culpability. Why should the fact that Baker is a government agent make all the difference? This the subjective approach fails to explain.

It is the failure of the subjective approach to provide a sufficient explanation of why the entrapment defense is acceptable that has led some proponents of the defense to favor the so-called objective approach. The California Supreme Court put the point as follows: "[We] are not concerned with who first conceived or who willingly, reluctantly acquiesced in a criminal project. What we do care about is how much and what manner of persuasion, pressure and cajoling are brought to bear by law enforcement officials to induce persons to commit crime."[9] Such, too, was the concern of Justice Frankfurter in the remark quoted at the beginning of this chapter. Granted, Abel may be as culpable in cases (1) and (2) as in the other cases, but the government, in entrapping him, is argued to have acted improperly.

8.2   THE OBJECTIVE APPROACH

In contrast to the subjective approach, the objective one focuses on the character of the state's involvement in the commission of the offense with which the defendant is charged: "The question is whether – regardless of the predisposition to crime of the particular defendant involved – the governmental agents have acted in such a way as is likely to instigate or create a criminal offense."[10] Or, again in the words of Justice Frankfurter, the question "is whether the police conduct revealed in the particular case falls below standards, to which common feelings respond, for the proper use of governmental power."[11]

This concern with governmental conduct has manifested itself in a number of different ways. In *Sorrells* and *Sherman*, a major issue – for the objective approach – was whether excessive persuasion had been used to induce the defendants to commit the crime. *Sorrells* was a Prohibition era case. The government agent, thinking that *Sorrells* might have been involved with bootleg liquor, introduced himself as an old buddy, and used his status to badger an initially reluctant Sorrells into obtaining some illicit liquor. In *Sherman*, the defendant, a recovering drug addict, was approached by another addict who confessed to difficulties in staying "clean." Drawing on Sherman's sympathies, he eventually persuaded Sherman to procure a small quantity of drugs for him. As the objectivists saw it, the problem in these cases was not – as it is in the subjective approach – with whether or not the persuasion was excessive in relation to the particular defendant, but with whether or not, in relation to some "objective" standard, it was excessive. As the California Supreme Court had posed the question: "Was the conduct of the law enforcement agent likely to induce a normally law-abiding person to commit the offense?"[12]

In *Russell* and *Hampton*, however, what seems to have been at issue – for objectivists – was the fact that the government had supplied something that was said to be essential to the commission of that kind of crime. In *Russell*, the defendants were already involved in the manufacture of illegal drugs. One of the necessary, though legal, ingredients was very difficult to obtain. They were approached by a government agent who offered to become their supplier for that ingredient, and they accepted his offer. The factual situation in *Hampton* was unclear, though it appears that here a government agent supplied the illegal substance that Hampton subsequently sold to another agent. In these cases it was acknowledged that the defendant may have been predisposed to commit a crime of the kind charged, but the objectivists claimed that its translation into reality depended crucially on the initiative and resources of government agents. "Federal agents play a debased role when they become the instigators of the crime, or partners in its commission, or the creative brain behind the illegal scheme."[13]

In all cases there appears to have been a further, supervenient, point of concern, namely, that in acting as it did the government operated in an *unseemly* manner. Not only had the government acted in a determinative and unfair manner, but in doing so it had also transgressed the bounds of decency. This is strongly suggested in many of Justice Frankfurter's remarks, but also in those of others.[14]

But if the subjective approach's terminology of "implanting" was problematic, the objective approach's talk of government's acting so as to "create" crime is no less so. For in what sense does the government "create" the crime in entrapment that it does not do when it uses decoys, stings, and other methods of undercover "detection"? Or, perhaps more radically, should government agents seriously reconsider the employment of decoys and stings? There are three, ultimately unsatisfactory, ways in which talk of government creating crime may be understood:

1. On one understanding of the charge, the government agent is claimed to have been the crime's sine qua non. Had it not been for the government agent's involvement, the prohibited conduct would (almost certainly) not have occurred. That, at least, is how some of the reasoning in *Russell* and *Hampton* reads. But if that is the contention, it is much too strong, for it would follow that in any case where the crime would not have occurred but for the government's involvement, a defense of entrapment would be sustainable. Not only would it rule out entrapment, but also many other practices in which the government seeks to divert the attention of criminals from innocent targets to waiting government agents. Although there is certainly a case for arguing that decoy and sting operations have often been badly

planned, to the detriment of innocent citizens, it is implausible to claim that every case in which the act of a government agent was a sine qua non of criminal activity is also an appropriate occasion for claiming that entrapment took place.

2. On another understanding, the claim is simply that the government agent has made the crime "easier." But this now seems too weak. If a defendant wants to manufacture counterfeit money, and the government agent helps by suggesting where a printing press can be bought, is the agent acting improperly? The argument, albeit questionable, in *Sorrells* was that the government did not make the crime easier to commit, but that there was reasonable doubt that it would have been committed had it not been for the government agent's involvement. Perhaps the only situation in which the government's making the crime easier would reflect badly would be if, when the government agent created the opportunity, he/she brought about the formation of a specific intent where none previously existed. But the objective approach eschews any direct concern with the defendant's specific intent.

3. A middle way can be plotted between (1) and (2). It might be claimed that when the government has played "the major part" in a crime's occurrence, then a defense of entrapment might be brought. However, it is difficult to know how one could determine whether entrapment has occurred without taking into account the so-called subjective factors that play a central role in the subjective approach. But since the objective approach explicitly excludes from consideration the mental state of the individual concerned, it is to be wondered whether it is seriously concerned with the issue of "creation" (that is, causation), or rather with something else. Sometimes it seems from the assertions of objectivist judges that the latter is the case.

Historically, the subjective approach has fared much better than the objective approach. By "fared better," I do not mean "had the better of the argument." The claim is about numbers rather than about quality of argument. Both approaches have their weaknesses, and seem to be expressive of more fundamental differences of standpoint than differences that are particular to the issue of entrapment.

8.3 THE JACOBSON REVERSAL

By the time *Jacobson* came up for review, the Supreme Court had already set a very firm precedent: On the four occasions on which it had considered the issue of entrapment it had favored the subjective approach. In the face of such a well-established precedent – and in view of what appeared to be an increasingly conservative Court – those members who might have been expected to favor an objective approach could not have been expected to carry the day.

But they did. And they did so by outflanking the more conservative members of the Court. Instead of challenging the premises of the subjective approach, they "commandeered it," interpreting it in a way that, in effect, gave voice to the concerns that had previously been expressed via the objective approach. The majority opinion was written by Justice White, with the concurrence of Justices Blackmun, Stevens, Souter, and Thomas. The dissenting opinion was written by Justice O'Connor, with the full concurrence of Chief Justice Rehnquist and Justice Kennedy, and the partial concurrence of Justice Scalia. What had previously been reasonably predictable coalitions were here broken up.

Where does this leave us with entrapment? Legally, the subjective approach has won out; but it has won out by recasting *disposition* in a way that enables the Court to draw upon what in Jacobson's case was clearly thought to be the overly intrusive hand of the government agents. The government agents should have been satisfied that Jacobson did not have the relevant disposition early on in the piece, and should have desisted from further approaches.

This crossing over is not really surprising. For, despite the rhetoric of clearly defined and opposing positions, it has not been uncommon for subjectivists to slip into objectivist language and for objectivists to draw on subjectivist concerns. Defenders of the subjective approach have argued that when the criminal design originates with the officials of the government, then "stealth and strategy become as objectionable police methods as the coerced confession and the unlawful search."[15] And defenders of the objective approach are willing to characterize entrapment as "the conception and planning of an offense by an officer, and his procurement of its commission by one who would not have perpetrated it except for the trickery, persuasion or fraud of the officer,"[16] in which implanting the crime in the mind of the defendant is clearly implied. This is not to deny any difference between the two approaches. There is certainly a difference in emphasis, for it is suggested by supporters of the objective approach and denied by supporters of the subjective approach that the conduct of the government agents is sufficiently egregious to violate the defendant's due process rights.

Nevertheless, the tendency for members of the opposing sides to draw on each others' reasons should make us suspicious of the categories into which the debate had been cast. This was manifest in *Jacobson*, which preserved the split, but not the categories in which it had been traditionally expressed.

Significantly, none of the Justices sought to articulate the entrapment defense in traditional objective terms. The weight of precedent had more or less settled that issue. They focused instead on Jacobson's predisposition. Speaking for the majority, Justice White argued that it was necessary to show that the predisposition antedated the government's solicitations. This, he claimed, could not be shown: Willingness to purchase a sexually explicit magazine while it was still legal could not be used to establish a predisposition to purchase such materials once they had been made illegal. It was strongly suggested that Jacobson's subsequent decision to order the materials came about only as the result of the underhanded tactics used by government agents – persistent solicitation, casting the issue of purchase as a vote for free speech and against oppressive government, assertion of the right to protest, and so on. Speaking for the dissent, Justice O'Connor argued that the majority had redefined "predisposition": "Not only must the Government show that a defendant was predisposed to engage in illegal conduct, . . . but also that the defendant was predisposed to break the law knowingly in order to do so." She therefore sees as "the crux of the Court's concern . . . that the Government went too far and 'abused' the 'processes of detection and enforcement' by luring an innocent person to violate the law."[17]

8.4   AN ALTERNATIVE APPROACH

It appears to me that casting the issue as one about whether the person was predisposed or whether the government acted in an underhanded manner has obscured a more significant consideration, one having to do with the epistemic basis that the government has for claiming that a defendant would have been involved in a crime of the kind for which it has sought to convict him.

Note first that proponents of both approaches hold that it is unacceptable for governments to operate in a manner that will induce defendants into committing crimes of a kind that they would not otherwise have committed. It is only when the defendants are charged with offenses of a type that they would have committed without the government's involvement that the government does not overreach itself.[18] It is from this shared starting point that the approaches differ. Subjectivists have held that the government has not behaved unacceptably if the person was predisposed to commit a crime of the particular type. Objectivists, on the other hand, have claimed that if the government has played too substantial a role in the crime's creation, then the bounds of acceptability will have been crossed.

I believe that we may do better if we do not focus exclusively on whether this or that responsibility-establishing or responsibility-defeating factor is present, but rather on the epistemic question of whether the situation has been such as to enable us to tell if the defendant would have acted in some such way had the government not been involved in the way it was. Sometimes the government's involvement *bulks so large* that we may no longer be able to have the requisite confidence that, absent its involvement, the individual concerned would have committed an offense of the kind in question. When that is so, I would suggest, the defense of entrapment should be available to the defendant.

My claim, then, is that what makes for entrapment is the government's involvement in criminal activity in a manner that *either* draws into it those who manifestly would not otherwise have engaged in conduct of that kind *or* leaves it unclear whether those who engaged in it would have otherwise engaged in conduct of that kind. In either case the defendant's conduct will not meet the evidentiary standards required to establish criminal guilt.

If we adopt this approach we can also accommodate the particular factors that gave the traditional approaches their appeal. The fact that a defendant was not, in some reasonably full-bodied sense, predisposed to criminal conduct of the kind charged will constitute a strong reason for believing that entrapment occurred. For it provides a fairly clear indication that without the government's involvement the defendant would not have engaged in that kind of criminal activity. This is the burden of the subjective approach. But even if the defendant was predisposed to engage in criminal conduct of the kind charged, a defense of entrapment may be available. For the government's involvement may bulk so large that it is no longer possible to tell, from the defendant's participation, whether he/she would have actually engaged in conduct of that kind. In recognizing this, we acknowledge a point emphasized by objectivists – the excessive involvement of government in the creation of crime.

8.4.1 *Some objections*

Admittedly, the way in which I have sought to accommodate the entrapment defense does not dispose of all the problems that have dogged the debate between subjectivists and objectivists. And it might not yield exactly the same legal solutions.[19] There are several standard objections – relics of that debate – that still need to be addressed.

1. Any approach that does give some weight to the matter of prior disposition might seem to work unfairly against prior offenders. For, will not the fact that they have offended in the past be used as evidence that in the current case they were disposed to criminal activity? This, at least, is what Justice Frankfurter claimed. An objectivist, he asserted that:

> Permissible police activity does not vary according to the particular defendant concerned; surely if two suspects have been solicited at the same time in the same manner, one should not go to jail simply because he has been convicted before and is said to have a criminal disposition. . . . [This] runs afoul of fundamental principles of equality under law, and would espouse the notion that when dealing with the criminal classes anything goes.[20]

Justice Stewart leveled a similar criticism when he claimed that the subjective approach

> allows the prosecution, in offering such proof [of disposition], to rely on the defendant's bad reputation or past criminal activities, including even rumored activities of which the prosecution may have insufficient evidence to obtain an indictment, and to present the agent's suspicions as to why they chose to tempt this defendant. This sort of evidence is not only unreliable, as the hearsay rule recognizes; but it is also highly prejudicial, especially if the matter is submitted to the jury.[21]

However, in pointing to the role of bad reputation, Justice Stewart seems to confuse two considerations: (1) what may be appealed to in decisions about whom to target for an undercover investigation; and (2) what can be taken in court to be sufficient evidence of a disposition to commit the crime with which the defendant is charged. With regard to (1), a bad reputation may have some relevance to targeting decisions.[22] But with regard to (2), which is where the entrapment defense becomes relevant, we may well argue that the hearsay rule should apply. Appeals to a bad reputation will not be good enough.

Does the appeal to a past criminal record do any better? The question to ask here is whether a previous criminal record constitutes appropriate evidence for a disposition to commit the crime with which the defendant is charged. I do not think so, but believe that both Stewart and Frankfurter overplay what is really only an abuse of the subjective account of predisposition. For one thing, the prior criminal activity may not have been of the same kind as that with which the defendant is now charged. We can hardly assume that if the defendant has manifested a past disposition to commit *y*-type crimes, he/she has a present disposition to commit *x*-type crimes. And even if the type of crime was similar, the past conduct at most provides a defeasible presumption of a *present* disposition. This indeed has been emphasized by defenders of the subjective account. For example, in *Russell*, Chief Justice Warren (a subjectivist) argued that a defendant's past record on identical and related offenses was not sufficient to establish that he/she was "ready and willing" to commit the offense with which he/she was being currently charged.[23]

2. In focusing on the evidentiary value of what the defendant did, I have, in contrast to the weight of tradition, eschewed the sufficiency of disposition. Shouldn't disposition be considered sufficient? This appeared to be the case in *Russell*, where Russell and his codefendants had sought to obtain from the agent an ingredient necessary to the manufacture of an illegal drug. The Supreme Court upheld their conviction. Surely no more was necessary.

I have questioned the sufficiency of disposition, and in fact I do not even believe that *Russell* stands as a counterexample. For one of the things that the majority was concerned to argue in that case was that even though the ingredient was difficult to get, the government agent only made it easier to obtain. There was evidence that Russell and his accomplices had already obtained some quantities of the chemical from other sources. In keeping with the spirit of that judgment, I have claimed that not only must the defendant be subjectively disposed to commit an offense of that kind, but also that, in relation to the particular offense for which he is charged, the circumstances of his involvement must be such as to provide sufficient evidence that the defendant would have actually committed a crime of that kind.[24]

3. It might appear that my epistemic approach diverts attention from the egregiousness of the police conduct in many of the cases in which entrapment is involved. It is, surely, one of the seemingly strong points of the objective approach that it focuses on the character of police conduct. It draws attention to the fact that the police sometimes engage in undercover tactics

that, however successful, are in themselves too offensive to be acceptable within a civilized society. Not only is this practically ignored by the subjective approach, but also by my own account. Where, for example, the police grossly abuse an intimate relationship, it might be thought that a defense of entrapment would be appropriate and that any evidence should be excluded.

I am sympathetic to this complaint, though I can also understand the view of traditional subjectivists that the police tactics have generally fallen short of what objectivists have wanted to establish – a "due process" defense. The tactics have not always been so unfair or shocking as to give plausibility to or to provide a constitutional backing for the defense. Nevertheless, the tactics sometimes employed are outrageous and abhorrent, and it would seem to be appropriate that there be some way of registering this. My view is that the entrapment defense is not the appropriate vehicle for this. There should be a separate Fourteenth Amendment violation that can be charged along with or instead of a claim of entrapment.[25] The entrapment defense is probably best left as is – as a defense that challenges the connection between the defendant's involvement in a particular x-type crime and the claim that the defendant would anyway have committed a crime of that type. The claim that certain government activities are in themselves improper should, I believe, be addressed as a separate issue, perhaps as a violation of due process.

However it is addressed, the issue of abhorrent government conduct is problematic. At what point does government conduct go beyond the pale? Does it vary with the kind of offense?[26] Some objectivists have argued that it becomes unacceptable when it is of a kind that would be sufficient to induce the average, normally law-abiding citizen to commit a crime. But this may be to pitch the limits too low, especially if it can be argued that more can be demanded of those in positions of great trust and responsibility than can be expected of the average, normally law-abiding citizen. A reasonable flexibility may be needed, not only to take account of the differing expectations we have of people, but also to avoid a situation in which the only criminals caught are the inexperienced.

Maybe the test suggested by Gerald Dworkin offers a way forward. The criminal law, he argues, is not a pricing system that is indifferent to the choices made by citizens – whether they obey or choose instead to disobey and pay the penalty. It is meant to be obeyed. Government goes too far when its actions have the effect of saying, not "Do not do x," but "Do x." When it does the latter, it not only violates the telos of the criminal law, but also deals unfairly with citizens. It becomes a tester of virtue rather than a detector of crime.[27]

The position I have argued for is that when people are entrapped we lack an evidentiary basis for thinking of them as criminals. Entrapment involves a structuring of circumstances such that the outcome possesses questionable evidentiary value. But doesn't this serve only to evacuate entrapment of all its pejorative overtones? Consider, for example, Justice Frankfurter's powerful but moralistic claim that: "The power of government is abused and directed to an end for which it was not constituted when employed to promote rather than detect crime and bring about the downfall of those who, left to themselves, might well have obeyed the law."[28] I am not unsympathetic to this claim, but believe that it overstates the objection to entrapment. What is a common concomitant of entrapment is elevated into its essence. Sometimes the effect of entrapment will be that crimes are committed that would not otherwise have occurred. And when government acts to prosecute acts of a kind that would not have occurred but for its scheming, it has abused its considerable powers. But it will not always have engaged in the abusive and ignoble conduct that concerns Frankfurter, for it will almost certainly sometimes be the case that an entrapped person would have committed – and maybe has already committed – a crime of the kind that he was set up to do. The problem with entrapment is that it leaves us without a proper basis for knowing whether that would have been so.

Behind Frankfurter's moralism there lies the earlier point that government, in conducting itself in a certain way, offends the standards of decent behavior. And that, I have suggested, is an issue distinct from that of entrapment. My point has not been to deny that in entrapment the government may be left with the stain of crime on its own hands, but to deny that this is what makes entrapment a proper defense. What makes it a proper defense is its evidentiary bankruptcy.

Chapter 9

Gratuities and corruption

Surely shoveling society's shit is worth something.

Police officer[1]

Don't take a dim view of criminals. *Remember, society's shit is your bread and butter.*

Nicholas Ross[2]

Corruption in police work has been a *pervasive* and *continuing* problem. Almost every serious history of policing and even of particular police departments has had to confront the issue of police corruptibility. Only the smallest and most vigilant departments have escaped its wasting effects. Corruption has been more virulent, visible and deep-rooted at some times and in some jurisdictions than at other times and in other jurisdictions. Large urban departments are more prone to corruption than most, though even in small communities police may be just as deeply corrupted. When, from time to time, police corruption has been uncovered, police spokespeople have usually been quick to speak of the rotten apple in every barrel. But it is clear that the corruption has often been much more extensive, claiming not simply lower-ranked officers, or officers on patrol, but involving officers of almost every rank in a network of intrigue, or at least disregard. Indeed, corruption is as much a top-down as a bottom-up problem.

Corruption is also a *serious* problem in police work. This is not only because it violates the ethical norms governing that work, but also because it impairs the ability of police to carry out their work successfully. Corruption is damaging to credibility, and police work, to be effective, needs the confidence and cooperation of the citizenry. It is not only external credibility that is damaged. The internal ethos of the organization is affected: "The officer who routinely profits by exploiting narcotics addicts and peddlers is not likely to take seriously a request to act with greater respect for minority interests and individual rights."[3] And as Frank Serpico noted, some of the corrupt officers with whom he was associated were first-class investigators,

163

and would have been highly effective as law enforcement officers had they not spent much of their time pursuing graft.[4]

Although corruption is by no means exclusive to police work, and the extent of police corruption is to some degree an index of wider civic corruption, there are, nevertheless, several factors that have made police work particularly vulnerable to corrupt practices:

1. In their law enforcement role, police are brought into contact with law-breakers who have an interest in police not doing what they have a duty to do. As possessors of considerable discretionary authority, authority that is not closely supervised, police have significant opportunities to succumb to temptation and pressures. Since those most interested in corrupting police may be people who have little to lose and much to gain from bribery and illegality, and may also be people who have access to substantial benefits and influence, the temptations and pressures may be considerable.

2. Police officers are regularly brought into contact with a side of life that inclines them to moral cynicism. Not only the obviously disreputable, but also many reputable citizens are seen to be corrupt – and corrupting. Police management too may be seen to be, if not corrupt, at least hypocritical. Corruption can come to be seen as a game in which everyone is out to get a larger share. To a certain extent, line officers may even be encouraged to participate. Why should we then expect them to be different? This may be reinforced by what are seen as the unpleasant features of the job. As this chapter's epigraphs suggest, minor corruption can be seen as compensation or even reward for some of "the Job's" more unpleasant, social sanitation dimensions.

3. Many kinds of minor corruption are tacitly encouraged by the wider community. Commercial establishments often have an interest in maximizing police presence or optimizing police service, and so inducements will be offered in the hope that they will be beneficiaries.[5] Many private individuals may also have interests that conduce to corruption. As frequent violators of traffic or parking laws, they will desire to be treated more leniently than would be justified by the facts of the case. They are likely to want a certain degree of openness to deviation.[6] In such cases there will generally be no complainant.

4. Police have frequently been unwilling to admit to significant corruption within their ranks. This has disabled them from confronting it openly and dealing with it head-on. Much corruption has gone undeclared and uninvestigated, because people have taken the view that reporting it will get you nowhere. Many have little faith in internal inquiries. As far as large-scale corruption is concerned, it has not usually been until the media have made an issue of it that it has been exposed. Even police management have not wanted to reveal known corruption, lest the media sensationalize it and create problems for the department's image.

9.1 CHARACTERIZING CORRUPTION

What is involved in corruption? The question is not a simple one. Not only is there disagreement about the nature of corruption, but there is also disagreement about the corruptness or otherwise of particular police practices. What one police officer sees as corrupt, another may consider legitimate. So, while there may be obvious cases of police corruption, from which we can distill a rough sense of its character, the fine-tuning process is made problematic by disagreements about the status of particular practices.

How might we define "corruption" as it pertains to police work? The following three accounts are fairly representative. According to McMullan's widely-quoted definition,

> A public official is corrupt if he accepts money or money's worth for doing something he is under a duty to do anyway, that he is under a duty not to do, or to exercise a legitimate discretion for improper reasons.[7]

Howard Cohen and Michael Feldberg suggest the following:

> Corruption involves accepting goods or services for performing or failing to perform duties which are a normal part of one's job. What makes a gift a gratuity is the reason it is given; what makes it corruption is the reason it is taken.[8]

And Herman Goldstein understands by "police corruption"

> the misuse of authority by a police officer in a manner designed to produce personal gain for the officer or for others.[9]

Despite their differences, none of these accounts equates police corruption with all forms of police misconduct or deviance. Various types of misconduct, such as use of the third degree to elicit a confession, informal punishments and brutality, perjury to secure a conviction, and petty theft or burglary where an exercise of authority is not involved, lie outside these characterizations. So too do deviations from occupational expectations, such as drinking, sleeping, or having sex while on duty. All three accounts of corruption are concerned with the exercise of police authority animated by the expectation of some form, usually, of material reward or gain. Yet there are significant differences between the three accounts.

In some respects the first two accounts are broader than the third. Goldstein's account focuses on two elements – a particular means (the misuse of authority) *and* a particular end (personal gain for self or others). But, as the other two accounts recognize, corruption need not involve any clear "misuse" of authority – not if it is understood as a deviation from doing what it is one's duty to *do*. Money or goods may be sought or accepted as a guarantee of "efficient" service. Behavior is not made less corrupt by the mere fact that officers do what they should be doing *because of* the inducements sought or accepted. Motivation is central to an understanding of corruption.

But on the other side, the first two definitions operate with a somewhat narrower understanding of personal gain than the third. Benefits for which the use of authority may be traded include not only tangibles such as money, goods, and services, but also less tangible items such as status, influence, prestige or future support. Indeed, it is only when we allow corruption to include the latter that we can understand how it is as much an issue for "white-collar" as for "blue-collar" policing.

There is a further dimension to Goldstein's account that is not acknowledged by the others. The gain need not be strictly or narrowly personal. The benefit might go to an officer's family or to the department. Officers who used to sell tickets to "the policeman's ball" were not exclusive beneficiaries of their solicitations. Nor would an officer who accepted help in regard to a relative's employment in return for a "break" or better service be doing it for narrow personal gain. However, it has to be allowed that, in this latter case, it is only because of the officer's "identification" with the direct beneficiary that the behavior constitutes corruption. An officer who agreed not to enforce the law if the violator made a sizable donation to charity would probably be acting improperly, but not corruptly.[10]

It may not be possible to give a neat overall characterization of corruption. Each of the definitions quoted above captures a good deal but not all of what would be considered corruption. Nevertheless, I offer the following as a general account of police corruption:

> Police officers act corruptly when, in exercising or failing to exercise their authority, they act with the primary intention of furthering private or departmental/divisional advantage.

In some respects, this is a very radical definition, since it covers many acts and practices that may never *show* themselves as corrupt – for example, doing what one is duty-bound to do solely for personal advancement (say, overtime collars or ignoring small jobs for the large, "visible" ones). Yet such practices are motivated by the *spirit* of corruption, and belong in the same moral category as corruption that is more visibly deleterious. The mistake involved in most discussions of corruption is to focus almost exclusively on kinds of acts, whereas corruption is primarily a problem of motivation. True, it is the kind of motivation that often manifests itself in deviant acts, but it need not do so.

In this sense corruption is an *ethical* problem before it is a *legal* or *administrative* problem. It becomes a legally and administratively significant problem only because it often expresses itself in deviant acts.

It is because corruption is to be conceived, at its heart, as a *motivational* transgression that the various catalogues and typologies of corruption common to sociological studies of corruption need to be qualified. It is not the deviant activities themselves that are corrupt. The deviance constitutes corruption only because it is animated by some desire for personal or departmental or divisional gain. An officer may fix a ticket for a friend without any thought of "gaining" from it, or shake down a drug dealer with a view to burning his money, or drop an investigation out of sheer laziness. These represent forms of misconduct, but not of corruption, though they are usually catalogued as forms of corruption. What may be true to say is that there are certain forms of deviant police conduct that are usually motivated by some benefit that will accrue to the officer or those with whom he or she identifies.

There are two further observations to be made about many of the standard catalogues of corrupt activities.[11] First, they focus for the most part on police–citizen interactions; and second, they are oriented to forms of corruption that are more likely to be found at lower levels of the police organization. Police corruption may be internal as well as external: There are personal or private gains that may be sought from personnel within a department as well as those that may come from those outside it. The desire for promotion benefits, pay increases, special rosters, convenient vacation arrangements, and so on, may all corrupt the exercise of authority. As well, equipment and funds may be used, and political assistance may be provided, for corrupt purposes. Indeed, there is some reason to think that the level of internal corruption may not be significantly lower than the level of external corruption. Much of the cynicism that develops in police circles and that contributes to external corruption has as one of its sources a cynicism about the integrity of the police organization (see Chapter 4, Section 4.3).

9.1.1 *Typologies of corruption*

Several typologies of police corruption have been developed, most thoroughly by Thomas Barker and his associates.[12] The purpose of such typologies has been to bring a certain explanatory and normative order and coherence into the multitude of acts that are usually denominated corrupt. Although, for reasons I have just outlined, I believe that such typologies focus on the wrong end of corruption – on the corrupted conduct rather than the corrupting motivation – they nevertheless provide us with a sense of the different public interests that may be corruptly subverted and therefore of the different levels of seriousness that may attach to different kinds of corrupt behavior.

Three features of the account that follows should be noted at the outset. First, the typology was initially constructed in response to the New York Police Department scandal of the early 1970s. However, the forms taken by police corruption are limited only by the imagination and opportunities that police have. Second, the authors see corruption as a group phenomenon, and not simply as an individual one. It arises, they believe, because of the character of an organization, and not just as the expression of an individual ego. Police corruption, as a phenomenon that attracts study, arises because departments are characterized by conflicting norms, the relative absence of external controls, impossible external demands, secretiveness, and bonds of loyalty that make "squealing" exceedingly difficult. Internal linguistic distinctions, such as those between clean and dirty money, help to sustain corrupt practices.[13] And third, the authors see their typology as hierarchical, manifesting "a progressive process in dynamics, accretion, and gravity, a process that might be checked at any one or more levels of progression by the tolerance limits of the police organization or the community."[14] I believe, however, that there is more contingency to this progression than the authors acknowledge.

9.1.1.1 Corruption of authority. Under this heading Barker gathers those unauthorized and unearned material benefits given an officer solely because he/she is a police officer. They include "free meals, booze, sex, services, free entertainment admissions, police discounts on merchandise, or other material inducements."[15] To what extent, if at all, the acceptance of these should be considered corruptions of authority we will discuss a little later in this chapter (Section 9.2). Less ambiguously, they include various "rewards" for extra services rendered – "payments by businessmen for property protection extending beyond routine patrol duties; secret payments by property owners to police for arresting robbers and burglars at their establishments; payments by bondsmen acting as bounty hunters to police for the arrest and notification of bond jumpers."[16]

Barker points out that in some of these cases, when the givers are "respectable citizens," there has been departmental condonation or acceptance, and a veiled rationalization of the "gratitude" that such gifts are intended to express.

9.1.1.2 Kickbacks. Included here are the goods, services, or money that police officers may receive for "referring business to towing companies, ambulances, garages, lawyers, doctors, bondsmen, undertakers, taxicab drivers, service stations, moving companies, and others who are anxious to sell services or goods to persons with whom the police interact during their routine patrol."[17] Like gratuities, kickbacks have sometimes been tacitly condoned, as long as the businesses concerned are legitimate and the rewards modest (cash rewards tend to be frowned upon): No laws are broken, and it is rationalized that the businesspersons are simply being "enterprising."

9.1.1.3 Opportunistic theft. As we reach this level, we cross the line of what has at times been seen as "ignorable" corruption. It takes a variety of forms: "Rolled arrestees, traffic accident victims, violent crime victims, and unconscious or dead citizens are generally unaware of the act. Officers investigating burglaries may take merchandise or money left behind by the original thief. Officers may also take items from unprotected property sites discovered during routine patrol; e.g., merchandise or money from unlocked businesses, building materials from construction locations, unguarded items from business or industrial establishments. Finally, policemen may keep a portion of the confiscated evidence they discover during vice raids, e.g., money, booze, narcotics, and property."[18]

9.1.1.4 Shakedowns. Although a shakedown is often seen as officer initiated, Barker understands it to include the opportunistic acceptance of payments for refraining from making an arrest (or issuing a summons) when it would otherwise have been called for. He therefore sees this as a sphere in which the "clean"/"dirty" graft distinction may operate. This is particularly the case where so-called victimless crimes (crimes without complainants) are involved. Although shakedowns connected with drug pushing, burglary, and other felonies may be "protected" by a code of silence, if found out they usually attract severe departmental condemnation.

9.1.1.5 Protection of illegal activities. It is important to those who engage in illegal enterprises that they operate with a minimum of official harassment. These operators have a strong reason for seeking to induce the police to turn a blind eye to their activities, or at least to go easy in constraining them. In the case of crimes without complainants, which are difficult enough to enforce and about which police may feel ambivalent anyway, there may even be a fair measure of public support for police leniency, albeit not for payments that police might accept or exact. Barker notes the great variety of forms of "protection" that police may provide: "Some cab companies and individual cab drivers pay police for illegal permission to operate outside prescribed routes and areas, to pick up and discharge fares at unauthorized sites, to operate cabs that do not meet safety and cleanliness standards, to operate without proper licensing procedures. Trucking firms pay for the privilege of hauling overloaded cargoes and driving off prescribed truck routes. . . . Legitimate businesses may also pay police to avoid Sunday 'blue' laws. . . . Construction companies may pay police to overlook violations of city regulations, e.g., trucks blocking traffic, violating pollution guidelines (burning trash, creating dust, etc.), destroying city property, blocking sidewalks."[19]

The fact that some of these illegal activities – those without complainants – are difficult to prosecute, effectively functions, according to Barker, "to drive many honest and dedicated police officers to resignation, ritualism, inaction, or corruption. Moreover, community approval of 'protected' illegal goods and services militates for a thoroughly deviant and criminal police organization."[20] He also suggests that if such protection is to be effective, it requires a fair measure of internal organization.[21]

We might also include within this category, though it does not appear in Barker's catalogue, the selling of confidential police information. Sometimes it might be to criminals, at other times to lawyers or employers who may wish to have it for more legitimate purposes.

9.1.1.6 The traffic fix. This involves the "taking up" or disposing of traffic citations for money or some other benefit. Apparently, this form of corruption was at one time so prevalent that one police agency proudly announced that it had succeeded in producing a "no-fix" ticket.[22]

9.1.1.7   The misdemeanor fix. In this case, the officer acts to quash misdemeanor court proceedings. This may take a number of forms: refraining from requesting prosecution, tampering with the existing evidence, or giving perjured testimony.

9.1.1.8   The felony fix. More seriously, but by some of the same means, an officer may act to ensure that a felony action is not proceeded with or will not result in a conviction.

9.1.1.9   Direct criminal activities. These occur when officers engage in burglary, robbery, larceny, and so on, for personal gain. Often it is solo, but sometimes a small ring operates. Generally such activities have little departmental sympathy or support, and officers who are involved generally shield their activities from others in the precinct.

9.1.1.10   Internal payoffs. Finally, Barker details various forms of internal corruption: "Internal payoffs regulate a market where police officers' prerogatives may be bought, bartered, or sold. Actors are exclusively police officers. Prerogatives negotiated encompass work assignments, off-days, holidays, vacation periods, control of evidence, and promotions. Officers who administer the distribution of assignments and personnel may collect fees for assigning officers to certain divisions, precincts, units, details, shifts, and beats; for insuring that selected personnel are retained in, transferred from, or excluded from certain work assignments. In departments taking protection money from vice operations, officers may contact command personnel and bid for 'good' (lucrative) assignments."[23]

As I noted earlier, Barker believes that these different forms of police corruption are progressively more serious. The order, however, is colored by his belief that the factors affecting corruption are to be construed in social rather than individual/psychological terms. It is for this reason that the various "internal payoffs," though apparently much less serious than some of the other acts of corruption that occur, nevertheless bespeak a much more deeply seated and serious corruption problem than those where criminals induce officers to go easy on them or in which officers opportunistically steal from premises that have already been burgled. A department that allows significant internal corruption is certain to be a department that has little control over the various forms of external corruption.

Like Lawrence Sherman, to whose views in "Becoming Bent" I shall soon turn, Barker sees something of a slide from one form of corruption to another. Those who engage in one of the less serious forms of corruption are likely to experience less difficulty in engaging in a more serious form of corruption than those who do not engage in any form of corruption. The slide is not inexorable, or the gradient even, but the slope is there.

The so-called slippery slope of police corruption is a persistent theme in both theoretical and biographical discussions of police corruption. It is so pervasive that most departments promulgate rules regarding what Barker sees as the least serious forms – particularly the acceptance of gratuities – and punish infractions with what seems to be a disproportionate ferocity. It is as though everything must be done to keep people off the "slope," because once on it, it is very difficult to reclaim the high ground. And so it is to that allegedly least serious form, the acceptance of gratuities, and the problem of a slippery slope that I shall now turn.

9.2 GRATUITIES: THE PROBLEM

Can we really say that the acceptance of gratuities, discounts, annual presents, and other "benefits" that police officers might be offered, qualify as corruption – that is, involve exercises of authority for the sake of private (or sectional) advantage?

There is nothing about a gratuity per se to imply that any (anticipated or actual) exercise of authority that has led to the gratuity being offered has been contingent on its being offered. Even if an officer performs an official service *in the expectation of receiving a gratuity,* it does not strictly follow that the service was provided with the intention of receiving the gratuity or that without the expectation of a gratuity the service would not have been provided or provided as efficiently.

In this respect, bribes differ significantly from gratuities. Bribes are offered and accepted in order to corrupt authority. At best this is a contingent feature of gratuities; indeed, many gratuities are offered as unsolicited and voluntary rewards for the proper, and even supererogatory, exercise of police authority. Gratuities also tend to involve smaller benefits than bribes. Because a bribe is offered or sought to deflect an officer from doing his duty, the inducement will need to be large enough to make the corruption of duty "worth it." A gratuity, on the other hand, is often just a token, a gesture of appreciation. When police management talk about gratuities, they tend to have in mind free cups of coffee and doughnuts no less than larger gifts; when they talk about bribes, the exchanges are almost always much larger.

Police officers are themselves strongly divided on the propriety or otherwise of gratuities and other gifts. At one end, there are those who see these as "perks" of the job, or as tokens of appreciation from a generally unappreciative citizenry, harmless benefits that make a somewhat humdrum existence more pleasant, or as rewards, perhaps, for doing some of society's dirty work. At the other end are those who see the acceptance of such benefits as corrupting, if not corrupt. O. W. Wilson is memorably quoted as saying that "a police officer should not be allowed to accept any gratuity, not even a free cup of coffee."[24]

Those who hold the first view are challenged to say where they would draw the line – at a free meal (at an expensive restaurant?[25]), $20, a TV? Those who hold the second are said to take their opposition to corruption to unrealistic and absurd lengths. Where does the truth lie?[26] In some ways, though the stakes are rather different, the debate parallels that which occurs in the case of abortion, each side seeking by means of structurally similar arguments to force the other into accepting the untenability of its position. So-called pro-lifers challenge pro-choicers to "draw a morally significant line" between an early and late abortion or even infanticide; pro-choicers suggest that it is patently absurd to accord to a "blob of jelly" the kind of regard we normally reserve for a person.

The major contentions of those who would tolerate the acceptance of gratuities and similar benefits are as follows:

1. It is very natural to show appreciation to those who benefit us in some way, even if it is their job to do so. When they do their job particularly well, or when we are particularly grateful, a mere "thank you" does not sufficiently express our gratitude. Something more is called for. Since police often attend us at critical times, we may have reason to be particularly grateful to them, and it is only natural that we express that gratitude by means of a gratuity. It would, moreover, be insulting were they not willing to accept it, since it would cast doubt on the spirit in which it was offered.[27]

2. The usual complaint against the offering and receiving of gratuities is that the practice will buy or cultivate favor. But those who believe that officers ought to be permitted to exercise discretion in the matter argue that most gratuities are not significant enough to be corrupting. Taking advantage of the offer of a half-priced Big Mac[28] or free cup of coffee is no big deal. It is too small to make a police officer beholden to the giver. No officer is going to put his job on the line for something so small.

3. In some cases, where the benefit (say, the half-priced Big Mac) is official company policy, there is nothing about the arrangement or individual transaction that would create a "personal" sense of obligation. For the company concerned, the arrangement is one way in which it can directly express its gratitude for a public service, increase its patronage, and in addition benefit from a police presence on its premises. These are all morally permissible goals. Since everything is "up front," there is no attempt or intention to deflect the officer from his/her duty.

4. Police on the beat depend for their effectiveness on establishing good relations with local businesspeople. That way they find out what is going on, who is believed to have done what, what might be in the air, and generally keep open the conduit between police and community. The acceptance of a free cup of coffee or piece of fruit is an integral part of the social give-and-take that is constitutive of effective street policing. An officer who knocks back such small gestures will be looked at as "unfriendly" and will not be confided in or shared with.[29]

5. The "free cup of coffee" is so deeply entrenched that attempts to root it out will be ineffective and will lead to alienation within and between the ranks. By line officers its prohibition is seen as expressing a "killjoy" attitude, and its enforcement is viewed as a waste of scarce departmental resources.[30] Cynicism will result.

6. Directives that forbid the acceptance of free cups of coffee treat police officers as fools who cannot distinguish between a friendly gesture or mark of appreciation and a bribe, as moral infants who cannot accept a token of respect and friendship without succumbing to favoritism, or as knaves or moochers who take every opportunity to exploit their position for personal advantage. On the contrary, it is argued, police are generally well aware of why gratuities are being offered. They are capable of exercising a proper discretion in accepting or refusing to accept them. And even if a cup of coffee is offered for the wrong reason, the reason for accepting it need not complement that for offering it.

The major contentions of those who oppose the acceptance of gratuities and similar benefits are:

1. Even the smallest gift, particularly if it becomes regularized, creates a sense of obligation. Or, if it does not create anything as strong as a sense of obligation, it gives at least a rose tint to the relationship. An officer who has previously accepted free cups of coffee will find it harder to take an impartial stand later if he/she is asked to do a "favor." Even if a stand is taken, it may be colored by the bond that has been cultivated: A warning might be given where otherwise a ticket would have been issued.

2. Those who accept gratuities find themselves on a slippery slope of corruption on which it becomes progressively more difficult to stop. There is the old saying: "Sow a thought and you reap an act; sow an act and you reap a habit; sow a habit and you reap a character; sow a character and you reap a destiny."[31] By accepting a gratuity, the officer is said to abandon a relationship with others that is motivated and directed solely by public duty to one in which private dealings and personal sentiment begin to play a part. The ground becomes softer, and the officer will find that little by little his/her actions come to be determined by personal, "self-interested" factors.

3. Although some, perhaps most, police are able to practice discernment with regard to the acceptance of gratuities, some are not able to do so. They will find that the free cup of coffee sets them on a path of accepting and then expecting gratuities that, because of the opportunities provided by police work, will eventually have few bounds. For the sake of these "weak" or "inexperienced" officers, inevitable in any organization, and because of the high trust that is placed in police officers, it is better for policing generally that the "strong" and "experienced" forgo what for them would be only a small and harmless benefit.[32]

4. Businesses that offer free cups of coffee, doughnuts, sandwiches, and meals to police officers do so with a partial view to attracting their presence. Naturally police officers are likely to spend more of their time in the vicinity of such businesses than elsewhere. While this may be beneficial to the businesses concerned, it leads to an unfair distribution of the police presence. It is "antidemocratic."[33]

9.2.1 *The slippery slope argument*

Most of the foregoing arguments lend themselves to further elaboration and defense, and some of them will be pursued a little later. For the moment, however, I want to focus on just one line of argument, that relating to the so-called slippery slope of corruption. Although there are many theories about the sources of police corruption – some relating to preexisting criminal tendencies and the attractions that police work may present to such people, and others to various aspects of police culture or to the dynamic of external and internal demands on police – it is still very common to find woven into these theories the suggestion that actual corruption starts off in a small way, and then becomes increasingly addictive. The acceptance of gratuities is seen as a major "small" thing that triggers the decline. And so, whether or not their acceptance is in itself corrupting, it is argued that a bright line needs to be drawn that excludes the acceptance of gratuities.

One thing, it is said, leads to another. And that, in essence, is the slippery slope argument, the general name for a cluster of related arguments, sometimes referred to as the "wedge," the "foot-in-the-door," or the "camel's-nose" *argument* by those who endorse it and as *fallacy* by those who oppose its use, the latter also frequently dubbing (a version of) it the "bald man" or "black-and-white" fallacy.[34] In this latter form it is related to what ancient logicians sometimes spoke of as the "sorites (heap) paradox." In the present context, it is claimed that the acceptance of small gratuities such as free cups of coffee by police officers will increase the likelihood of, or lead by degrees to, or is not significantly different from, corruption of the worst kind.

But not only does the slippery slope argument have a number of names, it also has a number of guises. And this sometimes makes it difficult to pin down. It will be useful to start off with James Rachels's distinction between "logical" and "psychological" versions of the argument:[35]

9.2.1.1 Logical. Although Rachels does not draw attention to the fact, there are at least two forms of the logical version of the slippery slope argument.[36] The first version states that once a certain practice is accepted, then, from a logical point of view, we are also committed to accepting certain other practices, since acceptance of the first practice removes any reason there might be for not going on to accept the additional practices. The additional practices, however, are patently and increasingly intolerable. Therefore, it is claimed, the first practice ought not to be permitted.

The argument is applied to police corruption in the following way. Although the acceptance of a free cup of coffee is not seriously wrong, and not in itself the sort of wrongdoing to make an issue of, it is, nevertheless, wrong. And since its implicit rationale – the compromise of impartiality for the sake of some personal benefit – is essentially the same as that involved in more serious forms of corruption, differing from them only in degree, the person who accepts a free cup of coffee has effectively undermined any moral ground he has for refusing to engage in corruption of a more serious kind.[37] The practical conclusion that is drawn from the "logical" version of the argument is that, in order to distance oneself morally from serious corruption, it is important not to engage in any corruption, albeit corruption of an apparently trivial kind.

According to the second version of the argument, although there appears to be a significant difference between one practice and some other, say p and z, where z is patently unacceptable,[38] closer inspection reveals that there is only an insignificant difference between p and q, an insignificant difference between q and r, an insignificant difference between r and s, . . . and between y and z. Therefore, the difference between q and z is more apparent than real, and any distinction between them must be arbitrary. Therefore p ought not to be permitted.

Applied to police corruption, the argument goes somewhat as follows: Although there appears to be a big difference between taking a free cup of coffee and, say, shaking down drug dealers and selling their drugs, that difference can be shown to be an arbitrary one. For there is only a slight difference between a cup of coffee and a cup of coffee and doughnut, and there is only a slight difference between a cup of coffee and doughnut and a free meal, and there is only a slight difference between a free meal and a gift, and . . . a shakedown. Since there is no precise, natural line to be drawn between the acceptance of a free cup of coffee and engaging in a shakedown, any distinction between them will be arbitrary. Therefore, the acceptance of free cups of coffee ought to be forbidden.

This second form of the logical version of the argument is almost certainly invalid. It is in this form that it has come to be known as an instantiation of the "bald man" or "black-and-white" fallacy, or, as Govier dubs it, "The Fallacy of Slippery Assimilation." The fallacy resides in refusing to recognize that there is a *cumulative* significance to the individually insignificant differences. This holds true and makes the difference between p and z significant, *even if* we cannot tell with any precision at what point what we want to say about z (say, that it is unacceptable and ought to be prohibited) applies also to a successor of p. The person who has 10,000 hairs on his head may not differ significantly from the person who has 9,999 hairs, and the person who has 9,999 hairs may not differ significantly from the person who has 9,998, . . . and the person who has no hair, but the cumulative effect of those differences makes for a very significant difference between a hairy person (with 10,000 hairs) and a bald one, even though we may not be able to state with any precision where we would draw the line.

9.2.1.2 Psychological. The "psychological" version of the slippery slope argument relies on an empirical connection between the acts or practices at the beginning of the slope and those at the bottom. It states that once a certain practice is accepted, people *are likely to* go on to accept other practices that are increasingly unacceptable. Unlike the previous version, which focuses on a logical or conceptual connection between the "trivial" and "serious" wrongdoing (since they can both be included under the same moral or conceptual maxim or label), this version focuses on a contingent but causal connection between the initial practice and the practices to which it is said its acceptance will lead.

One of the interesting features of this version is the ability of those who propound it to concede that the practice at the top of the slope (accepting a free cup of coffee) is not in itself "unacceptable" or morally troublesome. What they argue is that the practice of accepting a free cup of coffee is "empirically linked" to other (future) practices that will be morally unacceptable. One leads, if not inevitably, then "naturally" or easily, to the other. So, in contrast to the logical version of the argument, in which the case allegedly at the top of the slope is morally "of-a-piece" (at least in the sense of being immoral) with the case at the bottom of the slope, in the psychological version the case allegedly at the top of the slope is morally distinguishable from the case at the bottom of the slope. The difference is one of kind and not merely one of degree.

Those who employ the slippery slope argument may focus on one or both, though usually both, of two features of the metaphor. Some concentrate on the slope itself, how steep and slippery it is; others focus on the "abyss" or disaster that awaits at the bottom. Those who employ one of the logical versions generally focus on the gradient; those who resort to the psychological version generally focus on the result.[39]

Although both logical and psychological versions of the slippery slope argument are prevalent in the literature, it is the psychological version that gains most attention. Its status is also less easily determinable. Proponents claim that a transition from what we might call the "plateau" position (no free cups of coffee) to the "abyss" position is *much* harder to make than the transition from the "lip" position (free cups of coffee) to the "abyss" position (shakedowns, narcotics, graft, and so on). Better, then, to stay on the plateau. The argument usually trades very heavily on the disaster that awaits those who get onto the slope. But in order to give the specter of that abyss some realism, its proponents need to show why those who get onto the slope will find themselves faced with disaster. Or, to put it another way, they need to show that the metaphor of a *slope* – and a slippery one at that – is appropriate.

Proponents of the psychological version point to several factors that might be adduced to support their contention of a slope. One factor might be a certain linguistic or conceptual "fuzziness" in the distinction between the lip and abyss practices. For one thing, the edges of corruption may be very fuzzy. If, for example, there is considerable public controversy over whether and, if so, how the acceptance of gratuities such as free cups of coffee is to be distinguished from the engagement in corruption (albeit minor), or confusion over the distinction between a gift, a gratuity, and a bribe, there will be a less clear distinction between the acceptance of free cups of coffee and the acceptance of bribes than between the nonacceptance of free cups of coffee and the acceptance of bribes. This is not the same as the logical argument.

The point is not whether there *is* a significant moral distinction, but whether there is *controversy* about it. The "environment" in which the various practices take place encourages a certain blurring of boundaries.

The fuzziness may also be produced or exacerbated by the fact that the world does not come to us neatly packaged. Human activities form something of a continuum, and even if our conceptual distinctions are clear, it is not always clear how they are to be applied in particular cases. It is this feature of our experience that forms the centerpiece of the second form of the logical version of the argument. Here, however, the point is not to engage in some form of conceptual assimilation, but simply to note the *practical* difficulty of making the distinction.

A rather different source for the slide can be the "slippage" that naturally tends to occur in transfers between one person and another. If *a* understands a practice in a certain way, it is unlikely that if the practice is then explained to *b* it will be understood by *b* in exactly the same way. Some of the nuances for *a* may be lost in transit. So, while one police officer may be able to grasp the acceptance of a free cup of coffee in a way that keeps it firmly on the "lip," another to whom he teaches the practice may understand his engagement in it in a way that will begin the slide toward the "abyss" of corruption below. This transferential slippage may work with either a general account of "human finitude and limitedness" or a distinction between the "strong" and the "weak."

Perhaps this helps to explain why, very often, those who present the argument (say, police administrators) will claim that while *they* could engage in the practice at the top of the slope without sliding down, *others* will not be able to do so. A police chief may believe himself/herself able to resist the slide, but also think that (some) officers on the beat will not be capable of resisting it. Or the proponent may wish to claim that while he could *now* engage in the practice at the top of the slope without sliding down, nevertheless he might not be able to do so at some *future* time. Or maybe he will argue that because *he* would not be able to resist the slide, neither will others be able to. Clearly, there are problems about making such differentiations. If one is able to resist oneself, why not credit others with the same capacity? If one is able to resist now, why shouldn't one be able to resist later? If one is not able to resist now, why should one attribute a similar weakness to others? The reactions of such proponents need not reflect moral insensitivity, but the questions raised need to be addressed.

Is the psychological version of the argument valid? The question cannot be answered generally. It depends. It depends on the empirical plausibility of the transition from one point to another on the alleged slope. Each transition needs to be supported by arguments that will show why it is *likely* (and not merely possible) that a person who engages in practice *p* will then engage in practice *q* and then in practice *r* . . . and so on to practice *z*. Unfortunately, many who use the argument focus on the horrors of the abyss to deflect attention from the sparse support for the transitional stages.

Where, then, does this leave the free cup of coffee? In "Becoming Bent: Moral Careers of Corrupt Policemen," Lawrence Sherman argues that there is a relatively smooth descent ("a continuum of graft stages"[40]) from the acceptance of minor "perks," through accepting bribes in relation to bar closing hours, to taking graft for regulative crimes, gambling, prostitution, and ultimately involvement with narcotics. What prompts police officers to get onto this slope, and why, once on it, is it so difficult to stop? Sherman focuses on two factors: *affiliation* – the social considerations that bind police, both corrupt and noncorrupt, together; and *signification* – the way in which police represent their behavior to themselves to link the various stages of corruption.

As Sherman sees it, early in his career, the young recruit learns that being a police officer binds him to one social group and alienates him from another. Membership of the former includes peer pressure to accept minor "perks." Their acceptance has the effect of altering the rookie's self-image in a way that makes him vulnerable to slightly more substantial "graft": The young recruit who has accepted a free cup of coffee "has a different image of himself to contend with when a bar owner operating after closing hours offers him a drink."[41] The slide, though not inexorable, is made smoother by the relatively small moral gap between successive stages of the descent. One solution to the problem, Sherman suggests, is to make the grade on the slope steeper (and hence more daunting) by removing from the books those activities ("vice") that most easily tempt police into accepting graft and that then lead them easily on to more serious corruption.

Even if Sherman's solution to the problem is controversial, his analysis of the transition has a great deal of anecdotal support from corrupt police officers who have subsequently written about their decline.[42] It is not, however, universally shared, and, indeed, many line officers strongly resist its logic. That resistance is encapsulated in Michael Feldberg's rejection of Sherman's position. Most police, Feldberg claims, *are* able to make a firm distinction between minor "perks" and bribes intended to deflect them from their responsibilities, and invoking the slippery slope argument is "unrealistic, somewhat hypocritical, and insulting to a police officer's intelligence."[43] A ban on taking such perks will appear (and, in many cases, be) petty, because "what makes a gift a gratuity is the reason it is given; what makes it corruption is the reason it is taken."[44] There are many reasons why a police officer might accept a cup of coffee, and only a few of them will express a corrupt intent or tendency. Not that Feldberg is himself comfortable with the police acceptance of minor gratuities; but his unease does not lie in slippery slope considerations. Rather, their acceptance detracts from "the democratic ethos of policing": "Gratuities are simply an inducement to a police officer to distribute the benefit of his presence disproportionately to some taxpayers and not others."[45]

The dispute between Sherman and Feldberg is more subtle than appears at first reading. The point is not that one sees a slope where the other does not, but that they have a different understanding of its slipperiness. And they have a different understanding of its slipperiness mainly because they appeal (at least sometimes) to different versions of the argument.

Sherman believes that the police officer who accepts a free cup of coffee ipso facto compromises himself morally. His image of himself is changed, and the only issue now is how venal he is willing to be. Feldberg, on the other hand, does not see anything inherently wrong with accepting a free cup of coffee, though he is aware that there are certain risks involved. The issue of moral compromise need not be a pressing one at that stage (even though there may be different, distributional questions).

Sherman sees only a difference in degree between the officer who accepts a free cup of coffee and the officer who gets involved in drug trafficking. Moral compromise is already involved. The officer who accepts a free cup of coffee has already tarnished his self-image. Sherman, in other words, adopts what I referred to earlier as the "logical" version of the slippery slope argument. And the slope, not surprisingly, is much slipperier than Feldberg's. Feldberg, insofar as he sees the risk of a slide, has in mind the "psychological" version of the argument. There is a risk that the officer who accepts gratuities will lose a sense of where the line is to be drawn, but a conscientious officer will know when things are going too far, and at the free-cup-of-coffee stage, he/she will probably be well short of corruption. As has often been pointed out, experienced and/or cautious skiers are capable of stopping on quite steep slopes.

Let us note, however, that even though Sherman's slope is likely to be slipperier than Feldberg's, it is not perfectly smooth.[46] There may be plateaus on which it is fairly easy to stop. The person who is prepared to tell lies, is not ipso facto prepared to steal, to assault, and to murder. And even the person who is prepared to lie (inexcusably) about some things may not be prepared to lie about other things. All of us, even the not-so-virtuous among us, tend to draw lines beyond which we will not go. No doubt that was one of the functions of the grass-eater/meat-eater distinction drawn by New York City police in the 1960s.[47] The person who accepts free cups of coffee and sees this as wrong may nevertheless not be prepared to accept a free meal or a kickback. This is not to deny that it will be harder to refuse a free meal or kickback if a free cup of coffee is accepted (especially if they are believed to be wrong for the same reason), but it may not be too difficult. And where the acts or practices are believed to be wrong for different reasons, it will probably be much easier to draw the line.

Who is right? If corruption is thought of as an exercise of authority in which a person acts to further some private or sectional end, then the acceptance of a free cup of coffee may be too unimportant in itself to constitute a corrupt (or even corrupting) benefit. People commonly offer each other cups of coffee – whether as friends, business associates, clients, or benefactors – as a gesture of hospitality, friendship, gratitude, and so on. It is a small gesture, enough to express a measure of attentive recognition, but not really enough to create anything like a significant sense of obligation. To the extent that that is Feldberg's position, I think he is probably right.

But the free cup of coffee may not mean only that. Its symbolism may stretch further. It may be intended as a subtle lure, an attempt to create a rapport that can be drawn upon (exploited) at some future time. And if given regularly, it may give the officer who accepts it a slightly too generous view of the giver. Even though taking it will not be corrupting in itself, it may nevertheless pave the way for corrupting conduct in the future. And then, once that compromise has been made, other and larger compromises will more easily (though not inevitably) follow.

Even so, I think Feldberg has a better grasp of the moral relativities than Sherman. Police chiefs who make too big a deal of free cups of coffee, and treat their acceptance as a serious compromise or even only as a significant step in the direction of moral compromise, are likely to be seen as going overboard, and they risk losing the respect and confidence of their officers. Like parents who paint lurid pictures of the evils of pot and sex, only to find that their overdramatization has led to a loss of respect (their children experiment and find out that they are anything but dreadful), so police chiefs who make too much of a noise about free cups of coffee may find their authority undermined. And then, of course, like children who have lost respect for their parents and have thrown caution to the wind, only to discover the bedrock of truth in their parents' warnings, those officers who start ignoring warnings may find them coming true in unexpected ways.

It may be more prudent, as well as more realistic, if police chiefs do not pretend that there is something either inherently or inevitably (or even easily) corrupting about the acceptance of a free cup of coffee. That does not mean that it is all right to accept a free cup of coffee. Even if only a few officers succumb to the temptations involved, the serious public consequences may make for better policy if police do not accept gratuities. But beyond that there is Feldberg's argument that a no-gratuity policy assists in the more equitable distribution of police service.[48] If some establishments offer police free cups of coffee, police will be tempted to frequent them more often. Such is often the intention of those who run small businesses. The police presence helps to ensure their freedom from hoodlums, holdups, and may even help to secure a faster response in an emergency. The free cup of coffee is like a very cheap supplemental insurance premium. But it is achieved by getting for those establishments a disproportionate police presence, out of keeping with the equal protection and impartial service that it is the police's public role to provide. In a situation in which police resources are scarce anyway, it may breed competition and unfairly divert police attention.[49] Police, as beneficiaries of the public purse, and not fee-for-service providers, are responsible for the fair deployment of their resources, based on need rather than reward.

There is another reason for not overdoing the slippery slope potential of the free cup of coffee. If police chiefs insist on the corrupt and corrupting character of accepting free cups of coffee, then for that reason some officers who accept them may come to see themselves as having been compromised or at least as having something to hide. And insofar as they come to believe that, they may feel themselves on the logical slippery slope of which they have been warned. Believing themselves already compromised, they might then find it easier to make more significant compromises. This would not occur had they been told that the reason for not accepting gratuities was the "democratic" need to avoid a situation in which the police presence would become unfairly distributed.

For those who feel and thus find themselves on the slippery slope, the issue may now be to find a "branch" to cling to, such as the distinction between clean and dirty graft, or between active and passive graft. But some of these branches may not be very strong, the distinctions concerned having only secondary moral relevance.

9.3 WHISTLEBLOWING

What should officers do when they become aware of corrupt or illegal practices or other forms of misconduct on the part of their fellow officers? Consider the following scenarios:

A. A police officer becomes aware that one of his colleagues has a tendency to mistreat arrestees, particularly those from lower socioeconomic groups. He's told: "It's the only language they understand."
B. A police officer is transferred to a precinct in which there operates a fairly elaborate and extensive network of graft; even ranking officers are participants. He is under some pressure to join.
C. A police officer is involved in the investigation of a horrific child abuse/murder case that, if it goes to trial, will show gross dereliction by the Bureau of Child Welfare. High-ranking Bureau officials have intervened to arrange a plea bargain in which the parents get off very lightly.
D. A police officer is promoted into a specialist unit, known for its effectiveness. He discovers that this effectiveness is made possible because its members engage in various illegal activities – unauthorized wiretapping, withholding of confiscated drugs so that informants can be supplied, and so on. The officer becomes caught up in such activities until an internal investigation traps him. He is told that if he "cooperates" with the investigating officers – wears a wire, informs on his colleagues, and so on – his own position may be helped.

In each of these cases, the officer knows of and/or is involved in unethical conduct, whether engaged in by a colleague, a department, or an associated agency. What should the officer do?

In practice, there might be several broad options available to the officer. He/she might: (1) join in or actively assist in the unethical conduct; (2) turn a blind eye to it; (3) seek to dissuade those involved; (4) ask for a transfer away from the source of the unacceptable conduct; (5) report the conduct to superiors; (6) go public (by contacting the media or some authority outside the agency); (7) resign (and then go public?); and, if implicated himself/herself, (8) tough it out, or (9) cooperate with the investigating officers.

Not all these options are exclusive: for example, (3) might be followed by (4) and/or (5) and/or (6).

There may be no general "best solution"; it might depend on the kind of unethical conduct involved, the officer's own situation, and the prevailing conditions within a particular precinct, department, or even society. But whichever option is chosen, it will have its problems. It will have its problems because it brings into conflict two strong commitments: on the one hand, the professional (and personal) commitment to integrity; and on the other hand, the institutional or fraternal commitment to loyalty. Both of these may be felt as moral requirements.

Option (1) is of course no ethical "solution"; it is a sellout, an expedient rather than a principled response. It is most likely to arise where a police officer becomes aware of the unethical conduct by being asked to participate in it. Here, for whatever reason, personal integrity, or at least a basic obligation, is sacrificed – perhaps to the bonds of fraternity, but more likely to weakness of will, to moral cowardice, or, sometimes, to plain greed. Unless rationalized – and cynicism sometimes makes this possible – this option's psychological cost in guilt feelings may be very high.[50]

Option (2) may be the easiest to manage psychologically. Here the officer attempts (with questionable success) to keep a certain "moral distance" from the unethical conduct, without jeopardizing the bonds of loyalty. Of all such bonds, the police "code of silence" is one of the strongest, and corrupt police officers have sometimes persisted openly in their corruption in the confidence that even their disapproving colleagues will not "rat" on them.[51] It is not, however, a morally acceptable option. Turning a blind eye is culpable blindness.

Option (3) may be harder to pursue: In an individualistic culture, it could smack of busybodiness or sanctimoniousness and place considerable strain on fraternal bonds. Of all the advice we give to others, moral advice often seems to be the most intrusive and presumptuous, the least wanted. Unless the intervention is morally effective, trust may be lost, and the officer may find himself/herself suspect and isolated. The ability of an officer to be "morally effective" in this kind of situation may depend on skills, personality traits, and a preexisting relationship that few will possess.

Option (4) offers genuine distance, and probably will not be taken as betrayal. Of course, it may be costly to the officer if the transfer is unsatisfactory in other ways, and it may require that the officer lie about his or her reasons for seeking a transfer. However, this option may also be seen as cowardly, particularly if, as we presume, the transgressions of the other officer(s) are quite serious.

Option (5) may be a bit easier to accomplish psychologically, but it will usually be viewed as a betrayal, even though the complaint will be to another police officer. In police work, the prime loyalties are generally (albeit problematically) seen as horizontal, not vertical.[52] And the after-costs of perceived betrayal may be very great.[53]

But sometimes internal reporting may seem inadequate. Where systemic and serious corruption is involved, it may be very difficult to find any departmental responsiveness. And option (6) may be chosen. It is this option that generally constitutes "whistleblowing," though some writers would also include options (5), (7), and (8) under that head.[54] Whistleblowing is often seen by fellow officers as an unforgivable breach of loyalty, even if it has its basis in the officer's sense of integrity.[55] This reaction, based on our deep-seated aversion to "tattletales," is not confined to police work, but is found in almost any institution, both private and public.

The loyalty evident in option (8) looks admirable, since it is likely to be purchased at considerable personal cost (even though that cost might be said to be deserved). It is, nevertheless, arguable that a public responsibility is being passed over for what appears to be a blind, and misguided, loyalty.

On the other hand, if option (9) is taken, it will usually be argued that the whistleblowing lacks moral worth. Its roots will lie in the selfish desire to save one's skin rather than in any commitment to integrity. This may not be an argument for refusing to cooperate – an overriding public good may be accomplished; but such cooperation will not necessarily redound to the moral credit of the whistleblower.

Is whistleblowing justified, and if so, under what circumstances?

9.3.1   *Whistleblowing defined*

Whistleblowers, as the metaphorical characterization suggests, draw public attention to wrongdoing by blowing a whistle. Attempts to define whistleblowing more formally usually generate problems. Compare, for example, Norman Bowie's account with that of Frederick Elliston. According to Norman Bowie:

> A whistle blower is an employee or officer of any institution, profit or non-profit, private or public, who believes either that he/she has been ordered to perform some act[s] or he/she has obtained knowledge that the institution is engaged in activities which (a) are believed to cause unnecessary harm to third parties, (b) are in violation of human rights or (c) run counter to the defined purpose of the institution and who inform[s] the public of this fact.[56]

Elliston, on the other hand, writes that an act of whistleblowing occurs when:

1. an individual performs an action or series of actions intended to make information public;
2. the information is made a matter of public record;
3. the information is about possible or actual, nontrivial wrongdoing in an organization;
4. the individual who performs the action is a member or former member of the organization.[57]

There are several ways in which the two accounts differ. Elliston's appears to be the more embracing one. It includes former members of an organization as well as those currently employed by it. It allows that any "nontrivial wrongdoing" may provide an occasion for whistleblowing. However, Bowie's account gives us a better sense of why whistleblowing is seen as morally ambiguous, for it adverts to the tension between organizational and public responsibility. Elliston's account leaves it unclear why the "public" should be involved. Although it accommodates the reporting of conduct that lacks institutional connivance, its focus on "going public" makes it unclear why wrongdoing that lacks institutional connivance should be made "public."

In the context of policing, both accounts would probably be seen as too restrictive. Within police departments whistleblowing is often understood to involve any reporting outside the immediate circle of officers. Reporting to a high-ranking officer or to internal affairs is often treated as equivalent to whistleblowing in the more restrictive sense.[58] Nevertheless, there is a "soft" moral basis for restricting whistleblowing to cases in which someone "goes public." For the most part, whistleblowing occurs when public interests are being compromised: There is then a public interest in a wider public knowing about and ensuring discontinuance of the activity in question.

Although the foregoing accounts provide a reasonably useful informal account of whistleblowing, there are several issues that remain unclarified. The grounds for whistleblowing remain unclear. Elliston's reference to "nontrivial wrongdoing" cries out for greater specification; and Bowie's references to "unnecessary harm to third parties" and to activities that "run counter to the defined purposes of the institution" also lend themselves to seemingly endless extensions: It may be difficult to see why the *public* should have any interest in some of the violations that would fall under these categories. It is also unclear whether the relevant violations must be ongoing or imminent, or whether they might include past wrongs. In addition, it remains unclear what "going public" involves – going outside the organization? going to an appropriate external (public?) authority? going to the media? But perhaps this vagueness is as it should be. Unless we propose to define "whistleblowing" so narrowly that it necessarily refers to a justifiable activity, there is no strong reason to define it so that only those forms of justifiable going public will be included. Nevertheless, there is some reason for giving the practice enough structure to make it responsive to a reasonably unified justificatory argument. That we do when we see the major moral players to be organizational loyalty and the public interest.

9.3.2 *Occasions for whistleblowing*

The term "whistleblower" was coined about twenty-five years ago to provide a more neutral, if not actually positive, characterization of someone for whom there already existed a rich collection of derogatory terms – tattletale, whistler, snitch, rat, weasel, fink, squealer, sneak, and so on. It developed in response to a growing recognition that, on the one hand, the public has become increasingly vulnerable to the doings of large institutions and organizations and, on the other, that many of those institutions and organizations foster and demand a loyalty that can come into conflict with the public trust they seek to have and/or maintain.

Many organizations possess internal mechanisms for rectifying threats to the public interest, but some do not, and sometimes those that do have mechanisms that have become or have been rendered ineffective. A public-minded employee may believe that only if what is perceived to be a wrong within the organization is addressed from the outside will it be rectified. And so what is regarded within the organization as "confidential" or "restricted" will be disclosed to a person or persons outside. Such disclosure may have a very serious impact on the organization – on its profitability, its public standing, on the morale of its employees. The public interest that is served thereby may be minor compared to the disruption that is caused, and it may even turn out that what is perceived to be an unrectified wrong was not as it appeared to be. Furthermore, it may turn out that the motivation of the whistleblower is suspect, reflective of a desire to "get ahead" or "pay back."

And so it becomes important to establish conditions under which whistleblowing may constitute a justifiable activity. Norman Bowie suggests that whistleblowing may be morally justifiable if the following set of conditions can be satisfied:

1. It is done from the appropriate moral motive, namely, as provided in the definition of whistle blowing.
2. The whistle blower, except in special circumstances, has exhausted all internal channels for dissent before informing the public.
3. The whistle blower has made certain that his or her belief that inappropriate actions are ordered or have occurred is based on evidence that would persuade a reasonable person.
4. The whistle blower has acted after a careful analysis of the danger: (a) how serious is the moral violation, (b) how immediate is the moral violation, (c) is the moral violation one that can be specified?
5. The whistle blower's action is commensurate with one's responsibility for avoiding and/or exposing moral violations.
6. It has some chance of success.[59]

As can be seen from this fairly stringent set of conditions, organizational loyalty is here presumed to be a serious obligation, and the potentially detrimental impact of a public disclosure of wrongdoing is given full consideration. The first condition is designed to exclude revenge, personal advancement, and other self-interested reasons from the range of appropriate motivating considerations. Whistleblowing will be morally praiseworthy only if prompted by some other-regarding concern like the public interest. Although essential to the moral creditworthiness of whistleblowing, the reference to an appropriate motive may not figure quite as centrally in the development of whistleblowing policy. If the exposed threat is serious enough, protection against retaliation might be offered to whistleblowers *even though* their motives are suspect.

Condition 2 shows an awareness of the damage that whistleblowing may cause, and requires that other, less dramatic, alternative means of rectification be explored before the issue is taken to the public. It reflects the fact that the public interest is often best served if organizations possess their own mechanisms for ensuring that the public interest is secured. The damage that can be done by whistleblowing also informs the "sincerity is not enough" Condition 3. There will, obviously, be disputes about whether a subjective or objective criterion of reasonableness should be adopted. Public policy may favor an objective criterion, though a moral assessment of particular acts may be more amenable to one that is subjective. We may at least regard a misguided act of whistleblowing as morally excusable if it was based on subjectively reasonable grounds. Condition 4 links with Condition 2 in that it focuses on the necessity of going public. If the organizational or personal damage will exceed the public good, or if the danger is not so imminent that it can be averted only by blowing a whistle, or if the supposed danger does not have sufficient specificity, then alternative means of rectification should be pursued or created. Condition 5 is intended to accommodate a situation in which there may be differential responsibilities for dealing with wrongdoing or violations of different kinds. Its role is essentially a subsidiary one; those with specific responsibilities for dealing with violations are likely to be better placed to make decisions about the relevant factual and normative issues. Clearly, however, such organizational differentiation may break down, and any member of the organization who becomes aware of some imminent grave threat to the public interest will be justified in taking appropriate action, including blowing the whistle. Condition 6 acknowledges the essentially consequentialist purposes of whistleblowing: serving the public interest. If blowing the whistle is unlikely to accomplish any significant change for the better, then it will lack any justificatory point. Condition 6 also places a burden on the whistleblower to "go public" in a constructive and not merely retaliatory manner.

All of the foregoing considerations are relevant to police officers who become aware of various forms of corruption, misconduct, waste, and inefficiency within their departments. Not all such deviations will be serious enough or imminent enough to justify whistleblowing, and any act of whistleblowing – because it is indicative of a failure of the department to look after its own affairs – should be seen only as a last resort. Within most police departments, the "code of silence" will probably be sufficiently powerful to cast aspersions on the motives of any who would dare to blow the whistle. Yet it should be remembered that *even if* an officer's motives in going public do not reflect creditably on him, it may not follow that the whistleblowing was unjustified. Those failures warrant exposure whatever the motives of those who make them known. Too often police have attempted to deflect attention from the failures of their departments by casting aspersions on the motives of those who have exposed systemic corruption and complicity in corruption.

9.3.3 *Anonymous and implicated whistleblowing*

Whistleblowers have often paid a heavy price for their efforts.[60] They have been dismissed, demoted, discriminated against, ostracized, even assaulted. The organizations and institutions involved have often taken the view that that is as it should be. Whistleblowers have violated one of the central canons of organizational solidarity and confidentiality and, like civil disobedients, should be willing to accept the cost of their convictions.[61] What is more, exposing the whistleblower to the possibility of untoward consequences will provide a test of conviction and be a deterrent to self-interested exposures.

Yet, though we may wish to deter wrongly motivated and half-cocked or misguided whistleblowing, stories about the long-term consequences suffered by conscientious and public-spirited whistleblowers whose efforts to protect the public interest have often gone beyond the bounds of any moral duty they might have had make it inappropriate that the consequences be left to happenstance. Some protection should be offered. One option is to allow whistleblowers to hide under a cloak of anonymity. Another is to legislate to secure them against harassment, discrimination, and worse. The former option is often thought to play into the hands of unworthily motivated whistleblowers. But the latter option has often been ineffective. Harassment is often difficult to prove, and even if it can be proved, the whistleblower may have had to suffer considerably in the meantime. It is for that reason that some provisions for anonymity may be necessary. In general, it is probably better to encourage openness in complaint, so that those who are accused may, like those in court, be able to face their accusers. But just because the power and interests of those who have violated the public interest are often so great, disproportionate costs will be imposed on whistleblowers. Just as there are "witness protection programs" to shield those who testify in court, so there should be similar provisions for protecting whistleblowers in cases where vengeful reprisals are likely to occur and be difficult to monitor.

One of the things that has often excited the retaliatory anger of those who have had the whistle blown against them has been the fact that the whistleblower has been motivated by self-serving ends. This has been particularly true in the case of implicated whistleblowers. They have been "intercepted" in corrupt activities, and then been offered immunity or the opportunity to lighten their criminal burden in exchange for information that will assist in the conviction of others. It is understandable that others should feel aggrieved and betrayed by such conduct. Even if those involved cannot complain about their penalization, they might reasonably think that the whistleblower has been traitorous and should not be rewarded. In some cases that may be so – the trade-offs are themselves unseemly. But even where the trade-offs seem proportionate, it needs to be remembered that, even though little or no moral credit attaches to the person who blew the whistle, it may have been a good thing that the whistle was blown.[62]

Chapter 10

Public roles and private lives

Surely the fact that a uniformed police officer is wearing his hair below his collar will make him no less identifiable as a policeman.

Thurgood Marshall[1]

As a law enforcement officer . . . I will keep my private life unsullied as an example to all.

Law Enforcement Code of Ethics[2]

The distinction between public and private has never been clear either in theory or in practice.[3] Yet it has often been thought an important distinction for liberal theory. Liberalism seemingly acknowledges a sphere within which the individual should be permitted to act without interference from either the state or other parties. The great liberties – freedom of thought and religion, and freedom of speech – have been thought to belong to this protected sphere, along with all manner of other so-called self-regarding conduct, matters of lifestyle, to the extent that such conduct does not infringe on the legitimate interests of others.

But once we get beyond the elevating rhetoric, it becomes much more difficult to isolate a relevant "zone of privacy," or at least to isolate it in any stable manner. There are many reasons for this. One is to be found in the sheer complexity of the public/private distinction. There is no simple way of drawing it. As marital rape legislation has recognized, what is done in private in a relationship that is generally regarded as private may not be a private matter. A related problem is to be found in the interconnectedness of human life, in the fact that, as John Donne memorably phrased it, "No man is an island, entire of itself."[4] There is little that we do that does not or may not impinge on others, perhaps deleteriously, in some way. In addition, it is possible to argue that such privacy as people are entitled to is partially dependent on their public role.

All of these issues have some relevance to police work. Police officers in democratic countries, as products and bearers of a broadly liberal heritage, will probably wish to claim for themselves a sphere of private conduct. Yet it has been clear from the history of policing that they, along with other "public servants," have often been granted a much narrower sphere and held to much higher standards than other members of society. What claims might they reasonably make? What demands might others reasonably make of them? Do they have private concerns that should be honored just by virtue of their status as moral agents? May they be legitimately asked to waive certain rights to privacy as a result of their assumption of a particular public role?

These questions have arisen in a number of contexts. In the United States, they have arisen most often in the context of police officers' marital circumstances or sexual conduct. There was a time when divorcees or those whose living arrangements were not "sanctified" by marriage were unlikely to gain employment in the New York City Police Department. And police officers who are womanizers or have extramarital affairs or who are gay or have posed for sexually explicit magazines have often found entry denied them or departmental sanctions levied against them.[5] In addition, police officers have sometimes been prevented from engaging in certain "off-duty" social and economic arrangements – such as fraternizing with known criminals, entering into business partnerships with convicted felons, owning rental property in neighborhoods in which they live, living outside the jurisdiction in which they work, drinking in public bars, appearing in commercial advertisements. They have, moreover, sometimes been greatly restricted in their political activities – they have been forbidden from speaking in favor of particular political positions or candidates, or from soliciting political contributions, or from running for political office. And, finally, they have often been penalized for saying things critical or out of keeping with the ethos of their department.

Of course, there are many different distinctions to be drawn here. It is hardly surprising that police should be limited to *legal* off-duty activities. A police officer who engages in criminal activity can hardly expect that this will be ignored by his or her department. And where an off-duty activity affects or is likely to affect the ability of officers to perform their duties, it is not surprising that some action should be taken. But in many cases, even where there is no evidence that such links exist, there is yet thought to be a place for departmental discipline and control.

In this chapter I propose, first, to outline what I take to be the fundamental thrust of the demand for privacy. Then I will look at some of the ways in which those who assume a policing role might be thought to waive some of their claims to privacy. And finally, I will consider some of the specific constraints that have been placed on police officers.

10.1   FOUNDATIONS OF PRIVACY

When the United States Supreme Court in *Griswold* recognized a constitutional right to privacy, it gave public recognition to claims that for over half a century had already been made explicit in the legal literature[6] and that were arguably espoused by liberal writers of an earlier generation. The *Griswold* decision was itself a claim that privacy concerns were implicit in the very fabric of the United States Constitution. However, the correctness of the Supreme Court's position and the exact nature of the right in question, its foundations, and its limits have been matters of contention ever since.

In seeking to articulate bounds of privacy, and to provide some account of its foundations, we do well to keep this contentiousness in mind. Privacy is not some foundational rock whose precise composition and dimensions are matters of dispute, but a much less stable surface that might well turn out to be quicksand. This is not to deny that there are real concerns at stake (*Griswold* was, after all, concerned with the propriety of a law making the use of contraceptives by a married couple a criminal offense). But there is much dispute about the appropriateness of using the language of privacy to handle them.

In particular, what are called privacy rights are often viewed as, or are thought to be reducible to, liberty rights. Though I believe this to involve a misunderstanding of the notion of privacy – the view that the right to privacy is the right to be let alone rather than a right to retain control over certain kinds of personal information[7] – there is, nevertheless, a very close connection between privacy and liberty. And it is useful to approach privacy via liberty, for they emerge from similar normative concerns.

John Stuart Mill's classic essay *On Liberty* provides a useful starting point.[8] According to Mill, there is "a sphere of action in which society, as distinguished from an individual, has, if any, only an indirect interest." It is that "portion of a person's life and conduct which affects only himself or, if it also affects others, only with their free, voluntary and undeceived consent and participation." Society's interest in such "self-regarding" conduct is only indirect because, although what a person does may affect others, any effects that are of legitimate concern to others will be only contingently related to the conduct in question, and can be dealt with independently of it. The consumption of alcohol might interfere with a person's ability to perform his duties, and the latter may be of public concern. But we can prohibit being under the influence while on duty without prohibiting the consumption of alcohol altogether. A person whose gambling habits deprive his family of needed support fails in his duty to his family, and for this failure he may be penalized or otherwise constrained without gambling itself being outlawed.[9]

Mill held that self-regarding conduct is "the appropriate region of human liberty." Its core comprises "the inward domain of consciousness." We are entitled, he says, to "liberty of conscience in the most comprehensive sense, liberty of thought and feeling, absolute freedom of opinion and sentiment on all subjects, practical or speculative, scientific, moral or theological."

On the outer edge of this core is the expression and communication of the objects of consciousness. There ought to be "liberty of expressing and publishing opinions." Although such expressions impinge on others, they are, he says, "almost of as much importance as liberty of thought itself," and their liberty is justified by much the same considerations. Beyond the core, but still belonging to the domain of self-regarding conduct, are many acts and practices that do not violate the interests of others. We should, he writes, recognize "liberty of tastes and pursuits, of framing the plan of our life to suit our own character, of doing as we like, subject to such consequences as may follow, without impediment from our fellow creatures, so long as what we do does not harm them, even though they should think our conduct foolish, perverse, or wrong."[10]

As noted, Mill considers the domain of self-regarding conduct to be the appropriate domain of individual liberty. But why should we recognize such a domain, and how does it connect with a right to privacy? Mill's own answer to this question is influenced by his formal commitment to utilitarianism, and wish to "forego any advantage that could be derived by [his] argument from the idea of abstract right as a thing independent of utility." He states that he regards "utility as the ultimate appeal on all ethical questions, *but* it must be utility in the largest sense, grounded on the permanent interests of man as a progressive being." The qualification, however, is crucial and distinguishes Mill radically from other utilitarians such as Bentham.[11]

Mill's vision of "man as a progressive being" is developed in chapter 3 of *On Liberty*, "Of Individuality, As One Of The Elements Of Well-Being." There, with great rhetorical force, he articulates his conception of what human life ought to be – *a life in which a person's individual potentialities for reason and feeling are cultivated and encouraged to flourish and develop*:

> It is not by wearing down into uniformity all that is individual in themselves, but by cultivating it and calling it forth, within the limits imposed by the rights and interests of others, that human beings become a noble and beautiful object of contemplation; and as the works partake the character of those who do them, by the same process human life also becomes rich, diversified and animating, furnishing more abundant aliment to high thoughts and elevating feelings, and strengthening the tie which binds every individual to the race, by making the race infinitely better worth belonging to.

It is the normative claim of individuality – or, as we might now choose to phrase it – personal autonomy – that provides the raison d'être for liberty and the recognition of a domain of self-regarding conduct. It also provides the basis for recognizing a sphere of privacy, that is, of personal information and knowledge that should remain within a person's control. Knowledge concerning one's sex life or medical history or financial status is usually considered to be private. And the gaining and use of such knowledge by *unauthorized* others is generally considered a serious breach.

Of course, not all personal information qualifies as private. I can hardly claim that my privacy is breached if people look at me or notice what clothes I am wearing, though should they stare at me it may be a different matter. And there is also a certain relativity about the scope of the private, not only between cultures, but within cultures and between individuals. Some, indeed, would argue that privacy is simply a contingent value, a protective cocoon that is needed only until a person becomes robust enough to make his or her own way in the world. Whatever the truth in this, it does not follow that matters deemed to be private are arbitrarily determined. There is a common rationale behind the variations in knowledge.

Although the literature on privacy offers several rationales – for example, as a security against infringements of liberty or control by others, as a constitutive element in or causal precondition for personal autonomy (or individuality), as a means to increased happiness, and so on[12] – its deepest impulse lies in the relation that privacy bears to our securing and maintaining a conception of ourselves as moral agents, as beings who possess some significant measure of individuality or autonomy. Put simply, the demand for privacy is rooted in the need for moral space, that is, for conditions under which we can be, and can feel ourselves to be, acting authentically and independently. Our conception of personhood is one in which the capacity for autonomous activity is of central significance. And at the heart of this is the conception of ourselves as initiators of our acts, even when, as must often be the case, those acts are done in response to others. Moral space is necessary for the development and maintenance of individuality.

Liberty in self-regarding matters is one condition for ensuring moral space. But in addition we need control over certain kinds of information concerning ourselves. In some relationships of mutual intimacy, where another's knowledge of our person does not intrude itself in a threatening or distorting manner, there is a freedom for which privacy is not a precondition. The respect shown by others within such relationships includes their taking us as we are. There is a holistic appreciation that is sensitive to our self-understanding. In such contexts, where privacy serves no protective function, the right to privacy is likely to be waived or only selectively asserted. But not all relationships embody moral space. Where no relationship of mutual intimacy exists, moral space can be secured only if privacy is respected.[13] That is, it can be secured only if one is permitted to have control over one's self-presentation.

The demand for privacy can be seen as a consequence of the ineliminable and necessary tension that exists between personal autonomy and social existence. Specifically personal action is learned in a social context, and it bears the stamp of that context. What we do, how we describe what we do, and how we go about what we do tend to be specific to a particular social environment. But this need not negate the possibility of acting autonomously, for personal autonomy, even though ascribable to individuals, is a social concept. Some social environments, however, are more favorable to the development and maintenance of that autonomy than others. Where, for example, the meaning of one's acts is likely to be misunderstood or to be taken out of context, or where details about one's person or affairs could well affect one's standing as a person in the eyes of others, or where one is vulnerable to becoming simply an object (of curiosity, pity, or contempt) to others, one's autonomy will be at risk. In these situations people are likely to feel that the circumstances are inimical to their own initiatives. Consciousness of (the likelihood of) others' knowledge of one's person and affairs will (or is likely to) intrude upon one's understanding of the social meaning of one's acts, so that what is done will be done in response to a viewpoint that is alienated from one's own. By contrast, where there are relations of mutual trust, what is known about us will not threaten our acts with a significance we do not desire them to have. We can be ourselves and need not feel under pressure to recast our self-presentation to others. In such circumstances, the need for privacy will be correspondingly diminished. So, then, if our awareness of what others know or are able to come to know concerning ourselves places us under considerable pressure to restructure our self-presentation, lest it acquire an unwanted significance, or cause us shame or embarrassment, then our ability to achieve and maintain a unified awareness of ourselves as autonomous agents will be endangered. For we will no longer be free to be ourselves, to be our own person in relation to others. Of course, the privacy that enables us to control our self-presentation and thus to conceal our selves, also enables us to reveal those selves. But even intimacy is a matter of degree, and sometimes in very intimate relationships we may still wish to keep some matters private, lest knowledge of them obtrude unnecessarily and upset what is often a delicate balance.[14]

If what I have said is on the right track, we can see why privacy is a somewhat controversial value. Privatization is a sine qua non of moral space where the social ethos is individualistic or impersonal. Those who find no value in privacy are often committed to a communitarian moral framework in which everything is, so to speak, "within the family." Yet that too may be an excessive demand. We are not, and probably should not aspire to be, "one big family," and even within the family some private space is likely to be important to personal flourishing. The growth of community may diminish, but does not thereby dissolve, the need for a form of privacy.

Such, then, is the broad case for a "zone of privacy" that people ought to be able to claim, and that ought to be protected in various – legal and extralegal – ways. The case I have provided is general, and suggests that police officers, no less than others, have a need for and claim to privacy.

10.1.1 *Public office and private life*

It is one thing to say that individuals ought to be free with respect to their self-regarding conduct, and that privacy, as an aspect of that normative order, ought therefore to be respected. But liberty and privacy are not applicable to people in a completely undifferentiated way. Claims to liberty and privacy must compete with other claims, and individuals or holders of particular offices may find that both their liberties and their expectations of privacy are diminished. Public officials such as police officers, who are expected to foster public confidence in their role as social peacekeepers, may not be at liberty to dress as they please, or to engage in public conduct that we might tolerate in others (say, smoking, gum chewing). And public figures such as film and sports stars, who rely to some extent on public exposure and acclaim, can expect to have a more restricted sphere of privacy than those whose lives are of no particular public interest.

It has long been argued that public officers must be prepared to sacrifice some of their privacy in return for the public trust that they bear. The mandatory financial disclosure laws that apply to some holders of public office represent one such sacrifice. Requiring that they make known their financial holdings is a way in which we seek to ensure that conflicts of interest do not arise or are handled properly (usually by way of recusal) when they do. But what aspects of one's private life must one be prepared to sacrifice, and on what grounds might such invasions of privacy be justified? In particular, what sacrifices, if any, should police officers be expected to make?

One general and obvious enough occasion for removing the veil of privacy is when so-called private conduct renders a person incapable of satisfactorily performing his public duties satisfactorily. A police officer who regularly gets drunk off duty and appears for work with a severe hangover, can hardly complain if his private life is investigated and his freedom to do as he wishes behind closed doors is subsequently restricted.[15] Mill says of such cases that when, by virtue of conduct that might ordinarily be seen as self-regarding, "a person is led to violate a distinct and assignable obligation to any other person or persons, the case is taken out of the self-regarding class, and becomes amenable to moral disapprobation in the proper sense of the term."[16]

But the contingent consequences of a public official's conduct may be of different kinds. In the case of a police officer who gets drunk off duty, it may be that he is not himself rendered less able to perform his duties, but because of his notoriety the ability of others to perform theirs is affected, or the public's confidence in the ability of the department to accomplish its ends is diminished. Are these consequences of such significance that the officer in question ought to be held to account for what is done in his "private life"?

Enumerating and assessing the importance of these various consequentialist considerations is not easy. Their significance will be a function of what we consider to be reasonable expectations to have of the police and the actual (or perhaps only likely) impact that conduct of this or that kind will have on the fulfillment of those expectations. Against such consequentialist considerations there must be set the importance of the conduct for the person concerned.

In U.S. legal cases dealing with the private or off-duty conduct of police officers, three different standards have come to be employed. Where the courts have viewed the conduct in question as being of fundamental importance and constitutionally protected, interferences with it are subjected to "strict scrutiny." That is, the conduct may be interfered with *only* where it is necessary to promote some "compelling governmental interest."[17] Restraints on religious affiliations and speech are likely to be candidates for protection under this test. Where the problem conduct is not constitutionally protected, however, interferences with it are subjected only to a "rational basis" scrutiny. That is, it is required only that the regulation under which an officer has been penalized is "rationally related" to some legitimate governmental interest. Officer dress codes and the residence requirements might well be considered under this heading. In the large gap between these two forms of scrutiny there has grown up a third form, "heightened" scrutiny, which is applied in cases where the interests are regarded as "important" rather than "fundamental." In such cases, some effort is made to balance the competing interests involved. Restraints on the sexual activities of officers are sometimes thought to require scrutiny under this test.

These varied forms of scrutiny, and the reasons for adopting them, provide a useful, if controversial, insight into the constraints that may be placed on police expectations of privacy.

10.2 POLICE OFFICERS AND THEIR POLITICS

It is useful to begin with the political opinions and involvements of police officers, since it was the political activity of a police officer that for many years shaped the private lives of public officers.

It is to be expected that individual police officers, as human beings and citizens, will have political opinions and will want to express them in various practical ways. They may desire to make them known to others, or even want to participate in the work of a political party to which they feel sympathetic. They may even wish to stand for public office. In the early days of American policing, ties between police and local politics were very close. Sheriffs were oftentimes elected officials; police officers were frequently chosen by, and certainly their advancement depended upon, ward bosses; and police and civic corruption were deeply intertwined. Eventually efforts were made to sever or at least to discourage such ties, ostensibly in the name of reform, but probably also as part of a larger political shift and reorganization of the workplace. In some places all political activity beyond voting was forbidden. The position was formalized in the 1892 case of *McAuliffe v. Mayor of New Bedford*. Here a police officer failed in his appeal against dismissal for violating a regulation concerning political activities. In delivering the judgment of the Supreme Court of Massachusetts, Oliver Wendell Holmes, Jr., asserted: "The petitioner may have a constitutional right to talk politics, but he has no constitutional right to be a policeman."[18] Holmes's dictum was to hold sway for many years, and until 1967 police were discouraged from, or forbidden to take part in, political activities beyond the "secret" one of voting. The general position was captured by the nationally used *Eagle Police Manual*, which warned that police officers should not engage in political discussions "when off duty if in uniform or not, except to deposit such ballot as they prefer at the primaries and elections. They shall not solicit or make contribution in money, or otherwise, for political purposes, not [sic] be present at any rally, convention or other political gathering except as police officer there detailed for duty."[19] Although the *McAuliffe* doctrine has been considerably modified, there remains a great deal of resistance to many forms of political involvement by police.[20]

One of the things at stake here is the possibility that police officers who exercise their political freedom will undermine the public trust they are called upon to fulfill. There is the suspicion that an officer's exercise of discretion will be influenced by his/her political views and/or the political views of others. Given that political views are often strongly held, and have historically provided a basis for invidious discrimination, this might seem to be a real problem. Much, however, will depend on the nature of the particular involvement rather than involvement as such – whether or not it is party political, and whether it is disruptive or likely to be so. It is this recognition that led to the court decisions that overrode *McAuliffe*.

In *Garrity v. New Jersey*, in which the dismissal of a police officer for invoking the Fifth Amendment privilege against self-incrimination was overturned, the court drew on an earlier case involving a schoolteacher to argue that, along with teachers, "policemen . . . are not relegated to a watered down version of constitutional rights."[21] Even though public officials may have responsibilities that others lack, they do not thereby surrender their rights. The position was clarified the following year in *Pickering v. Board of Education*, another case involving a teacher. Here the Supreme Court emphasized the need to seek "a balance between the interests of the [public employee], as a citizen, in commenting upon matters of public concern and the interest of the State, as an employer, in promoting the efficiency of the public services it performs through its employees."[22] In Pickering's case, which involved a letter to a local newspaper that criticized the Board of Education and the Superintendent for the way in which bond elections had been handled and school funds allocated, the Court argued that the public interest served by Pickering's letter outweighed the discomfort and disruption that had been caused. But the Court also recognized that cases would differ and that the decision in Pickering's case could not be generalized.

When we go beyond general "political" speech to party-political speech and activities of a more concrete kind the difficulties increase, for the more partisan an officer's commitments, the greater might appear to be the likelihood of discrimination, with its undermining of public confidence and consequent effects on the "efficiency" of the service offered. The *appearance* of bias might be serious enough to justify placing some limits on political activity. A police officer who decides to run for political office, for example, might reasonably be required to resign before doing so, lest his political campaigning corrupt or be felt to corrupt his exercises of authority. But other forms of political activity might be more acceptable. Uniformed officers who appeared in "Law Enforcement for Bush" advertisements might be thought to have exercised their personal, professional, and political rights in an acceptable fashion, even if the views they expressed were controversial.

In addition to external problems with active party support or involvement, there might also be internal ones. Superior officers who actively express their political opinions might have a "chilling effect" on their subordinates' freedom, and it is not unreasonable to suppose that such views might sometimes be allowed to influence matters such as assignment, promotion, leave, and so on. Perhaps the best that can be said here is that verbal and other more practical expressions of political viewpoint and involvement need to be monitored lest they begin to corrupt the police role as *social* rather than partisan peacekeepers.

10.3 POLICE AND FREE SPEECH

Much of what we have said about police and their political involvements applies equally to their free speech rights. The *McAuliffe* doctrine, used to suppress police political activity, was also used to suppress police speech more generally, including speech that blew the whistle on agency wrongdoing. But *Pickering* established a more reasonable test that was subsequently refined in *Connick v. Myers*. In the latter case, an assistant district attorney was dismissd after she distributed a questionnaire in protest against her transfer to a different division. In the questionnaire she solicited her co-workers' opinions about office morale and personnel. The Court upheld her dismissal after applying a two-pronged test: (1) Does the speech in question address a matter of public concern? and (2) Is the employee's interest in making the statement outweighed by the agency's interest in suppressing it?[23] Each prong raises its own questions. What constitutes a matter of public concern? Does some particular statement *a* fall within its purview? How does one balance the employee's and agency's interests?

In a 1981 civil rights case in which certiorari was denied, the Fifth Circuit considered the situation of a lieutenant in the University of Georgia police department who was dismissed after revealing to others that his superiors had altered an accident report involving the chief of police.[24] The university claimed that the lieutenant's action was incompatible with the discipline necessary for a quasi-military organization and the working relationship that needed to exist between a superior and a subordinate. Although the court accepted the point, it argued that what the lieutenant had made known was of grave public concern, that what he had said thus fell within his First Amendment rights, and that it was therefore the *court's* task to balance the interests involved. It awarded the lieutenant compensatory and punitive damages. Where speech has not referred to matters of public concern and has been deemed disruptive, the courts have usually been unwilling to support it, at least where the speech has occurred in the ordinary course of an officer's duties.[25]

However, in a 1987 case, the United States Supreme Court decided that a deputy constable was improperly dismissed for making the remark: "If they go for him again, I hope they get him," following the shooting of then President Ronald Reagan. According to the majority, since the privately uttered (though overheard) remark did not constitute a threat and reflected the officer's disagreement with the President's domestic policies, thus qualifying it as being on a matter of public concern, and since the particular deputy did not have significant contact with the public and was only minimally involved in law enforcement, the statement was protected.[26]

When the statements in question concern departmental matters, the situation gets tricky. What if the statements concern the efficient and ordered running of the criminal justice system, or are reflective of an officer's position as a union member, or concern what is viewed as a display of racial discrimination against oneself? In such cases, the situation is much less clear. It is so, partly because the First Amendment has generally been interpreted as giving greatest protection to issues of public concern, and where the status of utterances becomes less clear, the protection tends to diminish. At the same time, the courts have not been oblivious to the "practical realities of running a government office," and have not wished to foster or defend a situation in which employee grievances are constitutionalized.[27] Crucial to a number of such decisions has been the identity of the *recipient* of the problematic speech – whether it has been an appropriate superior[28] and/or would be disruptive of good order or an effective working relationship.

Most of the court cases have concerned speech "on the job," and not remarks that are made off duty. If a police officer attends a public meeting in the neighborhood in which he resides, need he take account of the fact that utterances made as a private citizen might be construed somewhat differently because he is known to be a police officer? If his privately expressed views differ significantly from those of departmental policy, ought the officer to be held to account for them? Does it make a difference if the neighborhood in which the officer lives is not the same as the neighborhood in which he serves?

Although freedom of expression constitutes one of the most important requirements of personality, and lies at the heart of any tradition that places importance on individual moral agency, the acceptance of a public role also carries with it obligations that may sometimes stand in tension with an unfettered right of free expression. Though an officer who is off duty must certainly be accorded greater freedom to express his personal opinions than one who expresses them while on duty, especially if they will be "publicly" heard, there must still be some recognition of the fact that what is said off duty, if said in public, might affect the ability of a department to provide its services efficiently. Of course, *that* decision, namely, that a department's interests have been damaged by what an officer has said in an off-duty context, need not be taken at face value. Too often the interests of a department have in fact been little more than the interests of an officeholder who sees his position being challenged. That, as much as anything, probably lay behind the strongly split decision in *Connick v. Myers*.

An officer who attends a public meeting as a private citizen needs to take into account the fact that what he says may be interpreted by others in the light of their knowledge that he is a police officer. It counsels care rather than silence. And if the officer's own views are significantly different from those of his department, that should probably be made clear, albeit in a way that does not create problems for the department's ability to function effectively.

Officers have only so much responsibility for what they say as private citizens, and if others misinterpret or willfully misuse their off-duty statements, the officers should not be held responsible for all the consequences of what they have said.

10.4 POLICE OFFICERS AND SEXUAL PRIVACY

Regulation of the off-duty sexual conduct of police officers has generally been subject to only a rational basis test. That is, it has been sufficient for a police department to show that regulations prohibiting certain kinds of off-duty sexual conduct were not arbitrarily related to legitimate governmental objectives in order to sustain the dismissal of an officer for engaging in the prohibited conduct. In *Shawgo v. Spradlin*, where a patrol sergeant and police officer were disciplined for off-duty dating and inter-rank cohabitation, it was deemed sufficient for the department to show that the conduct in question could have resulted in unfavorable criticism and was thought to be prejudicial to good order.[29] There was in fact no evidence that there had been any such criticism or that the department's ability to function had been detrimentally affected or that the officers in question had been less diligent in the performance of their duties.

Use of this test for off-duty sexual conduct has been criticized. Michael Woronoff, for example, claims that some sort of heightened scrutiny ought to be applied in such cases. He believes that such regulations should be shown to be substantially (rather than reasonably) related to an important (rather than a merely legitimate) governmental interest.[30] His own view is that no important governmental interest is so served.

In the literature, however, several governmental interests have been asserted to be served by regulations relating to off-duty sexual conduct. Included among these have been (1) the promotion of public morality, (2) the promotion of respect for police officers, and (3) the promotion of an efficiently functioning police department. But none of these, Woronoff argues, is sufficiently important to justify special restrictions on the off-duty sexual behavior of police officers. For (a), unless conduct is seen as sufficiently immoral as to be illegal, there is not a sufficiently important public interest to override an officer's right to privacy. It is not generally for the government to promote morality. Moreover (b), it is, Woronoff believes, doubtful whether promotion of a high degree of respect for police officers is a sufficiently important governmental interest to justify an intrusion into officers' off-duty activities. In any case, any weakening of respect is contingent on the conduct in question being made public, something that he says is unlikely to happen if, as will often be the case, it occurs in private.[31] And finally, (c) he argues that it is unlikely that off-duty sexual conduct as such will significantly affect a department's good order and efficiency.[32]

1. Connected with the first interest is the view, frequently espoused by police management, that police officers should be considered role-models.

Support for this view is sometimes made quite explicit. In the IACP's Law Enforcement Code of Ethics, for example, an officer pledges: "I will keep my private life unsullied as an example to all . . . Honest in thought and deed in both my personal and official life."[33] And in the more recent statement of Values of the New York City Police Department, police officers pledge themselves to "maintain a higher standard of integrity than is generally expected of others because so much is expected of us."[34]

The argument has been considered at some length by Frederick Elliston. He contends that defenders of constricted privacy rights for police hold that "as public officials and bearers of a public trust, [police] must represent the public at all times."[35] Such representation carries with it the expectation that police function as "role models" – model citizens, bearers of community standards, perpetuators of the social mores. Elliston distinguishes two versions of this argument: (a) If police are to fulfill their proper social function, they must be role models; and (b) As a matter of fact, police are looked to as social role models; it is reasonable, therefore, to expect that they will live accordingly.

In the first version, Elliston complains, the crucial question is begged. He does not find it at all obvious that police should function as social role models. Though there may be some argument for expecting them to act in an exemplary fashion with respect to their specific duties – to be polite, efficient, law abiding, peaceable, and so on – he sees no reason why they (more than anyone else) should be *required* to have exemplary private lives. At least the burden is on those who maintain it to show why *police* should function as social role models.

In the second version, the propriety of the role model function is not argued for, but simply claimed as a social fact from which certain responsibilities should follow; that is, because many people do have these expectations of police, the police are under some obligation to live up to them. Elliston does not see why such social expectations should be binding or perpetuated. Others within the community might more reasonably be expected to be and to have a more effective role as behavioral models – teachers, clergy, and so on.[36] He knows of no evidence showing that police are or are considered to be more influential models than others. And, to give it something of a moral twist, he believes that a community that celebrates the joys of deviance in its entertainment industry is in no moral position to expect police to be effective role models.[37]

2. Elliston also has a version of the argument that bases itself on the respect police should have and which, it is alleged, might be lost should they engage in certain kinds of "inappropriate" sexual conduct.

He observes that police work, by its very nature, involves the exercise of considerable discretion, much of it unsupervised. It is important that police exercise their discretion wisely. Our confidence that they will do so will be assisted and sustained if we know them to be people of the highest character, upright and impartial. Of this we may be reasonably assured if they conduct themselves in an exemplary fashion at all times. If their private lives show weakness, it will not be as easy to maintain confidence in the integrity of their judgments as they carry out their largely unsupervised public roles. We may anticipate a "spillover" from one sphere to the other: Private failures will probably signal public failures. Excessive drinking or rowdiness in private is likely to indicate disabled judgment or abuse of authority in the work situation. "If married, he must be a disciplined family man, for if he cannot function acceptably in that role, he cannot be expected to control family disturbances to which he might be called."[38]

Elliston is no more impressed with this form of the argument than he was with the role model version. And to the extent that he does think it carries weight, he does not believe that it serves to single out police, or any other *public* officials, for higher standards of private conduct. In many cases, deviant private behavior will not affect efficiency, or will be extremely unlikely to do so. Any slope will not be very slippery. Is the police officer who poses for a (legal) *Playboy* or *Playgirl* centerfold likely to find his/her judgment affected as a result? Or be less able to police those who violate laws relating to sexual conduct? In those few cases where a police officer's ability to work is affected, then his/her situation is no different from that of anyone whose private life impinges on a public role. In that case, the behavior, even if engaged in *in private* (that is, away from the public gaze), is no longer *merely private* (that is, potent with respect to his/her interests alone). It becomes a matter of public concern, to be dealt with appropriately.

It is Elliston's belief, furthermore, that there is sufficient peer supervision to negate many of the public effects of private deviance. Police officers, concerned that they and their work not be brought into disrepute, will put pressure on their deviant colleagues to desist from unacceptable behavior. Police should not be placed under more stringent requirements than others.[39] They should be treated equally with others.

3. The third interest identified by Woronoff, that concerned with good order, is generally tied to a conception of the police as a paramilitary organization, in which hierarchical boundaries are to be observed and a particular esprit de corps is cultivated and sustained via dress and other regulations. In *Shawgo v. Spradlin*, the fact that Stanley Whisenhunt was a sergeant and Janet Shawgo only a patrol officer, and the fact that he was also sharing an apartment with a subordinate, figured significantly in the disciplinary action taken against him (and against Shawgo as well).

While there can be no doubt that good order and efficiency is essential to an effective police department, it is doubtful whether the full range of military observances is necessary for the task to which police are called. As we have observed on a number of occasions previously, battle discipline is required for only a small part of police work. As social peacekeepers rather than crimefighters pure and simple, much of their time is spent assisting the community in nonmilitary ways. Though it is reasonable that some form of hierarchy be maintained, and that efforts be made to minimize opportunities for conflicts of interest in relationships of the kind into which Shawgo and Whisenhunt entered, it seems morally unacceptable that they should be forbidden outright. It would seem to follow, from the *Shawgo* decision, that had Whisenhunt and Shawgo been husband and wife before Shawgo sought employment as a police officer, it would have been all right to reject her on the grounds of her relationship with Whisenhunt. What if they had both been employed as patrol officers, and one of them had subsequently been promoted? Would that be a cause for action?

In *Kelley v. Johnson*, a case that concerned the length of a patrol officer's hair, the Supreme Court argued that the paramilitary mode of organization that the Suffolk County police had chosen to enable its efficient handling of the duties assigned to it established a need for "discipline, esprit de corps and uniformity." The various rules and regulations it had promulgated to give effect to that choice were, the Court considered, to be viewed in the light of that choice, and not in isolation. It was not necessary for the department to "establish" a "genuine public need" for specific regulations. Instead, it was up to the respondent to demonstrate a lack of "rational connection between the regulation, based as it is on the county's method of organizing its police force, and the promotion of safety of persons and property."[40] In the Court's view, by failing to do that the respondent had also failed to show that his liberty interest under the Fourteenth Amendment had been improperly infringed.

It was to this argument that Justice Thurgood Marshall directed the remark quoted at the beginning of this chapter. It was his view that "an individual's personal appearance may reflect, sustain, and nourish his personality and may well be used as a means of expressing his attitude and lifestyle,"[41] and that it was therefore important to establish a rational connection between the specific regulation and goals such as officer identifiability and esprit de corps. As he considered it, the uniform satisfied the latter requirement, and any esprit de corps supposedly fostered by the regulation was negated by the fact that in regard to more substantial hairstyle matters – say the wearing of an Afro hair style or a crew cut – the department was neutral. The county's prohibition of hair touching the ears or collar was therefore unlikely to "create any increment in similarity of appearance among members of a uniformed police force."[42]

As before, I suspect that there is excessive rigidity in this area, born of an over-regard for a paramilitary style of management. Nevertheless, the legal arguments seem to leave out of account factors that are sometimes considered important in the provision of public services, namely, the level of confidence recipients can feel that they are being responsibly served. Presumably, uniformed officers on duty are required to wear their headgear, and so it makes little difference whether an officer has an Afro hair style or crew cut. But hair protruding from below the headgear will be visible and, admittedly for reasons of social prejudice, may lead some members of the public to feel that they are dealing with a "hippie" type. The clean-cut look may be one of the ways in which a department promotes confidence in its officers. No doubt it would be preferable were public confidence unrelated to such matters, and perhaps a police department should do what it can to counter social prejudice, but as long as such prejudices exist, then there is some case for police departments to take cognizance of them in considering such matters as officer appearance and behavior.[43]

It is Woronoff's contention that the equal protection clause of the Fourteenth Amendment sets the appropriate standard for police off-duty conduct. It does not rule out that police might have responsibilities that others do not, but it requires that any discrimination against police be subjected to some form of heightened scrutiny. Elliston advances a version of the same argument, based on the ethical requirement of fairness.

Taking his cue from the Aristotelian dictum that equals should be treated equally and unequals unequally, in proportion to their relevant differences,[44] Elliston notes that only if there are appropriate means for distinguishing between "equals" and "unequals" will the dictum carry any practical significance. To be implemented, the Aristotelian formula requires that we be able to determine "relevant" similarities and differences, a task that is notoriously difficult, though not for that reason to be shirked. Certain broad observations can be made. For example, when it comes to matters like hair color, texture, and growth, we are all likely to differ; but not in a way that will be relevant to our social obligations and privileges. For the most part, we can argue the same with respect to differences of gender, skin color, and social class.

It is Elliston's contention that so far as our social obligations and privileges are concerned, our being in *private* or *public* employment is also an irrelevant basis for discrimination. If privately employed people may conduct their private lives as they wish, so long as it does not affect the quality of their work or damage the interests of others, the same freedom ought also to extend to those in public employment. Moreover, any discrimination will harm not only them, but also those close to them, with whom they might be consenting parties in the deviant conduct.

Sometimes departments have used regulations prohibiting "conduct unbecoming an officer" to justify their penalization of off-duty sexual activity. This is open to a further objection, that of being too vague to protect officers from arbitrary and discriminatory treatment. Furthermore, it fails to provide officers with fair warning of what is and is not allowable.[45]

I believe that Elliston is right to think that constraints on police officers and other public officials, qua public officials, need to be justified. If a higher standard is not merely expected but required of police officers, some reason for this needs to be given. However, his appreciation of the rationales behind the higher demands made of police seems limited.

As we have observed again and again, police officers possess considerable power. They have been socially sanctioned to use necessary force in the fulfillment of their law enforcement, social service, and, more generally, peacekeeping roles. For the most part, however, that power is not exercised forcibly but authoritatively. It is publicly sanctioned or recognized power, and needs to be employed forcibly only when it is not acknowledged, and, even then, within appropriate limits. For most of us, the word of command is sufficient, though contingently so. Our confidence in its propriety will last as long as we believe that the police know what they are about.

The problem faced by a police officer whose private life deviates from the prevailing norms is that his/her authority may thereby be undermined. The recognition on which his/her authority depends may be lost. How is that so? As Elliston recognizes, police officers possess considerable discretionary authority. In their use of that authority, they must make complex decisions, requiring a considerable degree of good judgment and moral sensitivity. If in their private lives they engage in conduct which seems, at least to others, to be distinctly lacking in good judgment and/or moral sensitivity, then their public authority may be eroded. However wise their professional judgments may be, they may not be appreciated as such.[46]

The point I am making here has little to do with the thrust of the first two arguments that I considered. It is not that police should be role models. Being a role model is not obviously part of their function. With that much of Elliston's position I agree. But if they are to retain their authority, they may need to ensure that their claim to recognition, as people "in the know," is not belied or at least called into question by their private conduct. Since much of police discretionary decision making contains a significant moral component, there is a real possibility that what are seen as character defects, even if displayed only in private, will serve to undermine public authority. This is why Elliston's Aristotelian argument from fairness will not work. Police have a discretionary authority that most of us lack, and this is relevant to what may be expected of them. There may indeed, therefore, be relevant differences between the work of police officers (and other public officials with significant discretionary authority) and that of ordinary citizens which makes "unequal" treatment justified.

Nor am I suggesting that the private conduct of a police officer will "spill over" into public conduct, as this slippery slope argument suggests. It may, but that is not my point here. My contention is not so much that what the police officer does in private will *affect* his/her power to make appropriate judgments in his/her public role. Rather, what he/she does in private is believed to *manifest* an inability to make appropriate judgments in public.

This point can be dramatically underlined in court. If the particular police officer is called as a witness, the cross-examining defense lawyer may seek to use such private conduct to discredit the officer's testimony. Although it is probably not part of a police officer's task to be a role model, the fact that the social recognition that is constitutive of his authority is contingent upon expectations concerning the private as well as the public life of the officer, places a burden on the officer to conduct himself in private in a way that will not compromise his public standing.

The foregoing bears on an issue of ongoing contention in many departments, namely, whether officers should reside in the community in which they work. Although there are many considerations for and against residential requirements, one reason why many officers oppose the requirement is a desire to maintain privacy. They do not wish their private lives to be open to the scrutiny of those among whom they have to work.

PART III
Organizational ethics

Chapter 11

Authority and accountability

Quis custodiet ipsos custodes?

Juvenal[1]

Purely structural arrangements for achieving accountability do not, on their own, reach the problems citizens most want to reach.

Herman Goldstein[2]

Near the beginning of this book (Chapter 2, Section 2.2), I argued that authority is a social relation in which a form of deference is accorded to those who are perceived as being "in the know" with respect to the matters for which their authority is acknowledged. Police authority is no exception. Where their authority is acknowledged, police are generally believed to know what they are about. To the extent that we see their demands as being authoritatively issued, we comply with them because we believe that they know what they are doing. Even if we are reluctant to do what they ask of us, and we comply with their orders more out of concern for the consequences if we do not than out of a recognition of the propriety of what is demanded of us, there is still an acknowledgement that, so far as the threat and/or exercise of that force is concerned, it will be informed and appropriate. Compelled compliance or compliance to avoid the consequences does not automatically carry with it the implication that there was an exercise of force majeure or that what has been imposed upon us is morally equivalent to the threat of a gunman. The police use or threat of force is authoritative because it is taken to be proportioned to the demand that has been made on us. Only when we do not see it that way, as has occurred at times in our social history, will we view such uses or threats of force as indistinguishable from those of the bully or agent of a tyrannical state.

It is precisely because authority is a social relation rather than some inherent property that police are accountable to others for the authority they possess. Who are those others? In what does their accountability consist?

And how is it to be effected? These questions, particularly their moral underpinnings, will be the focus of this chapter.

The police are vested with authority in respect of a role that I have broadly characterized as social peacekeeping. This role (Chapter 2, Section 2.4) is partially articulated in terms of normative factors – rights or entitlements, privileges, powers, duties, and responsibilities – and it is with respect to the fulfillment of these normative expectations that "we" are concerned to hold them accountable.

The question of accountability can be raised at more than one level. Broadly, we can address it at the level of the police organization. Or we can look within the organization, at the individuals or units that comprise it, and consider their accountability. Presumably a satisfactory answer to one inquiry should cohere with that of the other, though the institutional nature of police work makes the former inquiry more critical. We can, if we like, talk about a structure of accountability within which individual, divisional, and organizational accountability can be coherently, efficiently, and acceptably pursued. Because individual and divisional accountability most often takes place within the broader context of organizational accountability, I shall pay more attention initially to issues of organizational accountability.

11.1   CONCEPTS OF ACCOUNTABILITY

Accountability can be thought of either normatively or structurally. It can characterize a demand that may be made or a condition that exists. To say that police are accountable for their authority can be to say either that they should be answerable (held to account) for what they do,[3] or that they are able to answer for what they do.

In both senses, accountability tends to be confused with liability or blame for shortcomings. That is commonly true in discussions of police accountability. Juvenal's much-quoted question displays a deep skepticism toward society's guardians. Can *they* be trusted any more than anybody else? The question is appropriately raised, and its focus is understandable, for our interest in accountability is often generated by untoward events for which there is a desire to allocate blame – for purposes of imposing punishment or exacting compensation, or, if not that, to provide a justification or excuse. Minimally, it tends to be generated by a desire to change things – to fix problems or ensure that they do not recur. Were human beings never to stray from what is judged to be an appropriate path, our interest in accountability would be greatly reduced, if not minimal.

Yet we ought not to forget that the question of accountability can be raised in relation to good as well as to evil, for the purposes of planning social policy and the giving of rewards as well as liability for disaster and the dispensing of penalties. Indeed, just because evil or its temptations are so familiar or attractive to us, accountability for good and the acknowledgment of those who do it should probably be given much greater importance. This is particularly true in police work, where officers often feel – and are – underappreciated.

Particularly in the case of police authority, though perhaps in that of social institutions generally, the scope of accountability is, or at least ought to be, very broad, encompassing every use of that authority, whether for good or ill. For wherever people seek to have influence over others, and have institutional authority and power to effect it, they should properly be held to account.

In its normative sense, police accountability is constituted by holding them, organizationally and / or individually, responsible for what they do, by seeing their policies and practices and what they claim authority to do as things that should be open to scrutiny and that they should be prepared to justify. Their social task and practices, along with their authority, are not timelessly determined "in the order of things," but socially determined and socially sustained. That is true of their role as social peacekeepers (if that is how we see them to be), and it is true of the ways in which they seek to embody that role in various organizational goals and objectives and regulations and practices. Authority is given, and that authority may evaporate or be taken away.

In its structural sense, police accountability is generally constituted by mechanisms that enable normative accountability to be determined. In large organizations such mechanisms are frequently missing, or their operation is seriously defective. There is a dispersal, diffusion, and dissipation of accountability that effectively undermines attributions of responsibility. Such organizations evade or avoid accountability.[4] And even if the mechanisms of accountability are in place, they may not be enough. As the opening quotation from Herman Goldstein indicates, the existence of mechanisms is no guarantee of their effectiveness. The telephone "runaround" is a prime example of this: More generally, it is the sapping of energy that bureaucratic lethargy is able to accomplish. Ultimately, whether structural accountability succeeds in providing normative accountability will depend significantly on the presence of a *willingness* to be held accountable so that such mechanisms can work. As Justice Holmes himself recognized, when enunciating his view that the law is there to give bad people a reason to be good,[5] unless you also think that there are people of good will, and that the law itself will "tend to make good citizens and good men," it will be an ineffective social instrument. It is only as the mechanisms of accountability are administered conscientiously and competently and encourage self-examination and self-improvement that they will be more than a political chip or public relations tool. Otherwise the mechanisms may even function as a shield against accountability, since they provide an appearance, but not the reality, of accountability. Goldstein has pointed out that accountability is not to be confused with mere responsiveness to demands.[6] An organization that is accountable may or may not be responsive to all the varied demands that are made of it. In a plural society, and in a society that is national as well as local, police hear many, and sometimes contradictory, voices and they cannot be responsive to all of them. They must decide which of those voices to heed. But the decision about which voices to respond to, and which not, is a decision for which they can be held normatively, and should be held structurally, accountable.

Perhaps another way of making the point is to note that responsiveness is a matter of degree. The degree to which police are or should be responsive to the demands made upon them is an issue of accountability. That, indeed, has been an important element in some current debates over the deployment of police resources. Whereas some departments have measured their success in terms of "response time" to emergency calls, others have figured that a community is better served by diverting more police resources to "broken windows" and the reversal of community decay.[7]

As will later become clear, holding police accountable for what they do is not the same as perusing, scrutinizing, or participating in all their decision-making processes. We are talking about openness to scrutiny or access to the participation of others rather than about actual involvement in their decision-making processes. How accountability is best implemented is a complex practical question that takes us beyond anything I can hope to cover here.

11.2   COMMUNAL ACCOUNTABILITY

It is natural to answer the general question, "To whom are the police normatively accountable?" by reference to the community that they are appointed to serve.[8] To the extent that some version of social contract theory can be accepted, and police can be said to have their authority because a community – and not some transcendent "order of things" – bestows it, they are answerable to that community. Their authority is conferred so that certain communally shared purposes can be achieved, and they are to be held accountable to the community for the way in which they apply themselves to those purposes.

As might be expected, this picture is far too simple. For one thing, as we have seen, communal consent tends to be configured by traditions of communal life. Police authority tends to be a "given" of the social life into which we are initiated. It was there before us and, presumably, it will continue after we have gone. Our consent to the institution is in some measure a form of acquiescence. Not that such authority is rigidly given: this is the important truth in contract theory. The traditions into which we have been initiated also provide for the questioning, and, to some extent, even the reconfiguration, of that authority. The community served by police is not so fixed in its ways that police can be simply presumed to know what they are about and to be about it well.

Although social contract theory, in either its actual or hypothetical forms, makes police ultimately accountable to the community, I do not want to suggest that it provides the only normative resource for that view. Nor should we too casually assume that it is the community, rather than God or the monarch or some oligarchy, to whom the police are accountable. But these are much larger questions of political theory than I can tackle here. And I must assume that what in broad terms social contract theory wishes to argue with respect to political and police authority is plausible.

There is a further problem, however. Who or what constitutes the community to which police are accountable? Is it some consensus, a majority, a ruling class or powerful group, or the bearers of its timeworn traditions? Is it some tenuously connected plurality or lowest common denominator? Social contract theory operates best against a background of relatively homogeneous social expectations, where there is some agreement about what values police are there to protect, and some agreement about how they are to be protected. For liberal societies, although there may be some broad procedural agreement that keeps them from fragmentation, at the level of substantive beliefs there is likely to be a great deal of disagreement. Even though many U.S. police departments are municipally based, and their members do not have to be responsive to some larger social collectivity (apart from the one that is enshrined in law and court decisions), even municipalities are often quite heterogeneous. In urban environments particularly, there may be little homogeneity of viewpoint or tradition, and police will often feel called upon to perform contradictory tasks. A police department that has to serve an area as diverse as Crown Heights in New York – with close-knit Hasidic and poor black and Hispanic communities jockeying for police resources – is likely to find itself pulled in incompatible directions. As well, police are expected to preserve the tolerability of public areas such as bus terminals and train stations, at the same time being sensitive to the needs and rights of the homeless and down-and-outs who may wish to seek refuge in them.[9]

Legal and court decisions complicate this even further. Police are expected to catch criminals, but at the same time to honor scrupulously the rights of suspects and other citizens. The U.S. exclusionary rules, whatever their merits as interpretations of the Constitution, mandate quite substantial constraints on police practice.[10] Police are expected to maintain order, but also to acknowledge the right of people to assemble, demonstrate, and protest. What are sometimes put forward as competing models of criminal justice – "crime control" and "due process"[11] – are reflective of competing communal concerns, and police as executors of "the" communal will are caught in the middle.

In such circumstances, one classic liberal appeal, enunciated more explicitly in the United Kingdom than in the United States, has been to "the rule of law," and to the police officer's role as an officer of the law. Law, it is said, stands above the narrowly political and partisan interests of a community, and constitutes its ongoing collective public will. The officer is a servant of that law. Thus a police officer's role responsibilities are circumscribed by the law and are to some extent focused on its enforcement. In English policing, some such understanding has been legally affirmed and is now part of a constable's oath of office.[12] It helps to explain the extreme position taken by a former Commissioner of the Metropolitan Police, Sir David McNee (1977–82):

> The political neutrality of the police service and the political independence and impartiality of chief police officers is central to the British policing system. I personally regard it as so important that I no longer exercise my right to vote, nor have I since I was appointed a chief officer of police. Police officers must be men and women of the middle, bound only by the rule of law.[13]

But although the symbolism is clear, there is a certain disingenuousness about McNee's understanding of being "bound only by the rule of law." No doubt the hierarchical structure of policing places a chief officer under pressure and provides him with significant opportunities to enforce the law in ways that are politically partial. Home Secretaries have been known to use their position to influence the activities of Chief Constables.[14] But many opportunities for partisan enforcement are available to other police, and one might wonder why Sir David did not think that he would be compromised or appear to be compromised *before* he took up his leadership position. And why should we think that not exercising his right to vote showed him to be politically independent and impartial? Refusing to vote is only one – and for a chief police officer probably a very minor – way of manifesting a certain kind of political independence and impartiality. No doubt with hindsight historians of policing will be able to locate Sir David on the political map. At best, his refusal to vote had a symbolic significance.

But there are other weaknesses in the idea that police, to serve the community, are servants only of the rule of law. We have already noted that a great deal of police work does not specifically concern law enforcement (Chapter 2, Section 2.4). Police are called upon to render a variety of emergency and other community services for which there are no specific legal solutions, for which discretion is required, and for which the sanction of "lawfulness" operates only as a broad side-constraint: As long as police do not break the law, it is for them to decide how they will act.[15] The rendering of those community services may well reflect the influence of partisan politics – and if not partisan politics, then class, religious, or other cultural values.

Indeed, even when police are engaged in law enforcement, they have and exercise considerable discretion with regard to whether and how the law is to be enforced. Law does not constitute an exclusive or higher reference point to which police can always determinatively appeal. Not only that, the very laws they will be called upon to enforce may be political and partial in just the sense that Sir David sought to avoid. Although legislation is democratic in the sense that it is the outcome of a democratic process conducted by democratically elected representatives, and, furthermore, does not automatically lose its authority with a change of government, even the most naïve observer of the legislative process knows that many laws reflect partisan values and interests, and that police will be expected to enforce at least some of these laws. Even the enforcement process might be influenced by ongoing political events and the expectations of an incumbent political power.

In the United States, where political involvement in police activity has a long and notorious history, and where even now police chiefs are often mayoral appointees or, in the case of sheriffs, sometimes elected to office, the interests of partisan politics may intrude even more powerfully. True, the argument for making a chief's appointment dependent on mayoral goodwill may be justified by reference to the latter's answerability to the voting community. But we should not confuse this with being apolitical or being above the influence of partisan interests. Indeed, police activity, or inactivity, may be quite sensitive to a mayoral desire for reelection.

The major problem for police, however, especially for line officers, may not be that they feel pressed into partisan service, but that they often have great difficulty in knowing what their communal reference should be, even when they are engaged in law enforcement. One reason for this is to be found in their frequent feeling that they are held accountable to values and a community that are alien to them.[16] They are called to show tolerance and impartiality and to defend civil rights in contexts where these values interfere with the pursuit of what they firmly believe to be right and the purging of what they firmly believe to be wrong. Why should perpetrators and others who promulgate alien values be treated with kid gloves and liberal tolerance? Why should those who have grown up in environments marked by clear standards of right and wrong, and a commitment to "traditional values," now be made the agents of the values of an intellectual élite?

Psychologically and socially, the problem is a difficult one, one that will continue so long as police are drawn from a segment of society that, though protected and in some ways sustained by its broader traditions, may not itself place much value on those traditions. There is a tension here that police have not always fully appreciated, though that may be changing. As urban and some suburban police departments broaden their horizons, and draw on a wider segment of the population, their social and cultural ethos will change and become more wisely responsive to the voices that make up the larger community. One of the possible benefits made available by current moves toward "professionalization," or at least through the exposure of police to a liberal arts education, is that they will learn to appreciate that the values they themselves hold dear are socially sustained in part because of a "liberal democratic" environment – in which diverse traditions, cultural integrity, and minority viewpoints are acknowledged and secured – and they will learn to differentiate between personal and social morality, between what may be privately believed and practiced and what may be imposed on others.

Unfortunately, even this is too simple. For the very traditions that may depend on liberal democratic values for their protection will probably embody beliefs about what values ought and ought not to be socially imposed, and these may be in tension with the liberal values they are expected to uphold. In such circumstances, the fact that their own traditions are secured by those liberal values may be seen as being of instrumental value at best, pending the wider propagation and recognition of their own. This "paradox of liberalism" is not easily resolved.[17]

At a wider social level, some of these tensions may be settled for police through legislation. Take, for example, the practices of clitoridectomy and infibulation, sometimes found in the communities that have relocated to Western liberal democracies.[18] Tolerated elsewhere, either as a rite of passage or as an exercise of marital right, "we" – as a diverse but broadly liberal community – may decide to reject these practices. The police, then, will not be required to exercise broad discretion about such matters should they become aware of them. But if they are called by neighbors to intervene in a marital dispute, in which a woman who is obviously being mistreated accepts that this is the way things are in her cultural community and is therefore unwilling to complain, the matter is more complicated. The officers' discretion will not be as limited as it may have been in the case of clitoridectomy, and they are being called upon to make a very difficult choice between two forms of social peacekeeping. Presumably their decision will have to take into account the seriousness of the assault, the options for the woman should they intervene, the alternatives available to them besides arrest, and so on.

Although problems such as these may be difficult for police, and will need to be addressed in recruitment and training, they are not unresolvable or essentially different from those faced by public servants generally. Those who enter into police work must do so with the expectation that their responsibility is to a diverse community, kept together (albeit, sometimes, tenuously) by certain broad traditions, and that they are responsible for maintaining the peace of that community. This is a conservative, but not rigidly conservative, task, for it is a characteristic of all communities, though perhaps especially of liberal communities, that traditions change over time. Police, in the prosecution of their peacekeeping role, and in the exercise of their discretion, need to be sensitive not only to the continuing traditions but also to change. Sometimes they may have to wait for that change; sometimes, in the exercise of their discretion, they may assist it.

Here at least police may benefit from membership in a department that has publicly articulated its mission, values, and goals in sufficient detail to forge some kind of community consensus and expectations with respect to the multifarious peacekeeping responsibilities that they are expected to fulfill.

11.3   EFFECTING ACCOUNTABILITY

It is one thing to claim that police are accountable to the community (or communities) they serve, and that we can identify that community through its legal, political, and cultural traditions, broadly conceived. It is another to specify how that accountability is to be ensured. Like most practical questions, it is probably not amenable to any timelessly valid and detailed response, but must be accommodated to particular social exigencies. Nevertheless, there are certain general observations and constraints that can inform detailed responses, and that are likely to possess some reasonably abiding relevance.

Most generally – and yet also most importantly – police accountability ought to be effected dispositionally. Although we may rightly demand that police be accountable for what they do, that demand ought not to come simply as an externally imposed obligation, but as an expectation that police officers will also have of themselves. Police are, after all, members of the very community that properly holds them to account. Police ought to be accountable for what they do out of an inner commitment to the ends of policing, and not simply as the product of externally imposed mechanisms of review and control. In an ideal world, the police would know and render the service expected of them. But then, in an ideal world police would probably not be necessary. In a nonideal world, external mechanisms may be necessary to foster such inner commitment or to supplement it when internal mechanisms are insufficient.

At their most fundamental level, human relations depend on significant goodwill and trust. We can hardly imagine what a society totally lacking in these qualities would be like: a Hobbesian state of nature, perhaps. We see the ravages of substantial breakdowns of goodwill and trust in some inner urban environments, especially in disaffected youth, though even here, for all their desolation, one can still find forms of goodwill and trust that keep them from total collapse into the condition that Hobbes spoke of as a "war of all against all." To the extent that goodwill and trust characterize human relations, individual and communal life is able to flourish, and the need for external mechanisms of accountability is lessened.

The kind of dispositional goodwill and trust we value in humans generally, and particularly in those who render public service, is not a simple outcome of maturation but a product of socialization. It is through our incorporation into and participation in a matrix of social relations that we come to possess the characteristics that constitute our distinctive and necessary heritage. Through educative socialization – the development of understanding, reflectiveness, and conscientiousness – we may come to possess the dispositions that foster normative accountability.

It is particularly important that police develop and foster such inner commitments. For even with the strong supervision that tends to characterize police work, police have a great deal of choice and discretion, choice and discretion that they will be under pressure to abuse. So varied are the demands made on them, and so geographically dispersed, that close supervision is well-nigh impossible, and they must simply be relied upon to respond in appropriate ways.

Obviously one hopes that police recruits will develop not only competence but also a sensitized and mature commitment to public service. In addition, however, there needs to be a sustaining organizational ethos. One

of the strongest arguments for police professionalism and professionalization has been the encouragement it should give to the fostering of attitudes
conducive to normative accountability, for professionals are ideally distinguished not only by their expertise but also by a spirit of public service.
Although the practical outworking of that ideal may prevent its full realization, to the extent that it can come to suffuse the organizational culture,
police will not stand in need of constant formal supervision, but will have
learned to direct their skills to the fulfillment of their professional ends.

Given, however, that the structure of police organizations does not fit
comfortably with the rhetoric of professionalization or even of professionalism, it becomes a matter of crucial importance that the police leadership
displays not only exemplary conduct but fosters those features of organizational life that will dispose officers to act accountably.

To the extent that the inner mechanism of educated commitment to public
service is lacking in a police organization, an increasing emphasis will need
to be placed on various institutional mechanisms of accountability, some
internal to the police organization, and others external to it. These mechanisms may and should be educative in intent. But to the extent that they are
not, and have to operate via the threat of sanctions, they will constitute at
best a holding operation, and will be unlikely to produce stable or long-term
benefits.

11.3.1 *Organizational mechanisms*

Within the professions, the major institutional mechanisms for accountability tend to be internal (see Chapter 3, Section 3.1.1.6). At least they are, for the
most part, felt to be that way. This is no accident. Members of the professions
claim that they form a community constituted, on the one hand, by a commitment to providing a particular public service, and on the other, by a
knowledge and expertise to which other members of the community are not
privy. They are, therefore, both motivated to provide the service for which
they claim authoritative recognition and uniquely positioned to ascertain
whether it has been competently and conscientiously provided.

Police organizations have wanted to claim the same privilege. They have
seen self-regulation as a key element in their push for professionalization.
But in addition they usually take the view that it is only they who have a
sufficiently large stake in, and understanding of, the work they do to enable
its policies and practices to be adequately developed and assessed. Indeed,
police officers are socialized early in their careers into believing that only
they can appreciate the difficulties under which they labor and that therefore
only' they can appreciate what is or is not an appropriate and reasonable
response to a situation. Sometimes this view is reinforced by the belief that
only they care sufficiently about crime to do something about it. To some
extent this position has reflected the alienation from the wider community
that often dominates police experience.

There is some basis for the police claim to self-regulative authority. Community pressures on police are often contradictory and unreasonable. Their smallest vices are paraded, whereas their virtues often go unsung. Many members of the community do not care to empathize with police, and are only too ready to criticize them. Nevertheless, there is little doubt that police have often abused their authority and have gone too far in their attempts to insulate themselves from scrutiny. As the recent Mollen Commission in New York has shown, that insulation has enabled them to conceal some of their most serious breaches of public trust. Even their own internal mechanisms have failed.[19] Some middle ground needs to be found.

It is precisely because police are responsible for rendering a public service that what they do and how they do it ought to be open to wider scrutiny. The wider public must have some access to police policy making and evaluation. This is not intended to deny that police are better situated to make some decisions and assessments; but not all decisions about what they do and how they do it and appraisals of what they have done are best made by them without a wider accountability.[20] Suppose we accept that police are far more skilled at crime prevention, crime detection, hostage negotiation, and arrest than other citizens could expect to be. There are, nevertheless, still questions about the importance to be given to "crimefighting" in relation to the other tasks that police are expected to perform, the risks to which police may put other members of the community when they perform their crimefighting functions, and so on, that are for the wider community – through its various voices (including that of the police) – to answer. This is not to say that the loudest communal voices will be correct in their assessments, but only that they have some right to participate in the decision-making process. Developing a mechanism for review that will have the right balance of communal and police input will always be a task of Solomonic proportions.

Nevertheless, there are other issues, particularly to do with micro-procedures and operational matters (such as arrest and handcuffing, dealing with the homeless, Mirandizing, and high-speed pursuits) for which it seems eminently reasonable that police should themselves have accountability mechanisms. When we look at those mechanisms, however, we notice that they are usually quite different from those covering professionals in institutions that employ professionals. Hospitals, architectural and legal firms, universities, and even ecclesiastical institutions have much looser structures than we find in most police departments. Paradoxically, the rigid paramilitary chain of command and internal affairs operations that characterize most police organizations have been seen – at least since the days of O. W. Wilson – as marks of professionalization, rather than its antithesis. Whereas professionals, even professionals employed by large organizations, are generally trusted to exercise their individual professional judgment in the tasks that they are given, and tend to be as answerable to their professional associations as they are to their administrative superiors, police officers tend not to be trusted by their superiors and (to the extent that it is practicable) are closely regulated and supervised. In this environment, orders and rules rather than professional discretion tend to be determinative of conduct.

11.3.1.1 Reporting and review. At its most general level, organizational accountability is handled through a process of regular reporting and review. Chiefs generally expect their divisional commanders, and the latter their subordinates, and so on, to provide regular and accurate information about the areas under their command. The results of this process are themselves reviewed, and recommendations are developed and discussed, and then – in the light of other forms of review – if accepted, are built into future policy and practice. The details of this process are the stuff of police administration, and of relevance here mainly because the review and reporting process constitutes as significant a part of organizational accountability as the rooting out of corruption, the handling of complaints, and so on, which are more commonly identified with "police accountability."

11.3.1.2 Clear structures of accountability. The accountability of the police organization will obviously be greatly enhanced if there are clear structures of accountability. It is a common problem of many bureaucratic organizations that accountability is diffused. This may arise because of the way in which labor is divided. No single person has responsibility for a "final product." Such responsibility as there is is linked to parts and not to wholes. The diffusion may arise because of rotating tours and frequent reassignments of personnel, so that by the time questions of accountability are raised, the person who was responsible is no longer available or in that position, and the person who is now responsible disclaims liability for whatever may have happened during another's tour or tenure. Whether such diffusion of responsibility is accidental or deliberate, it is nevertheless serious, and organizations that allow it to occur can hardly complain if they find themselves under pressure from outside and vulnerable to external regulation of some kind.

In police departments, the problem of diffusion of responsibility is often dealt with by means of a strict paramilitary chain of command. But this sits awkwardly with claims to foster professionalism. The path to police professionalism is not, as Wilson thought, through hierarchical centralization. Maintaining accountability by means of a centralization of authority represents the very antithesis of professionalism. Wilson confused the ordered efficiency and obedience of a military officer with the expertise and discretionary competence of the professional. In fact, too much centralization may be inefficient. Efficiency and accountability may be better served by clearly defined responsibilities. It has to be admitted, however, that in some large police departments where a centralized and hierarchical form of accountability has been relaxed, corruption has been and generally remains a serious problem. It is often argued that the notoriety of the NYPD's Special Investigating Unit, made famous through Robert Daley's *Prince of the City*,[21] arose largely because of an accountability structure that had become too loose. But even a "tight" accountability structure may need to evolve to accommodate itself to new forms of deviation.

But there are other reasons why a rigid accountability structure may not, after all, ensure accountability. For one thing, just because a rigid structure is less likely to foster a sense of professional responsibility, the more likely it is that cover-ups will occur. Chiefs are not generally willing to take the fall for a first line officer's misconduct. And perhaps they should not. What is needed is a clear articulation of duties that will enable line and ranking officers to know what can be expected of them and for what they will be held accountable. And in addition there needs to be an effective means of ensuring that those duties are fulfilled. The manifest problems of developing such a structure of organizational accountability reinforce the importance to an organization of dispositional accountability.

One neglected but important aspect of officer accountability is some formal recognition of the difference between a mistake or error of judgment and negligence or misconduct. Not every officer whose judgment turns out badly has judged badly. The world does not always conform to our reasonable expectations, and reasonable judgments may sometimes have bad consequences. Even if, because of their responsibilities, we may hold officers to a higher standard of performance than others, excusable errors and understandable misjudgments do occur. Officers who – because of an engineered public outcry and weak leadership – run a serious risk of censure or of being scapegoated for a nonblameworthy bad outcome are likely to become minimalists. It is not without reason that for many the primary rules of police culture are "cover your ass" and "when in doubt, don't do anything."[22]

11.3.1.3 Forward planning. Any large bureaucracy – and that includes most urban and state police departments – needs to be sensitive to social change and thus to changing demands on its services. It needs to be forward-looking as well as responsive to immediate needs. A properly accountable police organization will provide for ongoing planning and review, to allow for proactive and not merely reactive planning.[23] Such forward planning, taking account of demographic and social changes, the economic situation and recruitment initiatives, will be integral to departmental professionalism. Only if such planning occurs will departments be able to avoid lurching from crisis to crisis, a response that is not only unsatisfactory but also wasteful of resources. Unfortunately, effecting accountability of this sort is difficult. Planning requires the devotion of resources, and many police departments feel unable to keep up with present demands, let alone plan for future ones. This is exacerbated by the fact that mayoral horizons generally stretch no further than the next election, and a police management that offers a five- or ten-year plan is unlikely to encounter a responsive city hall.

Accountability at the organizational level also demands a review of police purposes and measures of accountability. In much recent writing on police operational policies, the focus has moved away from police as law enforcers and crisis managers to police as community problem solvers. If police success is measured in terms of response time and arrest statistics, it betokens a particular – but not necessarily the most appropriate – focus of police activity. Perhaps, as some writers have suggested, we need to look "beyond 911" to some of the larger local problems that generate repeated calls for police service but which seem to be nobody's responsibility. If police begin to address these problems instead, as brokers of social reconstruction, it may be that they will do more to fulfill their peacekeeping role than they are able to achieve via rapid response to the criminal manifestations of this social breakdown. Looking to the problems behind the emergencies may also diminish the pressure that is currently placed on rapid response services. Although the police themselves will almost certainly not be equipped to resolve these larger social problems, by identifying causal outcomes and social impacts and by initiating appropriate inquiries they may facilitate responsiveness on the part of those who are able to ameliorate them.[24]

11.3.1.4 Administrative rule making. An important and very practical organizational mechanism for enhancing accountability has been administrative rule making. The "policeman's bible," a handbook of administrative directives giving detailed guidance on matters affecting the delivery of police services, limits or channels police discretion in a quasi-legal manner. Such administratively promulgated rules help police officers to act appropriately in complex situations; but they may also regulate police conduct in a way that allows for internally administered sanctions should their provisions not be followed.

Administrative rule making has a number of things to be said in its favor:

1. Most obviously it helps to limit idiosyncrasy, thus contributing to administrative justice and predictability. Although first line officers must have some discretion in the way in which they do their job, administrative rule making encourages departmental consistency, and thus predictability – an important dimension of the "rule of law" that is intended to characterize liberal democracies.

2. Administrative rule making also allows for greater localization of police operational procedures. Large urban and small rural police departments generally operate under significantly different social conditions. Unlike state laws and judicial decisions, departmentally promulgated administrative rules are likely to be more responsive to local concerns and conditions.

3. Administrative rule making enables police to operate under rules that are sensitive to the exigencies of their work. Although police should not be the only judges of how their work is to be done, they will, by virtue of their doing that work, be aware of the practical problems confronting it, and to that extent they may be in a better position than external review agencies to shape its policies and practices. If they fail to develop their own operating procedures, the courts may well move to fill the void.

These are substantial benefits and contribute to accountability in two ways: Individual police officers are made more accountable to the police organization; and the police organization is made more accountable to the wider community.

Of course, like every measure of accountability, the effectiveness of administrative rule making as a mechanism of accountability will be contingent on other factors as well: the extent to which the guidelines have been sensitive to public and officer concerns; the willingness of officers to adhere to administrative guidelines; the effectiveness of monitoring and enforcement mechanisms.

The effectiveness of administrative rule making can be assisted if, as far as possible, rules are embedded in rationales, so that directives are not seen simply as deliverances from on high – from "the bosses" – but can be appreciated as reasonable responses to situational demands.[25] They should be educative as well as constraining (or permissive). Unfortunately, the paramilitary character of police organizations finds its natural expression in directives, and is not always comfortable with appeals to reasonableness. Providing rationales may be seen as an invitation (or as laying oneself open) to questioning, debate, and criticism; yet mere directives are generally perceived as veiled threats. And so an opportunity to foster in police the kind of commitment that is compatible with a professional rendering of service is forgone.[26]

11.3.1.5   Internal affairs. In relation to the general issue of misconduct and corruption, the most dramatic technique by which police seek to provide some form of organizational accountability is internal espionage. Most larger police departments have some form of internal affairs division through which police conduct is monitored. The focus is almost wholly negative – the rooting out of corruption and misconduct – and narrowly directed to ethical departures more than to failures due to incompetence. Sometimes internal affairs divisions have operated proactively, by setting up integrity tests or by recruiting officers (often during their academy training) who will keep their eyes open for and will report any conduct that they consider unbecoming;[27] more often, such divisions are content to respond to complaints, often from the general public, but sometimes to complaints emanating from within the organization.

The employment of internal spies distinguishes police organizations very dramatically from professional associations and organizations, where such oversight is almost wholly absent – though a number of them do have standing committees available to monitor and investigate complaints that are made against members. Such watchfulness seems totally antithetical to the spirit that infuses professionalism, which is an initial trust in the integrity, competence, and wise judgment of the professional. Even if professionals are notoriously overrated in these matters, there is still nothing like the naked distrust of police officers that is shown within larger police organizations.[28]

But unpleasant though internal espionage may be, many urban police executives would argue that it is necessary. They argue that operational police are uniquely situated. Not only are they singularly exposed to temptation and other pressures, but also, because of their peculiarly strong horizontal bonds of loyalty, they are not self-policing ("the blue wall of silence"). No breach of fraternal bonds is more deeply despised than "ratting." Only by means of internal auditing can the organization be kept free from systemic decline into corruption and misconduct.

However, even if some form of internal monitoring is necessary, there are important moral questions to be asked concerning the appropriate limits of surveillance. The costs to police privacy, dignity, morale, and ultimately to the encouragement of a professional attitude to their work may be considerable, and such methods ought not to be employed heavy-handedly, or as a matter of course, without a careful exploration of alternative ways of achieving ethical compliance. Requiring police to undertake drug tests is one thing; laying out traps is another. Responding to complaints is one thing; infiltrating precincts with spies is another. Sometimes the work of internal affairs divisions is compromised by their own corruption and self-servingness, thus feeding the very cynicism that is destructive of a genuinely professional service: Who watches those who watch the watchers?[29]

11.3.2 *External mechanisms*

The skepticism reflected in the foregoing extension of Juvenal's question points to the value of a diversity of checks and balances, to ensure that, as far as possible, holders of the public trust and dispensers of public coercive power are kept worthy of that trust and power. For all their merits, the organizational mechanisms that police have developed to ensure their accountability cannot by themselves sustain the public trust that is vested in them.

At one level, this failure does not reflect especially on police. No occupational group or social institution, including the most distinguished and the most intimate, has proved itself capable of fully adequate self-regulation. Even the medical profession, generally regarded as the most public spirited of the professions, can no longer count on deferential acquiescence in the unregulated monitoring of its policies and practices. But because police are repositories of such significant, and potentially oppressive, coercive power, there has probably been a greater public concern that they should be open to scrutiny from others.

The problem has been exacerbated by a somewhat turbulent history of police–public relations in which an "us–them" mentality has been developed, and police have become self-defensive and self-protective. Police unions, understandably and appropriately supportive of police interests, have sometimes been ridiculously defensive of the indefensible. And "the blue wall of silence," a centerpiece of police loyalty, has enabled police to be less accountable to their community or communities than they should have been. In the event, several external mechanisms of accountability have served, with varying degrees of success, as checks on the exercise of police authority.

11.3.2.1 Legislative review. Most, if not all, social institutions and organizations are accountable to the public authority vested in the law and legislature. The police are no exception. Police are not generally exempt from criminal and civil law, or from the regulatory power of a legislature. Police may be subject to tort actions and civil suits should they act recklessly or negligently in the performance of their duties. And the broad contours of police responsibility, the powers of police, the overall structure of responsibility for policing, and the allocation of social resources to police work might properly fall within the purview of public regulatory bodies. Crucially important though it is, police work constitutes just one of a number of public services, and a community has every right to expect that the provision of police services will be coordinated with, and to some extent limited by, other such services – trade, immigration, health, education, welfare, defense, and so on.

It is difficult to find fault with some such broad control over police work. Deficient though legislatures may be, they nevertheless constitute a vehicle through which communal voices may be heard and by which a communal will, to the extent that there is such, may be effected. There is no other way, in liberal democracies at least, in which to make the broad allocative and distributive decisions that are necessary to complex community life. We may well wish to improve legislative institutions – to make them more participatory or responsive – but it is hard to think of ways to replace them.

Yet at the same time the limitations of legislative control need to be recognized. Legislatures and other regulatory bodies are not competent to determine the more detailed policies and practical decisions that must direct departments, divisions, and officers. The task of a legislature is to secure and allocate social resources and to regulate social agencies by drawing boundaries that are consistent with the needs, ethos, and ongoing traditions of a community, leaving it to others to fill in the details. This is not grounded simply in a belief that the more specialized agencies that help to constitute a particular community are better placed to determine working policies and practices, but also in the conviction that a system in which control is staggered is likely to be more accountable than one in which it is concentrated in a single agency.

11.3.2.2 Judicial review. As Locke recognized, legislative decisions may leave boundaries unclear, since it is impossible that a legislature could anticipate every contingency that will confront an institution and its agents or the citizens of a community. Moreover, it may sometimes be wondered whether a legislature itself has not overstepped the boundaries of a community's fundamental traditions – as embodied, say, in its constitution. And so judicial review has functioned historically, and increasingly functions, as an accountability mechanism.

In American policing, judicial review has been of great significance, especially during the last thirty years. The U.S. Constitution, and particularly the amendments to it, have much to say about the government's police function and the constraints that ought to govern police operations. During the years of the Warren Court (1953–69), the Supreme Court of the United States reflected the activist social environment in which it found itself, and brought about dramatic changes in police procedure. The *Mapp* and *Miranda* decisions, excluding from the courtroom evidence and spoken testimony that had been obtained in violation of a defendant's constitutional rights, were only two of several judgments that constrained police activity. In some cases, the Warren Court was applying to the states constraints that had already limited federal law enforcement officials. But by virtue of such extensions to the jurisdictions in which most criminal offenses were prosecuted, the decisions impacted on the conduct of the vast majority of law enforcement officials.[30]

Many first line officers have resented the intrusion of (restrictive) judicial judgments into their modus operandi. Such judgments are generally seen as unsympathetic and unrealistic, a further example of the way in which "we" are misunderstood by "them." There may sometimes be truth in this, especially because judicial review has often generalized for police procedure what may have been more appropriate to the particular case than to police work in general. And it is no doubt the case that the higher courts, and some members of the Supreme Court, have sometimes shown what could be read as an antipolice stance. Herbert Packer's two models of criminal justice administration – the "due process" and "crime control" models[31] – have often been applied to periods of Supreme Court decision making. The due process model is often associated with the Warren court, where the dominant concerns appear to have been the preservation of suspects' rights and with ensuring that in the administration of justice the state does not overreach itself. As police have often seen it, upholders of the due process model are fundamentally skeptical about the good faith of police, and lack understanding of the demands of police work. The crime control model, on the other hand, has been more closely associated with the subsequent Burger and (to some extent) Rehnquist courts, where there has been a greater willingness to accept the good faith of law enforcement officials. In their desire to ensure efficiency and quick adjudication, proponents of the crime control model have shifted the emphasis from due process to reliability in judgment.[32]

Despite these fluctuations, judicial review almost certainly provides an important means for ensuring the accountability of police. The police have their own appropriate but limited agenda. The courts must consider those interests in the light of other governmental, societal, and individual interests, and in so doing may sometimes reflect the will and traditions of a community more faithfully than the police themselves might be capable of doing. There is something of a trade-off between crime control and the observance of due process. The more carefully suspects are cocooned against the possibility of mistreatment and mistake, the harder it is to "control" crime. The more concerned a community becomes about the level – or even the fear – of crime in its midst, the greater the risks it may be willing to take with respect to abuse and the conviction of innocents. What is important, however, is that the trade-off is not rigged: A trade-off ought to be considered only when police are doing the best they can with what they have got.[33] Sloppy police work is no reason for relaxing the protections to which suspects are currently entitled.

No less powerful than judicial review of police procedures have been some of the civil judgments handed down by courts in response to complaints against police. U.S. Federal Law Section 1983 provisions for civil and punitive damages against police (or the municipalities that employ them) who improperly carry out their duties have, in recent years, been appealed to with increasing frequency and success. The sizable judgments involved have forced police and city managers to review policies and practices regarding procedures, selection, and training, and to institute greater monitoring of officer conduct.

11.3.2.3 Civilian review. Probably the most controversial mechanism of police accountability has been some form of civilian review.[34] No doubt the wide psychic gulf that seems to have developed between police and community is partially responsible for this. It is also partially responsible for the vehement opposition to such review found in most police organizations. It is not helped by the fact that "civilian review" is generally limited to the adjudication of complaints against police. Opposition is also fed by the drive for professional recognition and the associated demand for self-regulation.

It is doubtful whether civilian review is as antagonistic and lacking in understanding as police have often suggested. Some writers, indeed, have claimed that civilian review boards frequently overcompensate for their distance, and are more willing than an internal police inquiry would be to accept that officers had to do what they did. Even so, the very idea of civilian review calls police operational autonomy into question, and, less flatteringly, appears to manifest a deep mistrust of police. For those very reasons it might be opposed.

Leaving aside the matters of autonomy and trust, it is initially difficult to see what might be the problem with civilian review. After all, the police provide a community service at a cost to the community. That is where their authority comes from. And it is only to be expected that the community should have some say about the service they receive, both prospectively and retrospectively. Operational autonomy is at best a contingent entitlement. Moreover, as the beneficiaries of those services, civilian members of the community might be expected to have some relevant input.

But clearly that is not the way it is perceived by the police themselves. After all, it is not as though the community that is served is – or is seen as being – sympathetically inclined to the police. And since civilian review boards concern themselves almost exclusively with the alleged misconduct of police officers, the gap is likely to be widened even further. Compounding this is the fact that the composition of civilian review boards is often fashioned as much by political as by competence-related factors, and police are (understandably) highly suspicious of "invasions" that may well be politically tainted. Furthermore, where a case for review has been sensationalized by the media, there is further reason for suspicion that any findings will be tainted.

All these are genuine enough concerns. But as experience has shown, exclusive reliance on internal mechanisms is also deficient. Perhaps civilian review boards that concern themselves exclusively with allegations of police misconduct give the wrong message, and should not be taken to represent the only form that civilian accountability can take. Citizens' crime commissions, civil rights groups, and police–community relations groups may all play a part in enhancing police accountability.

But what is true of organizational mechanisms of accountability is no less true of external ones: A mechanism is not likely to function well in the absence of a commitment to its working well. Citizens' groups are not necessarily less vulnerable to ideological and partisan concerns than those set up within the police organization. There is a lot to be said for some form of review that includes both police and citizen representation. Politically, at least, it will appear to be at least open to the perspectives of the two major "constituencies." Ethically, it gives (representatives of) those who may be affected by decisions a stake in the decisions that will be made. Whether it actually works out will depend on other factors: the investigative powers, expertise, and instruments available to the reviewing body, the standards of proof that are employed, the good will of those involved, and so on.

11.3.2.4 Ombudsmen. Another mechanism for ensuring accountability has been the appointment of "ombudsmen" – independent, statutorily authorized investigators with wide powers of inquiry into the conduct of public authorities.[35] Usually, of course, an ombudsman's brief will be limited to the investigation of public complaints, but as well as being an independent inquisitor with potentially wide powers of inquiry, the ombudsman provides written – and usually public – reasons for any opinions which he or she forms. Such opinions are then passed on to a body with powers to review and act on any recommendations made. A negative recommendation might be fed to a district attorney or to a police department tribunal in the expectation that it will be given immediate serious attention. [36]

11.3.2.5 Media review. Accountability need not be thought of exclusively as a formalized arrangement, even though some formal mechanisms of accountability may be necessary. To some extent it may be maintained in the ordinary ebb and flow of life as police go about their work. The publicization of police activities submits those activities to a wide audience, and allows for the interchange of ideas and opinions. The media constitute one of the powerful nonformalized instruments for police accountability.

They are also, in the view of some police, one of the most troublesome. For though the media enable police work to be broadly scrutinized, they may also constitute a distorting lens that prevents the police and public from fairly engaging each other. The popular media depend on sales, and this frequently encourages a form of pandering that is selective, ideological, overdramatizing, or otherwise unfair. Journalists sometimes display a singular insensitivity to facts and to the privacy, dignity, feelings, integrity, and reputations of those on whose activities they report.[37] And their desire to pursue a breaking story may be incompatible with the investigative needs of police. Understandably, the police are frequently suspicious of the media. On the other side, people in the media have sometimes had just as good reason to be suspicious of the police. The blue wall of silence, so difficult to penetrate, has often been used to conceal substantial and/or systemic abuses of authority. Sometimes only media attention has succeeded in forcing accountability upon the police.[38]

The power of the media is a fact of contemporary life. And whether they like it or not, police have to contend with media scrutiny. They have to contend with the fact that police work sells, and that what police do may be exposed to the public eye. The more secretive police become, the more fascinating is their work to the media, and greater is the danger of interference, distortion, and increasing alienation. Although many police executives now attempt to develop a relationship with the media that is productive and positive, the temptation to secrecy remains strong. By the same token, it is important that the media develop a relationship with the police that is sympathetic, sensitive, and truthful.[39]

Nevertheless, police–media relations will remain a risky and problematic business as long as communication remains a form of entertainment. The competition with other forms of entertainment will foster distortion and premature publicity, and fair and unfair reporting will exist side by side.[40] However, that tendency may be minimized if police adopt a more positive and open stance toward the media, in which trust can be cultivated and truth can become more important than sales and reputation. There are "success stories." But, as always, it will take two to tango, and it will not be in the (self-determined) "interests" of some media organizations, any more than it will be in the (self-determined) "interests" of some police departments, to cultivate better relations.

11.4 COMMUNITY POLICING

Many of the problems of police accountability are exacerbated, if not caused, by the cultural and social distance that often exists between police and the (urban) communities that they serve. And some of the mechanisms developed to ensure police accountability have the particular character they do because of this gap. Yet, as the Goldstein epigraph reminds us, "purely structural arrangements" for ensuring accountability are not sufficient. The root problem of police–community relations needs to be dealt with.

Unless police and community can be brought into dialogue, unless there is some empathetic bond, unless some commonality of purpose and expectation can be developed, achieving accountability will remain an adversarial and unsatisfactory process, constantly at risk of failure. Yet there is much in contemporary policing that has militated against their being productively brought together. The move from foot to motorized patrol was undoubtedly one such factor, though the alienation predates that. Police have an endemic public relations problem, for a good deal of their work involves the bearing of bad news – of injury, death, or arrest. Moreover, so long as they are seen primarily as law enforcers, and so long as their standard encounters with citizens reflect and feed their cynicism, it will be difficult to establish comfortable and cooperative police–community relations.

Nevertheless, the difficulties may be minimized, and the current interest in "community policing," particularly in those urban areas where police–community relations are poorest, could represent an important step in that direction. At least it should, once we get beyond the PR hype that confuses names with realities.

In certain respects, the move toward community policing revives an old, somewhat idealized stereotype – that of the local beat cop, knowing and known by his community, something of a neighborhood advisor and troubleshooter. Or, perhaps better, it seeks to implement a style of policing in urban situations that already operates to some extent in suburban and rural environments. But it is rather more than that. It also characterizes a philosophy, a departmental orientation, a form of departmental organization, in which police consider themselves not simply as publicly hired watchpersons, but as more generally responsible to a neighborhood, concerned with fostering and maintaining a public peace, in response to and *in coordination with* its residents and other bodies that have a stake in the community's well-being.

In theory at least, community policing is committed to an overcoming of the "us–them" distinction.[41] Or, to the extent that the distinction is retained, it is no longer "us over them" but "us and them together." It recognizes that effective policing must be a cooperative enterprise between police and their communities. Whether in their deterrent, investigative, or social service functions, police are "arms" of the community and dependent for their success on the cooperation of other citizens. Like lawyers, who need the trust and openness of their clients if they are to be adequate advocates of their cause, police too need to have the cooperative assistance of their "clients" if their various communal responsibilities are to be effectively prosecuted. More than that, the tasks of policing become shared tasks, as citizens take on peacekeeping functions through neighborhood watch, safe house, and community service associations.

Creating a more cooperative environment is a joint responsibility. The police themselves can do much to assist in the creation of a climate of cooperation. Putting police back on the streets is only part of that. Involvement in community programs and community organization is another part. Although this greater visibility and availability may expose police to greater public scrutiny, and is, therefore, risk-laden, it attempts to do so in a manner that is less alienating and more cognizant of what police work should represent.

Although community policing is often presented as a total philosophy of policing, it is most appropriately seen as a philosophy for urban policing, and if seriously implemented its impact is likely to be felt most noticeably in run-down and dispirited communities where police–community relations have to all intents become adversarial. Community policing is designed to provide not simply a partnership but also some form of empowerment for people who have lost – or who have never had – the ability to create for themselves an environment for betterment. In such circumstances, police can represent an infusion of knowledge and energy that is able to reverse the course of urban decay and demoralization.

How, in practice, a police department will best serve its community is most appropriately worked out at a local level. There is, however, much to be said for what has come to be known as a problem-oriented approach, in which calls on police services are not seen simply as discrete demands, but some effort is made to locate those demands within a wider framework or pattern of events. Where a pattern is perceived, it then becomes a target for action, if not by the police directly, then as public catalysts.[42]

As a way of enhancing urban police accountability, community policing has much to offer, at least to the communities for which it is proposed. It purports to bring police and community into a much more direct and open relationship, thus enabling a better appreciation of what police do. It attempts to make police more aware of and more responsive to community demands, and thus may enhance their rapport with and authority within their communities. In theory, too, it will contribute to a better allocation of police resources. Ultimately, should it work out, it also offers a great deal to police. The satisfactions of cooperation, of seeing a community regenerate itself, are antidotes to the cynicism engendered by a recurring status quo.

But, like most innovative strategies, community policing must face a number of problems, problems that could doom it to the fate of so many other strategies that have been attempted in the past.[43] For one thing, it runs the risk of faddishness – or of being a public relations panacea that exists on paper but is not seriously implemented in reality. Business as usual is simply given a different name. To the extent that this is so, the only question is: How long will it take before the emperor's new clothes are seen for what they are? This is a serious problem, because community policing does hold out the promise of a radically different form of policing. It is not simply, or even necessarily, that police are going to be put back on foot patrol, but that they are going to do and conceptualize what they do differently. However, some police managements are notorious for their unwillingness to accept and foster real, as distinct from cosmetic, change, especially when it may appear to loosen the reins of control and to risk trouble. Even goodwill, however, may not be sufficient if the police leadership lacks the skills necessary to foster support for change. More significantly, if chiefs of police are known to have a life of, say, five years, and others within the organization can expect to be policing for perhaps another fifteen years, both they and those under them may be unwilling to invest in changes that could be abandoned by the next incumbent. Community policing needs to be accepted as a Gestalt shift, and not simply as another new program.

There is another side to this coin that is equally problematic. A tension has traditionally existed between police line officers and police management. Managerial enthusiasm for community policing, where it exists, is generally not matched by an equal enthusiasm in the ranks. Line officers frequently resent the way in which armchair-bound management expects them to implement whatever – as they perceive it – happens to be politic or to strike the managerial fancy. Community policing, if it is to be successfully implemented, must have the support of both management and line officers. Line officers need to see it as a way of approaching what they do that not only improves their effectiveness, without increasing risk, but also enhances their job satisfaction. And, given traditional attitudes, that may not be easy to achieve. Indeed, there is a fair bit of evidence to suggest that in some of the larger departments in which community policing has become the catchword, line officers view it cynically as a creation of the bosses. It is considered to be low-status police work, a repository for officers who are not good enough to be promoted, but who are now being told they have greatly expanded discretionary powers. These cynical attitudes appear to be validated by the meager resources that have been devoted to training or otherwise preparing people for community policing. It is as though, at the behest of the hierarchy, line officers can abandon their traditional modus operandi and overnight become community organizers and empowerers. Money must match mouths.[44]

Although some of the current enthusiasm for community policing has come from police management, there has also been significant managerial reluctance to embrace it enthusiastically. In part this is a reflection of its perceived "academic" origins and academic support.[45] But a more practical reason can be discerned in the organizational risks that go with community policing. Police who become too closely identified with and involved in the community they serve often find it difficult to fulfill their law enforcement function. The risk of corruption must also be faced. Not only will associations be forged that make enforcement difficult, but police may start to share some of the perspectives of those whose activities they are expected to be curbing. Police departments may have to develop new strategies for dealing with the possibility of corruption.

But there is a more subtle problem that arises out of the specific orientation of community policing. If police do not see themselves simply as responders to crisis calls, but come to believe that they should take a more active and positive role in resolving the community problems that people believe they should tackle, they will very easily find themselves enmeshed in the concerns of partisan politics. Homelessness, abandoned buildings, run-down neighborhoods – problems that are often of immediate concern to members of a community, and are often directly linked to the fear and prevalence of crime – cannot be easily tackled without those involved becoming embroiled in local (or wider) politics. Just where does the police role end, and does it have a place for such political involvements?[46]

These are not easy questions, nor need they be. The open-endedness built into the police peacekeeping role is reflected in the fuzzy borders of the community policing concept. This may not be a bad thing. Different communities will have different resources available to them, and what is appropriate for police to involve themselves in in one community may not be appropriate for them in another. Although there is an inherent vagueness to the idea of social peacekeeping, it does not require too much imagination to see how, in one community, police will foster communal peace by tackling a particular social problem themselves, whereas in another, peace will be more effectively achieved by their leaving it to other agencies. Of course, even when police do involve themselves in some broader problem, such as helping to refurbish a run-down neighborhood, they will generally do this by utilizing their contacts with existing agencies. They will not take over what is the responsibility of others but broker the involvement of agencies that have the requisite resources.

Chapter 12

Ethics and codes of ethics[1]

Every code must be treated as a hypothesis to be tested and adapted while
following it.

John Kultgen[2]

Over the past hundred years – though particularly in the early decades of
this century and from the 1960s on – associations of engineers, accountants, insurance agents, financial planners, realtors, public administrators,
lobbyists, football coaches, journalists, social workers and psychologists,
and organizations such as hospitals, chain stores, and credit unions have
published "codes of ethics."[3] In these public statements, they have sought
to articulate standards that should characterize their membership or operations and that would therefore mediate their provision of goods or services.[4]

The precise reasons for this burgeoning interest in codes are probably
various, though a confluence of social factors is likely to have had considerable influence. Advances in technology, increasing specialization, occupational autonomy and professionalization, rising corporatism, population
growth, and rapid urbanization have considerably affected our social life.
We are required increasingly to put our trust in people and organizations to
whom we are significantly vulnerable and over whom we are able to exercise relatively little control. It is, as we have learned, a fragile trust, easily
and far too often betrayed. The formation of occupational and professional
associations, whose members are bound by a code of ethics, has been a
partial response to this social breakdown. These associations offer to a consuming public some assurance that the services on which it depends will be
delivered by its members in a manner that will not exploit or otherwise take
advantage of its vulnerability.

In this chapter I propose to trace the rise of police codes of ethics, and, by
setting them in the context of the more general flowering of such codes, will
consider their purposes, problems, and value.

12.1 HISTORY

Although something like a code of ethics was embedded in the 1829 *Instructions* given to Robert Peel's Metropolitan Police,[5] it was not until 1928 that a code of ethics was developed for U.S. police. Its background is interesting. On the recommendation of August Vollmer, the architect of the professionalization movement in American policing, his Californian protegé O. W. Wilson was appointed in 1928 as Chief of the Wichita (Kansas) Police Department. It was a troubled and much criticized department, and, full of Vollmer's spirit of professionalization, Wilson was provided with a context in which he could put into practice the ideas of his mentor. Among his early projects was what he called "Our 'Square Deal' Code," a public document designed in part to assure the citizens of Wichita that their much-criticized department was now there for them. Beyond that, Wilson rewrote the department's manual, establishing, in accordance with the conception of professionalization promoted by Vollmer, strict lines of authority, clear and efficient procedures, and rigid standards of conduct. The code did not replace the so-called ethical requirements that had traditionally been incorporated in departmental manuals. Rather, it gave public form to them.[6]

In 1937, the Federal Bureau of Investigation published its FBI Pledge for Law Enforcement Officers. Announced and printed in the December 1937 issue of the *FBI Law Enforcement Bulletin*, the director, J. Edgar Hoover, introduced the Pledge as being for "the voluntary consideration, acceptance, execution and adherence by all law enforcement officers." It was printed in poster format, and vigorously marketed to law enforcement agencies across the country. Police departments would get their sworn employees to sign, and then forward the signed pledges to the central office of the FBI, which then used the *Bulletin* to update the readership about its adoption across the country.

Then in 1955 the Police Officer's Research Association of California (PORAC), as part of a program to enhance the professional status of police, charged a subcommittee to prepare a code of ethics. Wilson, who had returned to Berkeley in 1947, was a member of PORAC and of its subcommittee. A final draft of the code was adopted by PORAC and the Californian Peace Officers Association in late 1955. Quite a bit of the phraseology comes from Wilson's 1928 code. The code gained wider attention, and in 1956 it was adopted by the National Conference of Police Associations. It was then considered for several months by an even more widely dispersed and prestigious body, the International Association of Chiefs of Police (IACP). Late in 1957, they too adopted the code, and published with it a short document called the Canons of Police Ethics, which sought to expand on some of the clauses and implications of the Code. Now known as the Law Enforcement Code of Ethics, the code was and still is adopted without change by many police departments, both in the United States and overseas.

Until the mid-1980s, the Code remained virtually unchallenged. But with the development of police accreditation in the early 1980s and the accreditation requirement that individual departments present a statement of their values, new ethical statements were formulated. There was, moreover, a growing discontent with the 1957 code. And so, in 1987 and 1989, the IACP adopted two new codes of ethics. The first was a Member Code of Ethics, tailored specifically to the situation of police executives. The second was designed to "replace" the 1957 code, which covered law enforcement officers generally. The attempt to replace the old code caused an unexpected uproar. Behind the uproar lay a sentimental grassroots attachment to the high-sounding phraseology of the 1957 code, though public attacks on the new code were couched in various ways: It was seen as an executive action that had not been properly considered by the wider membership; it was too long for recital at police graduations; and its pragmatism was no longer inspirational. In 1991 the IACP developed a compromise solution that found general acceptance. It renamed the so-called replacement code the Police Code of Conduct; it restored the 1957 code to its place as the Law Enforcement Code of Ethics, but revised it in a few places to take account of some of the most serious deficiencies of the original.

The Law Enforcement Code of Ethics, with the 1991 changes to the italicized parts noted in brackets, reads as follows:

As a Law Enforcement Officer, my fundamental duty is to serve *mankind* [the community]; to safeguard lives and property; to protect the innocent against deception, the weak against oppression or intimidation, and the peaceful against violence or disorder; and to respect the Constitutional rights of all *men* [ ] to liberty, equality and justice.

I will keep my private life unsullied as an example to all; [, and will behave in a manner that does not bring discredit to me or my agency. I will] maintain courageous calm in the face of danger, scorn or ridicule; develop self-restraint; and be constantly mindful of the welfare of others. Honest in thought and deed, in both my personal and official life, I will be exemplary in obeying the laws *of the land* [ ] and the regulations of my department. Whatever I see or hear of a confidential nature or that is confided to me in my official capacity will be kept ever secret unless revelation is necessary in the performance of my duty.

I will never act officiously or permit personal feelings, prejudices, [political beliefs, aspirations,] animosities or friendships to influence my decisions. With no compromise for crime and with relentless prosecution of criminals, I will enforce the law courteously and appropriately without fear or favor, malice or ill will, never employing unnecessary force or violence and never accepting gratuities.

I recognize the badge of my office as a symbol of public faith, and I accept it as a public trust to be held so long as I am true to the ethics of *the law enforcement* [police] service. [I will never engage in acts of corruption or bribery, nor will I condone such acts by other police officers. I will cooperate with all legally recognized agencies and their representatives in the pursuit of justice.

I know that I alone am responsible for my own standard of professional performance and will take every reasonable opportunity to enhance and improve my level of knowledge and competence.]

I will constantly strive to achieve these objectives and ideals, dedicating myself before God to my chosen profession . . . law enforcement.

There is just one further dimension to be added to this brief historical overview. Besides the IACP, which is United States-dominated, there have been a number of other international initiatives to formulate police codes of ethics. A United Nations code was first suggested as early as 1961, but serious work did not begin until 1975. In 1979, after much debate, the United Nations adopted its Code of Conduct for Law Enforcement Officials. It has been used as the basis for code formation in a number of other countries. At about the same time, the Legal Affairs Committee of the Council of Europe developed a Declaration on the Police for its twenty-plus constituent members. The declaration, however, although adopted by the Parliamentary Assembly, was criticized in some of its parts, and in the member states it has never achieved the acceptance that was sought for it.

12.2   CODES AND THEIR KINDRED

Codes of ethics are variously described and come in a variety of formats. Like Wittgenstein's rope, they hang together as much by family resemblance as by any more formal features. What I think may come close to linking them is their function as commitments intended to mediate the formal relations between providers of goods and services and their public recipients.[7]

But as I have already noted (Chapter 3, Section 3.1.1.1), this emphasis on the public or mediatorial function of codes has been challenged by Michael Davis. For him, a professional code is first and foremost an internal document, a set of morally binding conventions intended by members of a profession to regulate and guide the pursuit of their professional activities. The important truth in this, I believe, is that drawing up the terms of a code of ethics is essentially and ultimately the task of the members of the profession or occupation (albeit in consultation with a wider public), for it is they who appreciate best what excellence in their specialty requires, what are the peculiar temptations that providers face, and what compromises are acceptable in their provision to a wider public. A particular code of ethics cannot be imposed on the members of a profession or occupation. But at the same time, I believe that the pressure for codes of ethics has almost always come from outside the profession or occupation, and that what is generally sought, in the development of such codes, is a document that is oriented to the wider public of consumers of the goods or services that the profession or occupation provides.

Even if I am right about the generally public character of codes of ethics, any survey of codes makes it abundantly clear that their forms and foci vary considerably. Not only do we have "codes" of "ethics," we have "canons" of "professional responsibility," "statements" of "values," "principles" of "conduct," "standards" of "practice" or "performance," and "oaths" of "office," along with "pledges," "vows," "maxims," "credos," "prayers," "tenets," and "declarations," in varying combinations. The rubrics are not strictly interchangeable, but neither are they precisely defined nor always clearly separable. At the same time, such commitments are sometimes found in association with but distinguished from statements of "goals," "mission," "philosophy," and "objectives," in which the scope of the service is articulated and generally set in the context of some wider social purpose.

It would be overly fastidious to attempt a neat differentiation of these different forms and foci, since some of them are treated interchangeably by their promulgators, and even where distinguished they may be accounted for in different ways. Nevertheless, some broad distinguishing features may be noted.

12.2.1 *Codes*

Pledges, credos, prayers, and oaths generally take the form of personal affirmations. Prayers are directed to God, and oaths more generally to some superior. Codes, canons, standards, maxims, declarations, and principles may be expressed personally, but they may just as easily be expressed impersonally. Codes and standards are often regulatory, whereas pledges and oaths tend to be aspirational. But there are, as I indicated, no hard-and-fast lines here.

Despite these differences, I think it is fair to understand most of these codes as public promises, vows or at least commitments by the provider of goods or services that certain standards will be observed in their provision. Indeed, I believe that this constitutes something of a raison d'être. Some codes, such as the 1957 Law Enforcement Code of Ethics, are explicitly formulated in a promissory fashion. They are really pledges. Others, such as the 1989 code intended as its successor, are expressed declaratively, the promise here being implicit, or perhaps explicit, as one enters into associational or adopting agency membership.

If codes are seen as promises or commitments, then it is easy to see how they bind. But there is an important objection to this account, based on the fact that professional codes are now used by courts as a basis for appraising practitioners who have never, explicitly or implicitly, affirmed them.[8] Thus, the American Medical Association (AMA) Code of Ethics may be invoked against a physician who has never joined the AMA, and its obligations may not be avoided by refusal to join. As Michael Davis puts it, the obligations of a professional "do not seem to rest on anything so contingent as a promise, oath or vow."[9] Professional obligations are, he thinks, only quasi-contractual, "resting not on an actual agreement (whether express or tacit) but on what it is fair to require of someone given what he has voluntarily done, such as accepted the benefits that go with claiming to be a [professional]."[10]

There is much to commend Davis's position, though not, as I shall suggest, as an alternative to what I have already suggested. Davis is correct to think that it should not be open to the beneficiary of a privileged social position to claim that his refusal to join a professional or occupational association should exempt him from the obligations articulated in the professional code. Codes, after all, are intended to *reflect* and *express* but not to *create* the public obligations of professional or occupational life. In an important sense, the professional code is a secondary rather than a primary expression of professional obligations. Nevertheless, this need not gainsay the fact that the code itself is primarily promissory in character, and that it is intended, by those who *affirm* it, to manifest a commitment to honor what the profession or occupation requires.

It is understandable that for purposes of public accountability codes should acquire the more general function of articulating not simply what members of a professional or occupational association have committed themselves to, but what a society may reasonably expect of those engaged in those professions or occupations. For the privilege of controlling what they do and, in some cases, of having a social monopoly on their activity, professionals and members of many other occupational groups must expect that with their privilege will also go a commensurate responsibility. Professional codes articulate that responsibility in a public manner.

But there is more to it than that. Those who explicitly promise – that is, those whose concern for professional advancement has brought them together – will articulate values and standards that will not only foster public trust, but will also provide assurance of excellent work. That is why professional codes seek to foster that trust through a commitment to excellence. And to the extent that that is so, it is not unreasonable for outside assessors to see such codes as manifesting a standard of performance for anyone who provides the service.

12.2.2 *Ethics*

If the reference to "codes" is complex, no less complex is their object, "ethics." Although the language of ethics, values, conduct, and practice is sometimes used interchangeably, it is just as often distinguished.

Statements of values tend to be broader than statements of ethics, and both may focus more pointedly on dispositional attitudes and character than do principles of conduct or practice. But to some extent at least we are dealing here with a difference of emphasis, since the interiority of values and ethical standards is intended to have external expression, and the enunciated principles of conduct or practice are generally associated with the possession of practical virtues. Nevertheless, statements of values and ethical standards are likely to be briefer and more general than codes of conduct or practice. The latter usually spell out in some detail what and how acts may or may not be done by service providers or associational members. And codes of practice or performance, as distinct from codes of conduct, may also embody some reference to technical standards (levels of competence) that the provider is expected to maintain.

Some writers have gone further to distinguish moral from ethical standards, by according universality to the former and group relatedness to the latter.[11] Honesty is seen as a *moral* requirement, truth in advertising as an *ethical* standard for business. And if we are talking about the *morality* of business people, we are not likely to be talking about exactly the same thing as their *ethics*. These are distinctions that can be made, and that might appropriately be made in certain contexts, albeit with only partial linguistic support. What I think is central to such a distinction is the concern in ethical codes to articulate moral values as they are relevant to the provision of particular goods or services.

Michael Davis, however, has argued that there is more to an ethical code than the situating of moral requirements within a specific professional or occupational context. The ethical requirements of codes, he believes, demand more of those for whom they are intended than is expected of others: "A code of ethics must set standards beyond ordinary morality if it is to be a code of ethics at all."[12] Unless a code of ethics demands more of those to whom it applies than can be ordinarily expected of others, it has no point. It goes without saying, he argues, that members of the professions are subject to the ordinary constraints of morality, that is, "those standards of conduct each of us wants every other to follow even if everyone else's following them means we must do the same."[13] And thus something more must be demanded of those to whom the codes apply. For this to be acceptable to those involved, Davis suggests, there must be some payoff or return. Codes must "buy" obedience.[14] Davis explains the purchase by characterizing codes as conventions between those whose wish to pursue a particular occupation is coupled with the recognition that the activity is most fruitfully pursued as a cooperative undertaking. Higher standards are the price one pays for the cooperation of others. If we accept that the professions necessarily provide a public service,[15] then the public's cooperation will also be needed, and the code will contain requirements that constrain practitioners in relation to their clientele.

If, for a moment, we accept this account, what should we say about police codes of ethics? For, as Davis notes, such codes do *not* seem to require of police anything more than might be expected of any decent human being. Police are to treat people with courtesy and respect, to be honest, and to exhibit integrity; they are not to use unnecessary force or act inequitably. Are not these reasonable expectations of anybody? Are police codes then an exception to the rule? Or, more radically, are their "codes" not genuine ethical codes after all?

In a section on "the problem of the missing higher standard," Davis accepts that police codes may be exceptional and, if so, that a large part of the reason for this may be due to the kind of work in which police are engaged. They see a side of life that encourages cynicism, and are subject to considerable temptations, and thus they "will do well to remain decent human beings."[16] What is demanded of the rest of us is, therefore, in some sense "more" for them. Even so, Davis is not entirely happy to accept that this is sufficient to save police codes, and so he suggests that the positive requirement found in some codes, requiring police to combat the misconduct and corruption of fellow officers, might provide an appropriate "high-er" standard.

I believe, however, that, by assuming that there would be no point to a professional code of ethics were such a code not to demand a higher standard of conduct of practitioners, Davis has created his own problem. It is true that what is demanded of professionals differs from what is demanded of others. But I do not think it follows or that Davis has shown that *more* is demanded of professionals than can be expected from others in similar circumstances, or that they are held to a higher standard. Or, to put the point slightly differently, I believe that if professionals are held to a higher standard, this *is* because of situational factors. As bearers of a public trust, it is important that they act and be seen to act in certain ways. Anyone else bearing the same trust could also be expected to act in those ways. What a code of ethics articulates is how someone confronting the kinds of choices, pressures, and temptations that a professional does, and bearing the trust with which a professional is vested, can be expected to behave.

Consider the one instance of a police code provision that Davis suggests does go beyond "what law, market, and ordinary morality exact": prevent-ing and rigorously opposing violations of the code, reporting such violations to a superior or other appropriate authorities.[17] It is of course possible to question the propriety of such an expectation, seeing it as overzealous and maybe even insensitive to the loyalties that law enforcement work requires and fosters. But assuming that it is not an unreasonable expectation to have of police, might it not be argued that any person who is witness to the kinds of violations that are mentioned in the Code of Conduct (such as failures to respect human dignity or to be responsive to the suffering of those in one's care [custody], the infliction of torture or use of unnecessary force, or en-gagement in corruption) by someone in whom the public trust is vested – a witness who himself is a bearer of that trust – has a responsibility to prevent, oppose, or report such violations?

There is, however, a further distinction that Davis draws that has more importance for an understanding of ethical codes. He distinguishes between rules, principles, and ideals. It is a distinction between, roughly, those things that are to be regarded as mandatory or strictly obligatory, those that are to be seen as more general obligations or principles, and those forms of con-duct that are to be seen simply as desirable or as ideals to be aspired to. Some codes restrict themselves to requirements of just one kind, others include all three indiscriminately, and yet others, such as some of the Ameri-can Bar Association codes, have sometimes made an effort to distinguish them.[18]

Davis complains, properly so, that codes frequently confuse these differ-ent standards. What should be ideals are sometimes expressed as strict requirements, and what should be general principles are confused with rules.[19] Such confusions have practical significance. In the 1957 Law En-forcement Code of Ethics, for example, the pledge to "keep my private life unsullied as an example to all" is given the same status as obedience to the law and departmental regulations, hardly a reasonable expectation and liable to make the code an object of cynicism. It is, perhaps, reasonable for law enforcement officers to strive to keep their private lives "unsullied" and "an example to all," but this can hardly be demanded of them qua law enforcement officers. The 1989 Police Code of Conduct, though more discursive, manifests a similar failure to distinguish appropriate kinds of standards: "Force *should* be used only with the greatest restraint . . . ," an eminently reasonable principle, exists cheek by jowl with the statement: "The police officer's personal behavior *must* be beyond reproach" (emphases added).[20]

What drafters of codes need to ask themselves, Davis suggests, are the following questions: Does this provision state a minimum below which no officer may fall [except . . .]? Can an officer make good police decisions without giving some weight to this consideration? And if not, would it still be good for an officer qua officer to do as the provision suggests? Affirmative answers to the first question are likely to yield ethical rules; affirmative answers to the second are likely to yield ethical principles; and affirmative answers to the third are likely to yield ethical ideals.[21] Asking such questions, to anticipate what is to come, will not only inform a public of what it may and may not expect of police, and how to expect it, but also enables police to think through the ethical expectations associated with their role and to disentangle what is central and necessary from what must be taken into account and what is simply desirable.

12.3 CODES AND THEIR PUBLIC

I have suggested that it is a distinguishing feature of codes – as we currently understand them – that they do not function as purely internal documents, but manifest from within, or are intended to do so, the public accountability of organizations, agencies, and members of associations. Quite apart from various forms of external regulation and review to which the providers of goods and services are subject, codes are put forward as public evidence of a determination, on the part of the providers themselves, to serve in ways that are predictable and acceptable.

I referred earlier to Davis's distinction between morality and ethics, accepting that what is of significance in the distinction is the concern, in professional ethics, to articulate moral values in a manner that is relevant to the provision of particular goods or services. Professional ethics is not just general ethics writ small or in different garb, but ethical reflection that is articulated through the particular ideals and purposes that are constitutive of the profession. And it is precisely because of this that professionals are sometimes confronted with hard choices between the ethical demands of their professional excellence and other, or more general, ethical demands.[22]

Professional codes, too, are not to be seen as comprehensive codes of conduct. They view conduct primarily from the perspective of the professional services rendered. As Lon Fuller has expressed it, "a code of ethics must contain a sense of mission, some feeling for the peculiar role of the profession it seeks to regulate. A code that attempts to take the whole of right and wrong for its province breaks down inevitably into a mush of platitudes."[23] One unfortunate feature of some police codes of ethics is that they possess this platitudinous quality. What they commit their members to is not sufficiently articulated in terms of the services they provide. They uphold the virtues of public service, honesty, integrity, courtesy, nonpartisanship, and so on, without indicating in any significant way how these values might be expected to work themselves out in the concrete activities of police work.

12.4 THE PURPOSES OF POLICE CODES

When looking at the proliferation of occupational and professional codes, we need to keep distinct (though not completely separate) the issues of *explanation* and *justification*. Explanations of the formation of codes – whether in individual cases or as part of a general social phenomenon – look to the causal or historical factors in their production. Such factors might include the desire for social enhancement, the protection of turf, a defense against external controls, a heightened sense of moral and social accountability, or the desire to consolidate group identity and provide a group ethos. Explanatory factors may reflect well or badly or not at all on the organizations or associations in question. In other words, they may also function as justificatory reasons, though they need not do so.

Justificatory reasons, on the other hand, are directed to the question of normative desirability, to the legitimating grounds for promulgating or retaining a code. It is natural for organizations and associations to cast the reasons for formulating their codes in the language of justification, though in actual fact their motivations may be less commendable. Most likely, organizations will be moved to develop, retain, and revise their codes for a variety of reasons, some of which will be justificatory, but others of which will be of only explanatory significance – or, if also of justificatory significance, may serve only to call the organization's high purposes into question.

There is little doubt that one of the major impulses behind the development of police codes of ethics has been the desire for professional status. This was evident in O. W. Wilson's ambitions for his 1928 "Square Deal" Code, and has been behind subsequent initiatives of the IACP and other police organizations.

As noted earlier (Chapter 3, Section 3.1.1.2), codes of ethics are often taken to be a hallmark of professional status. Occupations aspiring to or claiming professional status frequently seek to display this determination or achievement by promulgating a code. But although codes of ethics may be central to professionalization, they are not constitutive of it; and so, while many organizations and associations may seek to improve their social standing through the development of a code of ethics, this will not, of itself, achieve that end.

12.4.1   *External functions*

Most codes of ethics are directed primarily to an indeterminate client public
– its size largely a function of the number of people who wish or need to
avail themselves of the goods or services provided. Sometimes, as in the case
of police, the code will be of indirect as well as direct significance. Even if an
individual does not actually require the direct services of a police officer, it
may be important to know that certain standards are affirmed by those who
provide police services. Otherwise one may be "caught in the crossfire" as
police perform their otherwise legitimate tasks. But there may also be other
groups to whom a code is partially directed. Codes of ethics sometimes seek
to determine the forms of contact that their adherents may have with the
media, with other professions, and even with government. More subtly,
but no less really, a code may be intended to deflect or pre-empt judicial
scrutiny.

What follows are some of the major external functions that codes are
expected to have. Obviously, not all codes will have all of these functions.
Indeed, most codes will not have all these functions, though most will have
more than one. And the importance given to these various functions will
differ from code to code. So will their justificatory value.

12.4.1.1   Assurance. Seekers and users of goods and services are to varying
degrees dependent on others for the provision of those goods and services.
For many goods and services the dependence can be very significant. And
obtaining the goods or service may require considerable sacrifice and / or
risk – of privacy, of resources, of effort, and / or of well-being. It is hardly
surprising that people should want to be assured that the goods and services
will meet certain expectations.

In the case of police, the need to provide assurance is demanded by the
enormous social power that is vested in them. That need is reinforced by the
media's relish for stories of police corruption and misconduct. Although
there is probably more public trust in the police than police themselves
recognize (for most of us there are, after all, few widely available alternatives), that trust must be secured in the face of ongoing (albeit uneven)
media scrutiny. It is no doubt for this reason that a number of police codes
(and regulations) restrict the liberty of first line officers in regard to their
dealings with the media.[24]

In many cases the code of ethics has the appearance of a compact between
the service-using public and the service provider. An exchange is involved.
Service providers are accorded certain social privileges in virtue of the service they provide. Police, for example, have certain entitlements in respect of
the use of coercive force, certain rights to command, and rights of entry. For
the granting of such privileges the public can expect a certain return. Although codes of ethics generally originate from within the association and
organizations to which they apply, and have not been formulated as the
result of a public interchange, they may be couched as an appropriate ex-

change for the privilege that is given. One of the main privileges may be that of being the (almost) exclusive provider of a particular range of services.[25]

Codes provide assurance, not simply by notifying a public of what standards they may expect to find observed, but also, through their being enshrined in a public document, by giving service users a "handle" in the event that the service fails to live up to expectations. In some cases, the codes themselves indicate resources that are available for the handling of dashed expectations.

12.4.1.2 Improved public relations. To say that codes of ethics provide assurance is to view them from the perspective of service users. There is a flip side to this in the perspective of service providers. That is a public relations function. Associations and organizations frequently view the promulgation of a code of ethics as one of the ways in which they can improve their public image and increase their clientele. By assuring the public they enhance their standing and make their services more attractive. Several major police codes were drawn up in the wake of the scandals of the early 1970s, at a time when trust in the police was under severe challenge. Although law enforcement associations were motivated by a genuine concern to lift police performance and to reestablish trust, there is little doubt that the promulgation of these codes was also an exercise in public relations.

Although there has often been a mercenary dimension to the public relations function of codes, the ends have been as much social as financial. It has become a hallmark of professional status that one is governed by a code. The code speaks of self-governance, autonomy, and dedication. The acquisition of professional status is important to the self-image and social acceptance of those who have it. Thus one of the first projects of an occupation seeking to improve its place in the world – socially, as well as economically – is the formulation, adoption, and promulgation of a code of ethics.

12.4.1.3 Liability limitation. To the extent that a police code of ethics sets out certain standards that are to operate in the provision of police services, it may be seen as constituting a constraint on excessive and unreasonable demands and in certain circumstances a hedge against liability for failures with which police may be charged. Where, as in the United States, the legal environment promotes contingency fee representation, and the judicial environment is often open to deep-pocket decision making, the police, as public employees with power to injure, are fair game for predators, both civilian and legal. In theory at least, and occasionally in practice, the code of ethics will constitute a public benchmark against which police conduct can be tested, and police can be secured against unwarranted – frivolous and vexatious – claims.[26]

There is a different way in which a code of ethics may limit liability. A hallmark of professionalism, at least in theory, is self-regulation. Those who provide professional services consider that they are best placed to appraise the delivery of those services. For the most part – except, perhaps, when blatantly criminal behavior is involved – professionals are strongly resistant to outside regulation. A code of ethics, particularly if it is associated with mechanisms for its monitoring and enforcement, is frequently appealed to as evidence that external review would be redundant and intrusive. Answerability within obviates the need for answerability without.

12.4.2 *Internal functions*

Although the paradigm code format tends to mediate between providers and users, assuring each in relation to the other, it is becoming increasingly common for codes to be used as internal documents, setting out guidelines for individual providers and managers, and developing organizational or professional commitment and cohesion.

12.4.2.1 A personal standard. From the point of view of those who are members of an association or who are employees of an organization, the code of ethics might be expected to represent at least a minimum commitment – a standard of behavior that service users may demand, a commitment to which the provider must adhere. What, externally, users may *expect*, internally, providers *promise* to deliver. Of course the code may also gesture toward a maximum – it may comprise ideals as well as duties. What, externally, users may *anticipate*, internally, providers *aspire to*.

In some cases these commitments may not seem to amount to very much. It is not uncommon for codes of ethics such as the 1957 Law Enforcement Code of Ethics to speak largely in generalities, pledging forms of conduct (self-restraint, courteousness, honesty) that might reasonably be expected of people in almost any situation. Nevertheless, we should not characterize them as merely platitudinous. For it is generally because the provision of a particular kind of service is associated with certain characteristic temptations that these ordinary forms of conduct are highlighted by a code.

In more detailed codes, declarations may involve distillations of practical wisdom that inexperienced practitioners are not likely to have, even if they are morally sensitive. As the working environment has become more complex and pluralistic, and traditions have become less evident, codes may constitute a beacon or anchor for service providers who do not yet or perhaps no longer have a sure sense of the normative constraints governing their work. There is an internal as well as external dimension to these normative constraints. In a complex and in some ways novel environment, providers of services may have no clear sense of "the thing to do." A code may help to crystallize issues and provide criteria for wise decision making. But as well as that, it may, in a pluralistic and normatively heterogeneous social milieu, provide something approaching a map of public expectations that will help the service provider to understand the social circumjacencies of decision making.

12.4.2.2 An organizational ethos. Codes, even if individually affirmed, are not constituted by individual declarations; they are associational and organizational constructs. And one function they try to serve is the unification of service providers through the creation or advancement of an associational or organizational ethos that is ostensibly promotive of the service to be provided. There are very few workplaces that can operate successfully simply by providing a location or vehicle for work. Associational ties and organizational cohesion generally require some sort of shared culture or ethos, and a code of ethics is frequently used to help foster that shared way of being. Where the providers of a service are at a geographical distance, and where there is a turnover of service providers, the code may be a major bonding agent, providing continuity from one generation to another. Professional and occupational loyalties are embedded in the ideology of code commitment.

The associational ethos usually involves a representation of the members to themselves that they are professionals. That may be interpreted in more than one way. One may see oneself as a privileged service provider; but equally one may understand it simply as a social status. For the social reality of being a professional is as much a matter of status as it is of expertise and service, even though the status purports to piggyback on expertise and service.

The duality here may create or at least embody a deep tension. On the one hand, the code serves the important sociopsychological purpose of binding and motivating service providers. On the other hand, it provides a moral framework and standard of conduct for what is done, one that is responsive to the concerns of a wider community. There is, therefore, an implicit tension between serving others as the binding raison d'être of the association or organization and a loyal commitment to fellow professionals or service providers. The stronger the organizational ethos, the more service to the public tends to be vulnerable to compromise, for personal loyalty to fellow professionals tends to take precedence over the commitment to a more impersonally construed public. In policing, this is a particularly acute problem; police officers will rarely turn in or testify against a fellow officer who violates the terms of his or her oath. This is so even if the code attempts to surmount the tension by explicitly demanding that police report violations by their fellows. Codes and other associational rituals may have a psychic and symbolic and social significance that is not strictly tied to their content. Many of those who bound themselves by and fought for the retention of the 1957 Law Enforcement Codes of Ethics not to "permit . . . friendships to influence [their] decisions" do not hesitate to exempt fellow officers from the normal consequences of traffic violations.

12.4.2.3 An organizational benchmark. Codes that are dedicated primarily to creating and promoting an organizational ethos tend to be aspirational. They enunciate ideals rather than establish obligatory standards. To the extent that a code's provisions are seen as aspirational, failure to live up to them may be viewed as a shortcoming, a reason for shame, perhaps, or even for others' social withdrawal. But where they are seen as benchmarks, as moral minima, they may serve a regulatory function. The more detailed and declarative a code is, the more likely it is that the standards it sets out will be regulatory (in intent, at least) rather than merely aspirational.

As an organizational benchmark, a code may function in any of at least four ways. (1) Generally the code is used to maintain membership quality control. By reference to its expectations, providers of a service may be admitted to or excluded from membership, and assessed, reprimanded, or ejected. Less formally, the code and its provisions may serve to deter unethical conduct. (2) The code may also be used to exercise control of a more political kind. Some years ago, Edwin T. Layton, Jr. observed that the AMA codes "have been used with great ruthlessness to punish dissidents who have taken the public's side on issues such as group medicine,"[27] and Philip Shuchman argued that the ABA Codes assert the power of "Big Law Firms" over "Little Lawyers."[28] In the policing context, the FBI Pledge was used to foster and assert the FBI's ideological dominance within American law enforcement. (3) There may, however, be a double edge to this, since ethics codes can also be used as vehicles for internal dissent, as means whereby members of an association or organization may hold their own hierarchy to account. (4) Less adversarially, codes may sometimes provide a basis for the adjudication of internal disputes.

12.4.2.4 A teaching device. It has not been uncommon for codes of ethics to function as the core of, or framework for, the ethical training of service providers. That at least has been one way in which medical and legal codes have been used in medical and law schools. Police academies have followed suit. A once widely used programmed text in police ethics, Allen P. Bristow's *You . . . and the Law Enforcement Code of Ethics*, is a particularly good expression of this approach.[29] Each of the clauses of the 1957 Law Enforcement Code of Ethics is articulated by means of problem cases in which trainee officers are called upon to think about what would constitute an ethically sensitive decision.

The use of professional codes in a teaching context has often left much to be desired. Whatever merit the codes themselves may have had, their use as a teaching device was often directed to keeping professionals out of trouble rather than to their ethical sensitization. The approach was legalistic rather than ethical.

In medical and legal ethics education, however, other less Sinaitic and self-serving approaches are now more common, and medical and law students are encouraged to develop ways of reflecting on what they are doing and on the hard cases that are likely to present themselves in the course of their work. They are taken behind and beyond what the traditional codes are able to provide. A similar change has been occurring in police training.[30]

12.5 CODES AND THEIR PROBLEMS

To say, as I have, that codes of ethics may have the various external and internal functions I have outlined is not to say that they always have or should have those functions, or that those functions are always compatible. Sometimes, indeed, individual codes give the appearance of being an uneasy compromise of several functions. But neither do I want to give the impression that these functions are always or easily separable. Thus, for example, unless there is some reasonable semblance of conformity with the provisions of a code, it is not likely that the code will constitute a very effective public relations document. Nevertheless, we should have no illusions that the foregoing catalogue provides an unproblematic justification for the promulgation of codes of ethics. Several difficulties need to be addressed.

Some of these problems tend to be associated with the code form itself, whereas others are more closely connected with contingent features of code formation and use. I will, somewhat artificially, distinguish the latter as contingent and the former as endemic problems.

12.5.1 *Contingent problems*

There are several problems that bedevil many ethical codes, but which are potentially correctible.

12.5.1.1 Enforceability. Occupational and professional codes are "necessitated" by the exigencies and temptations of social life – the need to give assurance to a consuming clientele or public that the goods or services it is seeking will be provided in a spirit of service. Yet, just because of the circumstances that generate the "need" for a code, its provisions are most likely to be observed only if there is also some recourse to sanctions.

In some codes, the need for sanctions is recognized, and procedures for their imposition are set out. The IACP Member Code of Ethics (1987) includes elaborate provisions for enforcement. In some other codes, sanctioning procedures are contained in a separate document. But even where this is so, and more so where sanctions are not explicitly indicated, members of occupational associations are often extremely reluctant to support their enforcement. There is great unwillingness to report breaches or to testify against those who are the subject of a complaint. This is particularly true of ideologically cohesive groups such as the professions, but it is also characteristic of law enforcement-related organizations. The so-called blue wall of silence is notorious. The very code that evokes and reinforces group loyalty also encourages its ineffectiveness.

12.5.1.2 Cynicism. Whereas some codes are pretty matter-of-fact and realistic in their demands, others, especially those that are aspirational, may place global, unnecessary, or unreasonable demands on those who are called to affirm them. Police codes, particularly where police are made out to be communal role models, may sometimes make excessive demands and thereby encourage a cynical response. Police cannot be expected to enforce "all" the laws or, qua police, to keep their private lives "unsullied." They can be expected to maintain the public peace through the enforcement of laws, and to conduct their private lives in a manner that will not derogate from their public authority.

Cynicism, however, may have its source not only in the content of code provisions, but also in the manner of their introduction. Very often, codes of ethics are top-down productions, creations of boards or management, and not the result of cooperative dialogue and community consultation. Rightly or wrongly, they are seen as alien impositions, motivated not by a commitment to service, but by the desire for control, political exigencies, or just plain arrogance. This may have very little to do with the content of the code. The *Principles of Policing*, produced for the (London) Metropolitan Police in 1985, is one of the most remarkable and thoughtful attempts to offer police general and specific ethical guidance. Yet it caused barely a ripple, and by 1988 had been replaced by a brief, unelaborated statement of values. One reason for this was undoubtedly the manner in which it was disseminated – as though it were a Sinaitic deliverance whose acceptability needed no participation by those for whom it was intended. London police felt no "ownership," and in regard to what they did not own they experienced no loss.

Another source of cynicism can be found in the "do as I say not as I do" ethos that may accompany management directives. If a code of ethics is to be taken seriously – especially if it is a top-down creation – it needs to have not merely the endorsement but also the commitment of management. In police departments, where the chain of command is central, leadership by example will have as much to do with the effectiveness of a code as any provisions of the code itself.

12.5.1.3 The danger of minimalism. Although aspirational codes tend to bespeak a self-sacrificial ideal of dedication and service, codes that focus instead on the "mandatory" requirements of professional life may dissuade sacrifice altogether. Practitioners may feel that so long as they stay within the mandated boundaries of the code they are doing all that may be expected of them. Though such requirements may deter conduct that is clearly detrimental to the users of goods and services, they may also discourage providers from giving more than is absolutely necessary. In occupations where the demands or competition are heavy and the threat of civil liability is constant, the pressure to stay with the minimum may be considerable.

12.5.2 *Endemic problems*

Some of the problems that codes confront are much more deep-seated, and function as permanent dangers.

12.5.2.1 The behavioral bias. One of the more obvious features of many codes of ethics is their focus on outcomes – on ensuring that behavior meets certain standards. The emphasis tends to be on *doing* rather than *being*.

Codes are not always of this form. The more confessional statements are often interlarded with the language of virtue. Those who uphold the IACP Law Enforcement Code of Ethics, for example, pledge themselves to show "courageous calm in the face of danger," to be "honest in thought and deed," and so on. And the recent move toward "statements of values" also reflects a concern for the possession of certain attitudes and not simply the performance of certain behaviors.

Nevertheless, there is a natural gravitation toward behavioral standards. It is, after all, not easy to test dispositions, intentions, and motivations apart from their behavioral manifestations, and, furthermore, those behavioral manifestations do represent some sort of "bottom line" so far as the public function of the code is concerned.

Given the general regulatory purpose of codes, the emphasis on conduct is probably to be expected. After all, what a public seeks are certain assurances about the delivery of services, and not (usually) some general statement of character or whole-of-life guarantee. It is concern with the *dealings* between police and public that leads to the construction of such statements in the first place. Yet we should not confuse a certain kind of outcome optimization with acting ethically. *Moral* worth attaches to conduct not just by virtue of the good that it does or the evil that it prevents, but because it was done for certain kinds of reasons or was expressive of a certain kind of character. If a police officer pursues and apprehends a fleeing mugger, what motivates him is not relevant to our assessment of the good that was done. Indeed the same good could have been accomplished by a falling piece of timber. But motivation is relevant to any *moral* assessment of what he did. Concern that a violator was escaping is one possible motivating factor; so was his doing his duty; so was his delight in pursuit and dislike for perpetrators who belong to a particular minority group. Why we do what we do is of central moral importance, not just that we do it. Not that it should not be done at all if it is not done for the right reasons, but that our assessment of moral worth must take our reasons into account. There is more to morality than an optimization of outcomes.[31] Indeed, part of the point of a professional code must be to inspire *service*, to point members beyond economic and personal reward as the basis for their conduct.

12.5.2.2 The encouragement of inauthenticity. Morality, I have claimed, is not just a matter of conduct but of conduct that is informed by some reasons rather than others. Some contribute to moral praiseworthiness, others do not. But there is a further issue beyond that of the appropriateness of reasons to moral merit. It is also important that the reasons be *one's own*. Codes encourage an externalization of conduct not just by divorcing conduct from its appropriate springs, but by detaching it from a certain kind of subjectivity that makes it an authentic expression of the person whose conduct it is. The reasons for engaging in ethical conduct must express what is within, and not conform simply to what is demanded without. True, a code may prompt one to reflect in certain ways that one might not otherwise have anticipated. That is not being questioned and may, in fact, be an important value to be preserved in codes of ethics. But unless what is ultimately done or not done is done or not done for reasons that are or have become one's own, rather than because "the conduct was prescribed or proscribed," it will lack authenticity and *moral* value, whatever other values it may possess. In some cases, no doubt, a person may be authentically committed to following the prescriptions and proscriptions of a code, and thus the conduct will possess an indirect authenticity. But there tends to be certain superficiality about this kind of authenticity, the kind of superficiality that made the Nuremberg defenses unworthy of human beings.

12.5.2.3 The danger of ossification. Associated with the foregoing deficiencies is a further one. Even if we grant – as I would – that ethical questions are generally amenable to definite and correct answers (there is a proper way to be, and a right thing to do), there is no decisive reason for assuming that those answers will be encapsulated in a given code of ethics. Actual codes do not usually exhaust the legitimate moral options and may even prescribe some illegitimate ones. Even if the provisions of a code reflect some widely shared understanding, that is no guarantee of their general correctness. We might, for example, consider how the Hippocratic Oath, for so long the physician's *Torah*, has now been "historicized" and called into question.[32] And although police officers who find their own understanding at variance with that of their code of ethics have a problem on their hands, we cannot just assume that all the provisions of a particular code are defensible. True, given the generality of most codified provisions, this is likely to be uncommon. But it will sometimes occur. And even when we are generally sympathetic to the provisions of a code, it is usually better to see them as presumptive than as absolute. For example, the commitment made in the IACP Law Enforcement Code of Ethics never to "permit personal feelings . . . or friendships to influence my decisions" and never to "accept gratuities" is probably reasonable enough if seen as a general statement of intent. But "never," as the code enjoins? We do not need to work too hard to think of situations in which conduct of the excluded kind would be, if not praiseworthy, then advisable, and even if not that, at least a matter for debate.[33] Few officers would ticket a fellow officer for a minor traffic violation. True, ticketing is discretionary, and there are surely limits to "professional courtesies,"[34] but when the renunciation is stated as baldly as it is in the Law Enforcement Code of Ethics it obscures the much finer nuancing that ethical reflection provides. And, of course, such absolutism lowers the code's status in the eyes of officers. There is an *ongoing* character to ethical reflection that is jeopardized by the institutionalized closure that often accompanies the adoption of a code.

12.5.2.4 The failure to prioritize. Even though codes sometimes provide fairly detailed guidance on specific issues, and may therefore assist the inexperienced, they are often of limited usefulness in those cases where assistance is most needed. "Hard cases" are not uncommon in police work. The very nature of the work often involves a careful assessment of individual and social interests that cannot be easily reconciled, and the wise exercise of discretion is required. Codes are rarely helpful to the making of such discretionary judgments. They enumerate goals and standards without indicating priorities or procedures for handling conflicts between code requirements. A police officer who must decide how to deal with a traffic violator needs to take into account not only the seriousness of the breach (itself a matter of judgment), but also the kinds of reasons that may have led to it, the sort of effects that a particular decision may have, the social and institutional environment in which the breach occurred, and so on. A police officer who has pledged to "keep the peace" and "enforce all the laws" is not likely to be greatly helped by such formulae. There is, after all, no simple choice between enforcing and not enforcing the law. There are several different ways in which the law may be enforced and not enforced, and though the officer's department may have, in addition to the code, some procedural regulations or rules of thumb, they are unlikely to accommodate all the complexities with which the officer will be confronted.

In some respects, it is not surprising that codes fail to give this kind of detailed attention to priorities, exceptions, and situational factors. To do so would undermine some of the functions they are generally intended to have. The more a code is prepared to address specific issues, the more likely it is to arouse controversy both outside and within. And since codes are usually intended to inspire confidence without and unity within, there is a certain counterproductivity associated with detail. Both the ABA and AMA have found that to their cost.[35]

Despite the foregoing problems – contingent and endemic – they do not in themselves support the conclusion that codes ought not to be promulgated. The absence of a code is also problematic, and some of the problems of codes, if recognized, can be diminished, even if not always eliminated. To anticipate, I do not believe there is any fixed formula for occupational and professional codes, and, provided that we are aware of what we intend of them and of their limitations, they may serve valuable external and internal functions. What the problems referred to may do is point us in the direction of codes that, on the one hand, provide a more systematic and integrated statement of the standards that can be expected of service providers, along with a recognition of their own limitations.

12.6 THE VALUE OF CODES

In some respects ethical codes are like firearms. They have their value; they have their dangers. It is often difficult to maintain their value without risking their dangers; and it is difficult to eliminate their dangers without sacrificing their value.

Codes of ethics remind us that the provision of public services involves certain kinds of social cooperation, certain sharings of experience and insight, and that if these services are to be provided in an orderly manner their providers need to create an environment of trust. They remind us that trust requires a measure of trustworthiness. At the same time, however, as we examine "the life and times" of professional codes, they also remind us of the power of ideology – of the way in which an appearance can mask reality, and self-interest can exploit the conditions for social living.

Codes of ethics are also like barometers. They register fluctuations of pressure, of social pressure, and reflect a society's or service association's dominant concerns. The promulgation of a code constitutes one means whereby service providers may look at themselves to see what they are responsive to, and it thus represents an opportunity for them to assess and refocus their endeavors.

One of the most important functions that a code can fulfill is a processual one. The very task of drawing up a code should be an opportunity for an organization or association to look at itself – to ask itself what it is really about, what is reasonable to expect of its members, what standards should determine its internal as well as its external affairs. It should also be an opportunity for a wider community to ask itself what it may reasonably expect of the providers of particular goods and services. Too often, unfortunately, codes of ethics are seen statically, as outcomes or products, as fixed determinations, and not as active expressions of the self-awareness of a community within a community. They are, moreover, viewed as the deliverances of police management and not as documents of common ownership. Only if officers as a whole are able to participate in their formulation are they likely to consider such codes as *theirs*, as embodiments of a commitment *they* have made.

In a helpful overview of professional ethics and of professional codes, John Kultgen has remarked, in the epigraph to this chapter, that every code should be treated as a hypothesis to be tested and adapted while following it. This contains just about the right amount of paradox. At the point where he makes this remark, Kultgen challenges the mechanical application of codified rules. For even if the rules are adequate to a situation at hand, they do not obviate the need for a personal acceptance that enables following them to be an authentic expression of the decision maker. The judgment that the rule is adequate must be a judgment that the service provider makes. Authenticity, however, is not enough. Judgment too is required in applying the rule to the situation at hand. Courtesy may be a reasonable expectation to have of police. But there are many ways of being courteous, and some situations make some expressions of courtesy more appropriate than others. Firmness is not necessarily excluded. A police officer who recognizes that courtesy is grounded in a respect for the persons of those with whom he or she must deal will not confuse it with gentility but will see in it an expectation of considerateness in dealing with others.

The paradox implicit in Kultgen's advice is to be found in the conjunction of rule following with the idea that rules are hypotheses to be tested. The conjunction is well chosen, however. There is no necessary opposition between fidelity to the standards that are implicit in the goals of a particular profession or occupation and a critical engagement with their articulation in specific provisions. A questioning faith need not be a doubting one. One may revise from within as from without.

In pledging themselves to their code of ethics, police officers signal their willingness to enter into an occupational culture that is defined by certain aims and standards. What is believed to justify this code – its creation and preservation – is the importance that a culture or ethos so defined has to the fulfillment of the ends of police service. In terms of their relations to each other and to their department and the public they serve, it is essential that there exists a framework of mutual understanding and trust. That at least seems to be something of the background to the pledge. But, as with other pledges, one does not sacrifice one's capacities and standing as a reflective being once the pledge has been made. And officers may well find, as they acclimatize themselves to their occupational environment, that their codes are not fully adequate to the situational and moral demands that are placed on them. To a degree, it is not inconsistent for them to press for some revision of their code. It is always appropriate for them to see the code itself as a resting point but not as the terminus in the ongoing deliberative enterprise that constitutes human life.

The very fact of variety in law enforcement (and other) codes should itself provide some reason for believing that, though codes may play a significant part in defining and preserving a police culture and in enabling police culture to flourish within a larger communal arrangement, they do not require a *sacrificium intellectus*. The police community is, as it must always be, a community of moral agents committed to the reflective and self-reflective task that is the task of every human being. That this reflection takes place within an environment shaped by the ends and tasks of policing need constitute no barrier to that deliberative enterprise, though it may well affect the way in which one goes about it. How one sets about repairing Theseus's ship will depend significantly on whether one is sailing in it on the high seas or one has it in dry dock.

Chapter 13

Ethical challenges for police management

> Police departments . . . are guided by implicit values that are often at odds
> with explicit values.
>
> Robert Wasserman and Mark H. Moore[1]

Many professionals are privately employed, either singly or as part of a
peer-run corporation. They are able to dispense their expertise without close
administrative direction and oversight. It is assumed that doctors and lawyers, whether self-employed or as members of larger practices, will exercise
good judgment and discretion when responding to the demands that are
placed upon them. Even where professionals are not privately employed,
and must dispense their expertise under the umbrella of a larger, non-peer-
operated organization, they are likely to be able to do so with little more
than peer accountability. Thus university professors work within space that
is secured by traditions of academic freedom, and physicians working in
large hospitals are for the most part shielded from administrative interference in the way they dispense their expertise.

Police officers, however, generally work in publicly supported organizations that are strongly hierarchical in character, and not known for democratic decision making or peer review. Naturally this impacts on their work
environment, on the possibilities that exist for professionalism, and on the
institutional structures that develop in response. Although the rhetoric of
professionalization is spouted by both management and rank and file, and
much managerial direction is justified in the name of professionalization, the
reality often seems quite otherwise. Management offers few opportunities
for professional autonomy, and, almost as a form of self-protection, police
organizations develop less as professional associations than as industrial
unions; for the most part they have been less concerned with raising the
quality of police service than with protecting and furthering the economic,
health, and welfare needs of employees.[2] Only the rhetoric of professionalization is left.

In this chapter I propose to consider some of the ethical challenges faced by police management, particularly in regard to its espousal of professionalism in policing. I shall limit myself to three issues: first, the uneasy relationship between police unions and police professionalism; second, the ethical and professional propriety of police industrial action (strikes, slowdowns, and so on); and third, the ethical and professional implications of demands for affirmative action in policing.

13.1 UNIONS AND PROFESSIONALISM

Professional associations usually see themselves as having a significant role to play in maintaining the integrity of a profession. By setting standards for admission to the profession (and often being influential in having those standards legislatively secured), by promulgating and securing compliance with a code of ethics, by providing for continuing education, and by representing the professional in his/her dealings with the public when issues of general relevance to the profession arise, professional associations can serve both the professional and the public interest. Of course, professional associations do not always live up to these expectations, nor do they pursue them in an uncorrupted form. From the perspective of an outsider, such associations seem often to be more intent on maintaining a certain kind of hegemony over the provision of services or on protecting the economic standing of members.

Professional associations of this kind do exist in the police world. In the United States, the International Association of Chiefs of Police (IACP), the Police Executive Research Forum (PERF), the National Organization of Black Law Enforcement Executives (NOBLE), the National Sheriffs' Association (NSA), and the American Society of Law Enforcement Trainers (ASLET) seek inter alia to establish and maintain standards for police officers and agencies nationwide. As I have already observed (Chapter 3, Section 3.1.1.4), some of these associations have collaborated in the development of accreditation standards for law enforcement agencies.

But beyond these largely national associations there are, in the United States, myriad other associations, such as the (various branches of the) Fraternal Order of Police, Patrolmen's Benevolent Association, Sergeant's Association, Lieutenant's Association, and so on, that are much more localized and function more like industrial trades or labor unions than as professional associations. Their concerns, though often social-welfare oriented, are also industrial. They endeavor to maximize negotiating power in dealings between, say, patrol officers and commissioners (over deployment policies and decisions), between police and the mayor or city managers or even legislature (over salary and wage provisions, equipment, legal constraints on working conditions), and in the defense of officers whose actions have attracted unfavorable attention, and so on. Often, unlike the broader associations, they have opposed moves that, on the surface at least, appear to be oriented to greater professionalism, and they have opposed these because of the disruption that would be caused to existing privileges or arrangements.[3]

Police unions of this more limited kind (local, industrial) had their beginnings in the late nineteenth and early twentieth centuries, during a period of considerable growth in the labor movement.[4] Though there were early conflicts between police unions and management it was not until the Boston police strike of 1919 that the issue of police unions was, at least for the time, decisively joined. Early in that year, the Boston Social Club (as the union referred to itself) sought to affiliate with the American Federation of Labor, so that it could negotiate collectively and supposedly more effectively for improved working conditions and salaries. At that time, no one could reasonably argue that police were adequately compensated for their work. But their efforts, which happen to have been in violation of city policy, were punitively rebuffed. When they struck in response, they were heavy-handedly repressed, and it was another fifty years before such unions nationwide were able to exercise significant power.[5]

Some of the resistance to police unions has taken the form of a charge that unionism is incompatible with professionalism and the aspirations of professional status. It is claimed that professionals do not generally belong to labor organizations, and that police involvement with them will inhibit their acceptance as professionals.[6] A simple response to this can be found in the very different work environment that first line police officers experience. Whereas most traditional professionals have a great deal of control over their working conditions and remuneration, police, as employees, have relatively little say about their conditions and salaries. It might be added that where physicians and lawyers have been employees, they, too, albeit rarely, have asserted their claims for better conditions via collective action.

Even so, the growth of police unionism is often seen, particularly by police management, as a threat to the recognition of police as professionals. Fundamental to this claim is the expectation that police unionization will lead to a shift in power within the police organization. As an institution that is hierarchically structured – presumably in the name of accountability, competence, and efficiency – the police organization would find its line of authority challenged by the collective power that the union represented, and would have to share its decision-making entitlements. This sharing, it is claimed, would have nothing to do with ability, and everything to do with industrial muscle.

But why should shared decision making militate against professionalism? On its face, there does not seem to be any problem at all, quite the contrary. The current hierarchization of decision-making power is itself problematic from the perspective of professionalism. And so its "taming" or moderation would not seem to be a bad thing. The problem, however, is seen as substantive rather than procedural. It is the belief that union involvement in decision making will show more concern with protecting and increasing employee benefits than with ensuring and raising occupational standards. A union agenda may well mean the preservation of promotion by seniority or sponsorship[7] instead of by merit, and a resistance to improved standards for promotion or other requirements designed to enhance performance. Some of these initiatives may not be opposed outright, but will come to be hedged about with conditions that make them impossible to implement. Acceptance of improved training requirements may be made contingent on the acceptance of paid leave, or of a new wage or health package.

Such complaints as these might be made, not from any opposition to unions as such, but simply in the belief that unions have a different role to play in occupational life. Whereas professionals, through their associations, are committed to providing the best possible service for public-spirited reasons, unions – it may be said – are concerned with providing benefits for service providers. Unions are bulwarks against exploitation. They are testimony to the fact that advantage is frequently taken of employees, and that some form of collective action will be the only way in which this situation can be avoided or rectified.

Unlike many who are considered professionals, police find themselves in the position of being employees who are highly vulnerable to political and economic factors. *Occupationally*, whatever one might want to say about their knowledge and expertise, they are in the position of employees who must work under difficult conditions and usually for modest compensation. This would indeed be a frustrating position to be in were their professional development not compatible with unionization.

But police are not the only group who claim or seek professional status while being employees. University professors and many engineers are in the employ of larger institutions or organizations. And they are frequently unionized. There is little doubt, however, that the conditions of their employment differ from those of police. Generally they have much more say in how they will organize their work. Their working conditions and financial compensation tend to be better. And in the case of professors, at least, the protections offered by a tradition of academic freedom are generally considerable. An effective police union is likely to be much more involved in the day-to-day operations of a police department, and if its concerns – rather than those of the relevant police professional association – are given priority, then professionalizing initiatives may well suffer.

We should not, however, compare the situation of police and other professional employees too closely. In part, though only in part, this is because police do not have a comparably educated grasp of the theory and principles that inform their work. The other side, and for police the more pressing fact, is the poor record of regard that police management (especially in larger departments) has for sworn employees. First line officers often consider that the rights they are required to recognize when dealing with other members of the community and the standards of integrity they are expected to observe are ignored by police management in its dealings with them. Police unions provide the only means whereby those at the bottom of a strongly hierarchical organization can get protection against managerial arbitrariness, oppression or corruption; are able to blow the whistle without recriminations; or can represent their concerns and viewpoint to the media. And because, they will argue, police management is so pervasively hierarchical, and with that, politicized, police unions will inevitably be called upon to play a much greater part in the day-to-day operations of a police department than will the relevant professional organization. Thus, even if police are less professionalized than others with whom they might be compared, it is not the greater influence of their unions that makes this so, since the latter provide a needed antidote to a chain of command that has historically abused its powers.

Richard M. Ayres has argued that the tension between unionization and professionalization is better seen as evolutionary than as ineradicable.[8] Drawing on the work of Frederick Herzberg, Ayres observes that the goals of unions can best be seen as the removal of work factors that "dissatisfy" employees. Included among such sources of dissatisfaction will be organizational policies and administrative practices, forms of supervision, general working conditions, money, and security. These are the things that unions will endeavor to alleviate or improve. Their alleviation or improvement, however, is not sufficient to make the work satisfying. Work factors that "satisfy" employees will include achievement, recognition, responsibility, growth, and tasks that are intrinsically interesting. And these factors are closely linked to the provision of professional service. Even though unions can help to remove sources of job dissatisfaction, they cannot make police work satisfying. And for this reason their goals should not be taken to constitute an alternative to or substitute for increased professionalism. Rather, they might better be viewed as clearing the ground for more professional performance.

In practice, however, what Ayres sees as compatible and evolutionarily related are unlikely to be so. In part this is because the communal resources for policing are scarce, and efforts to remove sources of dissatisfaction are likely to deplete resources that could be used to enhance work satisfaction. In this respect, police are comparable to school teachers, who constantly seek to improve their professional status, but always seem to be the victims of some political or budget crisis that diminishes their resources, opportunities, and energies. In addition to this, the factors that would help to make police work more satisfying are likely to be of a kind that calls into question the very system that is supposedly set up to promote those satisfactions. It is in significant part the hierarchical organization of police work that stifles responsibility, growth, recognition, and so on. Thus community policing – theoretically oriented to greater police initiative, improved recognition, and so on – is cramped by the very system that seeks to promote it.

13.2 POLICE AND THE RIGHT TO STRIKE

One of the historic functions of unions has been to provide collective representation for employees who are individually unable to achieve the equality in the negotiating process that is implicit in the employment contract. Where there is no great scarcity of workers – something that is generally true in lower-skilled occupations – those seeking employment may be confronted with a "take it or leave it" contract that, relative to need and capacity, is very unfavorable to the employee and unreasonably favorable to the employer. Unions, by virtue of the collective power that they bring to the negotiating table, may be able to correct such imbalances of bargaining power, and thus to ensure that the claims of employees are heard and taken seriously.

Collective representation, however, means very little, absent the ability to ensure that it is taken seriously. And that requires the capacity to take some form of industrial action. Just as employers can hold the threat of dismissal or sanction over employees as a condition for ensuring their compliance, so too must employees be capable of withdrawing their labor (or taking some other action) as a condition of ensuring that their concerns are taken seriously. The idea here is not so much that employees will forcibly secure their goals, though that is what often occurs, but that the ability to withdraw labor or to take some other action will secure an equal place for them at the negotiating table. Unions seldom enter into negotiations expecting to get everything they initially demand. The expectation is that each side in the negotiations will forgo some demands, and that, given the competing interests that are represented, a mutually acceptable compromise will be reached. Strike action is seen generally as a last resort, not a first one.

But this option, seemingly essential to the negotiating process in a situation where there are competing interests, has in the United States traditionally been denied to police – and indeed to many other public employees. Franklin D. Roosevelt wrote: "A strike of public employees manifests nothing less than an intent on their part to prevent or obstruct the operations of Government until their demands are satisfied. Such action, looking toward the paralysis of Government by those who have sworn to support it, is unthinkable and intolerable."[9]

Though addressed generally to "public employees," Roosevelt's remarks were directed more specifically at those "sworn to support" government, and the most concerted opposition has been directed at firefighters, police officers, the military, and others concerned with the maintenance of public order and safety. When the Boston police officers went on strike, the then Massachusetts Governor Calvin Coolidge telegraphed labor leader Samuel Gompers: "There is no right to strike against public safety by anybody, anywhere, at any time."[10] And in the wake of the disruption that followed, he was backed by President Woodrow Wilson, who stated in a speech: "A strike of the policemen of a great city, leaving that city at the mercy of an army of thugs, is a crime against civilization."[11] Public opinion, no doubt reinforced by fear, backed Coolidge and Wilson. And so it has often done since then.

During the 1970s, police unions managed to gain strength, and there were several significant, and in some cases effective, police strikes.[12] Nevertheless, police strikes have generally remained outlawed and unpopular, and police wishing to assert their claims in the face of intransigence (as they see it) have had to resort to less formal "job actions" – "blue flu," slowdowns, work-to-rules, speedups, ticket blitzes, and so on. The difference between these job actions and full-fledged strikes is generally one of degree rather than of legality. There is some tactical advantage to the former. Where there is a complete and coordinated withdrawal of labor without resignation, the situation is usually clear enough, but significant disruption can be caused if 30 percent of the workforce calls in "sick."

What is it, exactly, that makes police strikes, and perhaps lesser job actions, so problematic? And are these factors weighty enough to justify the disenfranchisement of police in this manner?

Some of the main concerns are reflected in the following statement of the court in *Board of Education v. Redding:*

> It is, so far as we can ascertain, the universal view that there is no inherent right in municipal employees to strike against their governmental employer, whether federal, state, or a political subdivision thereof, and that a strike of municipal employees for any purpose is illegal. . . . The underlying basis for the policy against strikes by public employees is the sound and demanding notion that governmental functions may not be impeded or obstructed, as well as the concept that the profit motive, inherent in the principle of free enterprise, is absent in the governmental function.[13]

The court takes the view that public employees not only lack a right to strike, but are also legally prohibited from doing so. It considers this a reasonable demand, given the importance of governmental functions and the absence of exploitative pressures of the kind found in market-oriented organizations.

Although the court in *Redding* views the prohibition of public employee strikes simply as an appropriate response in the light of some more general political and social considerations, it could have asserted, as some have done, that the fact of illegality may itself figure as the premise of a further argument against public employee strikes. It need not be seen simply as a conclusion. Consider, for example, the charges made by Joseph Herman:

> The most profound impact [of strikes], however, arises from the spectre of organized illegality which strikes by public employees present. Open defiance of the law by teachers and by the police themselves has a particularly telling impact. The corrosive effect of such conduct is aggravated by the failure to enforce the laws proscribing strikes by public employees. Even if the law is enforced initially against the strikers, "amnesty" is the usual price for settlement of the strike, and where strikers have been unable to obtain administrative or judicial suspension of the law, they frequently have obtained it from the legislature. In those instances where the law is enforced, it is often against relatively powerless groups of public employees who lack the "muscle" to obtain special dispensation from the law. Such non-enforcement or selective enforcement weakens the position of law in our society. It undermines the law's efficacy and mocks the ideal of equal treatment. The rule of law rests upon public expectations about the effectiveness of the law in securing order and about the state as the repository of a monopoly of power. It cannot survive repeated disappointment of these expectations.[14]

There is more than one consideration at work here. There is, first of all, a background commitment to the majesty of law, a belief in the dignity and obligatoriness of laws that have been promulgated by duly constituted authority. Those who flout the law do not violate what is merely a legal obligation, but the more fundamental political and moral commitments that are implicit in the notion of society governed by "the rule of law." For Herman, this flouting of law is exacerbated by the fact that, where strike action is concerned, the settlements that tend to be reached do not serve to reassert the law's majesty but only to undermine it further. The public disorder that illegal strike actions represent is aggravated through accommodations that bring the law into disrepute. We might add the further point that since, in the case of police strikes, those who break the law are precisely those who are pledged to uphold and enforce it, the erosion is exacerbated.

There is, certainly, a concern here that needs to be expressed. Yet we can hardly make a judgment about the matter without looking at the substantive issues involved. Whatever may be said about the "obligation to obey the law" – and there is much to be said on both sides of this issue[15] – our judgment about a specific breach of the law and the way in which it is subsequently handled cannot be properly determined without some consideration of the law's content, the reasons for breaching it, and the moral and social costs of handling its breach one way rather than another. Even if it is argued that there is some *moral* obligation to obey that which has been approved by society's duly constituted authority, the obligation is hardly strong enough on its own to rule out all disobedience. And so, if the law is judged to have been insensitive to the legitimate grievances of the striking party, and if the "amnesty" is seen to be warranted as part of the rectification precipitated by the strike, then this will not be as likely to impact unfavorably on respect for the law as would be the case were a settlement to be seen as capitulation to those "holding society to ransom." No doubt in any particular case there will be competing cries of "rectification" and "hostage holding," but it is likely that one will resonate more plausibly than the other.

What we really need to examine are the more substantive considerations at work. At least four seem to be implicit in the *Redding* judgment: (1) the absence of an inherent right to strike; (2) the unacceptability of impeding or obstructing governmental functions; (3) the freedom of public employees from vulnerability to exploitative market forces; and (4) the importance of a social policy against strikes by public employees.

13.2.1 *The right to strike*

In *Redding*, the court claimed that it could find no "inherent right" to strike, at least so far as public employees were concerned. This could be taken simply as a denial that public employees have such a right, though it is more likely that a broader claim was intended – namely, that no one has an inherent right to strike. The right to strike, if there is such, is not to be construed in the same way as the right to life or free speech or against self-incrimination.[16]

But we need not think of this in *constitutional* terms. Is there a *moral* right to strike, or if not a right, then a moral case for striking or even – in certain circumstances – a moral duty to strike?[17]

We should, perhaps, first address a general argument against any strike action. It is, simply, that the employer–employee relation is freely contracted, and that employees have an obligation to adhere to the terms of that contract by working for whatever remuneration, and under any conditions, it offered. If employees come to dislike what they agreed to, then they should leave and seek employment elsewhere under more favorable terms. Strike action is no option.

Although there are several variants of this kind of argument, here it will be sufficient to note some initial responses that shift the onus from strikers to employers. On a purely formal level, the legal system frequently recognizes that, despite the terms of the wage contract, workers may have a right to strike. It is true that this does not cover all workers; yet it is important to recognize that it does cover many. More substantively, the "freedom" with which employees enter into contracts is at best a qualified one. People have to live, they usually need jobs if their standard of living is to be at all acceptable, and, in most industrialized societies, there are fewer jobs available than people seeking them. Some have the skills and talent and opportunity to control the terms of their employment. Many do not. They are not equal bargainers in the wage contract, and employers, knowing their control, may make some of its terms unconscionable.[18] In any case, many strikes reflect either a change in the conditions that operated when the contract was first entered into (raising questions about its continued validity) or a change in the employer's demands (and thus reflect the employer's departure from its original conditions). It is much too superficial to claim that the wage contract per se excludes the possibility of legitimate strike action.

Fundamental to a case for the moral legitimacy of strike action is the idea that employees, by virtue of their status as persons *and* their contribution in labor, should enjoy certain terms and conditions of employment and receive certain returns from their employers. What these terms, conditions, and returns should be will be a complex matter to determine, though we might crudely distinguish terms, conditions, and benefits that employees might reasonably expect by virtue of their humanity from those that they might reasonably expect by virtue of their labor. We can see the former as establishing certain minimum terms, conditions, and returns, and the latter as bearing on above-baseline matters. The argument, in this form, has dual roots in respect and fairness. The former will have some bearing on a "minimum wage" structure, the latter will take account of features of the "wage contract" – its terms and expectations, as well as any relevant changes that have occurred since it was drawn up.

Where the terms, conditions, and returns of employment are judged to fall below their expectations, employees may consider what an appropriate response should be. In an ideal world, an employee would be able to present his or her complaint to management, it would be fairly adjudicated, and any needed action would be taken. In the world as we find it, these failures in expectations are less tractable, and are frequently endemic to the work environment. The interests of management may be incompatible with those of labor. In theory, workers who are dissatisfied may seek to do better for themselves elsewhere. But in practice there may be no elsewhere. Collective bargaining is a partial response to a situation in which individual employees have very little power to ensure a fair hearing for their claims.

As a response, however, collective bargaining may be no more effective than individual effort in ensuring that employees' concerns will be taken seriously unless it carries with it the capacity to engage in some form of collective sanction or coercive action. At what point is it appropriate that industrial action be taken? Given that the wage contract is intended to be a mutually agreeable and voluntary arrangement between rationally competent parties, it is reasonable to expect the threat of industrial action to be a latecomer in negotiations between employer and employee. Like the use of force by police, strike action should provide a background bargaining instrument; it should not constitute the preferred manner of asserting claims.

Several different justificatory strategies have been proposed for industrial action. In one view, it is justified as the "lesser evil" or "least restrictive alternative" in a conflict situation in which the parties have been unable to reach some consensus. In another view, industrial action is expected to meet the stringent standards that are required for a "just war."[19]

We probably do not need to pursue these very large questions here. Although they bear on the general issue of a right (or whatever) to strike, to consider them in general and at length would divert us from the related but more specific question of whether *public employees* such as police officers may avail themselves of this option in negotiating the terms, conditions, and returns of their employment. The court in *Redding* offered two reasons for excluding public employees from any right to strike – their importance to government functions and their insulation from market pressures.

13.2.2 *Hindering governmental functions*

Why is the view that "governmental functions may not be impeded or obstructed" a "sound and demanding" one? Two considerations seem to lie behind the claim. First, government is a condition for social order, and second, strike action by public employees is inconsistent with democratic process. The two considerations are not entirely separable.

1. For most liberal thinkers, government is not a convenient option but a necessity.[20] In complex societies, at least, government ensures a level of tolerability in human life. It is able to provide and guarantee a structure for social coordination in which the various activities, associations, and institutions that enable humans to realize their various goods can be organized and

secured. It therefore has a much more fundamental social role to play than a company or even an industry whose workers may, from time to time, strike to improve their terms, conditions, or returns.

Although there may be some symbolic significance to this way of distinguishing governmental from nongovernmental institutions, it is nevertheless too crude. Some strikes by public employees will not have nearly the impact of those by crucial workers in a large corporation. If it is no longer true that what is good for General Motors is good for America, it is still true that the effects of a strike in a large corporation or across a particular industry may be much more devastating than the withdrawal of labor by a group of government employees. Police, nevertheless, do have a critical role in the maintenance of public order, and this was no doubt one of the reasons why, despite the legitimacy of their claims, the Boston police in 1919 found such little public sympathy. The breakdown of order that was threatened and that occurred was seen as the consequence of an irresponsible act on their part (and not as the result of irresponsible provocation by the city).

Whether such breakdowns occur will of course depend significantly on the volatility of the social environment in which the strike takes place. Along with the Boston strike, the Montreal police strike of 1979 was accompanied by a steep increase in the incidence of crime. But several other police strikes have been accompanied by relatively little social disruption.[21] So although the potential for civil disruption in the face of a police strike is a reason for great caution before one is initiated, it does not of itself provide sufficient grounds for a total prohibition.

Those who have considered the justification of strike action to be in some way analogous to engagement in a just war have emphasized inter alia the need for proportionality and the likelihood of success. The disruption threatened by a strike of public employees must not be out of proportion to the gains sought by the striking workers. And a key ingredient in successful strike action by public employees will almost certainly be the degree of public support they can rally to their cause. If public support – in the form of a public appreciation of the justice of the strikers' cause – cannot be gained or sustained, public employee strike action will be seen as an act of naked self-interest, and it will be very difficult for the strikers to succeed in their claims.

2. The other complaint, perhaps a more symbolic one, is that the "manipulation" of government by a strategically placed interest group is incompatible with the idea of government promulgated by democratic theory. It is in this vein that Joseph Herman complains that "strikes by government employees are inconsistent with democratic politics. They constitute a direct attack upon the authority of democratic institutions by private interest groups which are not subject to public control."[22]

It is, of course, true that many "interest groups" seek to exert a disproportionate influence on government. And it is also true that in a democratic society governmental policies and practices ought to be determined by, or at least be accessible to, some more general mandate than that effected by means of industrial pressure. However, there is no necessary incompatibility between police or public employee strike action and broad social support. For a society may, through its legislative representatives, choose to provide for limited strike action by government employees.

There are similarities between this second complaint and the complaint often made against civil disobedience. Strike action, like civil disobedience, may represent an attempt to change the status quo by the exertion of certain kind of illegal pressure. But some of the same arguments that might justify the occasional resort to civil disobedience in a democratic society might also be employed in defense of strike action. Where negotiation has been tried and has failed, where the injustice involved is a serious one, where there is some preparedness to accept the costs of the action, and so on, strike action may represent a form of pressure that does not challenge the underlying institutions and values of a democratic society.[23]

Nevertheless, any such action would have to be carefully orchestrated – at least in the case of police – so that the broader public is not made, or made to feel, vulnerable to the forces of disorder that, at least in many urban communities, lie near the surface of social life. This would be a reason for taking only limited industrial action against the government body or representative whose actions are deemed intolerable. Some of the measures that police officers actually adopt have had just this character. The refusal to issue parking or traffic tickets or the exploitation of sickness provisions (blue flu) affect the ability of a police department to carry out its functions, but not usually in a manner that places the public at greatly increased risk.[24]

Where public employees are involved and strike action could be particularly disruptive, any contemplated action might need to be prefaced by some form of cooling-off period in which both sides are required to make good faith efforts to resolve their differences, and in which negotiations are mediated by some neutral party acceptable to them both.

13.2.3 *The absence of a profit motive*

According to some theorists of capitalism, private owners of capital, committed to maximizing profit, must extract from their employees maximum labor power for minimum outlay. Particularly in times of excess labor supply, employees are likely to find that they will be exploited. Such will be the pressure to maximize return on investment that workers, in no position to protect themselves, will find the terms, conditions, and returns of their employment made onerous or unreasonable. To rectify this, some form of collective industrial action may be necessary and justifiable. But, so the argument goes, public employees are not subject to the pressures of the marketplace, and cannot claim a similar necessity.

The contrast, however, is overdrawn. Even if a city or state is not in the "business" of making profits, it is almost certainly tied to the marketplace. To raise money for its projects and programs, it will issue bonds, and its investment rating will be affected by how well it is seen to manage its affairs. If it is seen as wasteful or inefficient, it may be unable to attract the investment it needs.

In addition, publicly and privately provided services often overlap or combine so significantly that substantive disparities between the terms, conditions, and returns of private and public sector employment will smack of comparative injustice. Schools and hospitals, and security, transport, and sanitation services, for example, tend to be shared between the private and public sectors, and if public employees in these areas are denied the option of striking, they may be placed at a serious disadvantage with respect to their privately employed peers. Robert Howlett has gone so far as to suggest that a restriction of this kind could be interpreted as violating the Fifth and Fourteenth Amendments to the Constitution, in which due process and equal protection are guaranteed.[25]

It is not necessary, however, to posit an intermingling of private and public to make a case for some kind of parity between the two sectors. In a minority opinion, Chief Justice DeBruler of the Indiana Supreme Court remarked that "we should note the basic similarities between the two categories of employees. They both involve people working for wages and seeking some control over their employment conditions. The potential for arbitrary and discriminatory practices against employees are [sic] the same."[26] This may be slightly overstated, given how the profit motive operates in the private sector. Nevertheless, there are many ways in which public employees may also be exploited or otherwise unfairly treated. High public expectations of police, for which a taxpaying public and city management may be prepared to provide only inadequate resources, political infighting in which line officers are made pawns, and political pressures or managerial insensitivity that place unreasonable burdens on lower-ranking officers may all be grounds for some collective assertion of claims.

In these contexts, it might be argued, the possibility of strike action is essential if there are to be effective negotiations between the parties involved. It is Herman's view, therefore, that "[s]trikes and lockouts are essential for collective bargaining because they provide the only means by which the parties may impose a cost of disagreement on each other. The possibility that such costs may be imposed is the only force which encourages the concessions and compromise which constitute bargaining."[27] This of course suggests a fundamentally adversarial relationship between employer and employee, and it may be claimed that this is a more plausible characterization of the private than of the public sector. I doubt, however, whether this is so. Some very large corporations are not unionized, but retain relatively good employee relations.[28] And very few, if any, public sector employees are nonunionized – a reflection, no doubt, of that fact that the need for "profits" represents only one possible source of employee discontent. Adversarial relations may develop just as easily within the public sector, and legal provisions are usually intended to cater to worst-case scenarios rather than best-case ones.

Pace Herman, however, I believe that we should see strike action as the ultimate recourse of employees and not as a pervasive threat in negotiations over the terms, conditions, and returns of employment. An adversarial stance should be taken only as a result of situational factors and not be assumed as a matter of ideology. We should, furthermore, take into account the fact that police officers provide an essential community service. In the initial stages, at least, private employees who strike will probably inconvenience management more than the general public. Unless there is a monopoly on particular goods or services, or employees are unionized on an industrywide basis, the public will probably have alternative sources for those goods or services. But in the case of public employees, particularly those like police officers and firefighters who have a monopoly on emergency services, the inconvenience of a strike will not be confined to "management" but will likely affect the wider community, and particularly those who are least able to fend for themselves. Although it is true that the actual effects of a police strike will differ considerably, depending on background social conditions, the risk of third-party damage could be considerable.

We should note, however, that the third-party damage caused by strike action is not to be automatically equated with damage to "innocent bystanders," any more than noncombatant casualties in wartime are to be seen – without further argument – as "innocent victims." We should remember that the discontent of public employees sometimes has its roots in the unwillingness of a recipient community to provide adequate resources for the services they demand, and that industrial action might be understood to be these chickens coming home to roost.

13.2.4 *The need for a restrictive social policy*

To this point much of the argument has focused on the extent to which, in individual cases, strike action might be defensible. The decision in *Redding*, however, was concerned with the right to strike as a matter of social policy. The issue was not whether, in the instant case, the strike hindered legitimate governmental functions, but whether those functions would be hindered if strike action were provided for or permitted as a matter of social policy. It was claimed that the bad consequences of a policy that allowed for strike action by public employees would outweigh any goods that might be achieved in particular instances.

Chief among those bad consequences have been the costs to third parties – sufficiently significant overall to make a restrictive policy very attractive. Even if in individual cases industrial action might be justified, its provision as a matter of public policy might create opportunities for overwhelmingly negative exploitation and abuse. But by the same token a formal ban on strikes imposes a cost on public employees that requires a responsible and responsive attitude on the part of legislators. The price of any ban on police strikes ought at least to be the setting up of effective mechanisms for negotiation and mediation, where this involves some parity of negotiating power.

Compulsory arbitration in the event of a deadlock might be one option that should be provided for. A legislature that is not prepared to make adequate provision for listening to the police voice may have itself partially to blame if, in the end, police defy the ban and strike anyway. And a judiciary that fails to require an employer to live up to bargaining agreements may also be partially to blame if employer intransigence precipitates a strike.

Of course, a ban on police strikes is just that. Although it will constitute a great disincentive to strike action, it need not prevent such action from occurring. If a police union is powerful enough or sufficiently well positioned, it may be able to strike without serious repercussions for its membership despite the absence of a legal privilege. True, the legal disincentives can be significant – unions and their membership may be subject to huge daily fines. Alternatively, police may find other ways of forcefully asserting their claims. The various job actions previously referred to – blue flu, ticket blitzes, slowdowns, and so on – may be difficult to establish in court as deliberate and coordinated, and yet provide enough pressure to force a recalcitrant management or city to the bargaining table.

13.3 AFFIRMATIVE ACTION

No less than police unionism, pressures for affirmative action in policing have created challenges for police management and for moves toward increased professionalism in the delivery of police services. Does the acceptance of affirmative action policies go counter to the demand for an increasingly professionalized police force? Are some affirmative action policies more acceptable than others?

For many years U.S. policing was a white, male preserve – more male than white, but nevertheless heavily skewed in that direction. In the late 1960s and early 1970s that began to change. The deep-seated racism and sexism of American society became increasingly embarrassing and difficult to sustain, and opportunities were created for minority groups and women to enter into fields from which they had previously been excluded or discouraged.

Yet the past has weighed heavily on the present, and change has been slow in coming, and there have been many calls for some form of organized rectification of the effects of past inequities – some form of "affirmative action," "reverse discrimination," "reparation," "compensatory justice," or "preferential treatment" (the terminology varies).[29] These policies have been highly controversial, in policing as in other areas.

Controversy has occurred at different levels. Most conservatively, the past status quo has been reaffirmed, though for reasons that are claimed to be nonsexist and/or nonracist. Less conservatively, past discrimination has been acknowledged and eschewed, but it has been argued that no special provisions (apart from a formal "equal opportunity") would be warranted. And most liberally, the need for "special provisions" has been acknowledged, though there is disagreement over the details.

13.3.1 *Exclusionary policies*

It is difficult to understand how members of minority groups could be intentionally excluded from policing except for racist reasons. In certain circumstances, reasons of national or local security might be thought to count in favor of a cautionary policy, but these are not relevant to the situation that generally confronts us. In fact, members of minority groups have for many years been represented (albeit underrepresented) in policing. That they have not been more significantly represented has generally reflected more subtle forms of discrimination – the compounding of educational disadvantage, biased testing procedures, and the cultural alienation of groups that have traditionally had poor relations with the police.

The situation for women has been more complicated. For many years, policing was thought to be an inappropriate career for women. Although there were "matrons" in police service from early days, detailed to handle certain police procedures relating to women prisoners, there was great reluctance to have them perform regular police duties.[30] To some extent, that prejudice against women police officers remains. There is a deep-seated tradition and belief among male police officers that policing is "man's work," and that it requires a toughness, physical and psychological, that women do not have and for which "by nature" they are not suited. The entry of women into patrol and detective work has not entirely dispelled that view. Indeed, to the extent that policing has remained modeled on paramilitary lines, it has not been thought an appropriate arena for female endeavor: Women do not belong on the battlefront. The issue here is not simply one of physical and psychological prowess but also of respect. Culturally, men are not used to taking orders from women, and the entry of women into policing has created opportunities for this to happen (though promotion and deployment practices have often minimized them). Women police officers have often found that, unless they "masculinize" their behavior, acceptance and respect are denied them.

But it is difficult to extract from the foregoing considerations an argument for excluding women from policing. There are several reasons: (1) Only a part, and probably not the major part, of policing requires the characteristics that women are said to lack; (2) if in fact women lack some of the characteristics said to be necessary for effective policing, the chances are that this has as much to do with their socialization as with their nature; (3) it is very difficult to argue that the reasons for their exclusion should apply to them as a group, and even if such reasons do apply (for example, their lesser upper-body strength), they are probably of marginal relevance to effective policing; and (4) some of the situations for which women are said to be unsuited (violent confrontations) may have become so precisely because male police officers and correspondingly "macho" attitudes have been involved. Women are probably socialized into dealing with conflict more effectively than men. This may be particularly true of what are among the more dangerous and volatile of situations – the handling of domestic disputes.

13.3.2 *Formal equality versus affirmative action*

It is one thing to say that minority groups and women should be able to pursue careers in policing, and to do so on the same formal terms as others. It is another to argue that, in view of past discrimination, and its contemporary residues, special provisions should be made, either for entry into police work or for advancement within the police agency.

"Special provisions" covers a wide range of possibilities: goals and quotas, an easing of entry requirements, treating group status as a positive factor, ensuring that applicants from the discriminated group are taken seriously, and so on. Some or all of these might be advocated, and some are more controversial than others. Here I shall briefly survey the major objections to some of these forms of affirmative action.

1. It is sometimes argued that injustice will be involved if all members of a particular group are favored, since only some will have been "victimized" by past discrimination. At the same time, victimized members of generally non-disadvantaged groups will be passed over. Color, ethnic background, and gender, it will be claimed, provide too crude an index of victimization. And compensatory justice, if it is to be what it claims to be, will need to be individualized rather than generalized.

There is some point to the complaint. If there is to be rectification of past injustices, then an argument exists for giving the same preference to, say, a discriminated-against white male as to a discriminated-against black female. To give preference to all black females because, as a group, they have been discriminated against, might be thought to favor unfairly those black females who have not been discriminated against and to neglect unfairly those white males who have been discriminated against.

One response here might be to argue that all women and members of minority groups have in fact suffered from past (and perhaps present) discrimination. For even though some of them have apparently done well, they are unlikely to have done as well as they would have had their groups not been discriminated against. Although there are black, Latino, and female millionaires, few if any of them are among the nation's Top 100 business leaders. Would this have been the case had not even the most successful of them suffered from some form of past discrimination?

Although it would be difficult to establish the truth of the foregoing rhetorical suggestion, it is not needed as part of a rejoinder to the initial argument. For, to the extent that affirmative action is seen as a matter of social or institutional policy, there may be reasons of fairness for making a group-based decision. If, as is likely, most members of one group have been discriminated against, and most members of the other group have not, then the practical difficulties involved in fairly establishing, in particular cases, whether a person has been discriminated against may make unfair decision making less likely where the basis for preference is group membership –

especially where that same group membership has, in the past, been used as the basis for discrimination.

But a variant of the original argument needs to be considered. It is that black and Latino group members and women are not the only members of society who experience or have experienced discrimination, and it is therefore unfair to single them out for preferential treatment. Have not Jews and Asians also been the objects of social discrimination?

Such an argument may provide a reason, though not a decisive one, for expanded categories for preferential treatment, rather than an argument against such treatment. Though the "singling out" of one rather than another group is no doubt less than ideal, it is surely arguable that within a country such as the United States blacks and Latinos have been subject to a much more systematic and destructive discrimination, and may therefore have a stronger claim than others to some form of reparation. In any case it is fallacious to assume that since every injustice cannot be redressed it would be improper to provide redress in those cases where redress is possible. Scarce social resources and the problems involved in identifying appropriate recipients will almost certainly result in less-than-ideal solutions to social need. But that is no reason for refraining from doing the best one can. True, the actual policies of preferential treatment that are developed may be less fair than they could have been in the circumstances. But that is a different objection. It is not an argument against affirmative action, but against the eligibility criteria used to implement it.

As it happens, many affirmative action policies do include in their statements a listing of "underrepresented groups" that extends beyond the focal categories of black, Latino and women. If some of the other groups that have suffered social discrimination have not been identified, this may also reflect the fact that the impact of social discrimination has not been as devastating as it has been in other cases.

2. It is often complained that preferential policies will lower the quality of police work. In support of this claim it is acknowledged that one reason why past discrimination tends to be perpetuated even in an environment of "formal equality" is that entry or promotional requirements contain conditions that either indirectly maintain the racial or gender status quo, or alternatively cannot be surmounted, given the social residues of past discrimination. Thus particular height, weight, and strength requirements will tend to exclude women, and particular educational requirements may militate against black and Latino applicants.[31] However, it is then claimed that any compromise of these requirements will diminish the effectiveness of policing.

I think it can be agreed that acceptable affirmative action policies should not result in a significant lowering of the quality of police work. Given the social importance of policing and the heavy responsibility borne by police officers, there is a strong public interest in achieving and maintaining a high level of police efficiency and integrity. However, it should not be assumed from this that any and every departure from or easing of existing standards of entry and promotion would lead to a serious decline in the standard of police service. The onus is on any who would use discriminatory criteria to show the real (and not merely supposed) relevance of those criteria to the position in question. In the landmark case of *Griggs v. Duke Power Company*, it was argued that tests used for hiring have "to measure the person for the job, and not the person in the abstract."[32] It is not enough to argue that men are generally physically stronger than women or that whites are generally better educated than blacks or Latinos. It must be shown that "absolute" measures of physical strength and educational achievement are necessary for successful job performance. That is very unlikely, at least in the case of policing. No doubt some standards are necessary, but a selection procedure that makes too much of rankings above the requirements appropriate for successful performance will wantonly discriminate against disadvantaged groups.

Even so, it might be insisted that the *best* qualified should be chosen, even if this would (as indeed it would) tend to favor the hiring and promotional *status quo*. However the theory here is rather better than the practice. In practice, hiring and promotion have been influenced by many other factors besides assessed merit. Old boy networks, friendships, ethnic and blood ties, rivalries, political advantage, and many other factors have intruded themselves into the selection process. That of course is not an argument for adding further irrelevant considerations, but it serves to call into question the highmindedness of the protest. More important, the various tests that are used to determine merit are too crude to allow anything but an approximate ranking, and it might be better to see all or at least most of those who qualify as standing on a roughly equal footing.[33]

Nevertheless, there could be a real problem here, one that needs to be seriously confronted. To the extent that police work is professionalized and demilitarized, then to that extent greater demands will be made of individual police officers, and training and promotional requirements may need to be tightened. As long as the prevailing tests for job-related skills tend to favor those who have been educationally and socially advantaged, the victims of past discrimination will once again lose out.

3. The previous objection, which argues against the use of employment standards that are not significantly job-related, might also be turned against any affirmative action policies that make group membership a *positive* factor in employment or promotion. It may be claimed that if race- or sex-based quotas are used, or race or sex is used as an affirmative factor in decision making, the mistake made in using irrelevant height or educational standards is simply repeated.

Or is it? If we allow that the proportion of women and some[34] minority group members within the general population is significantly greater than in the police force, and further that there are police problems faced by these groups that are (for the most part) best dealt with by police officers drawn from those groups, then gender and race might be seen as positive selection characteristics.

The first premise can be granted. The second is more problematic. It is true that much police work – for example, that which deals with domestic disputes and sexual assaults against women – might be handled more competently and humanely by women.[35] And perhaps the same could be claimed for the minority policing of areas with large minority populations.[36] But there is no guarantee that this will be the case, and in some cases the contrary position has been taken. Thus it has been argued that minority officers, rather than being more sympathetic to "their own," have little time for those who, unlike them, have gone astray, and further that, as if to reflect the social background from which they have come, they are liable to treat their own "in the only language they understand." The argument for treating group membership as a positive characteristic needs to be established and not merely asserted.[37]

Of course, even if it cannot be argued that members of the disadvantaged groups are significantly better suited to handle problems arising within their groups there might be other – say, sociopolitical – reasons for increasing their representation. A greater representation of women and minority group members might diminish social disaffection, envy, and instability; it might provide alternative role models and nurture cross-cultural and cross-sexual understanding.[38] If police hiring and promotional policies are not seen as racist and sexist, police effectiveness may be increased.[39] The influx of women may in fact help to transform police work from an excessively "macho" occupation to one that is more caring and respectful.[40]

It is important, however, that these benefits of affirmative action be not merely conjectured but shown to be probable. And the benefits of using a group characteristic affirmatively needs to be set against its drawbacks.

4. One significant drawback to an affirmative action policy is the strong likelihood that members of the relevant groups who are offered employment or promotion will, whether rightly or not, be seen as having achieved their goals by virtue of their group membership and not by virtue of their merits.[41] The effect will be a diminution rather than an enhancement of the respect in which they are held. In professions that rely heavily on mutual trust and respect between members, differential treatment could be particularly destructive.

This is a difficult problem, because it concerns the perception of affirmative action policies rather than any real consequences they may have. There is no reason why using gender or minority group membership as a positive factor in employment should detract from its meritoriousness more than the natural characteristic of being over 6 feet and 200 pounds. The real issue is whether those who are employed satisfy the relevant criteria; and if it can be argued that women and minority group members satisfy those criteria and/or that gender and minority group status constitute positive reasons for employment in police work, there is no cause for complaint or diminished respect. But public response to affirmative action programs need not be rational, and it is arguable that the social costs of affirmative action policies could be greater than their benefits.

All this shows, I suspect, is that social reforms, if they are to work, need to have adequate social support. Even the removal of a palpable injustice may not be warranted if the costs of its removal will foment even greater injustices. Perhaps the abolition of slavery warranted a Civil War; less dramatic affirmative action policies may be compatible with only a small amount of disruption. What need to be traded are the injustices involved, and the likelihood of their removal by affirmative and other means. This is not a simple consequentialist calculation, since injustices "demand" a rectification that is not offset by simple predictions of resistance, unrest, and so on. At the same time, *fiat justitia, ruat coelum* overrates the claims of justice for the world we must inhabit.

5. A further argument against affirmative action policies holds that the benefits to disadvantaged groups are purchased only at significant cost to members of the so-called advantaged group. If informal quotas are applied, equally or better qualified members of the latter group will be excluded. If assistance is given, it will be paid for by members of the advantaged group. Furthermore, it might be claimed, these costs will be exacted from a non-discriminatory present generation. Those not directly discriminated against will be recompensed by those who did not perpetrate the discriminations of the past.

Let us note, first, that these costs may be spread in different ways. If, for example, fifty places out of an existing hundred are reserved for members of minority groups who would otherwise gain only ten, then the costs of the additional forty minority group places will be borne by forty members of the advantaged group who will now be denied entry. If, however, the quota of fifty places is secured by adding forty additional places to the intake, then the costs will not be borne by forty unsuccessful members of the advantaged group, but will instead be spread more widely. The second alternative, if acceptable on other grounds, is less restrictive than the first, and for that reason may be preferred.[42]

Furthermore, whether the present generation referred to is in fact as non-discriminatory as the argument suggests is something of a moot point. Discrimination can take many forms, and the removal of the more blatant forms of past discrimination need not result and has not resulted in the removal of more subtle forms of discrimination. But even if we argue that active discrimination is a thing of the past, its residues remain, not only in the disadvantaged social backgrounds of some, but in the advantaged backgrounds of others. Contemporary white males are, for the most part, the beneficiaries of a past in which white males have been dominant and discriminatory.

Nevertheless, it might be argued in response that contemporary white males have neither sought the benefits of their social position nor voluntarily accepted them. They have been simply "given" as part of their social heritage; and it would therefore be unfair to exact from *them* the cost of reparation. But while it is true that, say, white males have had little control over the conditions of their upbringing, that same upbringing has placed them in a position where they have been able to exercise some control over their continued enjoyment of those benefits. And if, in those circumstances, they choose not to shoulder some of the costs of reparation, rhetoric about their earlier lack of control begins to ring hollow. It rings hollow because, unless they are willing to shoulder some of the burden of rectifying the past, the burden of that past will be borne unequally by those who have been disadvantaged by it.[43]

13.3.3 *Choosing between affirmative action policies*

As I mentioned earlier, affirmative action policies vary. They may take the form of goals and quotas,[44] of the expenditure of additional resources on the disadvantaged group (for recruitment or training), of changes to the criteria for employment or promotion, and so on. And within each of these possibilities there exist alternatives. A fair bit of the debate concerns the appropriateness of particular affirmative action policies (or features thereof).

I believe that we would be mistaken were we to look for some universally desirable affirmative action policy, even in relation to a particular group such as the police. Social situations vary considerably, and what works adequately in one context may be disastrous in another. Nevertheless, it is possible to indicate some of the factors that would need to be taken into account were an affirmative action policy to be developed for police work.

1. One constraint is embedded in the demands of police work. It is no good if an affirmative action policy results in the hiring or promotion of substantial numbers of people who cannot do the work that is reasonably expected of them. Nevertheless, it needs to be remembered that police work is very varied, and that not every police officer is suited to every kind of police work. Entry into police work should not be determined by a person's potential to be a police chief or detective inspector or member of a specialized unit, but by the regular demands of police work. Affirmative action policies should not diminish the quality of policing that the public is entitled to; but neither should entry into or promotion within police work depend on characteristics and skills that are minimally (or only occasionally) relevant to its successful performance.

There is a problem here, because it is difficult to specify and test the particular skills required by police work. Unlike many other occupations, policing does not require specialized skills prior to hiring. Needed skills are developed on the job, and entry requirements tend to be of a fairly general nature rather than highly specialized – common sense, integrity, an ability to communicate, good health, an ability to remain calm under pressure, and so on. And such tests as do exist for these are difficult to validate.[45]

2. It needs to be kept in mind that some kinds of capability develop with opportunity. It may be true that members of certain disadvantaged groups are less capable than most others of performing some of the tasks associated with police work (say, writing and reading skills, or driving and combat skills). These deficiencies will often result from the social background and socialization of the group members. Given opportunity, these deficiencies might be remedied, and an affirmative action policy could sometimes take the form of providing members of these groups with assistance in acquiring such skills.

This last point may be relevant to the problem almost universally encountered in recruitment drives – that even where job-related tests have been devised and applied, minority group members have done less well. Apart from the possibility that such results reflect "hidden" biases in the testing mechanisms, there is the further fact that, in a society that is beginning to accommodate its minorities within professions and at ranks from which they were previously excluded, better qualified minorities are being attracted into more promising work.

That said, I would issue the following caveat. It is by no means obvious what the most desirable or even an acceptable representation of women and minority group members in police work should be. No doubt discrimination can be appealed to in explanation of some current representations. But we should not ignore the possibility that some occupations will be less intrinsically desirable to members of some groups than to others.[46] I say "intrinsically," because there is little doubt that some of the reasons why women and minority group members do not seek employment in policing as readily as they seek employment elsewhere are merely contingent: they reflect the fact that attitudes and traditions within policing as it exists are unfriendly to their participation. Gender stereotypes, a history of police oppression of minorities, and so on, have made policing an unattractive occupational option for such people. And so there is, as Samuel Williams points out, a primary need to "reshape those elements of the current police experience that so frequently function to make the environment if not outrightly hostile, then subtly inhospitable to the minority group individual."[47] Unless this is undertaken and to some extent accomplished, affirmative action programs will face an uphill battle. Yet, lest this be used to justify a delay in those programs, we should not underrate the importance that the actual participation of women and minorities in policing may have in breaking down the barriers of prejudice. Much prejudice survives only through ignorance.

Notes

1 INTRODUCTION

1. Readers who are interested in the *teaching* of police ethics might care to consult my "Teaching and Learning Police Ethics: Competing and Complementary Approaches," *Journal of Criminal Justice* 18, 1 (January 1990), pp. 1–18.
2. The idea of judgment is none too clear, and needs further specification. A useful starting point is Henry S. Richardson, "Specifying Norms as a Way to Resolve Concrete Ethical Problems," *Philosophy & Public Affairs*, 19, 4 (Fall 1990), pp. 279–310.
3. Sidgwick's *The Methods of Ethics* was first published in 1874 (London: Macmillan Press); *Practical Ethics: A Collection of Addresses and Essays* was first published in 1898 (London: Swan Sonnenschein).
4. At this point I shall treat morality and ethics as the same. That is probably not quite right, though the various ways of making a distinction tend to be highly controversial. For many writers, ethics is seen as a more theoretical enterprise, morality being concerned instead with substantive practical principles and judgments. A further cut suggests that whereas morality is concerned with universal practical norms, ethics is contextualized – as in professional ethics or police ethics. We will return to this issue briefly in Chapter 12, Section 12.2.
5. Here I note simply that the various processes we have of choice making, indeed, of thinking more generally about the world in which we are embedded, are themselves mediated and appraised via evaluative concepts. The so-called intellectual virtues belong to this processual sphere.
6. I should perhaps note that for those who allow the legitimacy of religious interests and who accept the validity of some particular religious standpoint, the perspective provided by that standpoint will tend to be given priority in the government of life: Law, morality and politics will all be brought within the orbit of that religious understanding. Even so, the priority that is otherwise given to morality has generated one of the great debates of philosophy – the so-called Euthyphro problem: Is what God commands good because God commands only what is good, or is it good only because God commands it? If the former, morality retains a certain priority; if the latter, a reductio ad absurdum seems inevitable. The issue is too complex to pursue here. A useful entrée is Janine Marie Idziak (ed.) *Divine Command Morality: Historical and Contemporary Readings* (New York: Edwin Mellen Press, 1979).

7. See, for example, Philippa Foot, "Are Moral Considerations Overriding?" in *Virtues and Vices and Other Essays in Moral Philosophy* (Berkeley & Los Angeles: University of California Press, 1978), pp. 181–8.

8. Joseph Butler, Preface to *Fifteen Sermons*, in *Butler's Works*, ed. W. Gladstone (Oxford: Oxford University Press, 1896), vol. I, pp. 5–6.

9. Hare's statement of these claims is developed mainly in his *The Language of Morals* (Oxford: Oxford University Press [Clarendon Press], 1952), and *Freedom and Reason* (Oxford: Oxford University Press [Clarendon Press], 1963).

10. For a fascinating recent exploration of some facets of this, see Jonathan Lear, *Love and Its Place in Nature: A Philosophical Interpretation of Freudian Psychoanalysis* (New York: Farrar, Straus & Giroux, 1990).

11. Our moral concerns may encompass animals and the environment, independently of their impact on our human interactions.

12. I think this is what makes certain forms of moral relativism problematic. Of course, humans in different circumstances might reasonably have different expectations of each other, and the norms of interpersonal conduct that we come to learn as the result of our socialization tend to be colored by particular cultural traditions, and thus may not properly reflect ways of being and doing that are ultimately conducive to our flourishing. Moral relativism, at least in some of its forms, tends to be necessitated only by moral imperialism, our failure to see the extent to which the particular contours of our moral tradition have been distorted by cultural particularities.

13. See G. J. Warnock, *Contemporary Moral Philosophy* (London: Macmillan Press, 1967), ch. 5.

14. The distinction between deontology and consequentialism is itself so broad as to be practically meaningless. The former is a ragbag of intuitionist, natural law, divine command, and rationalistic theories, and the latter is often understood so broadly that it encompasses the very factors that are used to differentiate it from "deontological" theories. I take the view that there are elements of both "approaches" that need to be incorporated into any adequate understanding of moral life, and that domination by one rather than another approach is likely to distort not only our experience but also our judgment.

2 MORAL FOUNDATIONS OF POLICING

1. Jesse Rubin, "Police Identity and the Police Role," in Robert F. Steadman (ed.), *The Police and the Community* (Baltimore: Johns Hopkins University Press, 1972), p. 25.

2. Metropolitan Police, *General Instructions* (1829), part 1, excerpted in John Kleinig, with Yurong Zhang (comps. and eds.), *Professional Law Enforcement Codes: A Documentary Collection* (Westport, CT: Greenwood, 1993), p. 27. Usage of the term "police" was settled by Patrick Colquhoun's *A Treaty on the Police of the Metropolis* (London: C. Dilly, 1796), and the role of police as formulated in the *General Instructions*, had already been enunciated in Saunders Welch, *Observations on the Office of Constable: With Cautions for the More Safe Execution of That Duty: Drawn from Experience* (London: printed for A. Miller, 1754). For a history of the Metropolitan Police, see David Ascoli, *The Queen's Peace: The Origins and Development of the Metropolitan Police 1829–1979* (London: W. Hamilton, 1979). Policing in the United States is usefully chronicled in Robert Fogelson, *Big-City Police* (Cambridge, MA: Harvard University Press, 1977).

3. John Locke, *Second Treatise Of Civil Government* (1690). The material that follows is drawn particularly from chs. 2 and 9.
4. See, for example, Jeffrey H. Reiman, "The Social Contract and the Police Use of Deadly Force," in Frederick A. Elliston and Michael Feldberg (eds.), *Moral Issues in Police Work* (Totowa, NJ: Rowman & Allanheld, 1985), pp. 237–49; Howard Cohen and Michael Feldberg, *Power and Restraint: The Moral Dimension of Police Work* (New York: Praeger, 1991).
5. Locke, unlike Hobbes, does at least acknowledge that social life of a limited kind may preexist the conveniences of civil government. But it is not clear that he appreciates to what extent the individuals who subsequently come together in civil society are "socially constructed."
6. Albeit traditions that may have survived the scrutiny and obtained the consent of a past generation.
7. Locke, *Second Treatise*, ch. 8, sect. 119.
8. See, for example, the discussion in A. John Simmons, *Moral Principles and Political Obligations* (Princeton, NJ: Princeton University Press, 1979), ch. 4.
9. For failing to recognize this in his *A Theory of Justice* (Cambridge, MA: Harvard University Press [Belknap Press], 1971), John Rawls was strongly criticized. In subsequent work he has acknowledged that his argument needs to be understood against a background of liberal commitments. See, for example, his *Political Liberalism* (New York: Columbia University Press, 1993).
10. There is an impressive statement and defense of this general position in H. L. A. Hart's critique of John Austin. See his *The Concept of Law* (Oxford: Oxford University Press [Clarendon Press], 1961), ch. 1.
11. Embedded in the notion of *authoritative* coercion is the idea of proportionality.
12. Anyone can bully or tyrannize. Authoritarianism is a coercive abuse of authority. See my *Philosophical Issues in Education* (New York: St. Martin's, 1982), pp. 217–18.
13. See, for example, R. S. Peters, "Authority," *Proceedings of the Aristotelian Society* 32 (1958), pp. 207–24. Somewhat earlier, Max Weber made a slightly different distinction between "traditional," "legal-rational," and "charismatic" authority. See *The Theory of Social and Economic Organisation*, trans. A.M. Henderson and Talcott Parsons, rev. ed. (London: W. Hodge, 1947), pp. 324ff.
14. It used to be thought that police officers should meet certain height requirements, the idea being, in part, that an imposing figure would more likely command respect and obedience.
15. The causal connection probably works in the opposite direction as well. If police abuse their authority, this can lower the authoritative standing of the governing power.
16. In the film version of his story (*Serpico*, starring Al Pacino), Frank Serpico reports that what impressed him about police officers as a child, and influenced his decision to go into police work, was that, in a situation where others were confused, "they knew!"
17. See D. F. Gundersen, "Credibility and the Police Uniform," *Journal of Police Science and Administration* 15, 3 (September 1987), pp. 192–5.
18. See, for example, Clifford D. Shearing and Philip C. Stenning, "Modern Private Security: Its Growth and Implications," in Norval Morris and Michael Tonry (eds.), *Crime and Justice: An Annual Review of Research*, vol. 3 (Chicago: University of Chicago Press, 1981); Clifford D. Shearing and Philip Stenning (eds.), *Private Policing* (Beverly Hills, CA: Sage, 1987); Marcia Chaiken and Jan Chaiken, *Public Policing – Privately Provided* (Washington, DC: NIJ/OCRU, 1987).

19. We should, perhaps, not forget that the primary agent of arrest was originally "the private person." The balance in "power to arrest" shifts to constables, sheriffs, and so forth, only during the nineteenth century. See Jerome Hall, "Police and Law in a Democratic Society," *Indiana Law Journal* 28, 2 (Winter 1953), esp. pp. 135–7. Although it is not with this sense of "private policing" that I am here concerned, there are connections, since pre-nineteenth-century policing was "characterized" by a lack or limitedness of public control.

20. An acute discussion of its inadequacies, by someone who was ideologically inclined to it, can be found in Robert Nozick, *Anarchy, State and Utopia* (Oxford: Blackwell Publisher, 1974), pt. 1. Also, see John Hospers, *Libertarianism: A Political Philosophy for Tomorrow* (Los Angeles: Nash Publishing, 1971), ch. 11.

21. See Bill Lawson, "Crime, Minorities, and the Social Contract," *Criminal Justice Ethics* 9, 2 (Summer/Fall 1990), pp. 16–24.

22. For an argument to the effect that a policy of allowing the police acceptance of gratuities would be tantamount to encouragement of private and unequally distributed police services, see Michael Feldberg, "Gratuities, Corruption, and the Democratic Ethos of Policing: The Case of the Free Cup of Coffee," in Elliston and Feldberg, *Moral Issues in Police Work*, esp. pp. 270–6.

23. Adam Smith thought that the universal pursuit of self-interest would "frequently" do more to promote the good of society than a deliberate promotion of the public interest. By intending their own gain, individuals are "led by an invisible hand to promote an end which was no part of [their] intention" (*The Wealth of Nations* [Edinburgh: Adam & Charles Black, 1863], p. 199). For a critique, see Christopher McMahon, "Morality and the Invisible Hand," *Philosophy & Public Affairs* 10 (1981), pp. 247–77.

24. This was recently attempted, though the officers appointed were given considerably fewer powers than regular peace officers. See "Sussex Approves Use of Guards to Replace Police," *New York Times*, 21 April 1993, p. B7; Robert Hanley, "Sussex Force Only Looks Like Police," *New York Times*, 14 June 1993, pp. B1, B4.

25. The normative dimension of roles is often absent from sociological discussions. For a seminal treatment that emphasizes the normative character of roles, see Dorothy Emmet, *Rules, Roles and Relations* (London: Macmillan Press, 1967).

26. See James Q. Wilson, *The Varieties of Police Behavior* (Cambridge, MA: Harvard University Press, 1968), p. 19; Thomas Bercal, "Calls for Police Assistance," *American Behavioral Scientist*, 13 (1970), p. 682; Albert J. Reiss, Jr., *The Police and the Public* (New Haven, CT: Yale University Press, 1971), p. 75; Elaine Cumming, Ian M. Cumming, and Laura Edell, "The Policeman as Philosopher, Guide and Friend," *Social Problems*, 12 (Winter 1965), pp. 276–86. A British study yielded similar results: Maurice Punch and Trevor Naylor, "The Police: A Social Service," *New Society* 24 (17 May 1973), pp. 358–61. Although these studies are now somewhat dated, it is unlikely that the situation has changed significantly. See David H. Bayley, *Police for the Future* (New York : Oxford University Press, 1994), ch. 2.

27. For the most significant recent research on this particular issue, see Lawrence W. Sherman, with Janell D. Schmidt and Dennis P. Rogan, *Policing Domestic Violence: Experiments and Dilemmas*, New York: Free Press, 1992.

28. The fact that situations requiring a police presence do not divide neatly into community-service and law-enforcement categories constitutes the weakness of Bernard L. Garmire's suggestion that "contradictory roles that the police are expected to perform" be handled by a firm division of labor – "two agencies under one department," with staff selected on the basis of their suitability for one

or the other function. See "The Police Role in an Urban Society," in Steadman, *The Police and the Community*, pp. 1–11.

29. Models may be descriptive or normative; that is, some attempt to give a general characterization of the way in which police work *is* done, whereas others attempt to provide a characterization that will circumscribe the legitimate authority of the police role. Here I am concerned with normative models.

30. There is no decisive reason why police work should conform to any *one* model, though a single model may provide unity of understanding and help to obviate some of the role conflict that police often experience.

31. Sometimes this is referred to as the Law Enforcement or Military Model. Its dominance is suggested by (a) the fact that when officers refer to "real police work," they generally mean crimefighting, (b) the strongly hierarchical organization and trappings of many police departments – uniforms and badges of rank, salutes, inspections and parades, the carrying of weapons, and so forth, and (c) popular representations of police work on television and in movies. Although some recent TV series have attempted to take a broader view of the police role, most are still heavily slanted toward crimefighting.

32. Sometimes referred to as the Firefighter Model.

33. Howard Cohen, "Authority: The Limits of Discretion," in Elliston and Feldberg (eds), *Moral Issues in Police Work*, pp. 27–41. Though the purposes of peacekeeping and providing social services are stated rather than argued for, they are almost certainly broad enough to encompass the range of activities in which police currently find themselves engaged.

34. Cohen, "Authority: The Limits of Discretion," p. 38.

35. It is at least arguable that the kind of "stand-in authority" that Cohen accords to police is partially grounded in a more fundamental obligation that we all have when bystanders in crisis situations. Police will function somewhat as "professional citizens."

36. Joseph Betz, "Police Violence," in Elliston and Feldberg (eds.), *Moral Issues in Police Work*, p. 192. A similar point is made by Egon Bittner, "The Capacity to Use Force as the Core of the Police Role," in Elliston and Feldberg (eds.), *Moral Issues in Police Work*, p. 20.

37. Betz, "Police Violence," p. 187.

38. However, if we see community-oriented policing as problem-oriented policing – as a number of current writers do – then a rather more plausible rendition can be given of the social service role of police. They are there not just for "crises" and "emergencies" but for problem solving. See John E. Eck and William Spelman, "Who Ya Gonna Call? The Police as Problem-Busters," *Crime & Delinquency* 33, 1 (January 1987), pp. 31–52; Herman Goldstein, *Problem-Oriented Policing* (New York: McGraw-Hill, 1990); Malcolm K. Sparrow, Mark H. Moore, and David M. Kennedy, *Beyond 911: A New Era for Policing* (New York: Basic, 1990).

39. Bittner, "The Capacity to Use Force as the Core of the Police Role," p. 21. For a lengthier treatment, see his *The Functions of the Police in Modern Society* (Washington, DC: U.S. Government Printing Office, 1967). Cf. the very similar account of Peter Manning: "Police agencies may be defined as those agencies that stand ready to employ force upon the citizenry on the basis of situationally determined exigencies" (*Police Work: The Social Organization of Policing* [Cambridge, MA: MIT Press, 1977], p. 40).

40. Arthur Niederhoffer reports: "The new man is needled when he shows signs of diffidence in arresting or asserting his authority. Over and over again, well-

meaning old timers reiterate, 'Ya gotta be tough, kid, or you'll never last'" (*Behind the Shield: The Police in Urban Society* [New York: Doubleday, 1969], p. 56).

41. In order to sustain this peacekeeping function, various supporting personnel will no doubt have to be employed – forensic specialists, police surgeons, detectives, and various managerial and administrative staff. Some of them will properly have "peace officer" status, others will simply be civil service employees.

42. See Hubert Hall, "The King's Peace," *The Antiquary* 18 (November 1888), pp. 185–90; Sir Frederick Pollock, "The King's Peace," in *Oxford Lectures and Other Discourses* (London: Macmillan Press, 1890), pp. 65–82; Julius Goebel, Jr., *Felony and Misdemeanor: A Study in the History of Criminal Law* (1937; reprint, Philadelphia: University of Pennsylvania Press, 1976), pp. 7–12; Jack K. Weber, "The King's Peace: A Comparative Study," *The Journal of Legal History* 12 (September 1989), pp. 135–60.

43. Michael Banton distinguishes between police as "law officers" and "peace officers" (*The Policeman in the Community* [New York: Basic, 1964], pp. 6–7, 127ff), and is followed by Egon Bittner, who divides the police role into "law enforcement" and "keeping the peace" ("The Police on Skid-Row: A Study in Peace Keeping," *American Sociological Review* 32, 5 [October 1967], p. 700). Bernard L. Garmire distinguishes their "law-enforcement" and "community-service" functions ("The Police Role in an Urban Society," p. 4), Jesse Rubin their "peacekeeping," "crimefighting," and "community service" functions ("Police Identity and the Police Role," p. 23), and Maurice Punch and Trevor Naylor their "crime prevention and detection" and "social service" functions ("The Police: A Social Service," *New Society* [17 May 1973], p. 358).

44. Wayne B. Hanewicz, "Discretion and Order," in Elliston and Feldberg (eds.), *Moral Issues in Police Work*, pp. 43–54.

45. One of the original intentions of putting police into uniform was to deter public disorder. Police were not employed simply to catch criminals.

46. Hanewicz, "Discretion and Order," p. 47. The two levels are not separate. Conceptualization does not occur in vacuo, but only as we are incorporated into a social milieu characterized by language, culture, traditions, predictability, and so on.

3 PROFESSIONALISM, THE POLICE ROLE, AND OCCUPATIONAL ETHICS

1. Letter to Don Valentine de Feronda, 1809. A letter of 1810, to John B. Colvin, responding to the latter's inquiry "whether circumstances do not sometimes occur, which make it a duty in officers of high trust, to assume authorities beyond the law," suggests that Jefferson's views were somewhat more complex: "A strict observance of the written laws is doubtless *one* of the high duties of a good citizen, but it is not *the highest*. The laws of necessity, of self-preservation, of saving our country when in danger, are of higher obligation. . . . The officer who is called to act upon this superior ground, does indeed risk himself on the justice of the controlling powers of the constitution, and his station makes it his duty to incur that risk. . . . An officer is bound to obey orders; yet he would be a bad one who should do it in cases for which they were not intended, and which involved the most important consequences. The line of discrimination between cases may be difficult; but the good officer is bound to draw it at his own peril, and throw himself on the justice of his country and the rectitude of his motives." Despite the

practical difficulties here adverted to, Jefferson sees the issue as "easy of solution in principle, but sometimes embarrassing in practice." I am grateful to Kenneth Winston for drawing my attention to this letter, reprinted in Thomas Jefferson, *Public and Private Papers* (New York: Random House, 1990), pp. 1231-4.

2. Jean-Paul Sartre, *Les mains sales*, trans. Lionel Abel, as "Dirty Hands," in *No Exit and Three Other Plays* (New York: Random House, 1955), p. 218.
3. August Vollmer, *The Police and Modern Society* (Berkeley and Los Angeles: University of California Press, 1936).
4. This is probably the point at which to make it quite clear that there is a use of the terms "profession" and "professional" that, though related to the understandings that I shall discuss, is sufficiently distinct to be left to one side in the present context. In this distinctive use the focus is on *getting paid for doing something*. The view that prostitution is "the world's oldest profession" or that a sporting figure "has turned professional" probably focus on the financial dimension, though clearly one can see that this has not been totally dissociated from meanings that place more emphasis on the issue of knowledge, skill, and expertise. It is no mere accident that in popular parlance the terms have been extended in the direction that I will subsequently be ignoring.
5. Harold Wilensky, "The Professionalization of Everyone?" *American Journal of Sociology* 70 (September 1964), pp. 137–58.
6. See, for example, Michael Davis's account in "The Moral Authority of a Professional Code," in J. Roland Pennock and John W. Chapman (eds.), *Nomos XXIX: Authority Revisited* (New York: New York University Press, 1987), p. 323.
7. See Michael Davis, "Thinking Like an Engineer: The Place of a Code of Ethics in the Practice of a Profession," *Philosophy & Public Affairs* 20, 2 (Spring 1991), p. 153.
8. Though we may expect them to act professionally. This is an important distinction to which I shall return. I am of course ignoring the attempts to raise the status of these occupations to that of professions.
9. Davis, "Thinking Like an Engineer," p. 153.
10. Sometimes, however, there may be conflicts between the ways in which these various ends are to be achieved. The general goal of health may sometimes tempt medical practitioners to engage in risky experimental research on patients or to treat them without first obtaining their informed consent. Insofar as contemporary codes tend to make informed consent a prerequisite for treatment, or seriously limit what may be done by way of experimental therapy, a certain priority is accorded to the need to sustain public trust.
11. The "primary objects of police," embedded in the introductory chapter to the 1929 *General Instructions* issued to the London Metropolitan Police Force, came to have the force of a code in subsequent Metropolitan Police history, though brief digests of the *Instructions* were incorporated by other local and colonial constabularies as they were subsequently established. For one such example, see John Kleinig, with Yurong Zhang (comps. and eds.), *Professional Law Enforcement Codes of Ethics: A Documentary Collection* (Westport, CT: Greenwood, 1993), pp. 32–3.
12. Davis, "Thinking Like an Engineer," p. 154.
13. As is evidenced by the relatively short and "unsophisticated" training requirements for police work.
14. Howard Cohen, "Authority: The Limits of Discretion," in Frederick A. Elliston and Michael Feldberg (eds.), *Moral Issues in Police Work* (Totowa, NJ: Rowman & Allanheld, 1985), pp. 37–9.

15. In correspondence, Michael Davis has suggested that my account of a profession is too heavily skewed toward what might be called the "liberal" or "learned" professions, and that I fail to take account of the fact that, traditionally, "the military (the profession of arms) was ranked with the clergy, law and medicine as one of the professions of a gentleman." Yet it needs to be recognized that the profession of arms in question is that of an officer class, usually educated in the arts of war, and not simply that of the ranks of noncommissioned soldiers. Most police will be in the position of noncommissioned soldiers.

16. Not that a degree per se confers professional eligibility. But the professional degree is intended to signal an intensity, depth, and level of involvement in a sphere of activity that goes significantly beyond anything that a training program is intended and likely to provide.

17. It needs also to be noted that CALEA is meeting increasing resistance from police agencies, many of whom are now seeking accreditation from state or regional bodies. For an overview, see John W. Bizzack, *Professionalism and Law Enforcement Accreditation: The First Ten Years* (Lexington, KY: Autumn House, 1993).

18. Arthur Niederhoffer, *Behind the Shield: The Police in Urban Society* (New York: Doubleday, 1967), p. 3.

19. Interestingly, social service activities, though often thought to fail the test of "real" police work, may place much higher discretionary and judgmental demands on police than those involved in law enforcement. Certainly they expose police to a much more varied and complex range of decision-making situations.

20. See Gerald W. Lynch, "The Contribution of Higher Education to Ethical Behavior in Law Enforcement," *Journal of Criminal Justice* 4, 4 (Winter 1976), pp. 285–90.

21. For a good example of the latter, see Chief Superintendent John Murray, "Policy for Police Pursuits," *National Police Research Unit Review* 3, 2 (1987), esp. pp. 50–3.

22. Such has been the experience in the New York City Police Department.

23. By regulating the number of people admitted to the profession, professional associations have ensured that competition is managed, and that members' economic interests will not be threatened. This has been particularly true of the medical profession, where unreasonable barriers have been erected against a "threatened" influx of foreign medical practitioners.

24. Davis, "The Moral Authority of a Professional Code," p. 323.

25. Percy Bysshe Shelley, *Queen Mab* (1812–13), 3.

26. George Bernard Shaw, *The Doctor's Dilemma* (1906), Act I.

27. It may be argued that people would not go to doctors if they did not give overriding weight to their physical well-being. But this is much too quick.

28. Although there is no conceptual link between professionalization and specialization, the social tendency is for the professions to become increasingly specialized. Cf. Donald Kraybill: "Specialization intrudes on all professionals, and unfortunately fragmentation is an inherent part of the . . . process" (in Donald Kraybill and P. Pellman Good (eds.), *Perils of Professionalism* [Scottdale, PA: Herald Press, 1982], p. 114).

29. Professional jargon represents a common currency that enables them to engage in transactions from which others are effectively excluded. It is, however, not professionalization specifically that creates such esoterica, but the need for communal identity and solidarity. Police have a rich vocabulary of their own that reinforces their bonds and effectively excludes outsiders.

30. We might compare the attitude of traditional medicine toward alternative therapies with the attitude of police toward volunteer peacekeeping groups.

31. John Kultgen, *Ethics and Professionalism* (Philadelphia: University of Pennsylvania Press, 1988), ch. 14.
32. For a discussion of the role played by these maxims, see E. Reuss-Ianni and F. Ianni, "Street Cops and Management Cops: The Two Cultures of Policing," in Maurice Punch (ed.), *Control in the Police Organization* (Cambridge, MA: M.I.T. Press, 1983), pp. 266-9.
33. To some extent the following catalogue of possibilities is based on Mike W. Martin, "Professional and Ordinary Morality: A Reply," *Ethics* 91, 4 (July 1981), p. 631.
34. Alan Goldman, *The Moral Foundations of Professional Ethics* (Totowa, NJ: Rowman & Littlefield, 1980).
35. Benjamin Freedman, "A Meta-Ethics for Professional Morality," *Ethics* 89, 1 (October 1978), pp. 1-19.
36. Ibid., pp. 12-13.
37. Benjamin Freedman, "What Really Makes Professional Morality Different: Response to Martin," *Ethics* 91, 4 (July 1981), p. 629. In the article in question, Freedman is not prepared to indicate which of the alternatives he favors.
38. David Luban, *Lawyers and Justice: An Ethical Study* (Princeton, NJ: Princeton University Press, 1988), ch. 7.
39. An allusion to Arthur Schopenhauer's *The Fourfold Root of the Principle of Sufficient Reason*, ed. and trans. E. F. J. Payne (Peru, IL: Open Court, 1974).
40. What I mean by ordinary morality is not some sociological phenomenon (a summary of what people think) but something more critical and reflective – whether you want to call it critical morality (H. L. A. Hart), discriminatory morality (Ronald Dworkin), or rational morality (Alan Gewirth). See further, H. L. A. Hart, *Law, Liberty and Morality* (New York: Oxford University Press, 1973), pp. 17-24; Ronald Dworkin, "Liberty and Moralism," in *Taking Rights Seriously* (Cambridge, MA: Harvard University Press, 1977), ch. 10; Alan Gewirth, "Professional Ethics: The Separatist Thesis," *Ethics* 96, 2 (January 1986), pp. 282-300.
41. As Thomas Nagel terms it in *The View from Nowhere* (New York: Oxford University Press, 1986).
42. Sartre, *Les mains sales*. Sartre has Hoerderer, the revolutionary party's leader, saying to the idealistic Hugo, who is the butt of the epigraphical quotation at the beginning of this chapter: "You intellectuals and bourgeois anarchists use [purity] as a pretext for doing nothing. To do nothing, to remain motionless, arms at your sides, wearing kid gloves: Well, I have dirty hands. Right up to the elbows. I've plunged them in filth and blood. But what do you hope? Do you think you can govern innocently?" (p. 224).
43. As played by Clint Eastwood in Warner Brothers' 1971 film, *Dirty Harry* (screen play by H. J. Fink and Dean Reisner). It forms the basis of Carl B. Klockars's discussion in "The Dirty Harry Problem," *Annals of the American Academy of Political and Social Science* 452 (November 1980), pp. 33-47; reprinted in Frederick Elliston & Michael Feldberg (eds.), *Moral Issues in Police Work* (Totowa, NJ: Rowman & Allanheld, 1985), pp. 55-71.
44. Niccolò Machiavelli, *The Prince*, ch. 15.
45. Michael Walzer, "Political Action: The Problem of Dirty Hands," *Philosophy & Public Affairs* 2, 2 (Winter 1973), p. 164.
46. Some have argued that the British obliteration bombing of Dresden during World War II or President Truman's decision to A-bomb Hiroshima and Nagasaki had

this same character. Or, allegedly, the decision in 1941 not to warn the people of Coventry of an impending German air raid, lest it tip off the enemy that the Enigma Code had been broken. Sophie's "impossible" choice (in William Styron's novel) – to choose which of her two children the Nazis should spare, rather than have them kill both; Gertrude Schneider's account of Karel Besen, the Jewish hangman at Camp Salaspils (recounted in her collection, *Muted Voices: Jewish Survivors of Latvia Remember* [New York: Philosophical Library, 1987], p. 137); and Captain Vere's execution of Billy Budd (in Herman Melville's novel) are said to exemplify the same dilemma.

47. See the discussions in Gerald Caplan (ed.), *ABSCAM Ethics* (Cambridge, MA: Ballinger, 1983); and Robert W. Greene, *The Sting Man: Inside Abscam* (New York: Dutton, 1981).

48. Consider Sophie's situation in having to choose which of her children she will save, lest both are killed.

49. The (incorrectly) alleged decision to leave the people of Coventry unwarned and Dirty Harry's decision to violate Scorpio, are of this kind.

50. This is an enormously complex and highly contested issue. For an entrée to the discussion, see John Kleinig, "Criminal Liability for Failures to Act," *Law & Contemporary Problems* 49, 3 (Summer 1986), pp. 161–80. A subtle recent discussion can be found in Heidi M. Malm, "Killing, Letting Die, and Simple Conflicts," *Philosophy & Public Affairs* 18, 3 (Summer 1989), pp. 238–58.

51. Kenneth Winston has suggested a somewhat different way of distinguishing cases. He proposes a threefold distinction between cases in which the public official, faced with fortuitous happenstance, must dirty his hands as a matter of "moral opportunism, " cases in which, faced with the corruption and self-interest of others, the official must engage in "benign corruption," and those cases in which the official, in order to do what is required by one compelling moral standard, must violate another standard with independent moral force, and must thus make a "tragic choice." Winston believes that the choice is "tragic" in part because "no single standard or measure exists which renders all moral values commensurable, or more generally because moral justification is not unitary." See his "Necessity and Choice in Political Ethics: Varieties of Dirty Hands," in Daniel E. Wueste (ed.), *Professional Ethics and Social Responsibility* (Lanham, MD: Rowman & Littlefield, 1994), pp. 37–66.

52. For the assessment of dirty hands situations has also become an arena for some of the larger contests of moral theory. Critics of utilitarianism (Walzer, for example) have often seen the dirty hands phenomenon as a stumblingblock for utilitarian theory. The latter's seeming "bottom-line" approach to ethical questions appears to offer no room for moral "remainders." In response, utilitarians (such as R. M. Hare) have challenged the adequacy of dirty hands characterizations, and have treated such remainders as an illegitimate moral "double-counting" or evidence of a detached psychological residue. Although this is not really the place to attempt a resolution of these larger theoretical issues, they do not lie far behind some of my discussion.

53. Bernard Williams, "Ethical Consistency," reprinted in Christopher Gowans (ed.), *Moral Dilemmas* (New York: Oxford University Press, 1987), p. 123. Even earlier, Max Weber had said something much the same in "Politics as a Vocation," printed in H. H. Gerth and C. Wright Mills (eds. and trans.), *From Max Weber: Essays in Sociology* (New York: Oxford University Press, 1946), pp. 77–128.

54. Michael A.G. Stocker, *Plural and Conflicting Values* (Oxford: Oxford University Press [Clarendon Press], 1990), p. 22.
55. Matthew 10:16.
56. W. Kenneth Howard, "Must Public Hands Be Dirty?" *Journal of Value Inquiry* 11 (1977), p. 39. Compare C. A. J. Coady, "Messy Morality and the Art of the Possible," *Aristotelian Society Proceedings*, suppl. vol., 64 (1990), pp. 259–79; and Plato, *Republic*, 495–7.
57. Although there is a great deal to be said on the issue of moral coherence, most of it will have to be said in another place.
58. See Thomas E. Hill, Jr., "Moral Purity and the Lesser Evil," *The Monist* 66 (1983), p. 223.
59. This is acknowledged in Bas C. Van Fraassen, "Values and the Heart's Command," *Journal of Philosophy* 70 (1973), p. 14. See also Philippa Foot, "Moral Realism and Moral Dilemma," *Journal of Philosophy* 80, 7 (July 1983), pp. 388–9.
60. Cf. Hill, "Moral Purity and the Lesser Evil," p. 222.
61. This is not quite the issue of moral luck so fruitfully discussed by Bernard Williams; but it is related. See Bernard Williams, "Moral Luck," in *Moral Luck, and Other Essays* (New York: Cambridge University Press, 1981), ch. 2.
62. Coady, "Messy Morality and the Art of the Possible," p. 259.
63. Weber, "Politics as a Vocation," p. 123.
64. Klockars, "The Dirty Harry Problem," p. 70.
65. Walzer, "Political Action," p. 179.
66. Machiavelli, *The Prince*, ch. 18.
67. Walzer, "Political Action," p. 168.
68. The need for concealment if dirty hands are to be effective is one of the things that serves to distinguish what Walzer seeks to account for from the tradition of civil disobedience – from which he seeks to derive some moral sustenance.
69. Dennis F. Thompson, "Democratic Dirty Hands," in *Political Ethics and Public Office* (Cambridge, MA: Harvard University Press, 1987), ch. 1.
70. Alan Donagan, *The Theory of Morality* (Chicago: University of Chicago Press, 1977), p. 184; cf. Thompson, "Democratic Dirty Hands," pp. 15, 18.
71. Thompson, "Democratic Dirty Hands," pp. 23–4.
72. Ibid., p. 22.
73. Feinberg discusses a case in which someone caught in a blizzard breaks into a vacant cottage and proceeds to use the furniture as firewood ("Voluntary Euthanasia and the Inalienable Right to Life," *Philosophy & Public Affairs* 7 (1978), p. 102. Cf. also the discussion in Loren Lomasky, "Compensation and the Bounds of Rights," in John W. Chapman (ed.), *Nomos XXXIII: Compensatory Justice* (New York: New York University Press, 1991), pp. 13–44; and Hill, "Moral Purity and the Lesser Evil," pp. 217–18.

4 INSTITUTIONAL CULTURE AND INDIVIDUAL CHARACTER

1. I owe the quotation to Aaron Rosenthal, a former Deputy Chief of the New York City Police Department.
2. Bill McCarthy, with Mike Mallowe, *Vice Cop: My Twenty-Year Battle with New York's Dark Side* (New York: Morrow, 1991), p. 42.
3. James Ahern, *Police in Trouble* (New York: Hawthorne Books, 1972), p. 3.
4. See Maurice Punch, "Officers and Men: Occupational Culture, Inter-Rank Antag-

onism, and the Investigation of Corruption," and Elizabeth Reuss-Ianni and
Francis A. J. Ianni, "Street Cops and Management Cops: The Two Cultures of
Policing," in Maurice Punch (ed.), Control in the Police Organization (Cam-
bridge, MA: MIT Press, 1983), pp. 227–50, 251–74.

5. Former NYPD Police Commissioner Raymond Kelly, quoted in Eric Pooley,
   "Bulldog," *New York Magazine* (22 February, 1993), p. 39.
6. What is claimed in this paragraph holds more truly of larger urban departments
   than of many smaller suburban and rural departments. In addition, in many
   departments a significant proportion of uniformed officers can now work "regular" schedules.
7. Carsten Stroud, *Hot Pursuit: A Week in the Life of an NYPD Homicide Cop* (New
   York: Bantam, 1987), p. 111; also David Hansen, *Police Ethics* (Springfield, IL:
   Thomas, 1973), p. 73; Maurice Punch, "Officers and Men," and Reuss-Ianni and
   Ianni, "Street Cops and Management Cops."
8. Consider the generally unsuccessful attempts to prosecute police officers after
   the Tompkins Square Park riots in 1988, and the riotous New York police March
   on City Hall in 1993.
9. Epigraph to Donald O. Schultz (ed.), *Critical Issues in Criminal Justice* (Springfield,
   IL: Thomas, 1975).
10. McCarthy, *Vice Cop*, p. 42.
11. David Hume, *Treatise of Human Nature*, ed. L. A. Selby-Bigge (Oxford: Oxford
    University Press [Clarendon Press], 1888), p. 562.
12. Philip Pettit, "The Paradox of Loyalty," *American Philosophical Quarterly* 25, 2
    (April 1988), p. 163.
13. I owe this to a personal communication from Kenneth Strange, at that time a
    Precinct Commanding Officer in Brooklyn, New York.
14. The phrase originates with Dr Johnson. See James Boswell, *The Life of Samuel
    Johnson, LL.D.* (London: Macmillan Press, 1912), vol. 2, p. 115.
15. Harry Blamires, *The Christian Mind* (London: SPCK, 1963), p. 24. Joseph Agassi,
    who shares Blamires's position, nuances his criticism slightly differently:

    When an appeal is made for . . . any loyalty, it is because reasonable argu-
    ments have been tried and failed. This is so because loyalty at times when it is
    supportable by other considerations is simply redundant and thus usually
    not evoked [sic]. Logically, the question is not, do we ever have to be loyal,
    but rather, is loyalty a sufficient force to impose obligation on us. . . . The
    reason . . . for not seeing loyalty – to spouse, friend, or tribe – as a special
    category is the claim that the burden of responsibility lies in the individual,
    that *better a responsible individual who errs than a dependent one who is told to do
    the right thing and does it* ("The Last Refuge of the Scoundrel," *Philosophia* 4,
    2/3 [April–June 1974], pp. 315–16.)

    For Agassi, the loyalist manifests and appeals for an unseemly dependence, a
    sacrifice of autonomy to the object of loyalty.

16. In his toast given at Norfolk, Virginia, April 1816: "Our country! In her inter-
    course with foreign nations may she always be in the right; but our country, right
    or wrong."
17. Philippa Foot, "Virtues and Vices," in *Virtues and Vices and Other Essays* (Berkeley
    & Los Angeles: University of California Press, 1978), sect. 2.
18. Hirschman conceives of these broadly to include all kinds of social groupings –

families, educational and religious institutions, businesses, political parties, trades unions, voluntary organizations, government bureaucracies, and international corporations. See Albert O. Hirschman, *Exit, Voice, and Loyalty: Responses to Decline in Firms, Organizations, and States* (Cambridge, MA: Harvard University Press, 1970).

19. J. S. Mill, *On Liberty*, ch. 3.
20. There is some dispute about the "proper" objects of loyalty. Milton Konvitz, for example, suggests that we may be loyal to principles, causes, ideas, ideals, religions, ideologies, nations, governments, parties, leaders, families, friends, regions, racial groups – indeed, "anyone or anything to which one's heart can become attached or devoted" (s.v. "Loyalty," in Philip P. Wiener [ed.], *Encyclopedia of the History of Ideas* [New York: Scribner, 1973], vol. 3, p. 108). But others, such as John Ladd, argue that "in our common language, as well as historically, 'loyalty' is taken to refer to a relationship between persons," either individually or collectively (s.v. "Loyalty," in Paul Edwards [ed.] *Encyclopedia of Philosophy* [New York: Macmillan Press and The Free Press, 1967], vol. 5, p. 97). Marcia Baron is similarly minded: "Loyalty [is] to certain people or to a group of people, not loyalty to an ideal or cause. . . . When we speak of causes (or ideals) we are more apt to say that people are committed to them or devoted to them than that they are loyal to them" (*The Moral Status of Loyalty* [Dubuque, IA: Kendall/Hunt, 1984], p. 6). Our earliest and psychologically strongest loyalties are almost certainly personal, and those loyalties will often "embody" what we later differentiate more abstractly as values, causes, and ideals. But I think it incorrect (as a matter of logic) to restrict our loyalties to personal attachments.
21. New York: Doubleday, 1967.
22. Following Durkheim, Merton, and other sociologists, Niederhoffer portrays anomie as "a morbid condition of society characterized by the absence of standards, by apathy, confusion, frustration, alienation, and despair" (*Behind the Shield*, p. 94).
23. See, for example, Robert Michael Regoli, "Toward an Understanding of Police Cynicism," Ph.D. Diss., Washington State University, 1976; David M. Rafky, "Police Cynicism Reconsidered: An Application of Smallest Space Analysis," *Criminology* 13, 2 (August 1975), pp. 168–92.
24. See Rodney W. Lewis, "Toward an Understanding of Police Anomie," *Journal of Police Science and Administration* 1, 4 (1973), pp. 484-9.
25. Ibid., pp. 488–9. The point is not whether the dangers are real, but whether they are perceived to be there.

5 POLICE DISCRETION

1. *General Instructions*, London: Metropolitan Police, 1829, pt 1.
2. Samuel Walker, *Taming the System: The Control of Discretion in Criminal Justice 1950–1990* (New York: Oxford University Press, 1993), pp. 6, 16.
3. George P. Fletcher, "Some Unwise Reflections About Discretion," *Law and Contemporary Problems* 47, 4 (Autumn 1984), p. 270.
4. Kenneth Culp Davis, *Discretionary Justice: A Preliminary Inquiry* (Baton Rouge, LA: Louisiana State University Press, 1969), p. 4. A later book, *Police Discretion* (St.

Paul, MN: West, 1975), presupposes this account and focuses on the issue of selective enforcement.

5. Davis writes that "this phraseology ['*effective* limits'] is necessary because a good deal of discretion is illegal or of questionable legality" *(Discretionary Justice,* p. 4).

6. There is, however, some dispute about when the police must, and when they need not, intervene. See, for case reports, "Police Officers Have No Duty to Rescue Man from River," *Pennsylvania Law Journal – Reporter* 11, 10 (7 March, 1988), p. 9, col. 2; Linda M. Goodhand, "Police Officer Obligated to Help Disabled Motorist on Highway," *Pennsylvania Law Journal – Reporter* 12, 10 (13 March, 1989), p. 9, col. 2; Jay Judge and James R. Schirott, "Police Officer Had No Duty to Prevent Beating," *Chicago Daily Law Bulletin* 135, 72 (13 April, 1989), p. 3, col. 2. More generally, see Lisa McCabe, "Police Officers' Duty to Rescue or Aid: Are They Only Good Samaritans?" *California Law Review* 72, 4 (July 1984), pp. 661–96; Joseph M. Pellicioti, "Police Civil Liability for Failure to Protect: The Public Duty Doctrine Revisited," *American Journal of Police* 8, 1 (1989), pp. 37–69.

7. New York City Charter s. 435, as amended (1950).

8. Just because he believes that full enforcement is mandated and pledged, Heffernan resists speaking of these as exercises of police "discretion." See William C. Heffernan, "The Police and Their Rules of Office: An Ethical Analysis," in William C. Heffernan & Timothy Stroup (eds.), *Police Ethics: Hard Choices for Law Enforcement* (New York: John Jay Press, 1985), pp. 3–24.

9. Unless, that is, it can be argued that "preserving the rights of persons" and "protecting the public peace" are to be understood as goals of police work *only to the extent that they can be secured via the "arrest [of] all persons guilty of violating any law or ordinance."* But the oath gives no such priority to the latter.

10. Heffernan, "The Police and Their Rules of Office," p. 9.

11. Metropolitan Police, *General Instructions* (1829), Introduction.

12. Some such argument is suggested by the Frederick A. Elliston and Michael Feldberg, the editors of *Moral Issues in Police Work* (Totowa, NJ: Rowman & Allanheld, 1985), p. 11.

13. It is Heffernan's concern about these matters that makes him particularly chary of selective enforcement.

14. Our study of police codes of conduct has suggested that discretionary authority has almost always been given official recognition in police manuals. See John Kleinig, with Yurong Zhang (comps. and eds.), *Professional Law Enforcement Codes: A Documentary Collection* (Westport, CT: Greenwood, 1993).

15. Police officers frequently complain that they work in an environment in which "they [the Bosses] can always get you." Discretionary judgment is tolerated and even expected, so long as it causes no problems. If problems occur, a strict interpretation of the rules will suddenly be made, and the hapless officer must suffer for what he may have been "expected" to do. I do not want to say that this is necessarily a bad thing, though there are certainly occasions when, as a result of this strategy, an officer becomes virtually a scapegoat.

16. See Howard Cohen, "Authority: The Limits of Discretion," in Elliston and Feldberg (eds.), *Moral Issues in Police Work*, pp. 35–37.

17. Gary T. Marx, *Undercover: Police Surveillance in America,* (Berkeley and Los Angeles: University of California Press, 1988).

18. Davis, *Police Discretion,* pp. 143, 158.

19. Ibid., pp. 141–42.

6 THE USE OF FORCE

1. *Paradise Lost*, bk. 1, l. 648.
2. Egon Bittner, "The Capacity to Use Force as the Core of the Police Role," in Frederick A. Elliston and Michael Feldberg (eds.), *Moral Issues in Police Work* (Totowa, NJ: Rowman & Allanheld, 1985), p. 21.
3. It is a contingent matter that police are armed. Until recently, few police officers in the United Kingdom or Australia were armed. Indeed, it was originally believed that the police officer's most important "weapon" was his uniform, since it bespoke the authority of law, and served to deter the commission of crime. On a social peacekeeper understanding of the police role, the contingency of police officers being armed is manifest.
4. Religious believers may not see it that way. That perspective, however, cannot be presumed in this context; and in any case religious believers do not generally consider the prospect of a life after death as undermining respect for the present one.
5. For a good exposition of the Gandhian version of this argument, see Glyn Richards, *The Philosophy of Gandhi* (Totowa, NJ: Barnes & Noble Books, 1982), chs 3, 4.
6. Cf. Matthew 26:52. The epigraphical quote from Milton may suggest much the same. Force may enable one to subdue another physically, but the spirit may remain defiant – and ready to resist again when opportunity arises.
7. Reported by G. K. Chesterton in relation to "the Christian ideal" (*What's Wrong With the World?* 9th ed. [London: Cassell, 1910], pt I, ch. 5).
8. For a description, see Donald O. Schultz (ed.), *Critical Issues in Criminal Justice* (Springfield, IL: Thomas, 1975), p. 44.
9. For a description and discussion, see Jerome H. Skolnick and James J. Fyfe, *Above the Law: Police and the Excessive Use of Force* (New York: Free Press, 1993), pp. 166–70.
10. In addition to the foregoing, which have been "designed" with the purpose of applying force, police sometimes use other items of equipment (e.g., metal flashlights). Or perhaps they use equipment intended to be used for applying force in nonstandard ways. There may be significant risks associated with such deviations, and they should probably be discouraged. See Terry C. Cox, Jerry S. Vaughn, and William M. Nixon, "Police Use of Metal Flashlights as Weapons: An Analysis of Relevant Problems," *Journal of Police Science and Administration* 13, 3 (1985), pp. 244–50; also Terry C. Cox, Dennis J. Buchholz, and David J. Wolf, "Blunt Force Head Trauma from Police Impact Weapons: Some Skeletal and Neuropsychological Considerations," *Journal of Police Science and Administration* 15, 1 (1987), pp. 56–62.
11. It should be noted that, although I am focusing in this chapter on the use of *force*, the fact that it is the coerciveness of many uses of force that makes them particularly problematic raises similar questions about other police practices that do not have the *physical* connotations of the use of force, for example, browbeating and other forms of psychological pressure. On the scope of coercion, see Alan Wertheimer, *Coercion* (Princeton, NJ: Princeton University Press, 1987).
12. *Johnson v. Glick*, 481 F 2d 1028, at 1033 (2d Cir), *cert. denied*, 414 US 1033 (1973). The full *Johnson* test also contains "objective" as well as "subjective" factors: "the need for the application of force, the relationship between the need and the amount of force that was used, the extent of the injury inflicted, and whether the force was applied in a good faith effort to maintain or restore discipline or maliciously and sadistically for the very purpose of causing harm."

13. This was the test employed in *Tennessee v. Garner*, 471 US 1, 105 S Ct 1694, 85 L Ed 2d 1 (1985).

14. *Graham v. Connor et al.*, 109 S Ct 1865 (1989). In the course of its judgment the Court held:

> Where, as here, the excessive force claim arises in the context of an arrest or investigatory stop of a free citizen, it is most properly characterized as one invoking the protections of the Fourth Amendment, which guarantees citizens the right "to be secure in their persons . . . against unreasonable . . . seizures" of the person. . . .
>
> Determining whether the force used to effect a particular seizure is "reasonable" under the Fourth Amendment requires a careful balancing of "the nature and quality of the intrusion on the individual's Fourth Amendment interests" against the countervailing governmental interests at stake. Our Fourth Amendment jurisprudence has long recognized that the right to make an arrest or investigatory stop necessarily carries with it the right to use some degree of physical coercion or threat thereof to effect it. Because "[t]he test of reasonableness under the Fourth Amendment is not capable of precise definition or mechanical application," however, its proper application requires careful attention to the facts and circumstances of each particular case, including the severity of the crime at issue, whether the suspect poses an immediate threat to the safety of the officers or others, and whether he is actively resisting arrest or attempting to evade arrest by flight.
>
> The "reasonableness" of a particular use of force must be judged from the perspective of a reasonable officer on the scene, rather than with the 20/20 vision of hindsight. The calculus of reasonableness must embody allowance for the fact that police officers are often forced to make split-second judgments – in circumstances that are tense, uncertain and rapidly evolving – about the amount of force that is necessary in a particular situation.
>
> As in other Fourth Amendment contexts, however, the "reasonableness" inquiry in an excessive force case is an objective one: The question is whether the officers' actions are "objectively reasonable" in light of the facts and circumstances confronting them, without regard to their underlying intent or motivation (at 1871–2).

15. Cf. Joseph Betz, "Police Violence," in Elliston and Feldberg (eds.), *Moral Issues in Police Work*, pp. 177–8.

16. It needs to be pointed out, however, that the common resort to plea bargaining does not sit comfortably with this rationale.

17. *Rochin v. California*, 342 US 165, 72 S Ct 205 (1952). For discussions of *Rochin* and some post-*Rochin* decisions, see Note, "Nonconsensual Surgery: The Unkindest Cut of All," *Notre Dame Lawyer* 53 (1977), pp. 291–305; "Analyzing the Reasonableness of Bodily Intrusions," *Marquette Law Review* 68 (1984), pp. 130–53; William G. Eckhardt, "Intrusion into the Body," *Military Law Review* 52 (1971), pp. 141–67

18. The issue in *Rochin* was not simply one of seemliness. As Justice Frankfurter noted, "[It is anomalous] to hold that in order to convict a man the police cannot extract by force what is in his mind, but can extract what is in his stomach" (342 US 165, at 167 [1952]).

19. On the doctrine of proportionality, see Aristotle, *Nicomachean Ethics*, 1131a18ff; also Alan Gewirth, *Reason and Morality* (Chicago: University of Chicago Press, 1978), pp. 121–4, 141–4; Suzanne Uniacke, *Permissible Killing: The Self-Defence*

Justification of Homicide (New York: Cambridge University Press, 1994), pp. 132–7.

20. For a discussion of this principle, see Francis D. Wormuth and Harris G. Mirkin, "The Doctrine of the Reasonable Alternative," *Utah Law Review* 9 (1964), pp. 254–307.

21. See Betz, "Police Violence," pp. 179–80; also Frank G. Zarb, Jr., Note, "Police Liability for Creating the Need to Use Deadly Force in Self-Defense," *Michigan Law Review* 86 (August 1988), pp. 1,982–2,009. I believe that the dramatic events of February to April 1993, in Waco, Texas, illustrate this problem.

22. Pressure was placed on the NYPD to amend its policy, and so some small changes were made to allow for officer discretion, provided it was first cleared with a supervisor.

23. In many departments, however, handcuffing is discretionary where a misdemeanor is involved. For a general discussion of handcuffing policies and practices, see "Police Use of Handcuffs, Chemical Irritants and Dogs," *AELE Defense Manual* (1979), Brief 79–5, pp. 4–19.

24. This is, of course, to be distinguished from the over-tightening that might occur in the course of restraining a fiercely resistant arrestee.

25. In principle, it should be possible to file a complaint with Internal Affairs.

26. Though this may be voided if they are doctored by weighting or leading.

27. The stun gun is a small rectangular plastic box with two metal electrodes protruding from one end. It must come into contact with the body – or at least clothes – of the person against whom it is used. In Taser (Thomas A. Swift's Electric Rifle) guns, the electrodes are extendable wires with a barbed end, which can be fired from a distance of up to fifteen feet. Both are powered by rechargeable 9-volt nickel cadmium batteries.

28. Brian A. Felter, "The Nova XR-5000 Stun Gun. Hi-Tech Alternative Control Device," *Police Marksman* 10, 1 (January–February 1985), pp. 35–40. Quoted in Grafton H. Hull, Jr. and Joseph C. Frisbie, "The Stun Gun Debate: More Help than Hazard?" *Police Chief* 54, 2 (February 1987), p. 46.

29. Cf. the incident in Queens, NY, in 1985, and the Rodney King beating in Los Angeles in 1991. See "Alleged Torture Brings Focus on Police Use of Stun Guns," *New York Times*, 25 May 1985, pp.3–4; Greg Meyer, "LAPD Brutality Incident: Don't Blame the Taser," *Law Enforcement News* 17, 333 (31 March 1991), p. 8.

30. See, for example, James J. Fyfe, "The Los Angeles Chokehold Controversy," *Criminal Law Bulletin*, 19, 1 (January–February 1983), pp. 61–7.

31. Prior to the 1983 *Lyons* case, some sixteen people (including fourteen blacks) had died from chokeholds administered by officers of the Los Angeles Police Department. See *Los Angeles v. Lyons*, 461 US 95, 103 S Ct 1660, 75 L Ed 2d 675 (1983).

32. The number of chokehold deaths caused by LAPD officers more than doubled the combined number of deaths from chokeholds recorded in the twenty major U.S. police departments.

33. Barry Creighton, "Carotid Restraint: Useful Tool or Deadly Weapon?" *Trial* 19, 5 (May 1983), pp. 102–6.

34. After the Los Angeles chokehold controversy erupted, they were banned from departmental use though not, police spokesmen argued, because they were too dangerous, but because they were represented as "a symbol of police oppression." Before the resignation of Chief Daryl Gates, in the wake of the 1991 Rodney King beating, there were reports that their reintroduction was being

reconsidered ("Los Angeles Police Reconsider Using Choke Hold," *New York Times*, 3 September 1991, p. A18).

35. Fyfe, "The Los Angeles Chokehold Controversy," pp. 66–7.
36. This does not mean that police need not be trained in its "safe" use. If police can subdue a life-threatening attacker using a chokehold in a nonlethal manner, that option should be the preferred one.
37. Tear gases were first used in World War I, but two later forms, CN, or chemical mace (alpha-chloroacetophenone) and the more rapidly acting CS (2-chlorobenzylidene nalonotrile) have been in regular police use for only a couple of decades. A more recent addition is OC (oleoresin capsicum), a cayenne pepper-based spray that inflames the mucous membranes of the eyes, nose, and mouth, causing an excruciating burning sensation. Its severest effects last about twenty minutes. The effects are more localized than those of tear gas, so that arresting officers and others in the vicinity will not be affected. It is generally claimed that OC is less likely to cause permanent injury than both CS and CN, though there has been some controversy concerning this claim. See John Granfield, Jami Onnen, and Charles S. Petty, "Pepper Spray and In-Custody Deaths," *The Journal* 1, 2 (Summer 1994), pp. 30–5.
38. "Police Use of Handcuffs, Chemical Irritants and Dogs," p. 20. A. Pickles reports as follows: "Do you remember when Mace first hit the law enforcement scene? Then you must remember how many officers overused it. It was nonlethal, so most adopted a 'what the hell' attitude. It was used not just as a substitute for the nightstick, but even as a substitute for your hands. 'Hell, why get dirty. Mace the jerk,' was the common phrase" ("Nonlethal Weapons," *Police Product News* 5 (October 1981), pp. 54–61.
39. For some history on the use of dogs in police work, see "Police Use of Handcuffs, Chemical Irritants and Dogs," p. 30. See also J. T. Knutson & A. C. Revering, "Police Dogs: Their Use as Reasonable Force," *Police Chief* 50, 5 (May 1983), pp. 60–4.
40. They include incendiary devices, such as those used by the Philadelphia police in the MOVE siege. See the report and discussion in *Temple Law Quarterly* 59, 2 (Summer 1986), pp. 267–417.
41. *Tennessee v. Garner*, 471 US 1, 105 S Ct 1694, 85 L Ed 2d 1 (1985).
42. See the discussions in James J. Fyfe (ed.), *Readings on Police Use of Deadly Force* (Washington, DC: Police Foundation, 1982), pt. 4.
43. See James J. Fyfe, "Always Prepared: Police Off-Duty Guns," *The Annals of the American Academy of Political and Social Science* 452 (November 1980), pp. 72–81; reprinted in Fyfe (ed.), *Readings on Police Use of Deadly Force*, pp. 72–81.
44. Jeffrey Reiman, "The Social Contract and the Police Use of Deadly Force," in Elliston and Feldberg (eds.), *Moral Issues in Police Work*, pp. 237–49.
45. Ibid., pp. 238–9.
46. I leave aside – as does Reiman – military uses of deadly force, presumably directed to threats from without.
47. See, for example, Charles Black, *Capital Punishment: The Inevitability of Caprice and Mistake* (New York: Norton), 1974. Reiman himself appeals to a somewhat different argument against capital punishment in "Justice, Civilization, and the Death Penalty: Answering van den Haag," *Philosophy & Public Affairs* 14, 2 (Spring 1985), pp. 115–48.
48. Reiman, "The Social Contract and the Police Use of Deadly Force," p. 241.
49. Ibid., p. 243.

50. For some of the discussion, see Phillip Montague, "Self-Defense and Choosing Between Lives," *Philosophical Studies* 40 (1981), pp. 207–19; David Wasserman, "Justifying Self-Defense," *Philosophy & Public Affairs* 16, 4 (Fall, 1987), pp. 356–78; Phillip Montague, "The Morality of Self-Defense: A Reply to Wasserman," *Philosophy & Public Affairs* 18, 1 (Winter 1989), pp. 81–9; Judith Jarvis Thomson, "Self-Defense," *Philosophy & Public Affairs* 20, 4 (Fall 1991), pp. 283–310; George P. Fletcher, *A Crime of Self-Defense: Bernhard Goetz and the Law on Trial* (Chicago: University of Chicago Press, 1988); Jeff McMahan, "Self-Defense and the Problem of the Innocent Attacker," *Ethics* 104, 2 (January 1994), pp. 252–90; and Uniacke, *Permissible Killing*.

51. H. Lee Boatwright, "Legalized Murder of a Fleeing Felon," *Virginia Law Review* 15 (1929), p. 583.

52. *Petrie v. Cartwright*, 70 SW 297, at 299 (Ky. 1902). The *Petrie* dictum might be used to ground a further argument for the police use of deadly force, viz. that fleeing felons *forfeit* their right to life. At best this could be said with respect to the most extreme offenders; but even then it may not be appropriate to speak of "forfeiture." Where a person poses an immediate or imminent threat to the lives of others, we might speak of his right to life being "overridden" by others' competing and compelling claims. In other cases, what the felony warrants is a curb on the person's freedom rather than an overriding of his claim to life.

53. American Law Institute, *Model Penal Code – Proposed Official Draft* (Philadelphia: ALI, 1962), sect. 3.07.

54. The figures are based on those given in *Garner*.

55. Economic factors also played a part. On the matter of off-duty firearms, for example, police unions have often opposed the disarming of off-duty officers in part because of the bargaining advantage it provides in wage negotiations. If, unlike sanitation workers and firefighters, police officers are expected to be on the job and equipped with their tools of trade at all times, they have some claim to privileged treatment with respect to the groups with which they are traditionally compared.

56. The incident and quotations that follow are recorded in James J. Fyfe, "Police Use of Deadly Force: Research and Reform," *Justice Quarterly* 5, 2 (June 1988), p. 200.

57. To some extent this vote reflected political struggles within the IACP. Fyfe goes on to point out that only two years later the IACP was beginning to talk more restrictively.

58. *Tennessee v. Garner*, 471 US 1, 105 S Ct 1694, 85 L Ed 2d 1 (decided 27 March, 1985).

59. Majority: White, Brennan, Blackmun, Powell, Stevens. Minority: O'Connor, Burger, Rehnquist.

60. *Terry v. Ohio*, 392 US 1, 88 S Ct 1868, 20 L Ed 2d 917 (1968).

61. *United States v. Place*, 462 US 696, at 703 (1983).

62. *Tennessee v. Garner*, 471 US 1, 105 S Ct 1694, 85 L Ed 2d 1 (1985).

63. Ibid., at 11.

64. Ibid., at 21. The Court pointed out that less than 4 percent of burglaries involved violence. This was significant, because some states had denominated burglary a "forcible" offense, thus legitimating the use of deadly force to apprehend fleeing burglars.

65. Ibid., at 10.

66. Ibid.

67. See James J. Fyfe, "*Tennessee v. Garner*: The Issue Not Addressed," *New York University Review of Law & Social Change* 14, 3 (Summer 1986), pp. 721–31.

68. Lawrence W. Sherman, "Reducing Police Gun Use: Critical Events, Administrative Policy, and Organizational Change," in Maurice Punch (ed.), *Control in the Police Organization* (Cambridge, MA: MIT Press, 1983), pp. 98–125.
69. James Fyfe, however, indicates that accurate figures may not always be easy to obtain. See his "Police Use of Deadly Force: Research and Reform," p. 184, fn 23.
70. See A. Cohen, "I've Killed That Man Ten Thousand Times," *Police Magazine* 3 (July 1980), pp. 17–23; E. Donovan (issue ed.), "Post-Shooting Incidence of Traumatic Shock," *Police Stress* 6, 1 (Spring 1983).
71. The category is not well defined. Variously known as "hot pursuits" or "high-speed police/motor vehicle pursuits," the phenomenon is characterized by Scafe and Round as

   > an *active* attempt by a law enforcement officer operating a motor vehicle and utilizing simultaneously *all* emergency equipment to apprehend one or more occupants of another moving vehicle, when the driver of the fleeing vehicle is aware of that attempt and is resisting apprehension by maintaining or increasing his speed, ignoring the officer, or attempting to elude the officer while driving at speeds in excess of the legal speed limit (Myron E. Scafe and John E. Round, "High Speed Pursuits," *Police Chief* 46, 12 [December 1979], pp. 36–7).

   But useful though this characterization is, it does not accommodate every case in which, for moral purposes at least, we would talk about a hot pursuit. It could be that the driver of the "fleeing vehicle" is an innocent party, whose vehicle has been commandeered by a fleeing suspect. And circumstances can be envisaged in which the pursuit, though hot, does not exceed the legal speed limit: at peak hour on a crowded city street. Or consider the rather different situation of police officers responding to a 10-13 (officer in distress) call: here the attempt at apprehension has a quite different format. Yet most of the same moral problems would be posed.
72. Geoffrey P. Alpert and Patrick R. Anderson, "The Most Deadly Force: Police Pursuits," *Justice Quarterly* 3, 1 (March 1986), p. 2.
73. The earliest connections go back to 1977, but it is not until the mid-1980s that there is anything like a movement developing.
74. *Brower v. County of Inyo*, 109 S Ct 1378 (21 March 1989).
75. "Texas Court Ruling Gives Pursuits a New Wrinkle," *Law Enforcement News* 17, 331 (28 February 1991), p. 3.
76. The situation becomes more problematic when a minor vehicular infraction becomes the excuse for a fishing expedition, or when statistical profiles are used as the basis for stopping.
77. There are many reasons why a person might want to avoid being given a ticket, some more understandable than others. Yet such reasons will have a bearing on the moral acceptability of the risk to which the pursued person is put.
78. This, at least, is the argument used by police to support a discretionary approach. In one of the major studies of hot pursuits, it was concluded:

   > Attempted apprehension of motorists in violation of what appear to be minor traffic infractions is necessary for the preservation of order on the highways of California. If approximately 700 people will attempt to flee from the officers who participated in this six-month study, knowing full well that the officers would give chase, one can imagine what would happen if the police suddenly banned pursuits. Undoubtedly innocent people may be injured or

killed because an officer chooses to pursue a suspect, but this risk is necessary to avoid the even greater loss that would occur if law enforcement agencies were not allowed to aggressively pursue violators (Operational Planning Section, California Highway Patrol, *Pursuit Study* [July 1983], p. 21).

79. William Blackstone, *Commentaries on the Laws of England* bk. 4, ch. 27.
80. This issue is discussed in J. L. Mackie, "Responsibility and Language," *Australasian Journal of Philosophy* 33, 3 (December 1955), pp. 143–59.
81. Naturally, some of these alternatives will have costs attached to them – the vehicle may be stolen, evidence may be jettisoned, and so on.
82. It is, unfortunately, just such factors that can undermine or at least seriously compromise an otherwise good policy. In order to avoid constraints on their pursuit of a vehicle, officers may refuse to report it as a pursuit. It may be reported as such only when it takes them outside their jurisdiction.
83. Nor should we leave completely out of account the possible social ramifications of such post-pursuit beatings. A 1980 case in Dade County, Florida, in which a black man, Arthur McDuffie, was killed after a high-speed pursuit, left eighteen dead in the riot that it triggered. See the discussion in Skolnick and Fyfe, *Above the Law*, pp. 81–2.

7 THE USE OF DECEPTION

1. Benjamin Constant, "De réactions politiques," *France* 6, 1 (1797), p. 124, quoted in Immanuel Kant, "On a Supposed Right to Lie from Altruistic Motives," in *Critique of Practical Reason and Other Essays*, trans. Lewis White Beck (Chicago: University of Chicago Press, 1949), p. 346.
2. *The Metaphysical Principles of Virtue*, trans. James Ellington (Indianapolis: Bobbs-Merrill, 1964), pp. 90–1.
3. In some departments, interrogations are routinely videotaped, though, as the videotaped evidence shows, coercive tactics have not disappeared. Often it seems to be attributable to ineptitude rather than to any intentional ill will. See John Baldwin, "Police Interview Techniques: Establishing Truth or Proof?" *British Journal of Criminology* 33, 3 (Summer 1993), pp. 325–52. Sometimes, of course, especially where there are no safeguards, the third degree is still resorted to – if not by means of threat or physical force, then through persistent, prolonged questioning and/or deprivation of sleep, food, and so on. On the third degree, see Jerome H. Skolnick and James J. Fyfe, *Above the Law: Police and the Excessive Use of Force* (New York: Free Press, 1993), ch. 3.
4. Jerome H. Skolnick, "Deception by Police," *Criminal Justice Ethics* 1, 2 (Summer/Fall 1982), pp. 40–53.
5. The distinction goes back to Gilbert Ryle, *The Concept of Mind* (London: Hutchinson, 1949), esp. pp. 149–52.
6. René Descartes, *Meditations on First Philosophy*, I.
7. There is, in fact, an ongoing debate about the precise character of lying. For present purposes, though, what I have suggested is adequate. See further Frederick A. Siegler, "Lying," *American Philosophical Quarterly* 3 (April 1966), pp. 128–36; D. S. Mannison, "Lying and Lies," *Australasian Journal of Philosophy* 47 (August 1969), pp. 132–44; T. Foster Lindley, "Lying and Falsity," *Australasian Journal of Philosophy* 49 (August 1971), pp. 152–7; Sissela Bok, *Lying: Moral Choice in Public and Private Life* (New York: Pantheon, 1978); Garry Jones, "Lying and Intentions,"

Journal of Business Ethics 5 (August 1986), pp. 347–9. Similar debates surround the characterization of deception. See Leonard Linsky, "Deception," *Inquiry* 6 (1963), pp. 157–69; Roderick Chisholm and Thomas D. Feehan, "The Intent to Deceive," *Journal of Philosophy* 74 (1977), pp. 143–59; Annette Barnes, "When Do We Deceive Others?" *Analysis* 50, 3 (June 1990), pp. 197–202.

8. See Bok, *Lying: Moral Choice in Public and Private Life*, pp. 30–1. Although it need not be the case, many who speak of a duty of veracity interpret it as a contractarian duty – a duty of fidelity. See, for example, W. D. Ross, *The Right and the Good* (Oxford: Oxford University Press [Clarendon Press], 1930), pp. 19–22.

9. See, for example, Charles Fried, *Right and Wrong* (Cambridge, MA: Harvard University Press, 1978), ch. 3.

10. Kant believes that both coercion and lying violate the conditions under which we can assent to a course of action as our own. Physical coercion makes a tool of our bodily person. What Kant finds particularly odious about lying is that it makes a tool of our reason.

11. Kant discusses lying in several places. But see, particularly, *Foundations of the Metaphysics of Morals*, and "On a Supposed Right to Lie from Altruistic Motives," trans. Lewis White Beck, in *Immanuel Kant: Critique of Practical Reason and Other Writings in Moral Philosophy* (Chicago: Chicago University Press, 1949). The interpretation of Kant's position is a matter of some debate. For a particularly perceptive discussion, see Christine M. Korsgaard, "The Right to Lie: Kant on Dealing with Evil," *Philosophy & Public Affairs* 15 (Fall 1986), pp. 325–49.

12. Kant, *The Metaphysical Principles of Virtue*, pp. 90–1.

13. Consequentialist critiques of lying may be act- or practice-oriented. That is, lies might be assessed on an individual basis, their individual consequences being determinative of their moral status. Or they might be assessed by reference to the consequences of a practice of lying, or of a practice of telling lies of a particular kind.

14. Jeremy Bentham, *An Introduction to the Principles of Morals and Legislation*, ed. J. H. Burns & H. L. A. Hart (London: University of London / Athlone Press, 1970), p. 205.

15. Is it open to a utilitarian to argue that lying is presumptively wrong, because its consequences are normally bad? Perhaps, though this – even if cast in rule utilitarian terms – still fails to catch the wrongness we attribute to some lies despite their lack of evil consequences.

16. Hugo Grotius, *On the Law of War and Peace*, trans. Francis W. Kelsey (New York: Bobbs-Merrill, 1925), bk. 3, ch. 1.

17. Ross, *The Right and the Good*, p. 21; cf. idem, *The Foundations of Ethics* (New York: Oxford University Press, 1968), pp. 112–13.

18. Fried, *Right and Wrong*, p. 67.

19. For some of the literature, see Neil MacCormick, "Voluntary Obligations and Normative Powers," *Proceedings of the Aristotelian Society*, suppl. vol. 46 (1972), pp. 59–78 (and response by Joseph Raz); Joseph Raz, "Promises and Obligations," in P. M. S. Hacker and J. Raz (eds.), *Law, Morality and Society: Essays in Honour of H. L. A. Hart* (Oxford: Oxford University Press [Clarendon Press], 1977), pp. 210–28; Don Locke, "The Object of Morality and the Obligation to Keep a Promise," *Canadian Journal of Philosophy* 2 (1972), pp. 135–43.

20. I have, for example, left to one side various religious/theological arguments concerning lying. Some of these are closely related to some that I have already covered. Augustine's view that lying constitutes a misuse of God's gift is closely

tied to the view that speech was given so that we might communicate our thoughts to each other ("On Lying," in *Treatises on Various Subjects*, ed. R. J. Deferrari [New York: Catholic University of America Press, 1952], vol. 14, p. 66). Others are not so closely connected, for example, views that see lying as a breach of divine command, a form of insubordination.

21. Kant, however, is notorious for his brief essay, "On a Supposed Right to Lie from Altruistic Motives," where he argues that one is never justified in telling a lie. One of his reasons is that the liar, in contrast to the truthteller, must be held responsible for all the consequences of his lie, no matter how unexpected. Whereas some of Kant's critics have seen his attitude to lying as a reductio of his position, others have felt that there is a depth to his thinking that those critics have failed to plumb (see, particularly, Korsgaard, "The Right to Lie: Kant on Dealing with Evil").

22. Kant, *Lectures on Ethics*, p. 221.

23. Joseph Ellin, "Special Professional Morality and the Duty of Veracity," *Business and Professional Ethics Journal* 1, 2 (1982), pp. 75–90. The article is reprinted in Joan Callahan (ed.), *Ethical Issues in Professional Life* (New York: Oxford University Press, 1988), pp. 130–9. The quotations below are taken from Callahan.

24. Ibid., p. 133.

25. Ibid., p. 134.

26. Ibid.

27. Skolnick, "Deception by Police." Here "investigative" is used narrowly to refer to noncustodial investigation.

28. This, as I shall indicate later, is not a persuasive argument. Means are independently evaluable, and not just in relation to their ends.

29. Such was apparently the case with some of the investigations initiated by J. Edgar Hoover, though the purpose, often enough, was not to prosecute but to manipulate or destroy. See Curt Gentry, *J. Edgar Hoover: The Man and the Secrets* (New York: Norton, 1991). See also Lawrence W. Sherman, "Equity Against Truth: Value Choices in Deceptive Investigations," in William C. Heffernan and Timothy Stroup (eds.), *Police Ethics: Hard Choices in Law Enforcement* (New York: John Jay Press, 1985), pp. 117–32.

30. *United States v. Baldwin*, 621 F 2d 251 (6th Cir. 1980), *cert. denied* 450 US 1045, 101 S Ct 1767, 68 L Ed 2d 244 (1981). Justice Thurgood Marshall strongly dissented from the denial of certiorari: He argued that the government agent's conduct in this case was

> arguably more objectionable in constitutional terms than condemned in *Gouled*; the search was of a home rather than a business office, lasted for six months instead of several minutes, and appears to have been undertaken for the general purpose of gathering any incriminating evidence rather than the specific purpose of seizing any incriminating documents. . . . If the decision of the Memphis police to place an undercover agent in [Baldwin's] home for a six-month period, during which the agent rifled through his belongings in the search for incriminating evidence, does not implicate the "right of the people to be secure in their persons, houses, papers, and effects, against unreasonable searches and seizures," it is hard to imagine what sort of undercover activity would. Indeed, under the Sixth Circuit's approach, the Government need never satisfy the probable cause and warrant requirements of the Fourth Amendment if, by disguising its officers as repairmen, babysitters, neighbors, maids, and the like, it is able to gain entry to an individual's home

by ruse rather than force in order to conduct a search (450 US at 1048, 1049, 101 S Ct at 1769, 1770, 68 L Ed 2d at 245, 246 [1981], [J. Marshall, dissenting]).

The other case referred to is *Gouled v. United States*, 255 US 298, 41 S Ct 261, 65 L Ed 647 (1921).

31. In "Privacy and Police Undercover Work," Ferdinand Schoeman argued that legal error was involved (in Heffernan and Stroup (eds.), *Police Ethics: Hard Choices in Law Enforcement*, pp. 133–50). I believe, however, that Schoeman mistakenly confused a distinction that is sometimes drawn between "fraud in the *factum*" and "fraud in the inducement." Fraud in the *factum*, but not fraud in the inducement undermines a legally valid consent. The distinction, however, is not without problems of its own. See the discussion in Joel Feinberg, *Harm to Self* (New York: Oxford University Press, 1986), pp. 280–300.

32. Gary Marx, "Who Really Gets Stung? Some Issues Raised by the New Police Undercover Work," in Heffernan and Stroup (eds.), *Police Ethics*, pp. 112-15.

33. Ibid., p. 103.

34. See the discussions in Gerald M. Caplan (ed.), *ABSCAM Ethics: Moral Issues and Deception in Law Enforcement* (Cambridge, MA: Ballinger, 1983).

35. Marx, "Who Really Gets Stung?" p. 106. See also Sherman, "Equity Against Truth: Value Choices in Deceptive Investigations."

36. See, for example, Gary Marx, "Under-the-Covers Undercover Investigations: Some Reflections on the State's Use of Sex and Deception in Law Enforcement," *Criminal Justice Ethics* 11, 1 (Winter/Spring 1992), pp. 13–24. Put briefly, the more personal and intimate the deceptive technique, the stronger should be the constraints on its use.

37. See *United States v. Baldwin*, 621 F 2d 251 (1980), discussed in Schoeman, "Privacy and Police Undercover Work."

38. Skolnick, "Deception by Police," p. 94.

39. Gary Marx develops this point at some length in "Who Really Gets Stung?" pp. 108–10. See also Kim Wozencraft, *Rush: A Novel* (New York: Random House, 1990).

40. Marx, "Who Really Gets Stung?" pp. 110–13.

41. We need of course to distinguish what police *must* do, if they are to achieve their ends, from what it is *convenient* for them to do. It is easy for police to overstate the difficulties of investigation and to understate their capacity for developing imaginative investigative strategies.

42. Of course, not only undercover work but much police work is directed to this end. However, "the" solution to crime is not to be found in "more police on the streets." The battle is first to be fought elsewhere.

43. See, in particular, Sanford Levinson, "Under Cover: The Hidden Costs of Infiltration," in Caplan (ed.), *ABSCAM Ethics*, pp. 43-63.

44. Marx, "Who Really Gets Stung?" pp. 115–18.

45. See Skolnick, "Deception by Police," p. 83; also Yale Kamisar, *Police Interrogation and Confessions: Essays in Law and Policy* (Ann Arbor: University of Michigan Press, 1980); and John C. Hall, "Investigative Detention: An Intermediate Response, I, II, III," *FBI Law Enforcement Bulletin* 54 (November 1985, December 1985), pp. 25–31, 18–23; 55 (January, 1986), pp. 23–29.

46. In the United Kingdom, this approach is vigorously promoted by Eric Shepherd. See his *Investigative Interviewing: A Trainer's Workbook* (London: Investigative Science Associates, 1990); and "Ethical Interviewing," in *Policing* 7 (1991), pp. 42–60.

47. Fred E. Inbau and John E. Reid, *Criminal Interrogation and Confessions*, 2nd ed. (Baltimore: Williams & Wilkins, 1967), p. 218, and the discussion in Kamisar, *Police Interrogation and Confessions*.

48. Welsh S. White, "Police Trickery in Inducing Confessions," *University of Pennsylvania Law Review* 127 (January 1979), p. 583.

49. On the foundations of the right against self-incrimination, see Kent Greenawalt, "Silence as a Moral and Constitutional Right," *William and Mary Law Review* 23 (Fall 1981), pp. 15–71; Alan Donagan, "The Right Not to Incriminate Oneself," *Social Philosophy & Policy* 1, 2 (Spring 1984), pp. 137–48.

50. *Miranda v. Arizona*, 384 US 444 (1966).

51. This is one of the things that lies behind the Sixth Amendment to the U.S. Constitution. One of the dissenters from the *Miranda* decision complained that the *Miranda* commitment to voluntariness embodied a mélange of concerns: (a) an abhorrence of convictions based on unreliable confessions; (b) a belief that police practices used to obtain confessions should not impose an intolerable pressure on the will of suspects; and (c) a belief that police interrogatory practices should conform to certain basic standards of fairness (*Miranda v. Arizona*, 384 US 444, at 507 [1966], [Harlan, J, dissenting]). Though not identical, these concerns are, in this context, interlocking.

52. Ibid., at 476.

53. See Richard E. Ayers, "Confessions and the Court," *Yale Alumni Magazine* 32, 3 (December 1968), pp. 18, 20. Cf. Yale Kamisar: "*Miranda* wasn't really all that devastating. I don't deny that policemen give the warnings, but they can give it in the same tone [of voice] as asking 'How tall are you?' They can make it seem like part of just filling out another form. The suspect doesn't really absorb it. If I were giving the warnings, for example, I bet the number of suspects asserting their rights would go up phenomenally" (quoted in William Hart, "The Subtle Art of Persuasion," *Police Magazine* 4, 1 [January 1981], p. 8).

54. See, for example, Fred E. Inbau, "Over-Reaction – The Mischief of *Miranda v. Arizona*," *FBI Law Enforcement Bulletin* 52, 4 (April 1983), pp. 22–30 (reprinted from *Journal of Criminal Law and Criminology* 73, 2 [1982], pp. 797–810).

55. See Geoffrey R. Stone, "The Miranda Doctrine in the Burger Court," *1977 Supreme Court Review* (Chicago: University of Chicago Press, 1978), pp. 99–169; Jeffrey Higginbotham, "Interrogation: Post *Miranda* Refinements, I" *FBI Law Enforcement Bulletin* 55, 2 (February 1986), pp. 23–30.

56. Inbau and Reid, *Criminal Interrogation and Confessions*, p. 1.

57. White, "Police Trickery," pp. 596–601.

58. As in *Massiah v. United States*, 377 US 201 (1964). Although this case was decided prior to *Miranda*, it was held that the deception was unacceptable.

59. White, "Police Trickery," p. 605.

60. *Hoffa v. United States*, 385 US 283, at 302, 303 (1966) (quoting the dissent in *Lopez*).

61. In *Illinois v. Perkins*, 110 S Ct 2394 (1990), however, a prisoner who confessed to a murder to an undercover police officer posing as a recaptured escapee was not permitted to avail himself of this defense. The Court noted that the offense to which he confessed was not the offense for which he was in custody, and argued that since with respect to *that* offense he was not in custody he could not assert any Sixth Amendment *Massiah* rights.

62. See White, "Police Trickery," pp. 608–11. However, according to the recently passed U.K. Criminal Justice and Public Order Act (1994), suspects may find that their silence *is* interpreted negatively: "You do not have to say anything. But if

you do not mention now something which you later use in your defence, the court may decide that your failure to mention it now strengthens the case against you. A record will be made of anything you say and it may be given in evidence if you are brought to trial."

63. Such a tactic was upheld in *Colorado v. Spring*, 107 S Ct 851 (1987).
64. White, "Police Trickery," p. 614.
65. *Spano v. New York*, 360 US 323 (1959).
66. *State v. Reilly*, No. 5285 (Conn. Super. Ct. April 12 1974), *vacated*, 32 Conn Supp 349, 355 A 2d 324 (Super. Ct. 1976).
67. *State v. Biron*, 266 Minn 272, 123 NW 2d 392 (1963).
68. *State v. Miller*, 76 NJ 392, 388 A 2d 218 (1978).
69. *Miranda v. Arizona*, 384 US 444, at 469 (1966).
70. As long as the promises remain sufficiently vague, the courts will allow them. See, for example, *Miller v. Fenton*, 796 F 2d 598 (1986).
71. Explicit promises of leniency have been disallowed by the court. See *Bram v. United States*, 168 US 532 (1897).
72. See further David Abney, "Mutt and Jeff Meet the Constitution: The Propriety of Good Guy/Bad Guy Interrogation," *Criminal Law Bulletin* 22, 2 (March–April 1986), pp. 118–30.
73. White, "Police Trickery," pp. 620–1. Or at least the suspect is in no position to determine whether the bargain is illusory.
74. Inbau and Reid, *Criminal Interrogation and Confessions*, pp. 26–31.
75. Edwin H. Driver, "Confessions and the Social Psychology of Coercion," *Harvard Law Review* 82, 1 (1968), pp. 51–2. For an example, see Joan Barthel, *A Death in Canaan*, intro. William Styron (New York: Dutton, 1976).
76. For examples, see Barthel, *A Death in Canaan*; *State of Florida v. Tom Franklin Sawyer*, 561 So 2d 278 (1990).
77. *Frazier v. Cupp*, 394 US 731 (1969).
78. *Florida v. Cayward*, 552 So 2d 971 (1989).
79. There is a useful discussion of *Cayward* in Jerome H. Skolnick and Richard H. Leo, "The Ethics of Deceptive Interrogation," *Criminal Justice Ethics* 11, 1 (Winter/Spring 1992), pp. 7–10.
80. In this section I draw upon an earlier article, "Testimonial Deception by Police: An Ethical Analysis," *Philosophic Exchange* 17(1987), pp. 81–92, and a literature survey undertaken by William H. McDonald.
81. *Mapp v. Ohio*, 367 US 643, 81 S Ct 1684, 6 L Ed 2d 1081 (1961), where it was held that "all evidence obtained by searches and seizures in violation of the constitution is, by that same authority, inadmissible in a state court."
82. Irving Younger, "The Perjury Routine," *The Nation* 202 (8 May, 1967), pp. 596–97; Comment, "Effect of *Mapp v. Ohio* on Police Search-and-Seizure Practices in Narcotics Cases," *Columbia Journal of Law and Social Problems* 4, 1 (March 1968), pp. 87–104; Sarah Barlow, "Patterns of Arrest for Misdemeanor Narcotics Possession: Manhattan Police Practices 1960–62," *Criminal Law Bulletin* 4, 10 (December 1968), pp. 549–82; Comment, "Police Perjury in Narcotics 'Dropsy' Cases: A New Credibility Gap," *Georgetown Law Journal* 60, 2 (November 1971), pp. 507–23; J. S. Oteri, "Dropsy Evidence and the Viability of the Exclusionary Rule," *Contemporary Drug Problems* 1, 1 (1972), pp. 35–48; Lawrence Baum, "Impact of Court Decisions on Police Practices," in F. Meyer and R. Baker (eds.), *Determinants of Law Enforcement Policies* (Lexington, MA: Lexington Books, 1979), pp. 177–90; Myron Orfield, "The Exclusionary Rule and Deterrence: An Empirical Study of

Chicago Narcotics Officers," *University of Chicago Law Review* 54, 3 (Summer 1987), pp. 1,016–69.

83. Apparently, some police officers attempted to explain the discrepancy in terms of a change in the behavior of narcotics possessors:

> A person in possession of narcotics who sees a policeman approaching has a dilemma that grows out of the exclusionary rule. If the officer has a warrant for his arrest, the narcotics will be discovered and usable as evidence unless he can discard them. If the officer has no warrant, the person should retain the narcotics since any search necessary to discover them will probably be illegal and the exclusionary rule will prevent their use in evidence. Knowing the difficulty that an uncertain possessor will have in resolving this dilemma, a police officer without a warrant may rush a suspect, hoping to produce a panic in which the person will visibly discard the narcotics and give the officer cause to arrest him and a legitimate ground to use this evidence. (Cited in Dallin H. Oaks, "Studying the Exclusionary Rule in Search and Seizure," *University of Chicago Law Review* 37, 4 [Summer 1970], pp. 699–700.)

It is true, as Oaks points out (p. 740), that the Columbia study cited above assumes that what accounts for the differences is a change in police behavior rather than that of narcotics possessors, and a careful investigation should have investigated the latter possibility. However, the fact that explanations like the above have to be resorted to in order to lend credence to that possibility suggests that the methodological deficiency is not fatal. Barlow's study is more circumspect, though her figures are comparable to those in the Columbia study. She considers three alternative explanations for the increase in "dropsies," but indicates that although it is impossible to rule them out, an explanation in terms of perjurious testimony is the most plausible (pp. 556–60). That accords with Oaks's assessment.

84. See Fred Cohen, "Police Perjury: An Interview with Martin Garbus," *Criminal Law Bulletin* 8, 5 (June 1972), pp. 372–3; also Barlow, "Patterns of Arrest for Misdemeanor Narcotics Possession," pp. 554–5.

85. See Project, "Interrogations in New Haven: The Impact of Miranda," *Yale Law Journal* 76 (1967), pp. 1,551–8; and Ayers, "Confessions and the Court," pp. 18, 20.

86. See Myron Orfield, "The Exclusionary Rule in the Chicago Criminal Courts," *The Law School Record* (Spring 1989), pp. 35–37. Some idea of its frequency can be gained from City of New York, *Commission Report*, Commission to Investigate Allegations of Police Corruption and the Anti-Corruption Procedures of the Police Department (Milton Mollen, Chair), 7 July 1994, sect. 4.

87. Maurice Punch, *Conduct Unbecoming: The Social Construction of Police Deviance and Control* (New York: Tavistock, 1985); Thomas Barker and David L. Carter, "'Fluffing Up the Evidence' and 'Covering Your Ass': Some Conceptual Notes on Police Lying," *Deviant Behavior* 11, 1 (1990), pp. 61–73.

88. H. Richard Uviller, *Tempered Zeal* (New York: Contemporary Books, 1988), p. 113.

89. Cohen, "Police Perjury," p. 365.

90. *Commission Report*, p. 36.

91. It can sometimes work out differently. If the prosecutor's interest is simply in obtaining a conviction (the numbers count), or if the prosecutor does not think the case warrants the effort that it will require (the bigger the case the better), a plea bargain arrangement may be negotiated that will diminish the value of the

officer's work and perhaps lead to a sentence that, in the officer's eyes, will be seen as only "a slap on the wrist."

92. Of course, it might be argued that a just result *just is* what results from the application of just procedures (the adversarial process), but this is the "abstraction" from which officers frequently recoil.

93. Such was the view of Edwin Meese, III, the Reagan U.S. Attorney General, who, had he continued in office, would have set in motion proceedings intended to overthrow their rulings. See the report in *The New York Times*, 13 February 1987, p. A18.

94. Skolnick, "Deception by Police," p. 43.

8 ENTRAPMENT

1. *Sherman v. United States*, 356 US 384 (1958) (dissenting).

2. *Jacobson v. United States*, 893 F 2d 909, *rev'd*, 916 F 2d 467 (8th Cir., 1990), *cert. granted* 111 S Ct 1618 (1991).

3. *Jacobson v. United States*, 112 S Ct 1535 (1992).

4. *Sorrells v. United States*, 287 US 435, 53 S Ct 210, 77 L Ed 413 (1932); *Sherman v. United States*, 356 US 369, 78 S Ct 819, 2 L Ed 2d 848 (1958); *United States v. Russell*, 411 US 423, 93 S Ct 1637, 36 L Ed 2d 366 (1973); *Hampton v. United States*, 425 US 484, 96 S Ct 1646 (1976); *Jacobson v. United States*, 112 S Ct 1535 (1992).

5. *United States v. Russell*, 411 US 436 (1973).

6. *Sorrells v. United States*, 287 US 442 (1932). According to Chief Justice Hughes, the government's agent "lured" the defendant "by repeated and persistent solicitation in which he succeeded by taking advantage of the sentiment aroused by reminiscences of their experiences as companions in arms in the World War" (at 441). Much of Chief Justice Hughes's argument, however, turns on a point about original intent, viz. that it was most unlikely to have been "the intention of Congress in enacting [the violated] statute that its processes of detection and enforcement should be abused by the instigation by government officials of an act on the part of persons otherwise innocent in order to lure them to its commission and to punish them" (at 448). This aspect of Hughes's opinion was later strongly criticized by Justice Frankfurter (*Sherman v. United States*, 356 US 369, 2 L Ed 2d 848, at 855, 78 S Ct 819 [1958]).

7. *Sherman v. United States*, 356 US 369, at 372, 2 L Ed 2d 848, at 851, 78 S Ct 819 (1958).

8. The problem with (2) is that in law the net of "disposition" is cast broadly to encompass a person's "readiness and willingness" to commit an act of the kind with which he has been charged. Thus, in some of the Abscam cases, circumstances similar to (2) were not deemed to constitute entrapment. Even though there was no suggestion that the defendant had previously contemplated the corrupt behavior in question, or was on the lookout for an opportunity of the kind that was presented, nevertheless, the defendant's preparedness to set aside any initial reluctance, and the practical difficulties in the way of distinguishing (2) from (3), made the courts unsympathetic to an entrapment defense.

9. *People v. Barraza*, 23 Cal 3d 675 (1979).

10. *United States v. Russell*, 411 US 441 (1973) (J. Stewart, dissenting).

11. *Sherman v. United States*, 356 US 382 (1958).

12. *People v. Barraza*, 23 Cal 3d 675 (1979).

13. *United States v. Russell*, 411 US 423, at 439 (1972) (J. Stewart, dissenting).

14. Note Justice Stewart's reference above to the government's "debased" role. Justice Frankfurter quotes with approval Justice Holmes's dissenting argument in *Olmstead v. United States*, 277 US 438, at 470, 72 L Ed 944, at 952 (1928): "For my part I think it is a less evil that some criminals should escape than that the Government should play an ignoble part."
15. Chief Justice Warren, in *Sherman v. United States*, 356 US 369, 2 L Ed 2d 848, at 851, 78 S Ct 819 (1958).
16. *Sorrells v. United States*, 287 US 430, at 454 (1932) (J. Roberts, dissenting).
17. *Jacobson v. United States*, 112 S Ct 1535, at 1546, 1547 (1992).
18. The point is not that that particular instance of the offense would have been committed had the government not been involved, but that an offense *of that kind* would have been committed had the government not been involved. In some cases, it may be enough that the criminal conduct that the government makes available is "relevantly" similar, without being of the same kind. It would be much too demanding to insist (as a rule) that the particular offense would have occurred in the absence of government involvement, for that would severely and unnecessarily handicap undercover work. The important point is that the government's involvement be "light" enough to sustain the view that the person who committed the offense on this occasion had most probably committed it before and would do so again.
19. It may in fact make the defense more easily available. Emphasizing the issue as an epistemic one may allow more easily for "reasonable doubt."
20. *Sherman v. United States*, 356 US 383 (1958). See B. Grant Stitt and Gene G. James, "Entrapment: An Ethical Analysis," in Frederick Elliston and Michael Feldberg (eds.), *Moral Issues in Police Work* (Totowa, NJ: Rowman & Allanheld, 1985), p. 133.
21. *United States v. Russell*, 411 US 423, at 443 (1973). See Stitt & James, "Entrapment," p. 133. Justice Stewart's concerns were not altogether unfounded. In *Greene v. United States*, 454 F 2d 783 (9th Cir. 1971), in which Greene's conviction was reversed, the reversal was not granted because of entrapment, even though it was stated that "the same underlying objections which render entrapment objectionable to American criminal justice are operative." The reason for not accepting an entrapment defense was that Greene had a prior history of violations of a similar kind, and it was not thought possible to argue that he lacked the relevant "predisposition." In the particular instance, the defendant was reluctant to engage in the illicit activity, and the conviction was reversed because the government agent had engaged in excessive solicitation.
22. Though the strictures suggested in Lawrence Sherman, "Equity Against Truth: Value Choices in Deceptive Investigations," in William C. Heffernan and Timothy Stroup (eds.), *Police Ethics: Hard Cases in Law Enforcement* (New York: John Jay Press, 1985), pp. 117–32, need to be heeded.
23. *Sherman v. United States*, 356 US 375 (1958).
24. The situation was otherwise in *United States v. Twigg*, 558 F 2d 373 (3rd Cir. 1978), where the court reversed the conviction.
25. This possibility is raised by Justice Rehnquist in *United States v. Russell*, 411 US 423, at 431–2 (1973): "We may some day be presented with a situation in which the conduct of law enforcement agents is so outrageous that due process principles would absolutely bar the government from invoking judicial processes to obtain a conviction." In his view, the problem with the traditional "objectivist" approach is that the government conduct, even if unseemly, does not rise to the level of egregiousness necessary to justify a due process defense.

26. See the comments in Stitt and James, "Entrapment," pp. 135–6.
27. Gerald Dworkin, "The Serpent Beguiled Me and I Did Eat: Entrapment and the Creation of Crime," *Law and Philosophy* 4 (1985), pp. 30–4.
28. *Sherman v. United States*, 356 US 384 (1958).

9 GRATUITIES AND CORRUPTION

1. This remark was relayed to me by Mark H. Moore.
2. Nicholas Ross, *The Policeman's Bible: Or The Art of Taking a Bribe* (Chicago: Henry Regnery, 1976), p. 4.
3. Herman Goldstein, *Policing a Free Society* (Cambridge, MA: Ballinger, 1977), p. 191.
4. Peter Maas, *Serpico* (New York: Viking Press, 1973), p. 169.
5. It may not be the inducements that are corrupting, but the hypocrisy involved. Gratuities given to increase police presence are "advertised" as gestures of appreciation for the civic services provided by police and other uniformed personnel.
6. For a tongue-in-cheek discussion of corruption in this context, see Ross, *The Policeman's Bible* ch. 3.
7. M. McMullan, "A Theory of Corruption," *Sociological Review* 9 (1961), pp. 183–4.
8. Howard Cohen and Michael Feldberg, *Ethics for Law Enforcement Officers* (Boston: Wasserman Associates, 1983), p. 31, quoted in Feldberg, "Gratuities, Corruption, and the Democratic Ethos of Policing: The Case of the Free Cup of Coffee," in Frederick A. Elliston and Michael Feldberg (eds.), *Moral Issues in Police Work* (Totowa, NJ: Rowman & Allanheld, 1985), pp. 267–8.
9. Goldstein, *Policing in a Free Society*, p. 188.
10. A police chief who, against his better judgment, redeploys personnel to satisfy the political priorities of a mayor who makes it clear that the department's budget will thereby be enhanced does not act corruptly, though his behavior is in certain respects similar to that of the officer who massages his court testimony to secure a conviction. The situation is complicated, however, by the fact that the mayor, as an elected official, may have certain prerogatives so far as the determination of the "public interest" is concerned.
11. Herman Goldstein, for example, provides the following listing:

> (1) Failing to arrest and prosecute those the officer knows have violated the law. Examples are motorists parked overtime or illegally; traffic violators, including drunk drivers; gamblers, prostitutes, narcotics users, homosexuals; violators of minor regulatory ordinances, such as those regulating business hours; violators of the conditions of a license administered by the police agency; juvenile offenders; and more serious offenders, such as burglars and persons engaged in organized crime. (2) Agreeing to drop an investigation prematurely by not pursuing leads which would produce evidence supporting a criminal charge. (3) Agreeing not to inspect locations or premises where violations are known to occur and where an officer's presence might curtail the illegal activity – such as taverns in which prostitution or gambling flourishes and probably contributes to the volume of business. (4) Refraining from making arrests on licensed premises where an arrest results in license review that could lead to revocation. This includes taverns, night clubs, dance halls, and motion picture theaters. (5) Reducing the seriousness of a charge against an offender. (6) Agreeing to alter testimony at trial or to provide less than the

full amount of evidence available. (7) Providing more police protection or presence than is required by standard operating procedures. Examples are: more frequent and intensive checks of the security of private premises; more frequent presence in a store or other commercial establishment, such as a hotel, club, or restaurant where the officer's presence benefits the owner by keeping out "undesirables"; observation of parked cars while owners attend a social gathering or meeting in an area where cars are commonly stolen or damaged; and escorting businessmen making bank deposits. (8) Influencing departmental recommendations regarding the granting of licenses, for example, by recommending for or against continuance of a liquor or amusement license by either giving or suppressing derogatory information. (9) Arranging access to confidential departmental records or agreeing to alter such records. (10) Referring individuals caught in a new and stressful situation to persons who can assist them and who stand to profit from the referral. Police can get paid for making referrals to bondsmen or defense attorneys; placing accident victims in contact with physicians or attorneys specializing in the filing of personal injury claims; arranging for delivery of bodies to a funeral home; and selecting the ambulance or tow truck summoned to the scene of an accident or an illegally parked car. (11) Appropriating for personal use or disposal items of value acquired on the job, such as jewelry and goods from the scene of a burglary; narcotics confiscated from users or peddlers; funds used in gambling; items found at the scene of a fire; private property of a drunk or a deceased person; and confiscated weapons (Goldstein, *Policing in a Free Society*, pp. 194–5).

Apart from being somewhat dated, this list provides only a small window into the variety of ways in which police may be corrupted. As Goldstein comments: "One of the amazing things about police graft is the endless variety of schemes that come to light. Opportunities for personal profit in a corrupt agency seem to be limited only by the imagination and aggressiveness of those intent on realizing private gain" (p. 194).

12. See, for example, Thomas Barker and Julian B. Roebuck, *An Empirical Typology of Police Corruption* (Springfield, IL: Thomas, 1974); Julian B. Roebuck and Thomas Barker, "A Typology of Police Corruption," *Social Problems* 21, 3 (1974), pp. 423–37; Thomas Barker, "Social Definitions of Police Corruption: The Case of South City," *Criminal Justice Review* 2, 2, (1977), pp. 101–10; Tom Barker and Robert O. Wells, "Police Administrators' Attitudes Toward the Definition and Control of Police Deviance," *FBI Law Enforcement Bulletin* 51, 3 (March 1982), pp. 8–16; T. Barker and D. L. Carter, *Police Deviance* (Cincinnati, OH: Anderson Publishing Co., 1986).

13. The Knapp Commission Report referred to an almost equivalent distinction between "grass-eaters" and "meat-eaters," and noted: "One relatively strong impetus encouraging grass-eaters to continue to accept relatively petty graft is, ironically, their feeling of loyalty to their fellow officers. Accepting payoff money is one way for an officer to prove that he is one of the boys and that he can be trusted" (New York City Commission to Investigate Allegations of Police Corruption and the City's Anti-Corruption Procedures, *Commission Report* [Whitman Knapp, Chairman], [New York: Bar Press, 1972], p. 65.) Such distinctions possess considerable normative power. Compare the distinction more generally made between "souveniring" and "stealing."

14. Roebuck and Barker, "A Typology of Police Corruption," p. 435.

15. Ibid., p. 428.
16. Ibid., p. 429. I understand that the bondsmen scam has been cleaned up since their article was written.
17. Ibid.
18. Ibid., p. 430.
19. Ibid., p. 431.
20. Ibid., p. 432.
21. Ibid. See also Maas, *Serpico.*
22. See Michael Banton, *The Policeman in the Community* (New York: Basic, 1964), p. 195. However, as one former law enforcement officer drily commented: "It's nice you did it fellows, but it is nothing to shout about" (Jack E. Whitehouse, "Thou Shalt Not Be a Moocher" [typescript, n.d.], p. 5).
23. Roebuck and Barker, "A Typology of Police Corruption," p. 434.
24. Quoted in Feldberg, "Gratuities, Corruption, and the Democratic Ethos of Policing," p. 267. Cf. Patrick V. Murphy: "Except for your paycheck, there's no such thing as a clean buck," quoted in "Police Aides Told to Rid Commands of All Dishonesty," *New York Times*, 29 October 1970, p. A1.
25. In police argot, a "good" restaurant is not one that is expensive or provides good-quality food, but one that offers good discounts or free meals.
26. My talk here of "the truth" assumes that I am focusing on a fairly clearly defined phenomenon. And to some extent I am. However, the actual practices are much more varied than those I will focus on. My discussion will not consider discounts that might be available to police via their membership in a police union. These seem to me to have a rather different character from that of free cups of coffee. For one thing, such discounts are probably available to, and negotiated by, a number of other unions, and are seen as inducements to buy rather than – say – corrupt inducements to give favored treatment.
27. For a discussion of the moral etiquette of gratitude, and why saying "thank you" may not be enough, see Terrance McConnell, *Gratitude* (Philadelphia: Temple University Press, 1993).
28. In Australia, it is McDonald's policy to offer police officers and others in uniform half-price hamburgers. Ostensibly this is a public-spirited gesture intended to show appreciation for the good work that police and others do. More realistically, it is an investment in police presence.
29. This argument is developed in detail in Richard R. E. Kania, "Should We Tell the Police to Say 'Yes' to Gratuities?" *Criminal Justice Ethics* 7, 2 (Summer/Fall 1988), pp. 37–49.
30. Consider the contempt for management that followed reassignment of a police officer who accepted a double scoop of ice cream for the price of one. What angered many police officers was not simply the lack of understanding shown and the trivial character of the breach, but the fact that after the officer was reported, the ice cream shop was staked out no fewer than eighteen times over the next several months. See Bill Reel, "Corruption: Here's the Scoop," *Daily News* (21 February 1988), p. 49; "Never on Sundae," *Law Enforcement News* 14, 268 (15 April 1988), p. 4.
31. Quoted in Samuel Smiles, *Life and Labour; or Characteristics of Men of Industry, Culture & Genius* (London: John Murray, 1887), p. 9.
32. Cf. the "weaker brother" argument used in some religious contexts: I Cor. 8.
33. See Feldberg, "Gratuities, Corruption, and the Democratic Ethos of Policing."
34. There is, in fact more than one kind of argument here. Trudy Govier, who rejects

most slippery slope reasoning, distinguishes what she calls "the fallacy of slippery assimilation" (Where do you draw the line?) from "the fallacy of slippery precedent" (How do you stop?). See *A Practical Study of Argument*, 3rd ed. (Belmont, CA: Wadsworth, 1992), pp. 296–301. For a comprehensive review of slippery slope arguments, see Douglas N. Walton, *Slippery Slope Arguments* (Oxford: Oxford University Press [Clarendon Press], 1992).

35. James Rachels, *The End of Life* (New York: Oxford University Press, 1985), pp. 172–80.

36. The distinction is made, however, in Wibren van der Burg, "The Slippery Slope Argument," *Ethics* 102, 1 (October 1991), pp. 44–5.

37. There are two ways of construing the "logical" connection. One is to see the various practices on the slope connected by virtue of being wrong *for the same reason*. The other is to see them connected by virtue of their wrongness (though not necessarily wrong for the same reason). In the former case, the person, having accepted a particular maxim by virtue of engaging in one practice, is thereby committed to other practices in which the same maxim is operative. In the latter case, the person, having compromised his/her integrity in one instance, now no longer has an integrity to be compromised. This way of construing the connection is something of an amalgam of the logical and psychological versions.

38. I am assuming that z would be horrible. In the case of police corruption that may not be contentious. But we need to remember that what one person sees as "horrific" another may see as desirable. Cf. the slippery slope argument that starts with abortion and finishes up with euthanasia and infanticide. Not everyone would see those as unacceptable consequences. Cf. also the argument used twenty-five years ago that if motorcyclists were forced to wear safety helmets the time would come when the rest of us would be forced to wear seat belts! (*American Motorcycle Association v. Davids*, 158 NW 2d 72 [1968]).

39. See also Bernard Williams, "Which Slopes Are Slippery?" in Michael Lockwood (ed.), *Moral Dilemmas in Modern Medicine* (New York: Oxford University Press, 1985), pp. 126–7.

40. Lawrence Sherman, "Becoming Bent: Moral Careers of Corrupt Policemen," in Elliston and Feldberg (eds.), *Moral Issues in Police Work*, p. 259.

41. Ibid.

42. For example, Robert Leuci, of *Prince of the City* fame, has given two different accounts of his decline, each of which focuses on a slippery slope. See Myron Glazer, "Ten Whistleblowers and How They Fared," *Hastings Center Report* 13, 6 (December 1983), p. 33; Robert Leuci, "The Process of Erosion," in Dennis Jay Kenney (ed.), *Police and Policing: Contemporary Issues* (New York: Praeger, 1989), pp. 181–7.

43. Feldberg, "Gratuities, Corruption, and the Democratic Ethos of Policing," p. 268.

44. Ibid., pp. 267–8.

45. Ibid., p. 274.

46. Sherman himself recognizes this in "Becoming Bent," pp. 259–60.

47. Apparently the terms were coined – or at least made public – by the NYPD's Assistant Chief Inspector, Sydney Cooper, during the Knapp Commission hearings. See *The Knapp Commission Report on Police Corruption* (New York: George Braziller, 1972), p. 4.

48. A very similar position is developed in Howard Cohen, "Exploiting Police Authority," *Criminal Justice Ethics* 5, 2 (Summer/Fall 1986), pp. 23–31; and also David Hansen, *Police Ethics* (Springfield, IL: Thomas, 1973), chs. 1, 3.

49. And it may also turn police into moochers. The moocher is unseemly rather than corrupt. See Whitehouse, "Thou Shalt Not Be a Moocher."
50. See Michael Daley, "The Crack in the Shield: The Fall of the Seven-Seven," *New York* (8 December 1986), pp. 50–9.
51. This, no doubt, is one of the reasons for internal investigative mechanisms such as the NYPD "field associates" program. See Kevin Krajick, "Police vs Police," *Police Magazine*, May 1980, pp. 7–20; Vincent Henry, "Lifting the 'Blue Curtain': Some Controversial Strategies to Control Police Corruption," *National Police Research Unit Review* 6 (1990), pp. 48–55; and Gary T. Marx, "When the Guards Guard Themselves: Undercover Tactics Turned Inward," *Policing and Society* 2 (April 1992), pp. 158–72.
52. Cf. Carsten Stroud:

> In every masculine community there are three trials by which each male member will be judged and disposition carried out on his soul, and at none of these trials will a single word be spoken in open court. . . . [T]he third test is a trial of loyalty. Can this man be loyal, and if so, to whom is his loyalty given? If it's given to the Commissioner, the borough bosses, and the administration, then he fails. If it's placed on the anvil, between the Book and the Street, if he can step back and leave it there, at the mercy of the caprices of cop fate, knowing that there is no way to do a cop's job in the way the city truly calls for it to be done without placing his reputation and career and sometimes his freedom at risk – if he can leave his loyalty on that anvil, then he passes (*Close Pursuit: A Week in the Life of an NYPD Homicide Cop* [New York: Bantam, 1987], p.111).

The primarily horizontal character of police loyalty helps to explain the vehement dislike of internal investigators. Stroud's cop "hero" reacts: "Field Associate! What a name! Spy, snitch, stoolie, fink, rat, weasel – they were closer to the mark" (p. 117). The complexities of loyalty in police work are alluded to, but not grappled with in David A. Hansen's seminal *Police Ethics*:

> Loyalty is . . . a coin with more than one side. An officer must be loyal to his calling and to his department. Administrative loyalty comes into play here and unfortunately is the area in which loyalty sometimes dies. Loyalty flows upward and downward. When one flow ceases, so does the other. The chief and the department must be loyal to the officer, his desires, and his needs, and the officer needs to be loyal upward in turn. "Lateral loyalty" is sometimes a problem. The loyalty of the officer to his department is often strained as a result of competition between patrol and detective divisions, for example. This competition, when carried to extremes, is insidious. Of course the officer should be loyal to his primary unit, as with patrol, for example. Misplaced loyalty to the unit, however, can result in noncooperation, disloyalty vis-à-vis the department as an entity, or vis-à-vis some of the other components and divisions of the department (p. 73).

For more detailed studies of the vertical–horizontal loyalty problem, see Maurice Punch, "Officers and Men: Occupational Culture, Inter-Rank Antagonism, and the Investigation of Corruption," and Elizabeth Reuss-Ianni and Francis A. J. Ianni, "Street Cops and Management Cops: The Two Cultures of Policing," both in Maurice Punch (ed.), *Control in the Police Organization* (Cambridge, MA: MIT Press, 1983), pp. 227–50, 251–74.

53. See Maas, *Serpico*; Myron Glazer, "Ten Whistleblowers and How They Fared," pp. 33–41.
54. This seems to be the case with Thomas Wren, in "Whistle-Blowing and Loyalty to One's Friends," in William C. Heffernan and Timothy Stroup (eds.), *Police Ethics: Hard Choices in Law Enforcement* (New York: John Jay Press, 1985), pp. 25–43. Where, as in police work, the primary loyalty tends to be fraternal rather than institutional, reporting unethical activity to superiors may come to have many of the same overtones as "going public."
55. See Peter Maas, *Serpico*. Although Frank Serpico is now admired by many, for a long time there was thought to be a police "contract" on him, and Serpico spent some years in Switzerland. As we shall later see, defenders of "loyalty" frequently cast doubt on the genuineness of the "integrity" of whistleblowers. It is sometimes believed that only if option (7) is followed can the whistleblower's motives be trusted.
56. Norman Bowie, *Business Ethics* (Englewood Cliffs, NJ: Prentice-Hall, 1982), p. 142.
57. Frederick Elliston, John Keenan, Paula Lockhart and Jane van Schaick, *Whistleblowing Research: Methodological and Moral Issues* (New York: Praeger, 1985), p. 15.
58. See Wren, "Whistleblowing and Loyalty to One's Friends."
59. Bowie, *Business Ethics*, p. 143.
60. See Myron P. Glazer & Penina M. Glazer, *The Whistleblowers: Exposing Corruption in Government and Industry* (New York: Basic, 1989).
61. See further, Frederick Elliston, "Civil Disobedience and Whistleblowing: A Comparative Appraisal of Two Forms of Dissent," *Journal of Business Ethics* 1 (Spring 1982), pp. 23–8.
62. As part of the social shoring up that occurs after the whistle is blown, rumors about the motives of the whistleblower will almost inevitably begin to circulate. It is as though one could blow the whistle only for self-serving ends.

10 PUBLIC ROLES AND PRIVATE LIVES

1. Marshall was dissenting in *Kelley v. Johnson*, 425 US 238, at 254–5 (1976), a 6–2 opinion.
2. IACP, "Law Enforcement Code of Ethics," 1957; 1991. The phrasing is taken from O. W. Wilson's "Square Deal" Code, prepared for the Wichita Police Department, 1928.
3. For a good overview of the complexities, see Stanley I. Benn and Gerald F. Gaus, "The Public and the Private: Concepts and Action," in Stanley I. Benn & Gerald F. Gaus (eds.), *Public and Private in Social Life* (London: Croom Helm, 1983), pp. 3–27.
4. John Donne, "Devotions XVII" (1623). Cf. J. S. Mill, *On Liberty*, in J. M. Robson (ed.), *Collected Works of John Stuart Mill* (Toronto: University of Toronto Press, 1977), vol. 18, p. 280.
5. This is not to deny that there have been *traditions* of womanizing and extramarital conduct in some police departments. In such cases, action taken against those involved can usually be attributed to some specific factor – a zealous commander, a complaint, a particularly blatant incident – rather than to the regular operation of policy.
6. *Griswold v. Connecticut*, 381 US 479 (1965). Much of the legal discussion was initiated by S. Warren and L. Brandeis, "The Right to Privacy," *Harvard Law*

Review 4 (1890), pp. 193–220. But the public/private distinction, and even the idea that some matters are of only private concern, goes back much further.

7. This is how Warren and Brandeis saw it.

8. The quotations that immediately follow are taken from *On Liberty*, ch. 1.

9. These are examples used by Mill in ch. 4.

10. Even further beyond the core are various voluntary associations with others. From the "liberty of each individual follows the liberty, within the same limits, of combination among individuals; freedom to unite for any purpose not involving harm to others: the persons combining being supposed to be of full age and not forced or deceived" (*On Liberty*, p. 281).

11. See, in particular, C. L. Ten, *Mill on Liberty* (Oxford: Oxford University Press [Clarendon Press], 1980; also David Spitz, "Freedom and Individuality: Mill's *Liberty* in Retrospect," in C. J. Friedrich (ed.), *NOMOS IV: Liberty* (New York: Atherton Press), 1962, pp. 190–4.

12. For some of the main discussions, see, Special Issue on Privacy, *Law & Contemporary Problems* 31, 2 (Spring 1966), pp. 251–435; J. Roland Pennock & J.W. Chapman (eds.), *NOMOS XIII: Privacy*, Yearbook of the American Society for Political and Legal Philosophy (New York: Atherton Press, 1971); Ferdinand D. Schoeman (ed.), *Philosophical Dimensions of Privacy: An Anthology* (New York: Cambridge University Press, 1984).

13. Here I part company with Charles Fried, who believes that privacy makes intimacy possible. "Privacy," *Yale Law Journal* 77, 2 (January 1968), pp. 475–93.

14. Unfortunately, the demand for privacy may also function as a mask behind which our real self is concealed. That privacy is a value does not mean that it cannot be abused. In such contexts, we may wish to speak more neutrally of "secrecy."

15. What form any invasion of privacy and restriction on freedom should take is, of course, another matter. Should the officer be reprimanded, suspended, required to attend an alcohol treatment program, fired, or what?

16. Mill, *On Liberty*, ch. 4.

17. *Shapiro v. Thompson*, 394 US 618, at 634 (1969).

18. *McAuliffe v. Mayor of New Bedford*, 155 Mass 216, at 220, 29 NE 517 (1892).

19. Philip Sebold, "The Conduct of a Policeman," in Henry J. Lee (ed.), *Eagle Police Manual: A Handbook for Peace Officers; National in Scope* (New York: Eagle Library Publications, 1933), p. 41.

20. Reiner points out that "in Britain police were not even franchised until 1887 and are still forbidden to belong to any political party, or affiliate to any outside trade unions or the TUC (Trades Union Congress) on the grounds that this would threaten impartiality" (Robert Reiner, "The Politicization of the Police in Britain," in Maurice Punch [ed.], *Control in the Police Organization* (Cambridge, MA: MIT Press, 1983], p. 130).

21. *Garrity v. New Jersey*, 385 US 493, at 500 (1967). The earlier case was *Slochower v. Board of Higher Education*, 350 US 551 (1956). See also *Keyishian v. Board of Regents*, 385 US 589, at 605-6 (1967).

22. *Pickering v. Board of Education*, 391 US 563, at 568 (1968). In 1970 the Seventh Circuit applied *Pickering* to a police situation: *Muller v. Conlisk*, 429 F 2d 901 (7th Cir. 1970).

23. *Connick v. Myers*, 461 US 138 (1983). In a 5–4 decision, the Court stated that Myer's expression was "most accurately characterized as an employee grievance concerning internal office policy." A similar decision had been reached by the

Third Circuit in an earlier case, *Sprague v. Fitzpatrick*, where another assistant district attorney had revealed to the press that the district attorney's disclaimers regarding a sentencing recommendation had been untruthful. Here the damage to the working relationship was considered to outweigh the public's right to know this bit of information. In *Pickering* it was made clear that in working relationships that require a high degree of personal loyalty, there is a heavier burden on the employee to establish the public interest involved (546 F 2d 560 [3rd Cir. 1976], *cert. denied*, 431 US 937 (1977).

24. *Williams v. Board of Regents*, 629 F 2d 993 (5th Cir. 1970), *cert. denied*, 452 US 926 (1981). Justice Rehnquist dissented, claiming that the Appeals Court did not give sufficient weight to the need for discipline and control in a law enforcement agency.

25. See, for example, *Kannisto v. City and County of San Francisco*, 541 F 2d 841 (9th Cir. 1976), *cert. denied*, 430 US 931 (1977), in which a lieutenant made disparaging remarks about a superior to subordinates during a morning inspection; and *Key v. Rutherford*, 645 F 2d 880 (7th Cir. 1981), in which a police chief spoke with the mayor and city manager regarding budget grievances.

26. *Rankin v. McPherson*, 107 S Ct 2891 (1987). It was, however, a 5–4 decision, with Justices Scalia, Rehnquist, White, and O'Connor in dissent. They complained that no law enforcement agency should be required to allow one of its employees to "ride with the cops and cheer for the robbers." They also complained that the majority had confused the *motive* for the statement with its *content*.

27. *Connick v. Myers*, 461 US 138, at 154 (1983).

28. See *Clary v. Irvin*, 501 F Supp 706 (E.D. Tex. 1980).

29. *Shawgo v. Spradlin*, 701 F 2d 470 (5th Cir. 1983). Janet Shawgo was a patrol officer, and Stanley Whisenhunt, with whom she formed a romantic relationship, was a sergeant. They maintained separate apartments, though a seventeen-day surveillance of Whisenhunt's apartment ordered by Amarillo, Texas, Chief Lee Spradlin indicated that Shawgo sometimes slept over. In addition, Whisenhunt shared his apartment (and expenses) with a subordinate officer, John Edwards. The suspension and demotion imposed on Whisenhunt was ostensibly for inter-rank fraternization as well as the unfavorable criticism that might have occurred had the relationship become public. Whisenhunt had his immediate supervisor's permission for both activities, and received no warning. In the court case, there was some suggestion that the disciplining of Shawgo and Whisenhunt (who both subsequently resigned and married) was selective and not unconnected with unfavorable remarks that Whisenhunt was known to have made about the running of the department.

30. Michael A. Woronoff, "Public Employees or Private Citizens: The Off-Duty Sexual Activities of Police Officers and the Constitutional Right of Privacy," *Journal of Law Reform* 18, 1 (Fall 1984), p. 209.

31. Woronoff may be over-optimistic – especially if the sexual contact is between coworkers, as it was in *Shawgo v. Spradlin*.

32. There may have been a problem had Stanley Whisenhunt been Janet Shawgo's supervisor. But he was not.

33. Note, too, in the Canons of Police Ethics, adopted in 1957 at the same time as the IACP adopted the Law Enforcement Code of Ethics: "The law enforcement officer . . . will so conduct his private life that the public will regard him as an example of stability, fidelity and morality" (art. 6).

34. Compare also: "We are role models for the community" ("Values," Alexandria

Police Department, 1990; "Vision, Value and Mission Statements," Lawrence Police Department, 1991). All the above statements can be found in John Kleinig, with Yurong Zhang (eds.), *Professional Law Enforcement Codes: A Documentary Collection* (Westport, CT: Greenwood, 1993).

35. Frederick A. Elliston, "Police, Privacy, and the Double Standard," in Frederick A. Elliston and Michael Feldberg (eds.), *Moral Issues in Police Work* (Totowa, NJ: Rowman & Allanheld, 1985), p. 282.

36. Cf. the disclaimer of basketball star, Charles Barkley, accused of being a bad example: "I am not a role model. . . . I am paid to wreak havoc on the basketball court. Parents should be role models. Just because I dunk a basketball doesn't mean I should raise your kids" (quoted in Vern E. Smith and Aric Press, "Who You Calling Hero?" *Newsweek* 121, 21 [24 May, 1993], p. 64).

37. Elliston, "Police, Privacy, and the Double Standard," p. 283.

38. David A. Hansen, *Police Ethics* (Springfield, IL: Thomas, 1973), p. 58.

39. Elliston, "Police, Privacy, and the Double Standard," p. 285. I believe that Elliston is far too sanguine about the expectation that police peers will monitor and discipline each other.

40. *Kelley v. Johnson,* 425 US 238, at 247 (1976).

41. Ibid., at 250–1 (J. Marshall, dissenting).

42. Ibid., at 255.

43. The case is, however, a problematic one, since social prejudices may take other, and more pernicious, forms. Should a significant proportion of the citizens in a predominantly white neighborhood be prejudiced against black police officers serving there, ought the police department to accommodate itself to that prejudice?

44. *Nicomachean Ethics,* bk. 5.

45. Not all courts have taken this view, however.

46. Hansen hints at this sort of point when he writes: "Because the public relations image of his department is important, and because he directly affects that image, the officer must be disciplined. In avoiding both evil and the appearance of evil, the officer must be disciplined in his personal life" (*Police Ethics,* p. 56). It is factors like this that have been behind efforts to maintain a certain dress code in police work (including regulations about hair length, etc.), and to discourage certain lifestyles (at one time it was difficult for a divorced person to be accepted into the New York Police department; and there have been cases where police officers who have cohabited extramaritally have been disciplined). Whether these restrictions have been justifiably imposed is another matter.

11 AUTHORITY AND ACCOUNTABILITY

1. Juvenal, *Satires,* 6, l. 347: "Who then shall guard the guardians?"

2. Herman Goldstein, *Policing a Free Society* (Cambridge, MA: Ballinger, 1977), p. 144.

3. Some would argue for a broader and less unified statement of the normative understanding. Robert B. Wagner, for example, provides some grounds for thinking that "in saying that a particular agent is accountable we could imply that he is obligated to give a report, relation, description, explanation, justifying analysis, or some form of exposition. . . " (*Accountability in Education: A Philosophical Inquiry* [New York: Routledge, 1990], p. 8). Although I think that talk about answerability for what one does is broad enough to encompass these various alternative

expectations, Wagner is right to see that there is a difference between requiring a report or an explanation or a justification. My own belief, however, is that accountability for the authority one is accorded is almost always implicitly justificatory. A public trust is involved, and giving account is not merely a matter of reporting or explaining but of showing that the trust has been justified.

4. For a discussion of the problem of structuring accountability in large organizations, see Dennis Thompson, *Political Ethics and Public Office* (Cambridge, MA: Harvard University Press, 1987), Ch. 2.

5. See O. W. Holmes, Jr. "The Path of Law," *Harvard Law Review* 10 (1897), pp. 457–68.

6. Goldstein, *Policing a Free Society*, p. 143.

7. See, for example, James Q. Wilson and George L. Kelling, "The Police and Neighborhood Safety: Broken Windows," *Atlantic Monthly* (March 1982), pp. 29–38; Samuel Walker, "Broken Windows and Fractured History: The Use and Misuse of History in Recent Police Patrol Analysis," *Justice Quarterly* 1, 1 (1984), pp. 75–90; Malcolm Sparrow, Mark H. Moore, and David Kennedy, *Beyond 911: A New Era for Policing* (New York: Basic, 1990).

8. In the 1957 Law Enforcement Code of Ethics, police officers somewhat grandiloquently pledged themselves to serve "mankind." The 1992 revision has scaled this back to "the community."

9. For an exploration of some of the problems here, see my "Policing the Homeless: An Ethical Dilemma" *Journal of Social Distress & Homelessness* 2, 4 (1993), pp. 289–303; also, more recently, Martha R. Plotkin and Ortwin A. "Tony" Narr, *The Police Response to the Homeless: A Status Report* (Washington, DC: Police Executive Research Forum, 1993).

10. This is not to deny that officers sometimes find ways of getting around or neutralizing these limitations.

11. Herbert Packer, *The Limits of the Criminal Sanction* (Stanford, CA: Stanford University Press, 1968), ch. 8.

12. *Fisher v. Oldham Corporation*, 2 KB 364 (1930). The *ratio decidendi* employed in this case was reaffirmed – albeit only as obiter dicta – by Lord Denning in *R. v. Metropolitan Police Commissioner ex parte Blackburn*, 2 QB 118 (1968), where he asserted that the Commissioner of the Metropolitan Police was "answerable to the law and to the law alone." Every constable, too, was "independent of the executive." L. Lustgarten, however, has argued that "seldom have so many errors of law and logic been compressed into one paragraph" (*The Governance of Police* (London: Sweet & Maxwell, 1985), p. 64. The constable's oath reads in part: "I do solemnly and sincerely declare and affirm that I will well and truly serve Our Sovereign Lady the Queen in the office of constable . . . and that while I continue to hold the said office I will to the best of my skill and knowledge discharge all the duties thereof faithfully according to the law."

13. Sir David McNee, quoted in Robert Reiner, "The Politicization of the Police in Britain," in Maurice Punch (ed.), *Control in the Police Organization* (Cambridge, MA: MIT Press, 1983), p. 128.

14. See I. Oliver, *Police, Government and Accountability* (London: Macmillan Press, 1987), p. 96, where attention is drawn to the power to call the tune by the one who pays the piper.

15. See, for example, T. Jefferson and R. Grimshaw, *Controlling the Constable* (London: Frederic Muller, 1984), p. 142. It might be suggested that the police show their conformity with the rule of law when, in cases that have no explicit legal solution,

they act with fairness and without fear or favor. But for the observance of such procedural values to be considered as conformity to the rule of law, they need to be yoked in some way to the outworking of legal requirements.

16. Consider, for example, the large number of Irish (and Italian) Catholics who have entered into police work in urban America. See also Seymour Martin Lipsett, "Why Cops Hate Liberals – and Vice Versa," in Jack Goldsmith and Sharon S. Goldsmith (eds.), *The Police Community: Dimensions of an Occupational Subculture* (Pacific Palisades, CA: Palisades Publishers, 1974), ch. 9.

17. See, for discussions, J. Horton and Susan Mendus (eds.), *Aspects of Toleration: Philosophical Studies* (London: Methuen, 1985); Susan Mendus and David Edward (eds.), *On Toleration* (New York: Oxford University Press, 1987); Susan Mendus, *Toleration and the Limits of Liberalism* (Atlantic Highlands, NJ: Humanities Press, 1989).

18. For an account of the practices, and their social significance, see Olayinka Koso-Thomas, *The Circumcision of Women: A Strategy for Eradication* (Atlantic Highlands, NJ: Humanities Press, 1987). On the issue of its legality in a "liberal" society, see K. Hayter, "Female Circumcision – Is There a Legal Solution?" *Journal of Social Welfare Law* (November 1984), pp. 323–33. Because the practice occurs in many countries (perhaps twenty to thirty) some efforts have been made to bring UN pressure to bear on those countries that tolerate it. See Robyn Cerny Smith, "Female Circumcision: Bringing Women's Perspectives into the International Debate," *Southern California Law Review* 65, 5 (July 1992), pp. 2,449–504.

19. Commission to Investigate Allegations of Police Corruption and the Anti-Corruption Procedures of the Police Department, Milton Mollen – Chair, Report, 7 July, 1994.

20. I do not think that the police are alone in this. Even traditional professionals have not been given full control over the ways in which they render their service. Not only are they subject to legal scrutiny, but their actions are being increasingly reviewed by the wider community. The media, client groups, and even "internal" groups such as hospital review boards, with their community representatives, have called professionals to account for the services they provide.

21. Robert Daley, *Prince of the City: The Story of a Cop Who Knew Too Much* (Boston: Houghton Mifflin, 1978). Subsequently it was made into a film, starring Treat Williams. See also Leonard Shecter, with William Phillips, *On the Pad* (New York: Berkley Medallion Books, 1974).

22. This is well illustrated by an example that David Durk recites in James Lardner, "The Whistleblowers," *The New Yorker* 69 (5 July, 1993), p. 55. Why is it, when something goes "wrong," someone must be found to blame?

23. The recent promulgation of sixty-one performance indicators by the U.K. Home Office constitutes one step in this direction.

24. For studies that point in this direction, see Herman Goldstein, *Problem-Oriented Policing* (New York: McGraw-Hill, 1990); Malcolm K. Sparrow, Mark H. Moore, and David M. Kennedy, *Beyond 911: A New Era for Policing* (New York: Basic, 1990).

25. To this end, when management is developing policies, it might well provide opportunities for those who will have to implement the policies to have some input into their development.

26. In some departments this is changing, though it is rare to see the strategy of producing rationale-based rule making followed consistently. And sometimes the rationales are only superficially related to the statement of operating procedures.

27. The Field Associates program, commenced in the NYPD after the Knapp Commission, and subsequently exported to some other departments, takes this form. See Kevin Krajick, "Police vs. Police – No One Knows Much About Internal Affairs Bureaus, So Everyone Distrusts Them," *Police Magazine* 3, 3 (May 1980), pp. 6–15, 17–20.

28. There is really a continuum here. The Securities and Exchange Commission keeps a fairly close eye on the activities of its members, and some stores and organizations concerned with maintaining public good will will use "buying spies" and monitoring devices to check on the service that is being provided.

29. See, for example, Vincent Murano, with William Hoffer, *Cop Hunter* (New York: Simon & Schuster, 1990), where the willingness of a police department (the NYPD) to take its anticorruption task seriously is compromised by its concern to avoid a bad press (and, possibly along with that, executive accountability). In a recent NYPD scandal (investigated by the Mollen Commission), it was found that, although several officers involved in serious drug-related crime had come to the attention of its internal affairs division, nothing had been done. The men were arrested by police from a neighboring department. A shake-up of the NYPD's internal affairs division was subsequently undertaken.

30. The more activist the courts have been in interpreting the law and Constitution, the greater the problem they have posed for theorists of a democratic community. Because judges are usually appointed rather than elected – particularly at the higher levels – they are not as answerable to the community as other officials with legislative or regulatory powers. In practice, however, it may well be that the judiciary has been as sensitive (or insensitive) to communal voices as are elected officials.

31. Herbert Packer, *The Limits of the Criminal Sanction*, ch. 8.

32. Balancing the need to convict the guilty against the need to protect the innocent has, in Anglo-American law, generally been weighted in favor of protecting the innocent: "It is better that ten guilty persons escape than that one innocent suffer" (Blackstone). However, the rationale behind this truism of Anglo-American law is not altogether clear, and has sometimes been challenged. For a useful discussion of both sides, see Jeffrey Reiman and Ernest van den Haag, "On the Common Saying that it is Better that Ten Guilty Persons Escape than that One Innocent Suffer: *Pro* and *Con*," in Ellen Frankel Paul, Fred D. Miller, Jr. and Jeffrey Paul (eds.), *Crime, Culpability, and Remedy* (Oxford: Blackwell Publisher, 1990), pp. 226–48.

33. Even this may not justify a loosening of constraints on police. If police cannot do better because they lack the resources for doing better, maintaining the constraints may send a message to municipalities and legislatures that more resources should be devoted to their work.

34. For a history of civilian review, and of the fate of New York City's Civilian Complaint Review Board in 1966, see Algernon D. Black, *The People and the Police* (New York: McGraw-Hill, 1968); also James R. Hudson, "Police Review Boards and Police Accountability," *Law and Contemporary Problems* 36 (1971), pp. 515–38; D. C. Brown, *Civilian Review of Complaints Against the Police – A Survey of the United States Literature* (London: Home Office Research and Planning Unit, 1983); Douglas W. Perez, *Common Sense About Police Review* (Philadelphia: Temple University Press, 1994).

35. This form of review originated in Scandinavia. For some of the literature, see Donald C. Rowat, *The Spread of the Ombudsman Idea in the United States* (Edmon-

ton, Alberta: International Ombudsman Institute [1984?]); Victor Ayeni, *A Typology of Ombudsman Institutions* (Edmonton, Alberta: International Ombudsman Institute [1985]); Sam Zagoria, *The Ombudsman: How Good Governments Handle Citizens' Grievances* (Cabin John, MD: Seven Locks Press, 1988).

36. The office of ombudsman is used quite extensively in several countries. In the United States, however, where the politicization of public office seems almost all-pervasive, the idea has not caught on to any great degree. However, even where the ombudsman system has caught on, as in the United Kingdom, the investigation of complaints against police may be excluded from its purview (see G. Marshall, "Police Accountability Revisited," in D. E. Butler and A. H. Halsey [eds.], *Policy and Politics* [London: Methuen, 1978], p. 63).

37. This, no doubt, is one of the reasons for the burgeoning interest in journalistic ethics. See, for example, Stephen Klaidman and Tom L. Beauchamp, *The Virtuous Journalist* (New York: Oxford University Press, 1987).

38. See David Burnham, *The Role of the Media in Controlling Corruption*, CJC Monograph #3 (New York: Criminal Justice Center, John Jay College, 1977).

39. On this, see Jerome H. Skolnick and Candace McCoy, "Police Accountability and the Media," *American Bar Foundation Research Journal* (Summer (no. 3) 1984), pp. 521–57. The growing use, by police themselves, of video-recorded encounters with the public offers some protection against exaggerated charges.

40. Neither should we overlook the possibilities of collusion. To the extent that the police are able to benefit (or burden) the media, the media may sometimes be improperly persuaded to underreport or distort situations that would be disadvantageous to the police.

41. For an eirenic discussion of what community policing is about see Jerome Skolnick and David Bayley, *The New Blue Line: Police Innovation in Six American Cities* (New York: Free Press, 1986). They see it as having four dimensions: (1) police–community reciprocity; (2) area-based decentralization of command; (3) reorientation of patrol; and (4) civilianization. This, however, is but one, albeit fairly comprehensive, way of characterizing "community policing." Like "democracy," it has gathered up as many characterizations as advocates.

42. See Herman Goldstein, *Problem-Oriented Policing* (New York: McGraw-Hill, 1990).

43. For useful discussions of the problems that community policing must face, see Herman Goldstein, "Toward Community-Oriented Policing: Potential, Basic Requirements, and Threshold Questions," *Crime & Delinquency* 33, 1 (January 1987), pp. 6–30; Lisa Riechers and Roy Roberg, "Community Policing: A Critical Review of Underlying Assumptions," *Journal of Police Science and Administration* 17, 2 (1990), pp. 105–14; and the essays by Peter Manning, Stephen D. Mastrofski, Carl Klockars, and Jack R. Greene and Ralph Taylor in Jack R. Greene and Stephen D. Mastrofski (eds.), *Community Policing: Rhetoric or Reality* (New York: Praeger, 1988).

44. Beyond the informal reluctance that may exist, there is also the more formalized tightrope of union–management relations that will need to be negotiated. Unless line officers are involved in shaping the community policing process from an early stage, it may grind to a halt in formalities. Of course it may do this in any case if there is a history of union–management antagonism.

45. In the United States, much of the impetus for community policing has come through a jointly sponsored program of Harvard University's Kennedy School of Government and the National Institute of Justice. "Sector policing" in the United

Kingdom and community policing initiatives in Australia have also been influenced by the Kennedy School Program.

46. Is it acceptable – as occurred in Flint, Michigan – that a uniformed police officer lead a demonstration?

12 ETHICS AND CODES OF ETHICS

1. The material in this chapter overlaps with the Introduction to John Kleinig, with Yurong Zhang (comps. and eds.), *Professional Law Enforcement Codes: A Documentary Collection* (Westport, CT: Greenwood, 1993). All the police codes referred to in this chapter are reproduced in that collection.
2. John H. Kultgen, *Ethics and Professionalism* (Philadelphia: University of Pennsylvania Press, 1988), p. 216.
3. See Michael Davis, "The Ethics Boom: What and Why" *The Centennial Review* 34 (1990), pp. 163–86.
4. The earliest collection of which I am aware is Edgar L. Heermance's *Codes of Ethics: A Handbook* (Burlington, VT: Free Press Printing Co., 1924). Two significant recent collections are Rena A. Gorlin (ed.), *Codes of Professional Responsibility*, 3rd ed. (Edison, NJ: BNA Books, 1994); and Nigel G. E. Harris, *Professional Codes of Conduct in the United Kingdom: A Directory* (London: Mansell, 1989). None of them, however, contains any police code of ethics.
5. *Maxims for the General Guidance of Members of the Police Force* (Sydney: Thomas Richards, NSW Government Printer, 1870).
6. Wilson remained in Wichita for eleven years. For details, see William J. Bopp, *"O.W.": O.W. Wilson and the Search for a Police Profession* (New York: Kennikat Press, 1977), ch. 5.
7. Wittgenstein's metaphor is explicated in *Philosophical Investigations*, trans. G. E. M. Anscombe (Oxford: Blackwell, 1958), sects. 66ff. For a criticism, which I accept, and which accounts for my reference to a unifying function, see Julius Kovesi, *Moral Notions* (London: Routledge & Kegan Paul, 1967), p. 22.
8. As far as I know, police codes have not yet been used for this purpose. See, however, J. J. Fason, III, "Comment: The Georgia Code of Professional Responsibility: A Catalyst for Successful Malpractice Actions?" *Mercer Law Review*, 37 (1986), pp. 817–37; C.P. Edmonds, III and J. Shampton, "Codes of Ethics: A Basis for Evaluating Appraiser Liability," *Appraiser Journal* 58 (1990), pp. 168–79; C.A. Constantinides, "Note: Professional Ethics Codes in Court: Redefining the Social Contract Between the Public and the Professions," *Georgia Law Review* 25 (1991), pp. 1,327–73.
9. Michael Davis, "Thinking Like an Engineer: The Place of a Code of Ethics in the Practice of a Profession," *Philosophy & Public Affairs* 20 (1991), p. 156.
10. Ibid.
11. See Michael Davis, "Do Cops Really Need a Code of Ethics?" *Criminal Justice Ethics* 10, 2 (Summer / Fall 1991), pp. 15–17.
12. Davis, "Do Cops Really Need a Code of Ethics?" p. 20. Cf.: " . . . a code necessarily sets a standard higher than ordinary morality" (Davis, "Codes of Ethics, Professions, and Conflicts of Interest: A Case Study of an Emerging Profession, Clinical Engineering," *Professional Ethics* 1, 1 & 2 [Spring / Summer 1992], p. 186).
13. Davis, "Do Cops Really Need a Code of Ethics?" p. 15.
14. Ibid., p. 20.
15. A point that Davis appears to concede in ibid., p. 23.

16. Ibid., p. 24.
17. This is taken from Article 8 of the United Nations' "Code of Conduct for Law Enforcement Officials."
18. This is not the place to engage in an extended discussion of the appropriateness of each of these kinds of standards in an ethical code. Presumably, though, if a code is to have some practical bite, it will need to have some mandatory rules at its core. For an elaboration, see Davis, "Do Cops Really Need a Code of Ethics?"
19. Ibid., pp. 18–19.
20. I do not want to deny that a police officer's private life is of relevance to his or her public performance (see Chapter 10). However, the suggestion of these codified statements that a police officer must be a paragon of private virtue surely goes too far.
21. Ibid., p. 20.
22. See Davis, "Thinking Like an Engineer."
23. Lon L. Fuller, "The Philosophy of Codes of Ethics," in Bernard Baumrin and Benjamin Freedman (eds.), *Moral Responsibility and the Professions* (New York: Haven Press, 1984), p. 83.
24. Sometimes the restrictions are expressive of a fortress mentality. Yet there are quite legitimate concerns, such as the need to preserve the integrity and effectiveness of an investigation, and the correct representation of policy.
25. Occasionally – though I do not have examples from policing – codes spell out rights and duties not only of service providers but also of service users.
26. But of course a written document can be a two-edged sword. A document that may be used for protection in some situations may be used to convict in others. And so some organizations, including police departments, have at times shown an unwillingness to put standards (or more often procedures) in writing lest they be used against them at a later point. And, to the same end, when standards are reduced to written form, they are sometimes stated in a manner that will not allow breaches – even when they occur – to be easily established.
27. "Engineering Ethics and the Public Interest," in Robert Baum and Albert Flores (eds.), *Ethical Problems in Engineering*, 2nd ed. (Troy, NY: Rensselaer Polytechnic Institute, 1980), vol. 2, p. 26.
28. Philip Shuchman, "Ethics and Legal Ethics: The Propriety of the Canons as a Group Moral Code," *George Washington Law Review* 37 (1968), pp. 244–69. Cf. the cynical old-timer who is quoted as saying that "ethics are rules old men make to keep young men from getting any business" (in Jack McMinn, "Ethics Spun from Fairy Tales," in Baum and Flores [eds.], *Ethical Problems in Engineering*, vol. 1, p. 30).
29. A.P. Bristow, *You . . . and the Law Enforcement Code of Ethics* (Santa Cruz, CA: Davis Publishing Co., 1975). See also George T. Payton, *Patrol Procedure and Enforcement Concepts*, 6th ed. (Los Angeles: Legal Book Co., 1982), ch. 1.
30. It may, however, be occurring more slowly there, because police training is still academy-based rather than university-based. The openness to inquiry that should characterize university life is more difficult to create in the paramilitary environment of the police academy. This is a pity, since police on the street are still advised to "forget what you learned in academy."
31. There is also more to morality than taking motivation into account *only* because it bears on the optimization of outcomes. Bernard Williams points to some of these difficulties in *Ethics and the Limits of Philosophy* (Cambridge, MA: Harvard University Press, 1985), ch. 6. There are further subtleties concerning motivation that

make even apparently "moral" motivations inadequate. See Michael Stocker, "The Schizophrenia of Modern Ethical Theories," *Journal of Philosophy* 73, 14 (12 August, 1976), pp. 453–66.

32. See, for example, Robert M. Veatch, *A Theory of Medical Ethics* (New York: Basic, 1981).
33. See, for example, Richard Kania's discussion in "Should We Tell the Police to Say 'Yes' to Gratuities?" *Criminal Justice Ethics* 7, 2 (Summer/Fall 1988), pp. 37–49.
34. See John Kleinig and Albert J. Gorman, "Professional Courtesies: To Ticket or Not to Ticket," *American Journal of Police* 11, 4 (1992), pp. 97–113.
35. I would not, of course, want to deny that there have also been gains from such endeavors. One person's alienation is another's attraction.

13 ETHICAL CHALLENGES FOR POLICE MANAGEMENT

1. Robert Wasserman and Mark H. Moore, "Values in Policing," in *Perspectives on Policing, No. 8* (Washington, DC: National Institute of Justice, November, 1988), p. 1.
2. I will later modify this contrast, and hasten to point out that professional organizations frequently operate like industrial unions. Nevertheless, there is an initial difference of focus that I wish to capture before I seek to blur it.
3. Attempts to introduce merit-based promotion criteria to replace longstanding seniority-based promotion policies have often been opposed by police unions. Union officials argue, however, that a seniority-based system is less likely to be nepotistically manipulated than a supposedly merit-based one. In Western Australia, attempts to introduce a merit-based system were met by a staff room notice declaring: "MERIT = Mates Elevated Regardless (of) Intelligence or Training" ("No Talking Back to Top Cop," *The West Australian* [28 June 1994], p. 2).
4. For discussion, see John H. Burpo, *The Police Labor Movement* (Springfield, IL: Thomas, 1971); Hervey A. Juris and Peter Feuille, *Police Unionism: Power and Impact in Public-Sector Bargaining* (Lexington, MA: Lexington Books, 1973); Joseph D. Smith, "Police Unions: An Historical Perspective of Causes and Organizations," *Police Chief* 42, 11 (November 1975), pp. 24–8.
5. There are several accounts of this strike. The major discussion is Francis A. Russell, *A City in Terror: 1919, The Boston Police Strike* (New York: Penguin, 1975). But see also R. Lyons, "The Boston Police Strike of 1919," *The New England Quarterly* 20, 2 (June 1947), pp. 147–68; William J. Bopp, "The Boston Police Strike of 1919," *Police* 16, 11 (July 1972), pp. 54–8.
6. See, for example, "Report of the IACP Special Committee on Police Employee Organizations," *Police Chief* 36, 12 (December 1969), p. 54.
7. Note, however, note 3, *supra*. Even in large departments that have had a strong commitment to seniority, advancement (and sometimes survival) has often depended on a "hook" or "rabbi." See, for example, Bill McCarthy, with Mike Mallowe, *Vice Cop* (New York: Morrow, 1991), p. 39; Robert Daley, *Prince of the City* (New York: Berkley Books, 1981), p. 47.
8. Richard M. Ayres, "Police Unions: A Step Toward Professionalism?" *Journal of Police Science and Administration* 3, 4 (1975), pp. 400–4.
9. Letter to the President of the National Federation of Federal Employees, 16 August, 1937, in *The Public Papers and Addresses of Franklin D. Roosevelt* (New York: Russell & Russell, 1969), vol. 6, p. 325.
10. The full text of Coolidge's message is found in Russell, *A City in Terror*, pp. 191–2.

11. To an audience in Helena, Montana; quoted in ibid., p. 170.
12. See, generally, William D. Gentel & Martha L. Handman, *Police Strikes: Causes and Prevention* (Gaithersburg, MD: International Association of Chiefs of Police, 1979).
13. *Board of Education of Community Unit School District v. Redding*, 32 Ill 2d 567, 207 NE 2d 427, 430 (1965).
14. Joseph Herman, "Strikes by Public Employees: The Search for 'Right Principles,'" *Chicago Bar Record* 53 (November 1971), p. 58 (footnotes omitted).
15. See, for example, M. B. E. Smith, "Is There a Prima Facie Obligation to Obey the Law?" *Yale Law Journal* 82 (1973), pp. 950–76; Peter P. Nicholson, "The Internal Morality of Law: Fuller and His Critics," *Ethics* 84, 4 (July 1974), pp. 307–26.
16. Cf. Mr Justice Brandeis, who observed: "Neither the common law nor the Fourteenth Amendment confers the absolute right to strike" [*Dorchy v. Kansas*, 272 US 306, at 311 (1926)]. I don't think it can be inferred from Brandeis's remarks that he believed there may be an inherent right though no absolute right. His use of "absolute" is not far from what the court in *Redding* meant by "inherent."
17. There is not a very extensive literature on the morality of strike action. See, however, H. B. Acton, "Strikes, Trade Unions and the State," in Bhikhu Parekh and R. N. Berki (eds.), *The Morality of Politics* (London: Allen & Unwin, 1972), pp. 136–47; A. Aboud and G. Aboud, *The Right to Strike in Public Employment* (Ithaca, NY: Cornell University Press, 1974); Mary Gibson, *Workers' Rights* (Totowa, NJ: Rowman & Allanheld, 1983), pp. 108–21; and Don Locke, "The Right to Strike," in A. Phillips Griffiths (ed.), *Philosophy and Practice* (New York: Cambridge University Press, 1985), pp. 173–202.
18. Here I leave to one side the question whether the charge of unconscionability focuses on the coerciveness or the unfairness of contracts.
19. Some Catholic social thought has been particularly partial to the "just war" approach. See H.E. Manning, "Leo XIII on the Condition of Labour," *Dublin Review* 109 (July–October 1891), pp. 153–67. See also K. E. Kirk, *Conscience and its Problems: An Approach to Casuistry* (London: Longmans Group, 1927), pp. 254–362.
20. In some recent discussion, a distinction has been drawn between liberalism and republicanism. Liberals, it is claimed, see government as essentially problematic, a threat to individual freedom, whereas republicans see government as the context in which freedom can flourish. I would probably want to see these as two varieties of liberalism, one more individualistic or libertarian, and the other more communitarian. For an overview, see Philip Pettit, "Liberty in the Republic," *Political Theory Newsletter* 2, 2 (September 1990), pp. 159–77.
21. For discussion of the effects of police strikes, see Erdwin H. Pfuhl, "Police Strikes and Conventional Crime," *Criminology* 21, 4 (November 1983), pp. 489–503; and G. Clark, "What Happens When the Police Strike?" in W. J. Chambliss (ed.), *Criminal Law in Action* (Santa Barbara, CA: Hamilton, 1975), pp. 440–9.
22. Herman, "Strikes by Public Employees," p. 72.
23. I do not of course want to suggest that all strike action can be thought of in these terms. The potential similarities, however, should not be ignored. For discussions of the place of civil disobedience in a democratic community, see Alan Gewirth, *Human Rights: Essays on Justification and Applications* (Chicago: University of Chicago Press, 1982), ch 12; John Rawls, *A Theory of Justice* (Cambridge, MA: Harvard University Press [Belknap Press], 1971), ch. 6.
24. Minimal inconvenience to the public is probably not the actual reason why this

form of industrial action is preferred. The actual reason has more to do with the legal and economic advantages involved.

25. Robert G. Howlett, "The Right to Strike in the Public Sector," *Chicago Bar Record* 53 (December 1971), pp. 110–11.

26. *Anderson Federation of Teachers v. School City of Anderson*, 251 NE 2d 15 (S. Ct. Ind., 1969) (C. J. DeBruler, dissenting), *reh. denied*, 254 NE 2d 329, 73 LRRM 2601 (1970), *cert. denied*, 399 US 928, 74 LRRM 2552 (1970).

27. Herman, "Strikes by Public Employees," p. 61.

28. The desire for profitability may encourage good employer–employee relations just as much as it may discourage them: Productivity may be increased by incentives as much as by threats, and profit-sharing arrangements may give employees a stake in productivity.

29. Although there is some flexibility in the use of these terms, they are not completely interchangeable.

30. See Dorothy Moses Schulz, *From Social Worker to Crimefighter: Women in United States Municipal Policing* (Westport, CT: Praeger, 1995).

31. That the discrimination is not wholly "residual" is reinforced by the fact that in some departments ranking minority and women officers are more highly qualified than their white and male counterparts.

32. 401 US 424, 91 SCt 849 (1971).

33. See the discussion in Timothy Stroup, "Affirmative Action and the Police," in William C. Heffernan and Timothy Stroup (eds), *Police Ethics: Hard Choices in Law Enforcement* (New York: John Jay Press, 1985), pp. 192–93.

34. Nationwide, the proportion of blacks and Latinos in police work is about equal to that in the general population, though this is not true of some police departments, say, the NYPD. Should each police department aim to employ blacks and Latinos in roughly the proportion in which they are found in the local population?

35. See Barbara Raffel Price, "Sexual Integration in American Law Enforcement," in Heffernan and Stroup (eds.), *Police Ethics*, pp. 207–8.

36. For example, by Candace McCoy, "Affirmative Action in Police Organizations – Checklists for Supporting a Compelling State Interest," *Criminal Law Bulletin* 20, 3 (May–June 1984), pp. 245–54. This argument, of course, will work best when applied to first line officers. It will be less compelling where more specialized detective and forensic work is concerned.

37. Curiously enough, though understandably, sending minority officers to work in minority areas might itself be seen as unfair. Given the current social situation, these areas are likely to be much busier and harder to work than, say, white middle-class neighborhoods. Minority officers will have some reason to resent their work assignments.

38. See Stroup, "Affirmative Action and the Police," in Heffernan and Stroup (eds.), *Police Ethics*, p. 196, and Justice Powell in *The Regents of the University of California v. Allan Bakke*, 98 S Ct 3140 (1978).

39. See Price, "Sexual Integration in American Law Enforcement," in Heffernan and Stroup (eds.), *Police Ethics*, pp. 206–7.

40. See ibid., p. 207.

41. That there is such a perception is argued by Ellen Hochstedler, who claims that for many within policing affirmative action is "widely interpreted to mean that those who did not qualify were nevertheless hired," a "stigma from which many of those who were meant to be the beneficiaries wished to dissociate themselves"

("Impediments to Hiring Minorities in Public Police Agencies," *Journal of Police Science and Administration* 12, 2 [1984], p. 232). Stories about determining whether or not a new sergeant is a "quota boss" tend to confirm this view. Stroup, on the other hand, argues that since minority group members generally favor affirmative action policies, they do not see this objection as a very weighty one (Stroup, "Affirmative Action and the Police," in Heffernan and Stroup (eds.), *Police Ethics*, p. 203 fn.15).

42. The "if," unfortunately, is significant. What I view as the morally preferable policy is likely to be ruled out on economic grounds in the current fiscal environment. And even if the policy I favor is adopted, the "extra" money it will cost will be taken from some other program, within or outside of policing.

43. It has also been suggested that the moral distance between the past and present generation is probably less than it is commonly asserted to be. Try the following thought experiment: Were I (as I now am) in the position of my forebears, what would I have done?

44. The distinction between goals and quotas is problematic. See Stroup, "Affirmative Action and the Police," in Heffernan and Stroup (eds.), *Police Ethics*, pp. 201–2 fn.7; McCoy, "Affirmative Action in Police Organizations."

45. For discussion, see Marc R. Levinson, "Affirmative Action: Is It Just a Numbers Game?" *Police Magazine* 5, 2 (March 1982), p. 16. Also relevant here is the ongoing debate over maximum hiring and retirement ages, and discrimination against handicapped persons. See Emory A. Plitt, Jr., "Employment Discrimination and the Police Profession–An Update," *The Police Chief* 51, 3 (March 1984), pp. 88–94.

46. In the United States, policing does not seem to be a very attractive occupation for many Asians. Their lack of interest often has little to do with past discrimination, and more to do with other cultural expectations.

47. Samuel L. Williams, "Law Enforcement and Affirmative Action," *The Police Chief* 42, 2 (February 1975), p. 73. In the case of women, too, where the pattern of socialization has probably emphasized nonviolence, policing as it is currently portrayed may appear inhospitable. If, however, police work is reconceptualized as a form of social peacekeeping, and not glorified as crime fighting, it could become an increasingly attractive occupation for women.

Index of authors

Index of subjects